MOTIF PROGRAMMING

DIGITAL PRESS X AND MOTIF SERIES

Motif Programming

The Essentials . . . and More

Marshall Brain

X Window System Toolkit

The Complete Programmer's Guide and Specification

Paul J. Asente and Ralph R. Swick

X and Motif Quick Reference Guide

Randi J. Rost

X Window System

The Complete Reference to XLIB, X Protocol, ICCCM, XLFD
Third Edition

Robert W. Scheifler and James Gettys
With Jim Flowers, David Rosenthal

MOTIF PROGRAMMING

The Essentials . . . and More

MARSHALL BRAIN

 Digital Press

Printed in the United States of America.

9 8 7 6 5 4 3 2 1

Order number EY-J816E-DP

Design: David Ford
Production: Superscript Editorial Production Services
Composition: Paul C. Anagnostopoulos, Marsha Finley,
    and Alicia Quintano, using ZzTeX
Editing: Jonathan Weinert
Art: LM Graphics
Indexing: Ted Laux

PostScript is a trademark of Adobe Systems, Incorporated. Aldus PageMaker is a trademark of Aldus Corporation. TeX is a trademark of the American Mathematical Society. UNIX is a trademark of AT&T Laboratories, Incorporated. DECstation, Digital, the Digital logo, MicroVAX, and VAX are trademarks of Digital Equipment Corporation. X Window System is a trademark of The Massachusetts Institute of Technology. NeXT is a trademark of NeXT Computer, Incorporated. Motif, OSF, and OSF/Motif are trademarks of Open Software Foundation. Sun Workstation is a trademark of Sun MicroSystems, Incorporated. Mathematica is a trademark of Wolfram Research, Incorporated.

Library of Congress Cataloging-in-Publication Data

Brain, Marshall
    Motif programming: the essentials—and more / Marshall Brain.
        p.   cm.
    Includes bibliographical references and index.
    ISBN 1-55558-089-0
    1. X Window System (Computer System)   2. Motif (Computer program)
    I. Title.
    QA76.76.W56B73   1992   91–46975
    005.4'3—dc20   CIP

To **my Mother**, whose cookie shipments fueled this project

and to **Dr. Thomas L. Honeycutt**, who has cultivated my career for many years
and given me the environment in which I created this book

CONTENTS

vii

PREFACE

THE PURPOSE OF THIS BOOK

So you're sitting around one day minding your own business, when suddenly you are struck by an incredible need to understand how to write Motif programs on an X workstation. "I *must* learn how to write Motif programs!" you say to yourself. This remarkable compulsion has driven you to find and open this book.

What could inspire such a powerful desire? Perhaps you find yourself in one of the following situations:

1. Your boss walked into your office today and said, "Snydley, I want that program you wrote converted over to Motif by next week so it will look sharp on these new workstations."
2. The instructor of your "Introduction to Motif" class gave you your first assignment a month ago, and now, with two days left before the due date, you have decided to get started.
3. You need to write a program with a graphical user interface as quickly as possible, and X/Motif is the only thing available in the environment you are using. Typically, you need that program done yesterday.
4. You are an experienced programmer on the Macintosh or under Microsoft Windows, and you want to port one of your programs over to the UNIX world. Your major competitor will release its UNIX version tomorrow.
5. You are a student or a programmer, you have just been given a workstation to use, and you have a deep desire to learn Motif so that you can create snazzy graphical applications for the fun of it.

These scenarios have one thing in common: the need for a quick, thorough, and fairly painless introduction to Motif programming. The purpose of this book is to fill that need. This book covers all of the basic features of graphical user interfaces as implemented under Motif, starting at the beginning. It shows you how to get a program up and running in a short period of time and offers pointers to more advanced topics. It also shows you what Motif is capable of doing and how to do it.

This book will ease you into Motif programming as smoothly and as quickly as possible. It contains simple examples with simple explanations. It shows you how to design and build graphical applications with Motif in a reasonable amount of time.

THE PHILOSOPHY BEHIND THIS BOOK

There is one fundamental concept driving this book, and it is this: Motif is a very simple, beautifully designed way of creating graphical user interfaces.

It is hard to see the simplicity of Motif, however, because it is surrounded by a mass of complexity. In this way, Motif is rather like a power plant. The basic idea behind a power plant is very simple: Something generates heat, which creates steam, which drives a turbine connected to a generator. A power plant is elegant in its simplicity. However, power plants are ferociously complicated places, and if you tried to learn about them by walking around in one you would run into problems. The simplicity is masked by layers of complexity that have little or nothing to do with the basic concepts.

Motif is similar. This book will show you the fundamental forces that drive Motif so that you understand the big picture. Then you can start adding details to that picture and begin producing applications. Once you know and understand the fundamental concepts that drive Motif, you can easily add to that body of knowledge incrementally over time. As long as you understand the big picture, you will find that the rest comes easily.

PREREQUISITES

In order to use this book effectively, you need the following four prerequisites.

First, you need a good working knowledge of the C programming language. Although Motif binds to many languages, C is by far the most common for building Motif applications. The examples in this book, therefore, use C. Since many people who do not know C do know Pascal, or at least find Pascal code easier to read, Appendix E includes a set of C tutorials to help Pascal programmers make the jump to C. Occasional C programmers can also use these tutorials as a quick refresher course when necessary.

Second, you need access to a machine capable of compiling Motif code, for example, a UNIX workstation—preferably, a very fast one with abundant memory and disk space. Make sure that your workstation can compile Motif code, since some that run Motif applications and the Motif window manager do not. Your workstation must have access to X and Motif libraries. The examples in this book assume that you are running X11R4 or X11R5 and Motif version 1.1. If you are not sure which versions of X and Motif you have, or if you need to upgrade, see your system administrator or hardware vendor.

Third, you will need to have several reference books handy as your knowledge develops, since you will have to contend with a large amount of information. For instance, the Motif, X Toolkit, and X libraries contain hundreds of functions with thousands of variable names and types. See Appendix A for a list of recommended reference books and on-line resources.

Finally, you will find it very helpful to form friendships with programmers who know Motif, since they can be valuable sources of information and assistance. Because Motif and X are fairly complicated, program behavior sometimes seems to make no sense. A friend can point out simple mistakes that have serious repercussions and can answer questions in times of need.

HOW TO USE THIS BOOK

I have watched many people learn Motif, and I have learned Motif myself. From my observations, I can tell you that people learn to program in Motif by working with examples. Note that I did not say by *looking* at examples: You actually have to work with them. This is not the sort of book that you can take to bed with you. You need to use it while sitting in front of a workstation so that you can see what the code does, get familiar with the variable names and calling conventions, and modify code and observe the changes that occur.

This book contains many small, relatively simple pieces of example code. Especially in the early chapters, you should enter these examples yourself. The best way to learn Motif quickly is for Motif code to pass from your eyes to your brain to your fingers on a regular basis, so try to set a little (or a lot of) time aside every day to enter, run, and play with examples.

Students often learn Motif more quickly when they have projects of their own to work on. Once you have worked through the first few chapters, find a project that interests you and start working on it. Maybe you have a project at work that you could code with a graphical user interface. Maybe you have a videotape collection for which you could build a simple graphical database. Or maybe you could build a graphical front end to an existing character-based application to make that application easier to use. Find a little project that you can get excited about and start working on it.

As you work, questions will arise. Look in this book for similar situations and find the answers to those questions, and look at the applications it presents for ideas and suggestions. As you answer your own questions and design your own application, you will learn a lot about Motif. You will also enjoy it because you are working on something that excites you.

Every student I know who has learned Motif successfully has done so as the result of wanting to accomplish something else. Take advantage of this phenomenon, and you will learn Motif much more quickly.

THE ORGANIZATION OF THIS BOOK

This book follows a logical progression designed to teach you Motif starting at the beginning. It assumes that you have never seen X or Motif or event-driven programming before, and proceeds from there.

Chapter 1 begins with three very simple Motif programs and discusses the basic ideas and terminology you need to understand Motif programming. On the assumption that you are a beginner, this chapter does not contain in-depth theoretical discussions of the X Window System. A beginner simply has no way of understanding such material, so those in-depth discussions appear in Chapter 12 and beyond.

Chapter 2 contains a line-by-line discussion of a simple Motif program. This chapter will help you become familiar with the code you entered in Chapter 1, and it will make you comfortable with the different function calls used in every Motif application that you create.

Chapters 3, 4, and 5 introduce you to the three basic concepts that drive Motif: resources, callbacks, and managers. Once you thoroughly understand these concepts, you understand the heart of Motif programming.

Chapters 6 and 7 introduce you to two common graphical interface devices: menus and dialog boxes. These tools provide users of your programs with intuitive ways to enter commands, answer questions, and supply information.

Chapters 8 and 9 contain two simple examples that demonstrate and bind together the ideas presented earlier in the book. The example programs are a tic-tac-toe game, and an application called mkill, which kills background processes.

Chapter 10 introduces you to the text widget and creates a simple editor application using that widget. Code for a complete text editor is supplied in Appendix F.

Chapter 11 introduces the rest of the Motif widget set using a number of example programs and figures.

At this point in the book, you will have gained a great deal of knowledge about Motif and the creation of Motif applications. You are now ready to understand some of the details of the X Window system, resource files, the X toolkit, and so on. Chapter 12 covers resource-setting options such as resource files, fallback resources, and command line setting of resources. Chapter 13 covers the creation of custom dialog boxes. Chapter 14 discusses strings, font lists, gadgets, and the Clipboard. Chapter 15 discusses some of the capabilities available in the X layer, and Chapter 16 provides a similar overview of the Xt layer. Because the X and Xt layers are so large, Chapters 15 and 16 provide introductory material interspersed with numerous pointers to other sources of information. Finally Chapter 17 continues at the X level and provides an in-depth introduction to the drawing area widget and the X drawing model. Chapter 18 offers a brief conclusion.

This book also contains a number of appendixes. Browse through them periodically. Their importance to you will change as your knowledge of the subject evolves.

CODE AND COMMENTS

The example code used in this book is available for anonymous ftp, and the process for getting it is described at the beginning of Appendix A.

If for some reason you have trouble acquiring the code, or if you have any comments on this book, then please feel free to send me email at brain@adm.csc.ncsu.edu or brain@eos.ncsu.edu. I don't mind responding to questions and I welcome your suggestions because they will help to improve the book in later editions.

ACKNOWLEDGMENTS

This book would not exist without the work and support of a number of highly skilled people. I would like to acknowledge their help.

First, I would like to thank Mike Meehan, my publisher, who gave me the opportunity to create this book and talked me through every step of it. His patience is inexhaustible.

I thank Marsha Finley, Jonathan Weinert, David Ford, Chase Duffy, and Paul Anagnostopoulos for turning the manuscript into a book. There is a huge difference between a manuscript and a book, and their work propelled the transformation.

I would also like to thank Kevin Millsap, who cheerfully performed the thankless job of formatting and testing the more than 9,000 lines of code in this book. Phil Moore helped bring the code into compliance with Sun's compiler.

I am grateful to Carol Miller and Dorothy Strickland, my next-door neighbors at North Carolina State University, who provided infinite moral support and encouragement. They have an uncanny ability to say and do just the right thing at just the right time.

I thank Dr. Edward Davis for his patience and support.

Dr. William Willis, Bobby Pham, Ken Barnhouse, and David Smith all deserve my thanks for their work in implementing the Eos system at NCSU. The existence of the Eos system, and the amount of work they do to keep this huge and amazing beast running, has made my life extremely easy during the development of this book.

This book started out as a set of tutorials I wrote for students at NCSU. They were later released onto the network in the comp.windows.x.motif news group. I am grateful for all of the comments, corrections, and encouragement that students and the members of the news group provided.

My thanks go to those who reviewed the book, especially Jack Beidler, Chris DeLise, Don Merusi, Timothy Rice, and George Ross. The reviewer's comments significantly improved the book's quality.

Lance Lovette wrote the PostScript appendix. The ability to print is very important to a Motif programmer, and I thank Lance for clearly explaining how to add PostScript printing capabilities to your programs.

Kelly Campbell, Andy DeMaurice, Kevin Shay, and Lance Lovette contributed screen dumps for Chapter 1. I thank them for that and for asking me thousands of questions that forced me to think carefully about what I was doing.

I experienced one hard-disk anomaly during the development of this book. I get down on my knees and thank Joe Britt and Mike Braden for hard-disk recovery services offered at a very critical time in my life.

Finally, I would like to thank the following folks for being there when I needed them: Jay Lloyd, Steve Loyer, Toby Schaffer, Rob Ward, Dave Patterson, Dr. Alan Tharp, Duane Whitehurst, Trish Brezny, Mike and Beth Eddy, Perry Young, Molly Glander, Shari Brain, Katheryn Lee, Eric Scott, Jon Mauney, and Tim Lowman.

Marshall Brain
Zebulon, North Carolina
December 27, 1991

MOTIF PROGRAMMING

1 INTRODUCTION

This chapter will give you your first taste of Motif programming and introduce you to the basic ideas behind Motif and the X Window System. It will also describe how event-driven programming works in general and under X and Motif in particular.

1.1 GETTING STARTED: THREE SIMPLE MOTIF PROGRAMS

Motif is a collection of user interface objects called *widgets*. The Motif widget set includes all of the objects that programmers and users expect to find in a graphical user interface: pull-down menus, dialog boxes, scroll bars, push buttons, and so on. To build a Motif application, a programmer selects a group of widgets to create the user interface, and then writes code that makes those widgets appear on the screen and behave appropriately.

One of the best ways to begin building an understanding of Motif is to see it in action. Listing 1.1 uses a label widget to display the words "Hello World" on the screen. Enter this program using your favorite text editor and save it to a file named label.c. This code may seem rather intimidating at first, so enter it for now and we will examine it in detail in Chapter 2.

Listing 1.1 A Label Widget Demonstration

```
/* label.c */
#include <Xm/Xm.h>
#include <Xm/Label.h>

XtAppContext context;
XmStringCharSet char_set=XmSTRING_DEFAULT_CHARSET;

Widget toplevel, label;

main(argc,argv)
  int argc;
```

1

```
    char *argv[];
{
  Arg al[10];
  int ac;

  /* create the toplevel shell */
  toplevel = XtAppInitialize(&context,"",NULL,0,&argc,argv,NULL,NULL,0);

  /* create label widget */
  ac=0;
  XtSetArg(al[ac],XmNlabelString,
    XmStringCreateLtoR("Hello World", char_set)); ac++;
  label=XmCreateLabel(toplevel,"label",al,ac);
  XtManageChild(label);

  XtRealizeWidget(toplevel);
  XtAppMainLoop(context);
}
```

To compile this code, type

```
cc -o label label.c -lXm -lXt -lX11
```

This command compiles label.c, links it to the Motif, X Toolkit, and X11 libraries, and places the executable in a file named label. To run the program, type label.

This command demonstrates the standard way to compile and run a Motif program, and it should work if the libraries are all present and in their correct places. If it does not work, see the sidebar "Compilation Problems" on page 3.

When you run the program, a window containing the words "Hello World" should appear on the screen (see Figure 1.1). The object containing the words "Hello World" in this window is called a label widget. You can use label widgets in your own Motif programs to display static messages for the user. Note that you can resize the window, collapse it into an icon, overlay it with another window, and move it. Motif, or your window manager, handles the window's behavior for you gracefully and automatically.

Figure 1.1   The Output of Listing 1.1

Compilation Problems

You may be unable to compile the program label.c in the manner described on page 2. If so, you need to talk to a Motif-literate friend on your system, call your system administrator, fix it yourself by finding paths to the libraries and include files, or talk to the vendor. Since the problem may have a complex solution, the easiest way to solve it is to find someone on your system who knows how to compile a Motif program and ask for his or her standard makefile or compilation command. I recently worked on a system where the command to compile a Motif program was 200 characters long.

If you get error messages during compilation, make sure you have entered the code exactly as it appears in Listing 1.1. Also make sure that your system is running X11R4 or X11R5 and Motif 1.1.

Depending on the speed of your machine and the distance of the libraries from the CPU, this program may take from five seconds to five minutes to compile. Shortage of disk space may also cause problems. On my machine, a DECstation, this program's executable file consumes 1.75 megabytes of disk space. If space is critical, try compiling the executable to /tmp or /usr/tmp. For example, try typing cc -o /usr/tmp/label label.c -lXm -lXt -lX11. Make sure you erase the contents of the temporary directory when you are done.

To run the compiled program, type label. It may take some time to load the executable—for instance, up to a minute if you are loading a 1.75 MB executable over a busy network from a server.

To see another Motif widget in action, enter the code in Listing 1.2 and save it to a file named scale.c. This program demonstrates a scale widget.

Listing 1.2 A Scale Widget Demonstration

```
/* scale.c */
#include <Xm/Xm.h>
#include <Xm/Scale.h>

XtAppContext context;

Widget toplevel, scale;

main(argc,argv)
```

```
  int argc;
  char *argv[];
{
  Arg al[10];
  int ac;

  /* create the toplevel shell */
  toplevel = XtAppInitialize(&context,"",NULL,0,&argc,argv,NULL,NULL,0);

  /* create scale widget */
  ac=0;
  XtSetArg(al[ac],XmNshowValue,True); ac++;
  scale=XmCreateScale(toplevel,"scale",al,ac);
  XtManageChild(scale);

  XtRealizeWidget(toplevel);
  XtAppMainLoop(context);
}
```

To compile this code, type

```
cc -o scale scale.c -lXm -lXt -lX11
```

To run the program, type scale. An object appears on the screen whose behavior resembles that of a sliding control on a piece of stereo equipment (Figure 1.2). Use the mouse to slide the scale. A numeric display shows the scale's current setting. Again, a scale widget is a separate object on the screen, with a distinctive appearance and behavior. You can use scale widgets in your programs to let users enter both integer and real values.

Now, enter the final piece of code shown in Listing 1.3 and save it to a file named text.c. This code demonstrates a text widget.

Figure 1.2   The Output of Listing 1.2

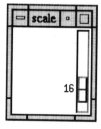

Listing 1.3   A Text Widget Demonstration

```
/* text.c */
#include <Xm/Xm.h>
#include <Xm/Text.h>

XtAppContext context;

Widget toplevel, text;

main(argc,argv)
  int argc;
  char *argv[];
{
  Arg al[10];
  int ac;

  /* create the toplevel shell */
  toplevel = XtAppInitialize(&context,"",NULL,0,&argc,argv,NULL,NULL,0);

  /* create text widget */
  ac=0;
  XtSetArg(al[ac],XmNeditMode,XmMULTI_LINE_EDIT); ac++;
  XtSetArg(al[ac],XmNheight,200); ac++;
  XtSetArg(al[ac],XmNwidth,200); ac++;
  text=XmCreateText(toplevel,"text",al,ac);
  XtManageChild(text);

  XtRealizeWidget(toplevel);
  XtAppMainLoop(context);
}
```

To compile this code, type

```
cc -o text text.c -lXm -lXt -lX11
```

To run the program, type text. A text widget appears on the screen (Figure 1.3). This widget contains a great deal of the functionality of a complete text editor.

   You can type characters into the text widget, use the arrow keys, position the cursor with the mouse, delete text, select areas of text, and so on. You can use text widgets in your own programs to provide users with regions in which they can enter and edit text.

Figure 1.3   The Output of Listing 1.3

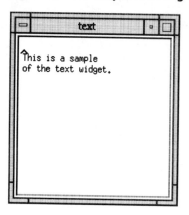

As these three pieces of code demonstrate, Motif provides you with a set of 40 or so objects that you can use to create programs with graphical user interfaces. You can combine these objects in many different ways.

1.2   WHAT IS MOTIF?

Imagine that you want to create a graphical application. Perhaps you wish to build a program that lets users draw circuit schematics, or one that provides a graphical view of a network, allowing users to click on a node or a network link to get more information. In creating either of these applications, you want to include certain user interface features such as pull-down menus, scroll bars, push buttons, text editing areas, and so on. How can the X Window System and Motif help you?

The X Window System allows you to create blank rectangular regions of any size on the screen. These regions are called *windows*. X also provides low-level drawing capabilities, so that you can draw in these windows. Of course, X supports many other capabilities, but this is primarily what it does.

Programming in X can be cumbersome. To create a scroll bar, a programmer must create a thin rectangular window on the screen and then draw the scroll bar in it. The programmer must then write code that manages the scroll bar when the user manipulates it—for example, if the user clicks or drags in the scroll bar, the program must animate it appropriately. Using X, a single scroll bar might require an immense amount of code. Furthermore, when many programmers create their own scroll bars in their own way, each will look

Table 1.1   A Summary of the Motif Widget Set

Widget	Chapter	Widget	Chapter
Arrow button	11	List, scrolled list	11
Bulletin board, bulletin		Main window	11
board		Menu bar	6
dialog	5, 13	Message box, message box	7
Cascade button	6	dialog	
Canned dialogs: error,		Option menu	11
file selection box,		Paned window	11
information, message,		Push button	4
prompt, question,		Radio box	11
selection box, warning,		RowColumn	5
working	7	Scale	4
Command	11	Scroll bar	11
Drawing area	17	Scrolled window	11
Drawn button	11	Selection box, selection	
File selection box, file		box	
selection		dialog	7
box dialog	7	Separator	5
Form, form dialog	5, 13	Shell	11, 14
Frame	11	Text, scrolled text	10
Label	3		

and behave slightly differently. This inconsistency annoys users as they move between applications.

Motif solves this problem. It sits on top of X and provides a set of preconstructed user interface objects—the widgets. These widgets can be placed on the screen by an application program. Table 1.1 provides a complete list of the widgets available in Motif and the chapters with information on them.

When you need a scroll bar in a Motif application, you call a function that creates one for you in the desired location. The scroll bar appears on the screen as a beautifully drawn object that is consistent across applications. Even better, Motif does all of the scroll bar management internally. When a user adjusts the scroll bar, Motif animates it appropriately on the screen: The slider moves, the arrow heads blink, and so on. When the user manipulates the scroll bar, Motif relays the new value chosen by the user to the program code.

The beauty of Motif is that almost all of the user interface overhead has already been programmed. You decide which widgets you need to use to create the user interface that you want. Motif functions position the widgets on the screen in the right location and at the right size. At the same time, Motif uses functions known as *callbacks* that notify the program when a user adjusts one of the widgets. The only additional code you must write is the "thinking" portion of the application: the part that makes the application respond correctly to user actions.

Figures 1.4 through 1.7 show examples of four typical programs created in Motif. Each uses its own assortment of user interface objects arranged on the screen in a unique way. As you can see, the figures illustrate the flexibility that Motif provides.

1.2.1   EVENT-DRIVEN PROGRAMMING

Motif is an event-driven programming environment. If you program on the Macintosh or under Microsoft Windows, this sort of environment is already familiar to you. If you are unfamiliar with it, the following introduction will provide a brief history. You must understand the basic concepts behind event-driven programming in order to fully understand Motif.

User interfaces have evolved through three stages. The first stage produced the command-driven user interface, which presents the user with a generally cryptic prompt such as this:

%

The user must know the set of commands that the interface recognizes and must enter those commands at the prompt.

The code required to implement a command-driven user interface is very simple. In pseudo-code, it looks something like

```
repeat
  display the prompt;
  wait for the user to type a command;
  parse off the first word of the command line;
  call the appropriate function to handle it, or print an
    error message;
until done;
```

From the programmer's standpoint, a command-driven interface is the simplest kind of interface because the code can be very straightforward and compact. From the user's standpoint, command-driven interfaces leave something to be desired, especially if the user is new to the system. The user must memorize a set of idiosyncratic commands that are often inconsistent.

Menu-driven user interfaces mark the next stage of user interface design. Structurally, menu-driven and command-driven interfaces are surprisingly

**Figure 1.4 Xcede, by Kelly Campbell and
Andy DeMaurice**
Kelly and Andy were college seniors when they created
Xcede, a schematic drawing application for digital
circuits. Note the use of buttons overlaid with icons,
scroll bars, and menus.

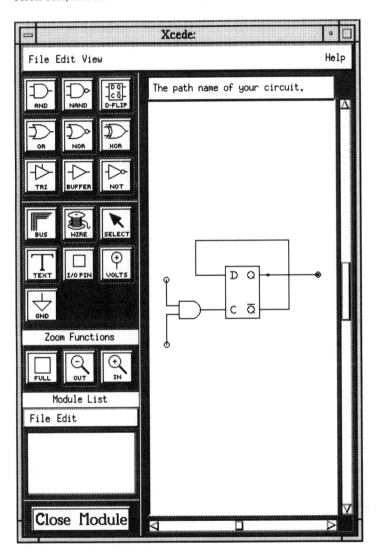

Figure 1.5   Xtracs, by Lance Lovette

Lance was a college freshman when he created the first version of Xtracs, and a sophomore when he created this version using wcl. Xtracs provides a graphical view of the week using different class schedules. Note the use of labeled text entry areas, buttons, and menus.

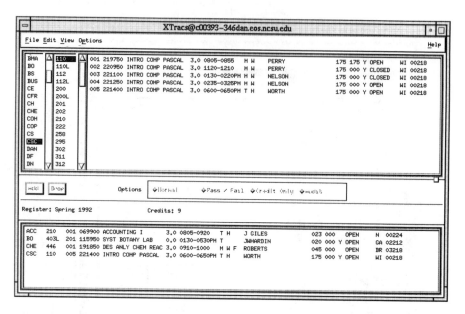

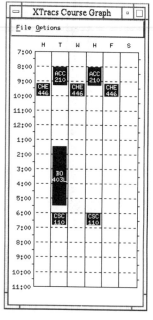

Figure 1.6   Xdesk, by Kevin Shay
Kevin was a college senior when he created Xdesk,
which provides a Macintosh-like front end for X.
Notice the use of multiple icons, drawing areas, and
menus.

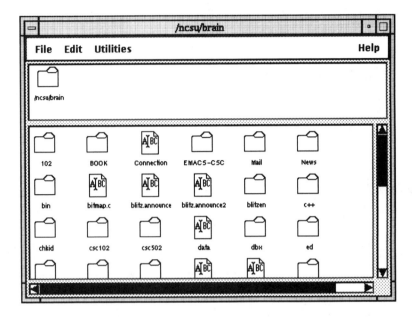

similar. The main difference is that menu-driven interfaces have much more
elaborate prompts. For example, the user might see a prompt such as

```
---Big Bank's Automatic-Teller System---

What would you like to do?
 1) Withdraw money
 2) Deposit money
 3) Pay us money
 4) Quit


Please enter the number of your choice:
```

The user enters the appropriate number, and a new menu appears. The
pseudo-code for a menu-driven program looks something like this:

```
repeat
  display the menu;
  wait for the user to type a number;
```

Figure 1.7   Blitzen Simulator, by Marshall Brain

Blitzen is a massively parallel processor. This application lets users simulate a Blitzen program's execution, examine the code, and see different views of memory and the processor array. Note the use of drawing, extensive text displays, scroll bars, and so on.

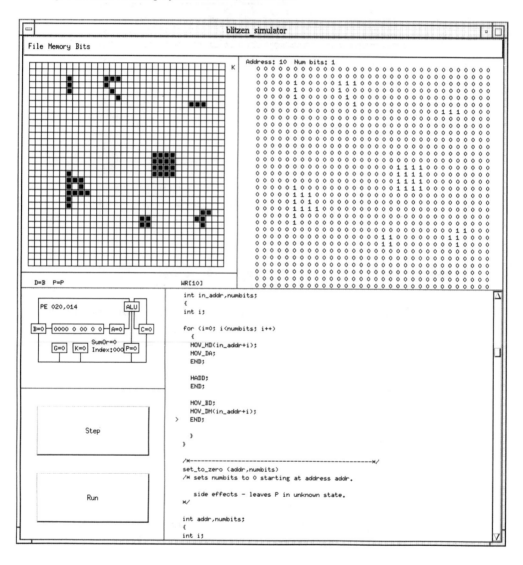

```
   parse the number;
   call the appropriate function to handle it, or print an
     error message;
until done;
```

Again, this code is fairly simple. It is less compact because all of the menus have to be displayed, but it does not pose a serious programming challenge.

Interfaces of the third stage are event-driven, and they provide programmers with plenty of challenges. The basic idea behind an event-driven environment is fairly simple, but the programming gets messy. An event-driven environment consists of some type of application program interface (API), which provides a library of functions that create user interface objects such as menus, windows, buttons, scroll bars, and the like. Users can manipulate these objects with the keyboard or mouse.

Each time a user presses a key or clicks the mouse, the API picks up the action and delivers it to the program as an *event*. Usually, events are held in an *event queue* so that the program does not have to handle them in real time. For example, each time a user presses a key on the keyboard, the appropriate character is placed into an *event record*, which is then placed in the event queue. Similarly, each time a user clicks the mouse, the click's location is packaged in an event record, which is also placed in the event queue. This behavior is typical of X, Microsoft Windows, and the Macintosh.

An event-driven program contains a loop that looks at the event queue to see if anything is there. If an event is pending, the program removes it from the queue, inspects its type, and handles it accordingly. The pseudo-code for an event-driven program might look like this:

```
Draw the graphical objects onto the screen to begin with;
repeat
   wait for an event to appear in the event queue;
   Parse the event;
   call the appropriate function to handle it;
until done;
```

The piece of looping code that receives and handles events like this is called an *event loop*.

Event-driven programs have two main sources of complexity. First, many objects appear simultaneously on the screen, and many of them have separate parts. When the code detects a mouse event, it has to determine which object, and which part of that object, it affects. On a Macintosh, code looks at a so-called "MouseDown" event and decides if it took place in a window, in the menu bar, in the background, or elsewhere. If it took place in a window, the code determines *which* window, and then explores which *region* of that window: the drag region, the close box, the zoom box, the content region, and so on. If the event took place in a scroll bar, the code has to decide which part of the scroll bar is affected. The Macintosh requires a great deal of code to manage all of these details.

The second source of complexity is the many internal events the windowing system itself can generate. When part of one window is exposed by the movement of another window, the program receives an expose event. When a window is resized, the code gets a resize event. Focus changes can generate focus events, and so on.

As you can see, you need many lines of code to parse out and handle all of these events. Much of this code is unique to each application, because each displays its own assortment of user interface objects. But don't get discouraged. The purpose of Motif is to make life as a programmer easier. The beauty of Motif is that it handles most of the low-level details, so you don't have to worry about them.

1.2.2   THE X WINDOW SYSTEM

Motif is a part of a UNIX library hierarchy which has four layers. At the bottom is UNIX and its standard libraries such as `stdio.h` and `math.h`. On top of UNIX sits the X Window System and its library, accessed through `Xlib.h`. On top of X sits the X Toolkit, accessed through `Intrinsics.h`. And finally, on top of the X Toolkit is Motif, accessed through `Xm.h`. The UNIX layer provides normal operating system support. The X layer provides basic windowing and event-handling capabilities. The X Toolkit layer provides support for the creation and use of widget sets. And Motif provides the widgets you need to create user interfaces easily.

It is possible to work with subsets of these layers. For example, UNIX programmers have been writing text-based C programs for decades. You can write programs that use only UNIX and the X layer, but this is the hard way to create a graphical program. You can also write programs that use a widget set such as Motif. Remember that the four layers are separate and can be used independently.

The X Window System provides a basic event-driven programming environment. It runs on a workstation or on an X terminal. It controls the mouse, the keyboard, and the screen; packages events, places them in an event queue, and allows programs to draw graphical items on the screen. The X library provides programming interface to the X Window System. You can access this library by including its header files in your code and then calling the appropriate routines to access the event queue, issue drawing commands, and so on.

The problem with X is that it provides little more than the core services you need to create a graphical user interface. X lets you create rectangular windows on the screen of any size or shape. Once you've created these windows, you can draw in them. But your code has to manage all of the events generated by the user, as well as all of the system events. Since X imposes absolutely no restrictions on the "look and feel" of what you create, and since X is so basic, you have the freedom to do nearly anything. On the other hand, even the simplest fully functional X program tends to become very long and complex.

1.2.3   THE OBJECT-ORIENTED NATURE OF MOTIF

To preserve the sanity of both programmers and users, it helps to restrict some of the freedom available in X through standardization. Users want different programs to work in similar ways—to have the same look and feel. Programmers prefer to ignore most of the low-level event-handling and drawing involved in the creation of common user interface objects.

To this end, another layer of libraries, called the X Toolkit, or Xt, sits on top of X. Xt is quite elegant. Like X, it is a general-purpose tool in that it does not enforce a particular look and feel. It allows programmers to design widget sets. There are several commonly used widget sets, among them the Athena widget set, the HP widget set, the Open Look widget set, and the Motif widget set. Because all of these widget sets use Xt, all of them work identically as far as the programmer is concerned. In fact, you can use widgets from different sets interchangeably. The widget sets likewise give users the impression of a distinct look and feel among applications that use them.

All widget sets provide the same basic objects, as well as special objects unique to each. The Motif set is typical: It contains scroll bar widgets, button widgets, menu widgets, text widgets, and so on.

By design, widget sets appear very object-oriented to the programmer. In practice, the Motif widget set looks much like an object-oriented programming environment. Nevertheless, because the programming is all done in C rather than in an object-oriented language like C++ or SmallTalk, it is not completely object-oriented. Thus, Xt carries most of object-oriented programming's advantages without requiring the programmer to learn a new language.

In Motif programming, each user interface object (or widget) is controlled by a set of variables called *resources*. By changing the resources, you can control the appearance and behavior of the widget. By reading the resources, you

The X Server/Client Model

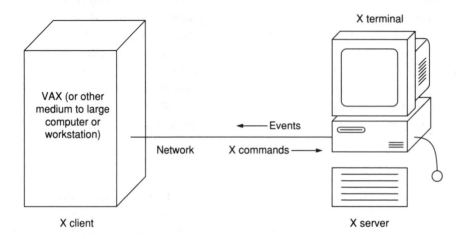

The X Window System provides a basic event-driven programming environment that runs on a workstation or on an X terminal. X controls the mouse, the keyboard, and the screen. Its job is to accept keyboard and mouse events from the user and also to allow applications to create windows on the screen and draw in them.

X is unique in that it is "network transparent." This means that an X terminal can package events and send them to another computer over the network, and the receiving computer can package drawing commands and send them back.

As shown in the diagram, the terminal acts as a "server" of X for the "client" program running on the VAX. At first, this may seem backward from the way it should be, but it makes sense once you think about it. The X server provides graphics services to multiple client machines that wish to draw graphical images on that server.

On a standalone X workstation, the server and client are running in the same box, but the separation is still there at the software level. The server is a complete, separate background program that runs independently of X programs that may also be running on the workstation.

Figure 1.8 The Motif/Xt/X/UNIX Hierarchy

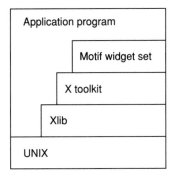

Accesses any layer in the hierarchy

Implements a specific set of widgets that gives applications a certain look and feel

Allows the creation and management of object-oriented user interface widget sets

Handles low-level window creation, drawing, and events.

can find out about the widget's state. The widget can also send out messages, known as callbacks, when it wants to communicate with your code.

Object-oriented programming environments support object hierarchies. To build a new object, you use and add to an existing object in a process called *inheritance*. The new object can do everything the original object can do, as well as anything else you add. You can also combine several existing objects into a new object. Similarly, Motif uses inheritance to build widgets on top of other widgets or out of groups of widgets. All Motif widgets use inheritance internally, as we will see in Chapter 3, although it is more difficult for a C programmer to take advantage of inheritance in a C program.

Let's use the scroll bar widget to illustrate these concepts. A scroll bar is a distinct object on the screen with a distinct appearance, behavior, size, and shape. The programmer creates a scroll bar on the screen by calling a function to create the widget. The scroll bar has a set of variables, or resources, associated with it. By setting values in the resource list, the programmer controls the appearance and behavior of the scroll bar—for example, altering the width and height by changing the **width** and **height** resources. By looking at resource values, the programmer can query the state of the scroll bar—for example, determining the position of the scroll bar's slider by looking at the **value** resource.

Each widget can send out messages, or callbacks, to functions in the program when a user manipulates the widget. When a user manipulates a scroll bar, the scroll bar calls a function in the program and says, essentially: "The user has changed me: Do something about it."

There are two immense advantages to handling user interface objects in this way. First, someone else has already coded the widget's appearance and behavior. Second, the widget handles *all* of the low-level event management. It animates itself and then, using callbacks, tells your code about it in a very controlled and simple way. Motif makes creating a graphical user interface extremely easy by doing most of the work for you.

2 ANALYZING A MOTIF PROGRAM

In this chapter we will examine the design of the simple "Hello World" program discussed in Chapter 1, and then discuss its implementation. Although short, this program introduces many new concepts.

This chapter should be read together with Chapter 3, where many concepts that may seem initially confusing are made much clearer by examples.

2.1 DESIGNING A "HELLO WORLD" PROGRAM

To create a Motif program, the programmer begins with a statement or image of the program's purpose and goals, and works from there to create a user interface using the widgets Motif offers. Once the programmer has designed the user interface, he or she writes code to place the widgets on the screen and to interconnect and animate them appropriately. Let's examine the Motif design process using the "Hello World" program from Chapter 1.

The purpose of this program is to display the words "Hello World" to the user. Motif provides many ways to accomplish this goal. For example, to display static text labels you can use a label widget. Or you can use a push-button widget, which also allows users to interact with the label by clicking on it. A text widget allows users to see and edit a piece of text. A message box widget shows users a text message in a pop-up dialog box and provides an OK button to click to clear the message. As you go through the book, you will become familiar with each of these widgets and their uses.

In our simple "Hello World" program, a label widget is an appropriate choice. The goals of the program do not require the user to edit or interact with the text, nor do they require the text to "go away" at any point.

To implement a Motif program that can display a label widget, a certain amount of standard code is required. You will find this standard code

19

in every Motif program you write. For example, all Motif programs must create a toplevel shell widget. The shell widget is the main application window for the program on the user's screen. It includes all of the decorations the user expects to see in an application window: a title bar, maximize and minimize buttons, resize areas, and so on. The standard code also "realizes" the toplevel shell and sets up the main event loop.

Listing 2.1 contains the code needed to create and display a label widget. Figure 2.1 shows the output of this program, and the following sections explain each line of the program in detail.

Listing 2.1   A "Hello World" Program in Motif

```
1      #include <Xm/Xm.h>
2      #include <Xm/Label.h>

3      XtAppContext context;
4      XmStringCharSet char_set=XmSTRING_DEFAULT_CHARSET;

5      Widget toplevel, label;

6      main(argc,argv)
7        int argc;
8        char *argv[];
9      {
10       Arg al[10];
11       int ac;

         /* Create the toplevel shell */
12       toplevel = XtAppInitialize(&context,"",NULL,0,&argc,argv,
            NULL,NULL,0);

         /* Create the label widget */
13       ac=0;
14       XtSetArg(al[ac],XmNlabelString,
            XmStringCreateLtoR("Hello World", char_set)); ac++;
15       label=XmCreateLabel(toplevel,"label",al,ac);
16       XtManageChild(label);

17       XtRealizeWidget(toplevel);
18       XtAppMainLoop(context);
19     }
```

Widgets

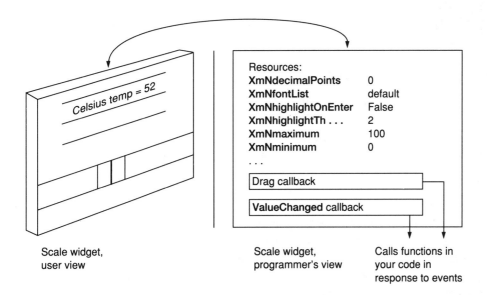

Scale widget,
user view

Scale widget,
programmer's view

Calls functions in
your code in
response to events

A widget is a user interface object that the user sees in one form—as a picture on-screen—and the programmer sees in another—as a set of resources and callbacks. The figure shows this dichotomy using a scale widget as an example.

The resources let the programmer control the appearance and behavior of the widget as seen by the user. For example, every widget has a **width** and a **height** resource, which determine the width and height of the widget on-screen. When you change a resource during the program's execution, the user sees a change in the appearance of the widget.

The callbacks let the widget communicate with your program as the user performs actions. You create code that tells the widget to call a specific function in response to a callback. The widget complies by calling that function whenever the callback is generated. For example, if the user changes the value of the scale's slider, the widget recognizes the change, updates the appearance of the widget on-screen, and generates a **valueChanged** callback. This causes the widget to call the function that the programmer specifies. The programmer writes this function so that the program responds appropriately to the user's action.

**Figure 2.1   The Output of the Program Shown
in Listing 2.1**

2.2   WHAT THE CODE MEANS

The code shown in Listing 2.1—in fact, Motif, Xt, and X code in general—has
a tendency to intimidate new programmers because of the unwieldy function
names, the long parameter lists, and the apparently random use of uppercase
and lowercase. Put this feeling aside for a moment and examine the code. You
should notice several things:

1. Two include files are used, `Xm.h` and `Label.h`. Both are Motif header files,
   hence the `Xm/` prefix. A large Motif program might include 20 or 30 header
   files from X, Xm, and so on. The inclusion of `Xm.h` brings in most of the
   Motif variable, constant, resource, and function names. It also brings in the
   Xt and X header files, making these libraries available as well. The inclusion
   of `Label.h` brings in functions and variables unique to the label widget,
   such as **XmCreateLabel**.

2. Six variables are defined, four globally and two locally to **main**. The four
   global variables are **context**, **char_set**, **toplevel**, and **label**. The two locals
   are **al** and **ac**. Two of the global variables are widgets: one is a **context**
   variable, and the other defines the character set to be used in the creation
   of an **XmString** variable. The local variables **al** and **ac** are be used to create
   an argument list that changes a widget's resource values and hence controls
   the behavior or appearance of a widget.

3. There is one function, **main**, with two parameters, **argv** and **argc**. All
   Motif programs, like all C programs, have one **main** function, which
   accepts the command line arguments as its parameters. Even if the code
   you write doesn't use any command line arguments, the **main** function
   needs to accept the parameters **argc** and **argv**. The X interface defines
   certain standard command line parameters that work the same way in all X
   applications, such as **-iconic** and **-geometry** (see Chapter 12 for a complete
   list of standard command line parameters). In practice, you will pass **argc**
   and **argv** off to the **XtAppInitialize** function so that it can extract and
   interpret all of the standard X command line options and then return what
   is left.

4. The code calls seven functions: **XtAppInitialize, XtSetArg, XmString-CreateLtoR, XmCreateLabel, XtManageChild, XtRealizeWidget**, and **XtAppMainLoop**. The functions beginning with the prefix **Xt** come from the X Toolkit libraries, while those beginning with **Xm** come from the Motif libraries. All widget sets use the **Xt** functions; the **Xm** functions are unique to the Motif widget set.

The following sections examine each line of code in the **main** function individually.

2.2.1 LINE 12

The first line of the **main** function (line 12) is extremely important. It creates a toplevel shell widget to hold the application, initializes all of X and the X Toolkit for you, sets up your main application window, and parses out standard X command line options:

```
toplevel = XtAppInitialize(&context,"",NULL,0,&argc,argv,NULL,NULL,0);
```

As the **Xt** prefix indicates, **XtAppInitialize** is a function in the X Toolkit library. It accepts several parameters, all but three of which are irrelevant in a simple program such as this. This is why **NULL**, **0**, and *""* appear so frequently in the function's parameter list. For completeness, all of the parameters are described below.

XtAppInitialize   *Creates the application's toplevel shell.*

```
Widget XtAppInitialize(XtAppContext *context,
    String application_class,
    XrmOptionDescRec options[],
    Cardinal num_options,
    Cardinal *argc,
    String *argv,
    String *fallback_resources,
    ArgList *args
    Cardinal num_args);
```

context	Returns the context value. Needed for calls to other XtApp functions.
application_class	The class name for loading resources (see Chapter 12).
options	Passed directly to the XrmParseCommand function (see Chapter 12).

num_options	Number of options.
argc	A pointer to the number of command line options (pass an address).
argv	The standard command line options array.
fallback_resources	A set of predefined resource strings (see Chapter 12).
args	An argument list for the toplevel shell.
num_args	The number of arguments in the argument list.

The first parameter is **context**. The context of an application is a structure that stores the information X needs to handle events and different displays. The **XtAppInitialize** function returns the **context** value because other **XtApp** functions need it (in this program, **XtAppMainLoop**).

The second parameter is the class name of the application, which determines which resource values are loaded from resource files as the application begins to run. Resource files are text files of resource values that the user, rather than the programmer, creates to customize applications (see Chapter 12). Resource values can be hard-coded into a program or read in from resource files. Since we are not concerned with resource files at this time, we pass in an empty string for this parameter.

The third and fourth parameters, **options** and **num_options**, are not used in this program and have been set to **NULL** and **0**, respectively. They have to do with command line parsing, which is discussed in detail in Chapter 12.

The next two parameters are **&argc** and **argv**. **XtAppInitialize** extracts the command line arguments that relate to X but leaves those that remain for your program to parse. Thus, **XtAppInitialize** has to be able to change **argc**. You *must* pass **argc** and **argv**—you cannot use **0** and **NULL**. Be sure to use the *address* of **argc**, since **XtAppInitialize** changes **argc** when X options are removed from **argv**.

The next parameter passes a set of fallback resources to **XtAppInitialize**. X uses fallback resources if the expected resource files cannot be found when the application begins to run. Fallback resources are also discussed in Chapter 12.

The last two parameters let you use an argument list to change resource values belonging to the toplevel shell (see Chapters 3 and 12). Since this feature is not being used during the creation of the toplevel shell, **NULL** and **0** are passed.

XtAppInitialize returns the toplevel shell widget for this program. A shell widget appears on the screen as a complete window, framed by decorations consisting of a border with a title area, resizing areas, and so on. All Motif programs have a shell that holds the application on the screen. The program places the widget value that **XtAppInitialize** returns into the widget variable named **toplevel**. Every time you need to change something about the toplevel shell widget, you reference it using the **toplevel** variable.

A call to **XtAppInitialize** should be the first line of all of your Motif programs. Be aware that it is easy to pass parameters improperly and create segmentation faults or addressing errors. All of the following lines of code cause segmentation faults that can be very hard to track down:

```
toplevel=XtAppInitialize(context,"",NULL,0,&argc,argv,NULL,NULL,0);
toplevel=XtAppInitialize(&context,NULL,NULL,0,&argc,argv,NULL,NULL,0);
toplevel=XtAppInitialize(&context,"",NULL,0,0,NULL,NULL,NULL,0);
toplevel=XtAppInitialize(&context,"",NULL,0,argc,argv,NULL,NULL,0);
```

You must pass Motif, Xt, and X functions exactly what they expect, or the program will not run.

2.2.2   LINES 13 AND 14

The toplevel shell, created by the call to **XtAppInitialize** in line 12 of the program, acts as the window for the application on-screen. It is empty until you place other widgets into it; doing so creates the user interface. This program creates one label widget and places it inside the toplevel shell. Lines 13 and 14 set the **labelString** resource of the label widget to a value, and the label widget displays that value on the screen. In this program, the value is the string "Hello World."

```
ac=0;
XtSetArg(al[ac],XmNlabelString,
    XmStringCreate("Hello World",char_set)); ac++;
```

Every label widget has a set of resources that you can change to customize the widget's appearance—for example, you can change the text, font, and size of the label. The code for our simple program changes the **labelString** resource of the label widget and leaves all of its other resources at their default values. For the names of the resources and their defaults, see Appendix J, (which contains summaries of the resource lists), the *Motif Programmer's Reference Manual*, or on-line manual pages on widgets.

To change the resources of any widget, your code needs to create an argument array, fill it with the names of resource values you want to change and their new values, and then pass it to the widget. Our program uses **ac** as a counter to keep track of the number of resource values stored in the array, and uses **al** as the argument list. Using the **XtSetArg** call, the code inserts the value "Hello World" into **al[0]** and specifies that the value should be used for the **XmNlabelString** resource. Make sure **ac** accurately reflects the number of resources in **al**.

The last point is very important. The incorrect code below shows how something seemingly straightforward can create unexpected problems in Motif:

```
XtSetArg(al[ac++],XmNlabelString,...);
```

You must place **ac++** on its own at the end of the statement, as shown in the program, because **XtSetArg** is a macro. When the macro is expanded, the following code is produced:

```
al[ac].name=XmNlabelString;
al[ac].value=...;
```

If you place **al[ac++]** within the call to **XtSetArg**, **ac** is increased two increments by the expanded macro, which is not what you intended.

You also have to contend with the **XmStringCreateLtoR** call. Motif strings are different from normal strings because they contain more information, so you must use a special procedure to create them. The first parameter is the value of the string, and the second is the character set for the string. Chapter 3 explains this process further.

You can commit errors easily when working with resource settings and argument lists. You can misspell the resource name, forget to initialize or increment **ac**, place too many values in **al** (as an array it can overflow), or forget to create an actual **XmString**.

The parameters of **XtSetArg** and **XmStringCreateLtoR** are described below.

XtSetArg *Sets a resource argument in the argument array.*

```
void XtSetArg(
    Arg arg,
    String resource_name,
    XtArgVal value);
```

arg   An argument variable. By convention, a location in an array.
resource_name   The name of the resource to set.
value   The value to which you want to set the resource.

XmStringCreateLtoR   *Creates an **XmString** from a normal, null-terminated C string.*

```
XmString XmStringCreateLtoR(
    char *text,
    XmStringCharSet charset);
```

text   The null-terminated C string.

charset   The character set to use during creation of the
           XmString.

2.2.3   LINE 15

Now that you have set up the argument list, you can create the label widget
itself.

```
label=XmCreateLabel(toplevel,"label",al,ac);
```

In this line, the parameter **label** is the name you choose for the widget. Use it
when setting the widget's resources from a resource file (see Chapter 12). It is
fairly common to give the same name to the widget and the widget variable.
Widget names should be unique and descriptive.

The **toplevel** parameter declares which widget is the parent of the label
widget. All widgets in an application except the toplevel shell must have a
parent. The toplevel shell can have only one child. As we will see in Chapter
5, Motif provides manager widgets that can hold many children.

The **al** and **ac** parameters let you modify the value of the widget's resources.
Since we have set up **al** and **ac** to contain resource values, the program passes
these variables to the widget here.

Once the widget is created, the function returns a value to the **label** variable.
This variable will be used later to refer to that widget individually.

As with line 12, there are many ways to make line 15 create segmentation
faults. Here, however, you can replace the **al** and **ac** parameters with **NULL**
and **0**, respectively, if you are not changing any resources at creation. An
extremely common mistake is to leave out the header file for the label widget
(`Label.h`). With many compilers, this omission generates irrational errors in
several places. Make sure you have included all the header files needed for all
of the widgets you use.

The description of **XmCreateLabel** follows.

XmCreateLabel   *Creates a label widget.*

```
Widget XmCreateLabel(
    Widget parent,
    String name,
    ArgList args,
    Cardinal num_args);
```

parent	The parent widget of the new widget.
name	The name of the widget, used when referring to its resources (see Chapter 12).
args	A resource argument array.
num_args	The number of arguments in the argument array.

2.2.4   LINE 16

Line 16 causes the widget's parent to manage its size and location on-screen.

```
XtManageChild(label)
```

If a widget is not managed, it will not appear on the screen. The widget will not actually appear until the code enters the event loop.

2.2.5   LINE 17

Line 17 realizes the **toplevel** widget.

```
XtRealizeWidget(toplevel);
```

When the toplevel shell is realized, the window frame that holds this application is created, along with the application's title, resizing borders, and so on. All of toplevel's child widgets are realized as well, and they too appear on screen (that is, all managed children become visible; unmanaged children do not). In general, a shell widget such as **toplevel** is the only widget you have to realize with an actual call, because the call to **XtRealizeWidget** recursively realizes all of the children of **toplevel**.

XtRealizeWidget   *Realizes a widget.*

```
void XtRealizeWidget(Widget w);
```

w   The shell widget to be realized.

It is useful to define the terms *manage, create,* and *realize,* and describe their differences. When you create a widget, you set up and initialize all of its resources. When you manage a widget, its parent is controlling its size and placement on the screen. When you realize a widget, you create its window (at the X level). A single realize call to **toplevel** recursively realizes all of its children.

2.2.6   LINE 18

Line 18 causes the event loop to begin processing events. The event loop removes events from the X event queue and passes them to the appropriate widget for processing.

```
XtAppMainLoop(context);
```

Since Motif manages the event loop for you, you do not have to worry about it. The main loop that **XtAppMainLoop** creates handles all events the application receives. From this point on, anything that happens in your code will happen because of callbacks triggered by user events passed to a specific widget. This topic is covered in detail in Chapter 4.

XtAppMainLoop   *Manages the Motif event loop.*

```
void XtAppMainLoop(XtAppContext context);
```

context   The context variable for the application received from
             XtAppInitialize.

---

3 RESOURCES

One of the keys to understanding Motif programming is understanding the concept of resources. The programmer designs a Motif application by selecting a set of widgets to compose the user interface. Every widget, in turn, has a set of associated resources that control its appearance and behavior. Resources are much like normal variables, except that you must access them in a special way. For example, a label widget has resources that determine such features as the string displayed by the label, the font used to display the string, and the margins around the string. These resources can be read or set to new values. The programmer changes the widgets in the user interface by adjusting resource values.

The label widget program described in Chapter 2 set only one resource of the label widget: it set the value of the label widget's **labelString** resource to "Hello World." The rest of the resources retained their default values. This chapter introduces you to resources by exploring some of the things you can accomplish by setting and getting resource values in a label widget.

3.1 GETTING STARTED

The program shown in Listing 3.1 demonstrates how to change the width and height resources of the label widget.

Listing 3.1 Changing the Width and Height of a Widget

```
    /* size1.c */
1   #include <Xm/Xm.h>
2   #include <Xm/Label.h>

3   XtAppContext context;
4   XmStringCharSet char_set=XmSTRING_DEFAULT_CHARSET;
```

```
5       Widget toplevel, label;

6       main(argc,argv)
7          int argc;
8          char *argv[];
9       {
10         Arg al[10];
11         int ac;

           /* create the toplevel shell */
12         toplevel = XtAppInitialize(&context,"",NULL,0,&argc,argv,
               NULL,NULL,0);

           /* create label widget */
13         ac=0;
14         XtSetArg(al[ac],XmNlabelString,
               XmStringCreateLtoR("Hello World", char_set)); ac++;
14a        XtSetArg(al[ac],XmNheight,300); ac++;
14b        XtSetArg(al[ac],XmNwidth,300); ac++;
15         label=XmCreateLabel(toplevel,"label",al,ac);
16         XtManageChild(label);

17         XtRealizeWidget(toplevel);
18         XtAppMainLoop(context);
19      }
```

This is the same program used in Chapters 1 and 2, with the addition of two new lines, 14a and 14b, that modify the **width** and **height** resources of the label widget. When you compile and run this code, note that the label widget contains the same string in the same font, but now the widget itself is much larger. Note also that the toplevel shell is larger to accommodate the larger label. This occurs because the toplevel shell is the parent of the label widget and therefore manages its size and position. When the shell is realized, it determines its own size based on the size of the label. The window should appear with a size of 300 × 300 pixels, as shown in Figure 3.1. Compare this figure with Figure 2.1, which shows the output of the program in Listing 2.1.

The modification of widget resources like **width** and **height** is the key to controlling the behavior and appearance of each widget in a Motif application. To use a widget effectively, you should be familiar with all of its resources, as well as the techniques for setting them. Resource lists provide this information for each widget.

**Figure 3.1   A 300-by-300-Pixel Label Widget
Produced by Listing 3.1**

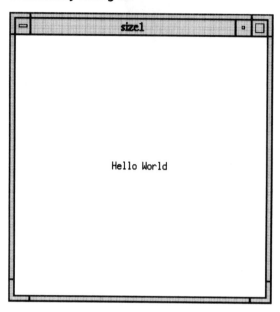

3.2   THE LABEL WIDGET'S RESOURCE LIST

Appendix J contains resource lists and brief descriptions of the resources for all
of the Motif widgets. The *Motif Programmer's Reference Manual* contains more
complete descriptions of all resources. Following is the description for the
label widget from Appendix J. It contains a lot of information, but it tells you
everything you need to know.

XmLabel Widget

Also available as a gadget.

Description	Displays a compound string or a pixmap
Class Pointer	xmLabelWidgetClass
Class Name	XmLabel
Include File	<Xm/Label.h>
Superclass	XmPrimitive

RESOURCES

Name	Type	Default
XmNaccelerator	String	NULL
XmNacceleratorText	XmString	NULL
XmNalignment	unsigned char	XmALIGNMENT_CENTER
XmNfontList	XmFontList	dynamic
XmNlabelInsensitive-Pixmap	Pixmap	XmUNSPECIFIED_PIXMAP
XmNlabelPixmap	Pixmap	XmUNSPECIFIED_PIXMAP
XmNlabelString	XmString	NULL
XmNlabelType	unsigned char	XmSTRING
XmNmarginBottom	Dimension	0
XmNmarginHeight	Dimension	2
XmNmarginLeft	Dimension	0
XmNmarginRight	Dimension	0
XmNmarginTop	Dimension	0
XmNmarginWidth	Dimension	2
XmNmnemonic	KeySym	NULL
XmNMnemonicCharSet	String	dynamic
XmNrecomputeSize	Boolean	True
XmNstringDirection	XmString-Direction	XmSTRING_DIRECTION_L_TO_R

RESOURCE DESCRIPTIONS

XmNaccelerator	The accelerator character to use when the label is used as part of a push-button or a toggle button in a menu. See Chapter 6.
XmNacceleratorText	Text that tells the user what the accelerator is. See Chapter 6.
XmNalignment	Alignment of string in the label. XmALIGNMENT_BEGINNING, XmALIGNMENT_CENTER, or XmALIGNMENT_END are valid.
XmNfontList	Font used to display labelString.
XmNlabelInsensitivePixmap	Used if label is insensitive and is displaying a pixmap (labelType = XmPIXMAP).
XmNlabelPixmap	Used if label is sensitive and is displaying a pixmap (labelType = XmPIXMAP).
XmNlabelString	String the label displays if labelType = XmSTRING.

XmNlabelType	Specifies whether label displays a string (Xm-STRING) or a pixmap (XmPIXMAP).
XmNmarginBottom	Space between the bottom of the label string and the top of the bottom margin.
XmNmarginHeight	Height of the margin above and below the label string.
XmNmarginLeft	Space to the left of the label string.
XmNmarginRight	Space to the right of the label string.
XmNmarginTop	Space above the label string.
XmNmarginWidth	Width of the margin to the left and right of the label string.
XmNmnemonic	The mnemonic character that activates the button when the label is part of a pushbutton or toggle button.
XmNmnemonicCharSet	The mnemonic's character set.
XmNrecomputeSize	When true, any change to the label will cause it to readjust its size immediately. When false, no readjustment takes place.
XmNstringDirection	Determines direction string is drawn. Xm-STRING_DIRECTION_L_TO_R and XmSTRING_DIRECTION_R_TO_L are valid.

CONVENIENCE FUNCTIONS

```
Widget XmCreateLabel(Widget parent,String name,ArgList arglist,
    Cardinal argcount);
Widget XmCreateLabelGadget(Widget parent,String name,ArgList arglist,
    Cardinal argcount);
```

The description field at the top describes what the label widget does. Note that a label widget is not restricted to text; it can also display a pixmap of any size (see Chapter 17). You use the class (or type) pointer and name when calling functions (**XtCreateManagedWidget**, for example) for which you need to know the type of the widget. You must include the include file at the top of any program that uses a label widget. The superclass specifies the widget from which the label widget inherits its behavior. Section 3.3 describes the implications of the superclass in more detail.

A summary table of resources comes next in the description. This table is important for three reasons: It lists the *names* of all available resources; it lists the *type* of each resource; and it lists the *default value* of each resource. Following the table is a set of brief descriptions to help the programmer better understand the purpose of each resource and a list of the convenience functions appropriate to the widget.

For example, the table provides the following information about the resource **XmNlabelType** (often written simply as **labelType**). The type of this resource is **unsigned char**, which means that it expects an integer constant value. The default value is the constant value **XmSTRING**. According to the description, you can also give the **labelType** resource the value **XmPIXMAP**, which means that the widget can display a text string or a pixmap.

The resource list demonstrates the flexibility of the label widget. As you can see, many of its features are customizable. For example, you can customize the label's text by changing the **labelString** resource, the alignment of the text by changing the **alignment** resource, or the font by changing the **fontList** resource.

3.3 UNDERSTANDING INHERITANCE

The *superclass* of a widget plays an important role in its behavior. In the case of a label widget, the superclass is a primitive widget. In other words, a label widget is built from a more fundamental widget called a primitive widget. The label widget *inherits* all of the resources and callbacks a primitive widget possesses.

When you look at the resource list for the label widget, you may note that there are some very obvious items missing. For example, Listing 3.1 set the **height** and **width** resources for the label, but the label widget's resource list mentions no **XmNheight** or **XmNwidth** resources. Why? The label widget is built from a primitive widget, and the primitive widget, in turn, is built from a core widget, as are all widgets in all widget sets. The core widget contains fundamental resources common to all widgets, such as **width** and **height**.

The resource lists for the primitive and core widgets appear in Appendix J. The width, height, foreground and background color, highlighting behavior, borders, and so on, are all declared here. Because of the inheritance from core widget to primitive widget to label widget, there are a total of 51 resources that affect a label widget's behavior (18 core, 16 primitive, and 17 of its own). Figure 3.2 summarizes the inheritance hierarchy for label widgets.

In the remainder of this chapter, we will manipulate several of the resources that control the label widget to gain a better understanding of how to use resources.

Figure 3.2   The Inheritance Hierarchy for Label Widgets

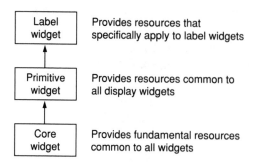

Label widget	Provides resources that specifically apply to label widgets
Primitive widget	Provides resources common to all display widgets
Core widget	Provides fundamental resources common to all widgets

3.4   A SIMPLE EXAMPLE REVISITED: CHANGING THE HEIGHT AND WIDTH OF A WIDGET

All widgets have resources that control their height and width. These resources are inherited from the core widget, from which all widgets are built. If you do not specifically set its **width** and **height** resources, a label widget will automatically adjust to the size of the string or pixmap it displays. If you want it to have a specific size, however, you can specify this through the resources.

Several different techniques can be used to set the value of a widget's resources. You can set resources from the command line, from resource files, or from within a program (see Chapter 12). From within a program, you have two options: You can specify the values as the widget is created by passing an argument list into the function that creates the widget; or you can set the values of the widget after it has been created using the **XtSetValues** function.

The code in Listing 3.1 illustrated the first option, but it might also have been written using **XtSetValues**, as shown in Listing 3.2.

Listing 3.2   Using XtSetValues to Set Resource Values

```
      /* size2.c */
1     #include <Xm/Xm.h>
2     #include <Xm/Label.h>

3     XtAppContext context;
4     XmStringCharSet char_set=XmSTRING_DEFAULT_CHARSET;

5     Widget toplevel, label;
```

Setting and Getting Resources

al

	al	
al[0]	XmNLabelString	"Hello World"
al[1]	XmNalignment	Xm_ALIGNMENT_END
al[2]	XmNrecomputeSize	False
al[3]		
al[4]		

◄— ac is 3 (pointing to al[2] row)

and so on

When you set resources, you make use of a structure called an argument list. This list is an array that contains pairs of items; the first item in a pair is the resource's name, and the second is the resource's new value.

In the figure above, **al** is the array. It contains pairs of items, three of which are currently in use. The **ac** variable keeps track of the number of valid items in the argument list.

Following is the code that creates the argument list and sends it to an existing label widget:

```
ac=0;
XtSetArg(al[ac],XmNlabelString,
    XmStringCreateLtoR("Hello World",
    char_set)); ac++;
XtSetArg(al[ac],XmNalignment,
    XmALIGNMENT_END); ac++;
XtSetArg(al[ac],XmNrecomputeSize,
    False); ac++;
XtSetValues(label,al,ac);
```

The Xt layer supports a second way to pass argument lists to an existing widget, using the **XtVaSetValues** function. In this case, the argument list is passed directly:

```
XtVaSetValues (label,
    XmNlabelString,XmStringCreateLtoR
    ("Hello World",char_set),
    XmNalignment,XmALIGNMENT_END,
    XmNrecomputeSize,False,
    NULL);
```

The Xt layer also supports an **XtVaGet-Values** function, which you can use to retrieve values from a widget:

```
XtVaGetValues(label,
    XmNwidth,&w,
    XmNheight,&h,
    NULL);
```

The **Va** capability does not exist in the Motif widget creation functions, so you must use **al** and **ac** to change resource values during widget creation.

```
6    main(argc,argv)
7        int argc;
8        char *argv[];
9    {
10       Arg al[10];
11       int ac;

         /* create the toplevel shell */
12       toplevel = XtAppInitialize(&context,"",NULL,0,&argc,argv,
             NULL,NULL,0);

         /* create label widget */
13       ac=0;
14       XtSetArg(al[ac],XmNlabelString,
             XmStringCreateLtoR("Hello World", char_set)); ac++;
15       label=XmCreateLabel(toplevel,"label",al,ac);
16       XtManageChild(label);

         /* Set resources in the label widget. */
16a      ac=0;
16b      XtSetArg(al[ac],XmNheight,300); ac++;
16c      XtSetArg(al[ac],XmNwidth,300); ac++;
16d      XtSetValues(label,al,ac);

17       XtRealizeWidget(toplevel);
18       XtAppMainLoop(context);
19   }
```

Listing 3.2 contains four new lines (16a–16d). These lines load an argument list with the new values for the **height** and **width** resources. They then use the argument list to set the values of those resources in the label widget using the **XtSetValues** function. **XtSetValues** accepts three parameters: the widget to set, the argument list, and a count. When you run this code, it will behave identically to the code that generated Figure 3.1.

XtSetValues   *Passes an Arg list to a widget.*

```
void XtSetValues(Widget widget,
    ArgList arg,
    Cardinal num_args)
```

widget   The widget you want to set.

arg   The argument array of resources and values.

num_args   The number of arguments in the array.

Watch for the following problems when setting resources:

1. Make sure you initialize and increment **ac** correctly. It is *extremely* easy to forget line 13, which can cause very strange behavior.
2. Make sure you spell the resource names correctly. Case matters.
3. Make sure you use only resource names valid for the widget in question. For example, if you try to set the **autoUnmanage** resource for the label widget, the code will compile because the bulletin board widget uses that resource name and makes it valid. However, the code will ignore **autoUnmanage** because the label widget does not have a resource of this name anywhere in its inheritance hierarchy.
4. Make sure you pass **al** and **ac** to **XtSetValues** in the correct order, or you will get a bus error or segmentation fault when you run the program, even though the code will compile correctly on many machines.

As you can see, changing the **height** and **width** of a widget is straightforward. Several other resources in the label widget's resource list have integer values, and you can change them all easily.

3.5   CHANGING THE LABELSTRING RESOURCE, REVISITED

In all of the examples so far, we have been changing the **labelString** resource. It is important to look at this process closely and understand how it works.

The C programming language defines a string as a null-terminated array of characters. Motif uses a somewhat more complicated string type called an **Xm-String**, often referred to as a compound string (see Chapter 14). In order to use C strings with Motif widgets, you must first convert them to the **XmString** format. Motif provides functions to convert C strings to **XmStrings** and **Xm-Strings** to C strings.

Recall that when we set the width resource in the previous section, we used a call to **XtSetArg**, as shown here:

```
XtSetArg(al[ac],XmNwidth,300); ac++;
```

The **XtSetArg** function accepts three parameters: the argument to be set, the name of a resource, and the value to be used for that resource. The call to

XtSetArg specifies that the **width** resource be set to the value 300. This specification is placed at location **ac** in the argument list (array) **al**, and **ac** is incremented.

To set the **labelString** resource, **XtSetArg** is used in the same way. To do this, we have been using the line:

```
XtSetArg(al[ac],XmNlabelString,
    XmStringCreateLtoR("Hello World",char_set)); ac++;
```

It might be clearer to declare a specific **XmString** variable (I will use **s** for it here) and break the above line into two parts, as shown below:

```
XmString s; /*declare s somewhere in the program */
    .
    .
    .
s=XmStringCreateLtoR("Hello World",char_set);
XtSetArg(al[ac],XmNlabelString,s); ac++;
```

Now the **XtSetArg** line looks just as it did for **XmNwidth**: **labelString** is set to the value **s**.

The conversion process demonstrated here is extremely important. (It is very easy to forget the conversion and innocently try to pass a normal C string in the **XtSetArg** call. The code will compile correctly on many machines, but it will not work correctly because the resource type for the **labelString** resource is **XmString**.) **XmStringCreateLtoR** converts a C string to an **XmString**. The call to **XmStringCreateLtoR** accepts two parameters: the C string you want to convert, and the character set for the conversion. In this example, the character set is represented by the variable **char_set**, which is set to the value **Xm-STRING_DEFAULT_CHARSET**. In Chapter 14, you will learn about character sets and **char_set**.

You can display long messages in label widgets, but if the message contains 120 characters, the label widget that ends up holding it will become extremely long and narrow. To get around this problem, you can embed new-line characters within the C string to break up the text into several lines inside the label widget:

```
XtSetArg(al[ac],XmNlabelString,
    XmStringCreateLtoR("line one\nline two\nline three\nline four",
    char_set)); ac++;
```

The function **XmStringCreateLtoR** recognizes the **\n** characters and converts them properly into separate components within the **XmString** variable. Each component will appear in its own line in the label when the label is displayed.

The **alignment** resource controls the positioning of **labelString** in the label. You can set the alignment resource to the values **XmALIGNMENT_ BEGINNING, XmALIGNMENT_CENTER** (the default), or **XmALIGNMENT_ END.** The following code provides an example:

```
XtSetArg(al[ac],XmNalignment,XmALIGNMENT_BEGINNING); ac++;
```

Pass this argument into the widget when you create it or use an **XtSetValues** call.

Exercises

1. Try replacing the line

```
XtSetArg(al[ac],XmNlabelString,
    XmStringCreateLtoR("Hello World",char_set)); ac++;
```

with the line

```
XtSetArg(al[ac],XmNlabelString,"Hello World"); ac++;
```

Note the result when the program fails to execute.
2. Try all three different values for the **alignment** resource with a long multiline string (a string containing \n characters) to see what effect this resource has on the string the label widget displays.

3.6 CHANGING THE FONT USED

The label widget allows you to specify a font list for the label in your code. Setting **fontList** is somewhat more involved than setting the width and height of a widget, but you follow the same general procedure. An example is shown in Listing 3.3.

Listing 3.3 Changing a Label Widget's fontList Resource

```
    /* font.c */
1   #include <Xm/Xm.h>
2   #include <Xm/Label.h>

3   XtAppContext context;
4   XmStringCharSet char_set=XmSTRING_DEFAULT_CHARSET;

5   Widget toplevel, label;
```

```
6     main(argc,argv)
7        int argc;
8        char *argv[];
9     {
10       Arg al[10];
11       int ac;
11a      XFontStruct *font=NULL;
11b      XmFontList fontlist=NULL;
11c      char *namestring=NULL;

         /* create the toplevel shell */
12       toplevel = XtAppInitialize(&context,"",NULL,0,&argc,argv,
             NULL,NULL,0);

         /* create label widget */
13       ac=0;
14       XtSetArg(al[ac],XmNlabelString,
             XmStringCreateLtoR("Hello World", char_set)); ac++;
15       label=XmCreateLabel(toplevel,"label",al,ac);
16       XtManageChild(label);

         /* Set fontList resource in the label widget. */
16a      namestring="*times*24*"; /* you may need to change this. */
16b      font=XLoadQueryFont(XtDisplay(label),namestring);
16c      fontlist=XmFontListCreate(font,char_set);
16d      ac=0;
16e      XtSetArg(al[ac],XmNfontList,fontlist); ac++;
16f      XtSetValues(label,al,ac);

17       XtRealizeWidget(toplevel);
18       XtAppMainLoop(context);
19    }
```

Lines 16a through 16f create a font list and set the **fontList** resource of the label widget. Line 16a takes the name of the font and points **namestring** at it. Line 16b loads the font using the X function **XLoadQueryFont**. Line 16c creates a Motif font list from the X font structure using **XmFontListCreate**. Lines 16d-16f set the value of the **fontList** resource. This process is similar to the one that creates an **XmString** from a C string, as shown in the previous section: Motif uses a special font list structure, so **XmFontListCreate** translates the X form of the font list created by **XLoadQueryFont** into a Motif font list. See Chapter 14 for more details on this process.

**Figure 3.3 A Label Widget Displaying the Label
String in 24-Point Times**

When you run this code, you should see the label displayed in a 24-point Times font, as shown in Figure 3.3. If not, see below for an explanation and a fix.

To find the font names that are valid on your system, type the following command at the UNIX prompt:

```
xlsfonts -fn "*" > out
```

The file out will contain all of the font names known to your system. Some of them are short, such as "6x10", but others are monsters, as the following fragment of my out file shows:

```
-adobe-times-bold-i-normal---24-240-75-75-p-128-iso8859-1
-adobe-times-bold-i-normal---25-180-100-100-p-128-iso8859-1
-adobe-times-bold-i-normal---34-240-100-100-p-170-iso8859-1
```

To avoid having to type long font names such as these, you can use asterisks (*) as wildcards when setting **namestring**:

```
namestring="*times*24*";
```

This line of code will set the font of the label widget to 24-point Times. However, there may be many 24-point Times fonts that match the wildcard description. If so, the code uses the first match it finds. On the system I am using, the first match to "***times*24***" happens to be

```
-adobe-times-bold-i-normal---24-240-75-75-p-128-iso8859-1
```

This font is bold and italic. If you want a specific Times font, use a more specific argument, such as "***times*bold*-24-***".

If the code finds no matching font, nothing happens. For example, if you use the sample code on page 43, and your system does not have a 24-point Times font, the code will leave the font at its default value. In such a case, look at the file containing the fonts available on your system, pick one, and use it for the value of **namestring**.

Exercise

1. Try several different fonts, using more and less specific font names, and see how the font changes the label's appearance.

3.7   AN ANOMALY

Motif is a very rich programming environment. At times, however, its richness can lead to internal interactions that result in what appears to be incorrect program behavior. Run the code in Listing 3.4 to see an example of such an anomaly.

Listing 3.4   A Resource-Setting Anomaly

```
     /* anomaly.c */
1    #include <Xm/Xm.h>
2    #include <Xm/Label.h>

3    XtAppContext context;
4    XmStringCharSet char_set=XmSTRING_DEFAULT_CHARSET;

5    Widget toplevel, label;

6    main(argc,argv)
7      int argc;
8      char *argv[];
9    {
10     Arg al[10];
11     int ac;
11a    XFontStruct *font=NULL;
11b    XmFontList fontlist=NULL;
11c    char *namestring=NULL;

       /* create the toplevel shell */
12     toplevel = XtAppInitialize(&context,"",NULL,0,&argc,argv,
          NULL,NULL,0);

       /* create label widget */
13     ac=0;
14     XtSetArg(al[ac],XmNlabelString,
          XmStringCreateLtoR("Hello World", char_set)); ac++;
14a    XtSetArg(al[ac],XmNheight,300); ac++;
14b    XtSetArg(al[ac],XmNwidth,300); ac++;
```

```
15      label=XmCreateLabel(toplevel,"label",al,ac);
16      XtManageChild(label);

        /* Set fontList resource in the label widget. */
16a     namestring="*times*24*"; /* you may need to change this. */
16b     font=XLoadQueryFont(XtDisplay(label),namestring);
16c     fontlist=XmFontListCreate(font,char_set);
16d     ac=0;
16e     XtSetArg(al[ac],XmNfontList,fontlist); ac++;
16f     XtSetValues(label,al,ac);

17      XtRealizeWidget(toplevel);
18      XtAppMainLoop(context);
19   }
```

This code changes the size of the label widget to 300 × 300 when it creates the label. It also changes the font of the label to 24-point Times after creation. When you run this program, you expect it to display the string "Hello World" in 24-point Times in a label widget of 300 × 300 pixels. Instead, the label appears as it does in Figure 3.3, as if the changes to the **width** and **height** resources had no effect.

Why does this occur? If you examine the resource list for the label widget (see Appendix J), you will find that it contains a resource named **recompute-Size**. This is a Boolean resource with a default value of true. When true, this resource causes the label widget to recompute its size each time the pixmap, accelerator text, margins, font list, or label string resource types are set. The label widget in the above code resized itself when the **fontList** resource changed, negating the effect of setting the widget's width and height. You can solve this problem by setting **recomputeSize** to false.

This example demonstrates an important fact about Motif programming: Unexpected behavior can result from seemingly straightforward code. When unexpected behavior occurs, search for a rational cause.

3.8 READING RESOURCE VALUES

It is often useful to read the value of a resource when responding to a callback or when retrieving what a user has done to a user-modifiable widget such as a scroll bar. The code in Listing 3.5 demonstrates how to read the height and width of a label widget.

**Listing 3.5   Reading the height and width Resources
of a Label Widget**

```
      /* getsize.c */
1     #include <Xm/Xm.h>
2     #include <Xm/Label.h>

3     XtAppContext context;
4     XmStringCharSet char_set=XmSTRING_DEFAULT_CHARSET;

5     Widget toplevel, label;

6     main(argc,argv)
7       int argc;
8       char *argv[];
9     {
10      Arg al[10];
11      int ac;
12      Dimension w,h;

13      toplevel = XtAppInitialize(&context,"",NULL,0,&argc,argv,
            NULL,NULL,0);

      /* Create a label widget */
14      ac=0;
15      XtSetArg(al[ac],XmNlabelString,
            XmStringCreateLtoR("Hello Hello Hello Hello",char_set)); ac++;
16      label=XmCreateLabel(toplevel,"label",al,ac);
17      XtManageChild(label);

      /* Get the height and width */
18a     ac=0;
18b     XtSetArg(al[ac],XmNheight,&h); ac++;
18c     XtSetArg(al[ac],XmNwidth,&w); ac++;
18d     XtGetValues(label,al,ac);
18e     printf("%d %d \n",w,h);

19      XtRealizeWidget(toplevel);
20      XtAppMainLoop(context);
21    }
```

Here, the string "Hello Hello Hello Hello" controls the height and width of the
widget, which will automatically size itself to hold this string.

To read a resource value, you create an argument list using **XtSetArg** in a manner very similar to that used in the previous examples. To **XtSetArg** is passed the argument, the name of the resource to be read, and the *address* of the variable into which the resource value should be placed after it is read. Then **XtGetValues** is called to get the resource values requested.

XtGetValues   *Retrieves resource values to a widget.*

```
void XtGetValues(
    Widget widget,
    ArgList arg,
    Cardinal num_args)
```

widget   The widget you want to set.

arg   The argument array of resources and values.

num_args   The number of arguments in the array.

Note that the variables **w** and **h** are declared as type **Dimension**—the type **int** won't work, or produces unexpected results, on many machines. Make sure that variables you use to read resource values have exactly the same type as the resource being read. Use the resource lists in Appendix J to determine the correct type for a resource.

3.9   READING BACK THE LABEL WIDGET'S LABELSTRING

To see a more complicated example, let's read back the label widget's **label-String** resource. Beginning with the code above, declare the variables **s** and **cstring**, then replace lines 16a through 16e with the code shown in Listing 3.6.

Listing 3.6   Reading the labelString Resource

```
XmString s;
char *cstring;
  .
  .
  .
ac=0;
XtSetArg(al[ac],XmNlabelString,&s); ac++;
XtGetValues(label,al,ac);
XmStringGetLtoR(s,char_set,&cstring);
printf("%s\n",cstring);
```

This code gets the **XmString** in **labelString** and then converts it back to a normal C string so that it can be printed to standard out (stdout).

Any experienced C programmer who looks at this code hears a small voice in the back of his or her head whispering two dreaded words: "memory leaks." The first tip-off is the fact that the code declares **cstring** as a pointer. Something is allocating the block to which it eventually points but nothing is freeing that block up. To prevent memory leaks, add these two lines following the **printf** statement:

```
XmStringFree(s);
XtFree(cstring);
```

Since the variable **s** is specifically an **XmString**, this code uses a special **XmStringFree** function to free that block: Use **XtFree** on the **cstring** block. You can use **XtFree** interchangeably with the normal C **free** function (see Chapter 16).

While on the subject of memory leaks, notice that the following statement, which is used frequently in this book and others, leaks:

```
XtSetArg(al[ac],XmNlabelString,
    XmStringCreateLtoR("Hello", char_set)); ac++;
```

The call to **XmStringCreateLtoR** returns a pointer, and that pointer is never freed. In general, this leak is considered acceptable because the **labelString** is changed only once in most cases. A label whose **labelString** resource changes frequently, however, can present problems. You can use the code in Listing 3.7 as a solution.

Listing 3.7   Preventing Memory Leaks in XmStrings

```
XmString s; /*declare s somewhere in the program */
  .
  .
  .
s=XmStringCreateLtoR("Hello World",char_set);
XtSetArg(al[ac],XmNlabelString,s); ac++;
XtSetValues(label,al,ac);
XmStringFree(s);
```

Note that the string **s** cannot be freed until after the call to **XtSetValues**. A copy of the string is made at that point.

3.10   A NOTE OF CAUTION

XtSetArg, combined with **XtSetValues**, can set a resource to a four-byte value. That is all it can do. If the resource is an integer or Boolean value, it passes the integer or value as the four-byte value. Otherwise, it passes a pointer. No checking is done on this pointer, as we saw in the exercise where we set **labelString**. If a normal C string pointer is passed in as the value of **labelString**, with the necessary call to **XmStringCreateLtoR** omitted, the code compiles properly on many machines but fails to run. You must take care while programming to avoid pitfalls such as this.

In the same way, you can use **XtGetValues** to get a four-byte resource value. **XtGetValues** either gets the value directly, in the case of integers and Booleans, or returns a pointer. Misuse of these pointers can cause memory leaks, as we have just seen, and you should take care with them as well.

4 CALLBACKS

All Motif widgets have callbacks, which they use to trigger specific actions in response to user events. In this chapter we will work with a push-button widget to gain an understanding of how callbacks work, and then we will look at a more advanced example using a scale widget.

4.1   THE BASIC IDEA BEHIND CALLBACKS

The idea behind callbacks is extremely straightforward. If a user manipulates a widget on-screen, something needs to notify the program of the change. For example, if an application displays a push-button widget, the user will eventually click the push button and expect some specific action to result. For example, the user will expect the program to quit after clicking the button labeled "Quit." The program needs to know about the click so that it can generate the appropriate action.

Motif handles a mouse-click event in its main event loop (which is established by the call to the **XtAppMainLoop** function) and routes the event to the push-button widget. The push-button widget handles the event appropriately by making the button flash, but it also needs a way to communicate this event to the program. Motif provides a way with a callback function. A callback function is a normal C function that performs an appropriate action. The address of the callback function is passed to the widget with the function **XtAddCallback**, and thereby registered as a callback function for that widget. Whenever the widget detects a mouse event, it calls that function and the action occurs.

4.2   WORKING WITH THE PUSH-BUTTON WIDGET

In order to understand callbacks, you must use a widget capable of producing them in response to user events. A label widget cannot do this (although like all widgets, it produces a callback when destroyed). A push-button widget is the simplest widget that responds to user events, so we will use it here.

Look through the description of the push-button widget in Appendix J. Note that you must use the PushB.h include file. Also note that its superclass is the label widget, so it inherits all of the label widget's resources and callbacks. By extension, the push-button widget inherits all the resources and callbacks from the primitive and core widgets, because the label widget inherits them. It also adds three callbacks of its own: **activate**, **arm**, and **disarm**.

To try a push button, enter and run the code shown in Listing 4.1. Then try clicking the push button labeled "Push Me" several times.

Listing 4.1   The Creation of a Push-Button Widget

```
/* button.c */

#include <Xm/Xm.h>
#include <Xm/PushB.h>

XtAppContext context;
XmStringCharSet char_set=XmSTRING_DEFAULT_CHARSET;

Widget toplevel, button;

void main(argc,argv)
    int argc;
    char *argv[];
{
    Arg al[10];
    int ac;

    /* create the toplevel shell */
    toplevel = XtAppInitialize(&context,"",NULL,0,&argc,argv,
        NULL,NULL,0);

    /* create the button widget */
    ac=0;
    XtSetArg(al[ac],XmNlabelString,
        XmStringCreate("Push Me",char_set)); ac++;
    button=XmCreatePushButton(toplevel,"button",al,ac);
    XtManageChild(button);

    XtRealizeWidget(toplevel);
    XtAppMainLoop(context);
}
```

Figure 4.1 A Push-Button Widget

The code in Listing 4.1 is exactly the same code we used for the label widget in Chapters 1, 2 and 3, except that the **XmCreate** function has been changed from **XmCreateLabel** to **XmCreatePushButton**, and the include file at the top of the code has changed from Label.h to PushB.h. When you run this code, you should see a push button with the words "Push Me" in a window, as shown in Figure 4.1. Clicking this push button should highlight it. The button doesn't "do" anything useful yet, because we haven't told it what to do.

To make the push button do something, we have to use its callbacks. We can demonstrate this by modifying the code in Listing 4.1 so that it prints the words "button pushed" to standard out (stdout) whenever the button is pushed. Listing 4.2 shows the new code.

Listing 4.2 Wiring in the Activate Callback for the Push-Button Widget

```
/* callback.c*/

#include <Xm/Xm.h>
#include <Xm/PushB.h>

XtAppContext context;
XmStringCharSet char_set=XmSTRING_DEFAULT_CHARSET;

Widget toplevel, button;

void handle_button(w,client_data,call_data)
    Widget w;
    XtPointer client_data;
    XmPushButtonCallbackStruct *call_data;
/* handles the pushbutton's activate callback. */
{
    printf("button pushed\n");
}
```

```
void main(argc,argv)
    int argc;
    char *argv[];
{
    Arg al[10];
    int ac;

    /* create the toplevel shell */
    toplevel = XtAppInitialize(&context,"",NULL,0,&argc,argv,
        NULL,NULL,0);

    /* create the button widget */
    ac=0;
    XtSetArg(al[ac],XmNlabelString,
        XmStringCreate("Push Me",char_set)); ac++;
    button=XmCreatePushButton(toplevel,"button",al,ac);
    XtManageChild(button);
    XtAddCallback(button,XmNactivateCallback,handle_button,NULL);

    XtRealizeWidget(toplevel);
    XtAppMainLoop(context);
}
```

This modified program calls the **XtAddCallback** function after it creates the push-button widget. **XtAddCallback** tells the push-button widget to call the function named **handle_button** whenever its **activate** callback is triggered.

XtAddCallback   *Adds a callback function to a widget.*

```
void XtAddCallback(
    Widget w,
    String callback_name,
    XtCallbackProc callback,
    XtPointer client_data);
```

w	The widget.
callback_name	The name of the callback.
callback	The function to call when the callback is triggered.
client_data	Programmer-specified data sent to the callback function.

Now when a user clicks the button, the widget automatically calls **handle_button** which prints the words "button pushed" to stdout. As you can see, **handle_button** is nothing more than a standard C function and therefore can contain anything you like.

When called, callback functions receive three pieces of information as parameters. The first parameter is the widget that triggered the callback. The second is a piece of programmer-defined data, which can be anything that fits in four bytes, say an integer or a pointer. The **XtPointer** type is a generic C pointer type available in Xt and used by convention when you need a generic four-byte type. We use it here because at this point we are not doing anything with **client_data** in the code and therefore need to declare it as something generic. The third parameter is a pointer to the push-button callback structure, which contains an integer holding the reason for the callback and the complete event structure describing the event that triggered the callback. Section 4.4 describes the **call_data** Parameter in detail.

4.3   USING THE CLIENT_DATA FIELD

The **client_data** field can be extremely useful when you need to differentiate between multiple callbacks or when you need to send in a pointer to a record that contains information the callback needs. The code in Listing 4.3 demonstrates the former and will also help you to learn the difference between the **arm**, **disarm**, and **activate** callbacks generated by a push button.

Listing 4.3   Wiring in All Callbacks for the Push-Button Widget Using the client_data Parameter

```
/* all_callbacks.c */

#include <Xm/Xm.h>
#include <Xm/PushB.h>

XtAppContext context;
XmStringCharSet char_set=XmSTRING_DEFAULT_CHARSET;

Widget toplevel, button;

void handle_button(w,client_data,call_data)
    Widget w;
    int client_data;
    XmPushButtonCallbackStruct *call_data;
```

```
/* handles callbacks generated by the pushbutton */
{
    switch (client_data)
    {
        case 1:
            printf("activate\n");
            break;
        case 2:
            printf("arm\n");
            break;
        case 3:
            printf("disarm\n");
            break;
    }
}

void main(argc,argv)
    int argc;
    char *argv[];
{
    Arg al[10];
    int ac;

    /* create the toplevel shell */
    toplevel = XtAppInitialize(&context,"",NULL,0,&argc,argv,
        NULL,NULL,0);

    /* create the button widget */
    ac=0;
    XtSetArg(al[ac],XmNlabelString,
        XmStringCreate("Push Me",char_set)); ac++;
    button=XmCreatePushButton(toplevel,"button",al,ac);
    XtManageChild(button);
    XtAddCallback(button,XmNactivateCallback,handle_button,1);
    XtAddCallback(button,XmNarmCallback,handle_button,2);
    XtAddCallback(button,XmNdisarmCallback,handle_button,3);

    XtRealizeWidget(toplevel);
    XtAppMainLoop(context);
}
```

This code is similar to the previous code, except that all three of the call-backs a push-button widget can generate are now active, because of the three calls to **XtAddCallback** that appear immediately after the widget creation function. All of these callbacks call the same function (**handle_button**), but each one passes a different integer to the callback function through the **client_ data** parameter. In the callback function **handle_button**, the **client_data** parameter has been declared as an integer and guides a switch statement.

You can use this code to see the differences between the **arm**, **disarm**, and **activate** callbacks. Run the program, position the cursor inside the push button, and hold the mouse button down without releasing it. The word "arm" appears in stdout, because the **arm** callback was activated. Clicking the mouse button inside the push button arms the push button. Arming highlights it, and it remains highlighted as long as the mouse button stays clicked there.

Now move the cursor outside the push button while holding the mouse button down. The highlighting disappears, but the button is still armed. Now release the mouse button. A **disarm** callback is generated and a message to this effect prints to stdout. Since you released the mouse button outside the push button, however, the button was never activated.

Now click the push button again, and this time release the mouse button inside the highlighted push button. The **arm** callback is triggered, followed by the **activate** and **disarm** callbacks. The **activate** callback is generated only if the cursor is inside the push button when the mouse button is released.

As you can see, an **arm** callback is generated when you click the mouse button inside the push button, and a **disarm** callback is generated when the mouse button is subsequently released. The **activate** callback occurs only if the button is disarmed while the cursor is inside the button. **Activate** tends to be used far more frequently than **arm** or **disarm** in a program. The **arm** and **disarm** callbacks can be useful, however. For example, you may want some action to begin when the user first clicks the button and stop when the user releases it.

Is it better to use three separate callback functions or one callback function and a switch statement triggered off a **client_data** value, as shown above? This is really a matter of personal choice. If several callback functions contain similar code, I try to combine them and trigger the unique portions with a switch statement. This approach reuses code and can make the program shorter. If callback functions have nothing to do with each other, I tend to leave them separate.

You can declare the **client_data** parameter as any type that will fit in four bytes. For example, a program could have a structure called **data** of the type **struct data_type data**, which must be passed into a callback function via

client_data. Since the **client_data** parameter only accepts four bytes, a pointer to **data** must be passed. The following code will create the callback:

```
XtAddCallback(button,XmNactivateCallback,handle_button,&data);
```

You can declare the **client_data** parameter in the callback function as follows:

```
struct data_type *client_data
```

And you can use the **client_data** parameter in the callback function by referring to it as a pointer. Use either of the following:

```
client_data->fieldname = whatever;
```

```
(*client_data).fieldname = whatever;
```

where **fieldname** is the name of one of the fields in **data** and **whatever** is a value of that type.

4.4   WORKING WITH THE CALL_DATA PARAMETER

The **call_data** parameter passed to a callback function contains a great deal of information. The declaration of the **XmPushButtonCallbackStruct** structure is as follows:

```
typedef struct
{
    int reason;
    XEvent *event;
    int click_count;
} XmPushButtonCallbackStruct;
```

The **reason** field contains the reason for the callback, as listed in the callback list in Appendix J. In the case of a push-button widget, three reasons are possible:

Callback List	Call Data Type	Reason
XmNactivateCallback	XmPushButtonCallback-Struct	XmCR_ACTIVATE
XmNarmCallback	XmPushButtonCallback-Struct	XmCR_ARM
XmNdisarmCallback	XmPushButtonCallback-Struct	XmCR_DISARM

Inside the callback function, you can use the **reason** integer in much the same way as the integer **client_data** value in the previous piece of code:

```
void handle_button(w,client_data,call_data)
    Widget w;
    int client_data;
    XmPushButtonCallbackStruct *call_data;
/* handles callbacks generated by the pushbutton */
{
    switch (call_data->reason)
    {
        case XmCR_ACTIVATE:
            printf("activate\n");
            break;
        case XmCR_ARM:
            printf("arm\n");
            break;
        case XmCR_DISARM:
            printf("disarm\n");
            break;
    }
}
```

The **event** field of the **call_data** structure contains a copy of the actual X event that led to the callback. You can often ignore this field since Motif allows you to ignore events, but there are times when it contains useful information.

In order to use the **event** field effectively, you need to understand events in X (see Chapter 15). Briefly, X recognizes 25 different types of events. When a user clicks and then releases the mouse button, for example, X events of the type **ButtonPress** and **ButtonRelease** are generated. The information surrounding the event is packaged in an **XEvent** structure and delivered to Motif, which passes it to your code in the **event** field of **call_data**. Each different event type has a different event structure. The type **XEvent** is a union of all of these event structures (see Chapter 15). One of the fields of this union, **Xbutton**, contains the structure that corresponds to **ButtonPress** and **Button-Release** events.

The structure declaration for an **XButtonEvent** is as follows:

```
typedef struct {
    int type;              /* of event */
    unsigned long serial;  /* # of last request processed by server */
    Bool send_event;       /* true if this came from a SendEvent
                              request */
```

```
    Display *display;      /* Display the event was read from */
    Window window;         /* event window it's reported relative to */
    Window root;           /* root window that the event occurred on */
    Window subwindow;      /* child window */
    Time time;             /* milliseconds */
    int x, y;              /* pointer x, y coordinates in event
                                 window */
    int x_root, y_root;    /* coordinates relative to root */
    unsigned int state;    /* key or button mask */
    unsigned int button;   /* detail */
    Bool same_screen;      /* same screen flag */
} XButtonEvent;
typedef XButtonEvent XButtonPressedEvent;
typedef XButtonEvent XButtonReleasedEvent;
```

The x and y fields contain the x and y coordinates of the cursor at the moment
the user released the mouse button. The following code shows how to extract
these values:

```
void handle_button(w,client_data,call_data)
    Widget w;
    XtPointer client_data;
    XmPushButtonCallbackStruct *call_data;
/* handles the pushbutton's activate callback. */
{
    printf("X=%d Y=%d\n",
        call_data->event->xbutton.x,
        call_data->event->xbutton.y);
}
```

The **click_count** field of the **call_data** parameter of the callback function is
unique to Motif buttons. It indicates the number of times the button has been
clicked within the display's multiclick time. The code in Listing 4.4 illustrates
the use of the **click_count** field.

Listing 4.4 Understanding the click_count Field of the call_data Parameter

```
/* clickcount.c*/

#include <Xm/Xm.h>
#include <Xm/PushB.h>

XtAppContext context;
XmStringCharSet char_set=XmSTRING_DEFAULT_CHARSET;
```

```
Widget toplevel, button;

void handle_button(w,client_data,call_data)
    Widget w;
    XtPointer client_data;
    XmPushButtonCallbackStruct *call_data;
/* handles the pushbutton's activate callback. */
{
    printf("click_count=%d\n",call_data->click_count);
}

void main(argc,argv)
    int argc;
    char *argv[];
{
    Arg al[10];
    int ac;

    /* create toplevel shell */
    toplevel = XtAppInitialize(&context,"",NULL,0,&argc,argv,
        NULL,NULL,0);

    /* create button */
    ac=0;
    XtSetArg(al[ac],XmNlabelString,
        XmStringCreate("Push Me",char_set)); ac++;
    XtSetArg(al[ac],XmNmultiClick,XmMULTICLICK_KEEP); ac++;
    button=XmCreatePushButton(toplevel,"button",al,ac);
    XtManageChild(button);
    XtAddCallback(button,XmNactivateCallback,
        handle_button,NULL);

    XtRealizeWidget(toplevel);
    XtAppMainLoop(context);
}
```

In the **main** function, the **multiClick** resource has been set to the value **XmMULTICLICK_KEEP** (which is the default). The callback function has been coded so that the value of the **click_count** field is printed to stdout. If you run this program and click the button, the value 1 will appear, and if you click the button several seconds later, the value 1 will appear again. However, if you click the button rapidly, the **click_count** field will keep track of the number of clicks.

Exercises

1. Try changing the **multiClick** resource to **XmMULTICLICK_DISCARD** in Listing 4.4 and observe the result of multiple clicks.
2. Modify Listing 4.4 to print out different fields of the event structure.

4.5   WORKING WITH THE SCALE WIDGET

A scale widget acts like a slider on a graphic equalizer. When a user slides the scale widget's control with the mouse, its value changes. Scale widgets allow users to adjust the values of variables easily and intuitively. Figure 4.2 shows a scale widget in action. This figure was generated from the code shown in Listing 4.5.

Listing 4.5   Code for Creating and Responding to a Scale Widget

```
/* scale_callback.c */

#include <Xm/Xm.h>
#include <Xm/Scale.h>

XtAppContext context;
XmStringCharSet char_set=XmSTRING_DEFAULT_CHARSET;

Widget toplevel, scale;

void handle_scale(w,client_data,call_data)
    Widget w;
    caddr_t client_data;
    XmScaleCallbackStruct *call_data;
/* handles the scale widget's callbacks. */
{
    Arg al[10];
    int ac;
    int value;

    ac=0;
    XtSetArg(al[ac],XmNvalue,&value); ac++;
    XtGetValues(w,al,ac);
    printf("value = %d\n",value);
}

void main(argc,argv)
    int argc;
```

```
    char *argv[];
{

    Arg al[10];
    int ac;

    /* create the toplevel shell */
    toplevel = XtAppInitialize(&context,"",NULL,0,&argc,argv,
        NULL,NULL,0);

    /* create the scale widget */
    ac=0;
    XtSetArg(al[ac],XmNtitleString,
        XmStringCreate("Slide Me",char_set)); ac++;
    XtSetArg(al[ac],XmNorientation,XmHORIZONTAL); ac++;
    scale=XmCreateScale(toplevel,"scale",al,ac);
    XtManageChild(scale);
    XtAddCallback(scale,XmNvalueChangedCallback,handle_scale,NULL);

    XtRealizeWidget(toplevel);
    XtAppMainLoop(context);
}
```

By now, the style of this code should be familiar. In Listing 4.5, the **title** and the **orientation** resources of the scale are changed and the **valueChanged** callback is registered.

A scale widget works as follows: When a user drags the slider and releases it, the **valueChanged** callback is activated. You can retrieve the new value from one of two locations: from the **value** resource of the scale widget using a call to **XtGetValues,** or from the **XmScaleCallbackStruct** structure, which contains a field called **value** that holds the new value (see the callback structure section of the scale widget in Appendix J). In either case, the **minimum** and **maximum** resources bound this value and the slider's position controls it. In the code shown in Listing 4.5, the value is retrieved in the callback function with a call to **XtGetValues,** and then dumped to stdout with a **printf** statement.

Figure 4.2   A Scale Widget

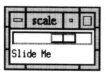

The following rewrite of the **handle_scale** function gets the value of the **value** resource from the event record instead:

```
void handle_scale(w,client_data,call_data)
    Widget w;
    XtPointer client_data;
    XmScaleCallbackStruct *call_data;
/* handles the scale widget's callbacks. */
{
    Arg al[10];
    int ac;
    int value;

    printf("value = %d\n",call_data->value);
}
```

As you can see, Motif's callback structure makes something fairly complicated, such as a scale widget, very easy to use in a program.

Exercises

1. Create a callback function to handle the **drag** callback. Print out the **value** resource both from the **call_data** parameter and through the use of **XtGetValues**.
2. Change various resources in the scale widget and note the effect. Change the **minimum** and **maximum** resources to see how they affect scaling. Also change **decimalPoints, orientation, processingDirection, scaleHeight, scaleWidth, scaleMultiple,** and **titleString**.

4.6   A WARNING ABOUT CALLBACK FUNCTIONS

Any callback function that you create must finish and return within a short period of time (on the order of milliseconds). A quick return time is important because, while your code is processing a callback in the callback function, none of the widgets on the screen can handle events. To handle the callback, the program jumps out of its Motif-handled event loop and into your callback function. If the callback function requires 20 seconds to complete its task, the entire user interface will stall, or freeze up, during that time. When the callback function returns, it returns to the main event loop. Only then can the loop start handling user events inside the widgets again. Your application can process user events only when it is inside the main event loop, not when it is inside one of your callback functions.

Failure to avoid this problem can lead to user interfaces that are very annoying. Chapter 16 shows how to work around this problem with the **XtApp-WorkProc** and **XtAppTimeOut** functions.

Exercise

To get a feeling for the stalling problem, modify Listing 4.2 in this chapter so that its callback function looks like this:

```
void handle_button(w,client_data,call_data)
    Widget w;
    XtPointer client_data;
    XmPushButtonCallbackStruct *call_data;
/* handles the pushbutton's activate callback. */
{
    printf("button clicked\n");
    sleep(5);
}
```

In this callback, a call to the **sleep** function simulates five seconds of processing time. Click the button once and then try to click it a second time. Nothing happens until five seconds pass and the callback function returns. Try changing the sleep value to 10 as well. Try placing a sleep statement in the **handle_scale** function of Listing 4.5 as well.

5   MANAGER WIDGETS

The programs we have created so far consist of a single widget displayed in a toplevel shell. However, most real applications need to display a number of widgets simultaneously. In Motif, manager widgets handle the placement of multiple widgets in a single window.

In this chapter, we will look at three manager widgets—the bulletin board widget, the form widget, and the RowColumn widget—and see how to apply them to a variety of multiwidget programming situations.

5.1   DESIGNING A CELSIUS-TO-FAHRENHEIT CONVERSION PROGRAM

Let's look at a typical programming task: You have been asked to port an existing text-based application to Motif. The existing application is a Celsius-to-Fahrenheit conversion program that prompts the user for a Celsius temperature between 0 and 100 degrees and converts it to the equivalent Fahrenheit temperature.

The design process in Motif begins by deciding on what functionality the program needs. In a Celsius-to-Fahrenheit converter, the user has to enter the Celsius temperature, and the program has to display the Fahrenheit equivalent. The user also needs a way to quit the application easily. Once you have determined the functionality, you need to combine different Motif widgets to create the best user interface.

At this point, you have experience with the label, push-button, and scale widgets. You can combine the three to implement this application, using the scale widget to accept the Celsius temperature, the label widget to display the Fahrenheit temperature, and the push button to provide the ability to quit. Figure 5.1 shows a rough sketch of the proposed interface.

One problem arises: A toplevel shell widget can hold only one child widget, but now we need it to hold three. We can solve this problem by using

Figure 5.1   A Rough Sketch of a Celsius-to-Fahrenheit Converter

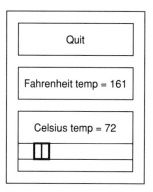

manager widgets. A simple manager widget contains other widgets statically. More complicated widgets constrain other widgets dynamically: As the manager changes size and shape, it rearranges its children appropriately. If the toplevel shell holds a manager widget as its single child, the toplevel widget can display many children.

5.2   IMPLEMENTING THE PROGRAM WITH A BULLETIN BOARD

The code shown in Listing 5.1 demonstrates the Celsius-to-Fahrenheit application. The code places a push-button, a label, and a scale widget into a manager widget called a *bulletin board* widget. You can place a widget into a manager by making the manager the parent of the widget when you create it. Because the bulletin board is the parent, it controls the placement of the children. The bulletin board determines each child's position by examining the values found in the x and y resources of each child. This process is described in more detail below.

Listing 5.1   A Celsius-to-Fahrenheit Conversion Program Using a Bulletin Board

```
/* c2f.bb.c */

#include <Xm/Xm.h>
#include <Xm/PushB.h>
#include <Xm/Label.h>
#include <Xm/Scale.h>
#include <Xm/BulletinB.h>
```

```
XtAppContext context;
XmStringCharSet char_set=XmSTRING_DEFAULT_CHARSET;

Widget toplevel, button, bb, label, scale;

void buttonCB(w, client_data, call_data)
    Widget w;
    int client_data;
    XmPushButtonCallbackStruct *call_data;
/* handles the pushbutton's activate callback. */
{
    exit(0);
}

void scaleCB(w, client_data, call_data)
    Widget w;
    int client_data;
    XmScaleCallbackStruct *call_data;
/* handles the scale's callback. */
{
    char s[100];
    Arg al[10];
    int ac;

    sprintf(s,"farenheit=%d",call_data->value*9/5+32);
    ac=0;
    XtSetArg(al[ac],XmNlabelString,
        XmStringCreate(s,char_set)); ac++;
    XtSetValues(label,al,ac);
}

void main(argc,argv)
    int argc;
    char *argv[];
{
    Arg al[10];
    int ac;

    /* create the toplevel shell */
    toplevel = XtAppInitialize(&context,"",NULL,0,&argc,argv,
        NULL,NULL,0);

    /* resize toplevel */
    ac=0;
    XtSetArg(al[ac],XmNheight,300); ac++;
```

```
XtSetArg(al[ac],XmNwidth,200); ac++;
XtSetValues(toplevel,al,ac);

/* create a bulletin board to hold the three widgets */
ac=0;
bb=XmCreateBulletinBoard(toplevel,"bb",al,ac);
XtManageChild(bb);

/* create a push button */
ac=0;
XtSetArg(al[ac],XmNlabelString,
    XmStringCreate("Quit",char_set)); ac++;
button=XmCreatePushButton(bb,"button",al,ac);
XtManageChild(button);
XtAddCallback(button,XmNactivateCallback,buttonCB,NULL);

/* create a scale */
ac=0;
XtSetArg(al[ac],XmNtitleString,
    XmStringCreate("Celsius Temperature",char_set)); ac++;
XtSetArg(al[ac],XmNorientation,XmHORIZONTAL); ac++;
XtSetArg(al[ac],XmNshowValue,True); ac++;
scale=XmCreateScale(bb,"scale",al,ac);
XtManageChild(scale);
XtAddCallback(scale,XmNdragCallback,scaleCB,NULL);

/* create a label */
ac=0;
XtSetArg(al[ac],XmNlabelString,
    XmStringCreate("Farenheit = 32",char_set)); ac++;
label=XmCreateLabel(bb,"label",al,ac);
XtManageChild(label);

/* position widgets on the bulletin board */
ac=0;
XtSetArg(al[ac],XmNx,10); ac++;
XtSetArg(al[ac],XmNy,10); ac++;
XtSetValues(button,al,ac);

ac=0;
XtSetArg(al[ac],XmNx,1); ac++;
XtSetArg(al[ac],XmNy,100); ac++;
XtSetValues(scale,al,ac);
```

```
ac=0;
XtSetArg(al[ac],XmNx,10); ac++;
XtSetArg(al[ac],XmNy,200); ac++;
XtSetValues(label,al,ac);


XtRealizeWidget(toplevel);
XtAppMainLoop(context);
}
```

Although the code in Listing 5.1 is somewhat larger than in previous listings (note especially how the number of include files is growing), all of its elements should be familiar to you by now.

In the first section of the program, the toplevel widget is created with the usual **XtAppInitialize** call and is resized by a change to its **width** and **height** resources. A bulletin board widget is created as a child of the toplevel shell, and then the push-button, scale, and label widgets are created as children of the bulletin board. As the parent, the bulletin board manages the placement of its three children. The parentage in this program can be illustrated in a figure known as a widget tree (Figure 5.2), which shows the hierarchy of widgets in an application.

The next section of the program determines the placement of the three children on the bulletin board by setting each child's **x** and **y** resources (inherited from the core widget). The bulletin board uses the **x** and **y** resources of each child to manage its location. For example, the label widget's **x** resource is set to 10, while its **y** resource is set to 200. This means that the label widget's upper-left corner will appear 200 pixels down from and 10 pixels to the right of the bulletin board's upper left corner.

Two extremely brief callback functions handle the Celsius-to-Farhrenheit conversion process and the quit function in this program. The **activate** callback for the push-button widget is wired to the **buttonCB** function. When a user clicks the push button, the program quits immediately. The **drag** callback for the scale widget is wired to the **scaleCB** function. When a user drags the scale's control, the **labelString** resource for the label widget changes to reflect the new Fahrenheit temperature.

When you run this program, the three widgets appear in the specified positions, as shown in Figure 5.3. As the scale changes, the correct Fahrenheit temperature appears, and a click of the quit button quits the program.

Form Attachments

You can attach widgets to a form in many different ways. The figures below demonstrate some of the possibilities. Section 5.3 shows how to create code to implement these attachments.

In the figure at the bottom of this page, the bottom of the label is attached to the vertical midpoint of the form by attaching to postion 50. When the form changes size, the midpoint changes and the bottom of the label follows.

In the following figure, the two labels are attached to each other.

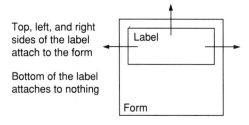

Top, left, and right sides of the label attach to the form

Bottom of the label attaches to nothing

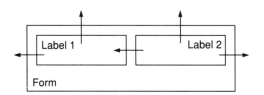

Here the left, top, and right sides of the label are attached to the form. As the form's sides move in response to resizing commands, the attached sides of the label move also, and the label changes width to accommodate the form's size. Since the bottom of the label attaches to nothing, the height of the label does not change, but retains its default height as determined by the label's string and its attributes.

Label 1's left and top sides attach to the form, and its bottom and right sides attach to nothing. The label defaults to its natural width and height. The top and right sides of label 2 attach to the form, the

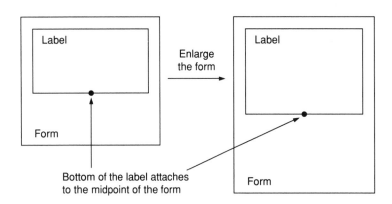

Bottom of the label attaches to the midpoint of the form

Form Attachments (continued)

bottom attaches to nothing, and the left side attaches to label 1. As the form changes width, label 2 resizes to fill the space between the right side of label 1 and the right side of the form.

In the following figure, all four widgets align on their right sides.

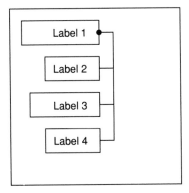

Label 1's right side is attached to the horizontal midpoint of the form. Labels 2, 3, and 4 attach their right sides, using the **XmATTACH_OPPOSITE_WIDGET** attachment, to label 1. As the right side of label 1 moves, the right sides of the other three labels follow. Thus, all of the right sides remain aligned.

Form widgets also add offset resources to their children. Each child of a form acquires left, top, right, and bottom offset values, which determine the offset between the specified side of the widget and the attachment point, as shown below.

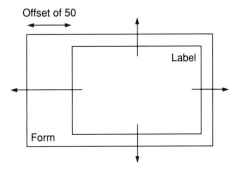

All four sides of the label attach to the form. The label's **leftOffset** resource is set to 50, so its left side remains 50 pixels away from the side of the form to which it is attached. You can create interesting and useful spacing effects using negative offset values as well.

Figure 5.2   The Widget Tree for the Bulletin Board Code

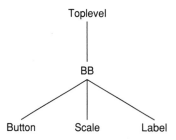

Figure 5.3   A Bulletin Board Widget Used for the Celsius-to-Fahrenheit Conversion Program

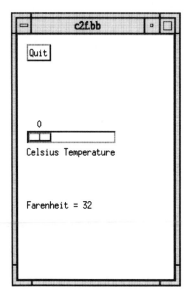

Exercises

1. Arrange the three widgets horizontally on the bulletin board by modifying the **orientation** resource of the scale and the **x** and **y** resource values.
2. Remove the code that sizes the toplevel shell and see what happens.

5.3   RESIZING GRACEFULLY WITH THE FORM WIDGET

Run the bulletin board code again, and this time try to resize the window. Users tend to resize windows often but a bulletin board doesn't handle resizing very well. The bulletin board changes in size, but the widgets it holds remain fixed. To solve this problem, you can either set the window so that users cannot resize it or choose a different manager. Form widgets are the best choice because they automatically resize and reposition the widgets they hold when a user resizes the form.

The program shown in Listing 5.2 demonstrates the use of a form widget. This code is a modification of the bulletin board program in Listing 5.1: It creates the same label, scale, and push-button widgets but makes them children of a form widget rather than of a bulletin board widget. This program also adds a fourth widget—a separator—to make the application look better. The separator simply adds a line between the scale widget and the label widget to separate them.

Listing 5.2   A Celsius-to-Fahrenheit Conversion Program Using a Form Widget

```
/* c2f.form.c */

#include <Xm/Xm.h>
#include <Xm/PushB.h>
#include <Xm/Label.h>
#include <Xm/Scale.h>
#include <Xm/Separator.h>
#include <Xm/Form.h>

XtAppContext context;
XmStringCharSet char_set=XmSTRING_DEFAULT_CHARSET;

Widget toplevel, button, form, label, scale, sep;

void buttonCB(w, client_data, call_data)
    Widget w;
    int client_data;
    XmPushButtonCallbackStruct *call_data;
/* handles the pushbutton's activate callback. */
{
    exit(0);
}

void scaleCB(w, client_data, call_data)
    Widget w;
    int client_data;
    XmScaleCallbackStruct *call_data;
```

```
/* handles the scale's callback. */
{
    char s[100];
    Arg al[10];
    int ac;

    sprintf(s,"farenheit=%d",call_data->value*9/5+32);
    ac=0;
    XtSetArg(al[ac],XmNlabelString,
        XmStringCreate(s,char_set)); ac++;
    XtSetValues(label,al,ac);
}

void main(argc,argv)
    int argc;
    char *argv[];
{
    Arg al[10];
    int ac;

    /* create the toplevel shell */
    toplevel = XtAppInitialize(&context,"",NULL,0,&argc,argv,
        NULL,NULL,0);

    /* resize toplevel */
    ac=0;
    XtSetArg(al[ac],XmNheight,300); ac++;
    XtSetArg(al[ac],XmNwidth,200); ac++;
    XtSetValues(toplevel,al,ac);

    /* create a form to hold the other widgets */
    ac=0;
    form=XmCreateForm(toplevel,"form",al,ac);
    XtManageChild(form);

    /* create a push button */
    ac=0;
    XtSetArg(al[ac],XmNlabelString,
        XmStringCreate("Quit",char_set)); ac++;
    button=XmCreatePushButton(form,"button",al,ac);
    XtManageChild(button);
    XtAddCallback(button,XmNactivateCallback,buttonCB,NULL);

    /* create a scale */
    ac=0;
```

```
XtSetArg(al[ac],XmNtitleString,
    XmStringCreate("Celsius Temperature",char_set)); ac++;
XtSetArg(al[ac],XmNorientation,XmHORIZONTAL); ac++;
XtSetArg(al[ac],XmNshowValue,True); ac++;
scale=XmCreateScale(form,"scale",al,ac);
XtManageChild(scale);
XtAddCallback(scale,XmNdragCallback,scaleCB,NULL);

/* create a label */
ac=0;
XtSetArg(al[ac],XmNlabelString,
    XmStringCreate("Farenheit = 32",char_set)); ac++;
label=XmCreateLabel(form,"label",al,ac);
XtManageChild(label);

/* create a separator */
ac=0;
sep=XmCreateSeparator(form,"sep",al,ac);
XtManageChild(sep);

/* attach the children to the form */
ac=0;
XtSetArg(al[ac], XmNtopAttachment, XmATTACH_FORM); ac++;
XtSetArg(al[ac], XmNrightAttachment, XmATTACH_FORM); ac++;
XtSetArg(al[ac], XmNleftAttachment, XmATTACH_FORM); ac++;
XtSetArg(al[ac], XmNbottomAttachment, XmATTACH_POSITION); ac++;
XtSetArg(al[ac], XmNbottomPosition, 30); ac++; /* 30 = a percent */
XtSetValues(button,al,ac);

ac=0;
XtSetArg(al[ac], XmNtopAttachment, XmATTACH_WIDGET); ac++;
XtSetArg(al[ac], XmNtopWidget, button); ac++;
XtSetArg(al[ac], XmNrightAttachment, XmATTACH_FORM); ac++;
XtSetArg(al[ac], XmNleftAttachment, XmATTACH_FORM); ac++;
XtSetArg(al[ac], XmNbottomAttachment, XmATTACH_NONE); ac++;
XtSetValues(scale,al,ac);

ac=0;
XtSetArg(al[ac], XmNtopAttachment, XmATTACH_WIDGET); ac++;
XtSetArg(al[ac], XmNtopWidget, scale); ac++;
XtSetArg(al[ac], XmNrightAttachment, XmATTACH_FORM); ac++;
XtSetArg(al[ac], XmNleftAttachment, XmATTACH_FORM); ac++;
XtSetArg(al[ac], XmNbottomAttachment, XmATTACH_NONE); ac++;
XtSetValues(sep,al,ac);
```

```
    ac=0;
    XtSetArg(al[ac], XmNtopAttachment, XmATTACH_WIDGET); ac++;
    XtSetArg(al[ac], XmNtopWidget, sep); ac++;
    XtSetArg(al[ac], XmNrightAttachment, XmATTACH_FORM); ac++;
    XtSetArg(al[ac], XmNleftAttachment, XmATTACH_FORM); ac++;
    XtSetArg(al[ac], XmNbottomAttachment, XmATTACH_FORM); ac++;
    XtSetValues(label,al,ac);

    XtRealizeWidget(toplevel);
    XtAppMainLoop(context);
}
```

When you run this program and resize the window, all of the widgets in the form are resized appropriately, as shown in Figure 5.4.

Note that the program in Listing 5.2 does not declare resources such as **topWidget**, **leftAttachment**, and **bottomPosition**. Nor do they appear in the resource list for the label widget, the primitive widget, or the core widget. These attachment resources come from the form widget itself. The form widget is a constraint widget and can therefore impart new resources to its children. See Appendix J for a list of constraint resources for the **XmForm** widget. Note that the constraint resources are made available to every immediate child of

Figure 5.4 Multiple Widgets Attached to a Form Widget

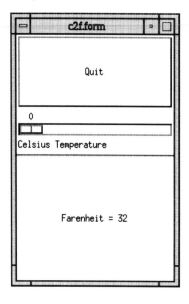

the form widget. Once you create a child of a form widget, the child widget picks up the constraint resource list of the form widget and adds it to its own list of resources.

When you attach other widgets to a form widget, these attached widgets change shape and size along with the form widget. Four types of attachments are demonstrated in Listing 5.2: attachment to the form's edges, attachment to a position on the form, attachment to other widgets, and no attachment. Examples from the program appear below.

Attachment to the form's edges:

```
XtSetArg(al[ac], XmNleftAttachment, XmATTACH_FORM); ac++;
```

Attachment to another widget:

```
XtSetArg(al[ac], XmNtopAttachment, XmATTACH_WIDGET); ac++;
XtSetArg(al[ac], XmNtopWidget, sep); ac++;
```

Attachment to a position on the form:

```
XtSetArg(al[ac], XmNbottomAttachment, XmATTACH_POSITION); ac++;
XtSetArg(al[ac], XmNbottomPosition, 30); ac++; /*30 is a percentage*/
```

Attachment to nothing:

```
XtSetArg(al[ac], XmNbottomAttachment, XmATTACH_NONE); ac++;
```

Note that when attaching to another widget or attaching to a position, you must set a pair of resources for the attachment to work.

Looking at the code, you can see that the push button is attached by its top, left, and right sides to the form's edges. When the form's edges move in response to resizing, the attached widget moves in the same way. The bottom edge of the push button is attached to a position a third of the way down the form widget. As the form grows and shrinks, this attachment point moves, and the bottom of the push button is adjusted accordingly. Similarly, the scale's top edge is attached to the bottom of the push button, and its sides are attached to the form's edges. The separator's top is attached to the scale, and its sides are attached to the form. The label widget is attached to the separator on the top and to the form's edges on its sides and bottom.

Note that the bottom of the separator is not attached to anything. When a widget has a fixed height as a separator does, you do not need to attach its bottom edge since the bottom edge is already fixed by the height of the widget. You can leave the bottom edge of the push button or label unattached as well, so that these widgets default to their natural heights.

It is easy to create bugs when attaching objects to a form widget, especially if the form has many children. You can avoid problems by working from the top down and from left to right. You can also place forms inside of forms to modularize attachments.

Exercises

1. Set the bottom attachment of the button widget to **XmATTACH_NONE** and note the change in the button's behavior.
2. Remove the separator from the code and note the difference in appearance.
3. Modify the program so that the widgets appear horizontally on the form rather than vertically.
4. Add a second button to the form, placing it and the quit button side by side. This button should allow the user to change the program between Celsius-to-Fahrenheit and Fahrenheit-to-Celsius conversion modes.

5.4   ROWCOLUMN WIDGETS

Both the form widget and the bulletin board widget require you to explicitly manage the placement of the individual widgets they contain. In the bulletin board widget, you set the x and y coordinates of each child of the bulletin board. In the form widget, you must attach all of the child widgets appropriately.

At times all of this attaching and placing can become bothersome. If, for example, an application contains 20 buttons, you would probably prefer a manager widget that manages the placement of all 20 children automatically. The RowColumn widget can do this for you.

The code shown in Listing 5.3 demonstrates the capabilities of a RowColumn widget by creating 10 push buttons as children of a RowColumn widget (see Figure 5.5).

Listing 5.3   Working with a RowColumn Widget

```
/* rowcolumn.c */

#include <Xm/Xm.h>
#include <Xm/PushB.h>
#include <Xm/RowColumn.h>
```

Managers Inside of Managers

Motif lets you place managers inside of managers to almost any depth. This capability can simplify the arrangement of large numbers of widgets in a complex application by subdividing the placement tasks into smaller modules. For example, the following figure represents a typical drawing program. In this illustration, a form widget holds the drawing area as well as another form, which in turn holds a palette of drawing tools.

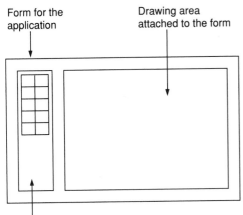

Form for the application

Drawing area attached to the form

Second form attached to the application form, which holds a palette of drawing tools

The following figure shows a schematic representation of the Motif news reader. In this case, a form widget holds a number of other widgets. Two RowColumn widgets function as containers for groups of push buttons, an arrangement that greatly simplifies the placement of the buttons.

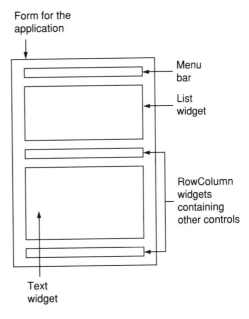

Form for the application

Menu bar

List widget

RowColumn widgets containing other controls

Text widget

You attach managers to a form or another manager in the same way that you attach simple widgets to the manager. However, you should pay attention to parentage when creating the widgets so that the appropriate widgets end up in the appropriate managers.

```
XtAppContext context;
XmStringCharSet char_set=XmSTRING_DEFAULT_CHARSET;

Widget toplevel, rowcol, buttons[10];

void main(argc,argv)
    int argc;
    char *argv[];
{
    Arg al[10];
    int ac;
    int x;

    /* create the toplevel shell */
    toplevel = XtAppInitialize(&context,"",NULL,0,&argc,argv,
        NULL,NULL,0);

    /* resize toplevel */
    ac=0;
    XtSetArg(al[ac],XmNheight,120); ac++;
    XtSetArg(al[ac],XmNwidth,480); ac++;
    XtSetValues(toplevel,al,ac);

    /* create a RowColumn container to hold widgets */
    ac=0;
    XtSetArg(al[ac], XmNpacking, XmPACK_TIGHT); ac++;
    XtSetArg(al[ac], XmNorientation, XmHORIZONTAL); ac++;
    XtSetArg(al[ac], XmNadjustLast, False); ac++;
    rowcol=XmCreateRowColumn(toplevel,"rowcol",al,ac);
    XtManageChild(rowcol);

    /* create 10 push buttons */
    for (x=0; x<10; x++)
    {
        ac=0;
        XtSetArg(al[ac],XmNlabelString,
            XmStringCreate("I'm a button",char_set)); ac++;
        buttons[x]=XmCreatePushButton(rowcol,"button",al,ac);
        XtManageChild(buttons[x]);
    }

    XtRealizeWidget(toplevel);
    XtAppMainLoop(context);
}
```

Figure 5.5 A RowColumn Widget in Action

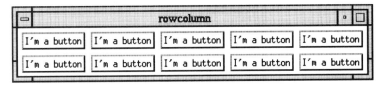

When you run this code and resize the window, the arrangement of the buttons in the window changes to match the window's new shape.

The code is similar to that in previous listings. It creates a RowColumn widget, and then 10 button widgets as its children. The array of button widgets used here makes the program shorter, but is not a requirement. For simplicity, the code uses no callbacks, but you would handle callbacks here as elsewhere. Note that no code is required to place or attach the objects in the RowColumn widget, since it manages the placement of its children for you.

A RowColumn widget provides a number of resources, and also comes in several different flavors depending on its application (see Appendix J). The RowColumn demonstration code shown in Listing 5.3 sets two of the available resources, **orientation** and **adjustLast**, which affect the way the RowColumn widget manages its children. Consider them as "hints"—the RowColumn widget is managing the placement of its children on its own, but you may want the container to behave in a certain way in different situations. Resources like **adjustLast**, **orientation**, **numColumns**, **spacing**, and **packing** are useful in controlling a RowColumn widget's general behavior, as summarized below:

adjustLast if true, causes widgets at the end of a row or column to attach themselves to the edge of the RowColumn widget. If false, these widgets default to their natural size.

orientation determines whether or not the RowColumn widget favors filling rows or columns as the container is resized.

numColumns determines the number of columns or rows, depending on the orientation, that the RowColumn widget will naturally favor.

spacing determines the space between child widgets, in pixels.

packing controls how widgets align. **PACK_TIGHT** causes widgets to default to their natural sizes and packs them as tightly as possible. **PACK_COLUMN** places widgets in same-size boxes based on the largest child widget. **PACK_NONE** makes the RowColumn widget behave like a bulletin board widget: it performs no automatic placement.

You can use the RowColumn widget whenever you need to manage sets of widgets as a group. In Motif, both menu bars and menu panes are made from RowColumn widgets. Radio boxes are RowColumn widgets tuned to handle groups of toggle buttons.

Exercises

1. Modify the five hinting resources of a RowColumn widget in different ways to understand their capabilities.
2. Place a RowColumn widget within a form widget to get a feel for placing managers inside of managers. For example, replace the push button in the Listing 5.2 program with a RowColumn widget full of push buttons.
3. Create a set of 10 buttons, each of which has a different-size label, and place them in a RowColumn widget. Change the **packing** resource to different values and note the behavior.

6 MENUS

The tools presented in the last three chapters are sufficient for you to create many complete Motif applications. You can use push buttons and scales for command and data input, and label widgets for output. You can also combine these widgets using manager widgets. The Celsius-to-Fahrenheit converter demonstrated in Chapter 5 is a good example of what these widgets can do.

Menus and dialog boxes are somewhat more complicated to use, but once implemented they provide easy and intuitive ways to get commands and information from the user. After you have seen several examples, you can begin to incorporate menus and dialogs into your programs to provide more advanced application interfaces.

This chapter describes how to build simple menu bars and menus. The goal of this chapter is to create a piece of generic menu-creation code that you can easily copy to new applications. The applications in Chapters 8 and 10 use this generic menu code.

6.1   MENU BARS AND MENUS

Menus are not necessary. Instead, you could make all of the menu options available to the user through push buttons. The problem with this approach is that large programs might require you to display 30 or 40 push buttons at once, and these buttons would take up quite a bit of space.

Menus economize space when you have a large number of program options and commands. They organize different options in groups. The menu bar displays the name of each group at the top of the application window. Clicking a name in the menu bar pulls down a menu pane containing the options associated with the menu name. The menu bar takes up very little space in the application, but it gives users access to a large number of program options organized by category.

Figure 6.1   The Elements of a Menu

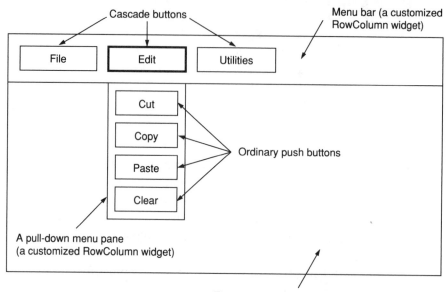

In Motif, you create menu bars and menu panes with specially tuned Row-Column widgets (see Chapter 5 and Appendix J). You can create menu bars with the **XmCreateMenuBar** convenience function, and you can create a pull-down menu pane with the **XmCreatePulidownMenu** convenience function. Each of these functions creates a RowColumn widget and sets its resources so that it works well as a menu. You create the menu options displayed in the individual menu panes with normal push buttons. You create the items in the menu bar itself using specialized push-button-like widgets called cascade buttons. Figure 6.1 shows these different elements.

To create a menu, you must follow several steps. First, you create the menu bar. Then, for each name that appears in the menu bar, you create a cascade button along with a pull-down menu pane. You create each cascade button using the menu bar as its parent. The order in which you create the cascade buttons determines the order in which they appear in the menu bar.

Next, you create a pull-down menu pane for each cascade button. Cascade buttons have a resource named **subMenuID:** You set this resource to the pull-down menu pane you will use for the cascade button. When a user clicks the cascade button, it manages the widget in the **subMenuID** resource, making the menu pane visible. When you create the pull-down menu pane, do *not* manage the pane.

**Figure 6.2   View During Execution of the Menu Code,
Showing the Menu Bar and Label Widget Attached to
a Form Widget**

You create the options for individual menu panes using push buttons, with the pull-down menu pane as their parent. The order in which you create the push buttons determines the order in which they will appear in the pane. These buttons *should* be managed.

The creation of the Edit menu shown in Figure 6.1 requires the following steps, assuming that the menu bar already exists:

1. Create and manage a cascade button labeled Edit, with the menu bar as its parent.
2. Create but do *not* manage a pull-down menu pane, with the menu bar as its parent.
3. Set the **subMenuID** resource of the cascade button to the pane.
4. Create and manage the push buttons for the four Edit menu buttons with the pane as their parent.

When you use this structure, the following occurs during program execution:

1. The user clicks the Edit cascade button.
2. The cascade button manages the widget in its **subMenuID** resource.
3. The menu pane, along with its child push buttons, becomes visible.
4. The user clicks one of the push buttons, and its callback function causes the desired action to occur.

The program shown in Listing 6.1 demonstrates how to create a simple Motif menu consisting of a menu bar attached to a form widget. The menu bar this program creates consists of a pair of menus (see Figure 6.2). One is a standard File menu containing the commands Open, Close, and Quit, and the other is a standard Edit menu containing the commands Copy, Cut, and Paste.

Every time a user selects one of these commands, the program sends a message
to stdout.

Listing 6.1   Generic Menu Creation Code

```
/* menu.c */

#include <Xm/Xm.h>
#include <Xm/Label.h>
#include <Xm/Form.h>
#include <Xm/PushB.h>
#include <Xm/RowColumn.h>
#include <Xm/CascadeB.h>

XtAppContext context;
XmStringCharSet char_set=XmSTRING_DEFAULT_CHARSET;

Widget toplevel, form, label, menu_bar;
Widget file_menu;
Widget open_item;
Widget close_item;
Widget quit_item;
Widget edit_menu;
Widget copy_item;
Widget cut_item;
Widget paste_item;

void menuCB(w,client_data,call_data)
    Widget w;
    char *client_data;
    XmAnyCallbackStruct *call_data;
/* callback routine used for all menus */
{
    printf("%s\n",client_data);
    if (strcmp(client_data,"Quit")==0) /* if quit seen, then exit */
        exit(0);
}

Widget make_menu_item(item_name,client_data,menu)
    char *item_name;
    caddr_t client_data;
    Widget menu;
/* adds an item into a menu. */
{
    int ac;
```

```
    Arg al[10];
    Widget item;

    ac = 0;
    XtSetArg(al[ac],XmNlabelString,
        XmStringCreateLtoR(item_name,char_set)); ac++;
    item=XmCreatePushButton(menu,item_name,al,ac);
    XtManageChild(item);
    XtAddCallback(item,XmNactivateCallback,menuCB,client_data);
    XtSetSensitive(item,True);
    return(item);
}


Widget make_menu(menu_name,menu_bar)
    char *menu_name;
    Widget menu_bar;
/* creates a menu on the menu bar */
{
    int ac;
    Arg al[10];
    Widget menu, cascade;

    menu=XmCreatePulldownMenu(menu_bar,menu_name,NULL,0);
    ac=0;
    XtSetArg (al[ac],XmNsubMenuId, menu); ac++;
    XtSetArg(al[ac],XmNlabelString,
        XmStringCreateLtoR(menu_name,char_set)); ac++;
    cascade=XmCreateCascadeButton(menu_bar,menu_name,al,ac);
    XtManageChild(cascade);
    return(menu);
}


void create_menus(menu_bar)
    Widget menu_bar;
/* creates all the menus for this program */
{
    /* create the file menu */
    file_menu=make_menu("File",menu_bar);
    open_item=make_menu_item("Open","Open selected",file_menu);
    close_item=make_menu_item("Close","Close selected",file_menu);
    quit_item=make_menu_item("Quit","Quit",file_menu);

    /* create the edit menu */
    edit_menu=make_menu("Edit",menu_bar);
    copy_item=make_menu_item("Copy","Copy selected",edit_menu);
```

```
        cut_item=make_menu_item("Cut","Cut Selected",edit_menu);
        paste_item=make_menu_item("Paste","Paste Selected",edit_menu);
}

void main(argc,argv)
    int argc;
    char *argv[];
{
    Arg al[10];
    int ac;

    /* create the toplevel shell */
    toplevel = XtAppInitialize(&context,"",NULL,0,&argc,argv,
        NULL,NULL,0);

    /* resize the window */
    ac=0;
    XtSetArg(al[ac],XmNheight,200); ac++;
    XtSetArg(al[ac],XmNwidth,200); ac++;
    XtSetValues(toplevel,al,ac);

    /* create a form widget */
    ac=0;
    form=XmCreateForm(toplevel,"form",al,ac);
    XtManageChild(form);

    /* create a label widget */
    ac=0;
    XtSetArg(al[ac],XmNlabelString,
        XmStringCreate("I'm a label", char_set)); ac++;
    label=XmCreateLabel(form,"label",al,ac);
    XtManageChild(label);

    /* create the menu bar */
    ac=0;
    menu_bar=XmCreateMenuBar(form,"menu_bar",al,ac);
    XtManageChild(menu_bar);

    /* attach the menu bar to the form */
    ac=0;
    XtSetArg(al[ac],XmNtopAttachment,XmATTACH_FORM); ac++;
    XtSetArg(al[ac],XmNrightAttachment,XmATTACH_FORM); ac++;
    XtSetArg(al[ac],XmNleftAttachment,XmATTACH_FORM); ac++;
    XtSetValues(menu_bar,al,ac);
```

```
/* attach the label to the form */
ac=0;
XtSetArg(al[ac],XmNtopAttachment,XmATTACH_WIDGET); ac++;
XtSetArg(al[ac],XmNtopWidget,menu_bar); ac++;
XtSetArg(al[ac],XmNrightAttachment,XmATTACH_FORM); ac++;
XtSetArg(al[ac],XmNleftAttachment,XmATTACH_FORM); ac++;
XtSetArg(al[ac],XmNbottomAttachment,XmATTACH_FORM); ac++;
XtSetValues(label,al,ac);

create_menus(menu_bar);

XtRealizeWidget(toplevel);
XtAppMainLoop(context);
}
```

Listing 6.1 is a large, but well-modularized, program. It consists of five functions:

1. The **main** function contains nothing you have not seen before. It creates and attaches the form, menu bar, and label widgets.
2. The function **create_menus** creates the two menus and adds the appropriate items to them.
3. The function **make_menu** adds a new cascade button and menu pane to the menu bar.
4. The function **make_menu_item** adds a new item (a push button) to a menu pane created in **make_menu**.
5. The function **menuCB** is the callback function that all of the menu items use.

This program uses the callback function **menuCB** for all menu items. You might use other structures in more involved programs—for example, a different callback function for each of the menus or even for each menu item.

The **main** function starts out by creating **toplevel** and resizing it. Then it creates a form widget, and a menu bar and a label widget as the form's children. The menu bar widget is a specialized RowColumn widget used for menus. The **main** function then attaches the label and the menu bar widgets to the form. The call to the **create_menus** function creates all of the menus and their items.

The **make_menu** function creates individual menu entries on the menu bar. Each menu name appears on the menu bar as the result of a call to **make_menu**. This function starts by creating a pull-down menu widget. The pull-down menu widget is made from a RowColumn widget and will eventually hold the items in the menu. It is hooked into a cascade button widget. The cascade button places the menu's name on the menu bar in a push-button-like device. When the user clicks the menu's cascade button, it manages the pull-down menu.

You add the actual menu items to the menus with the function **make_menu_item**. The order in which you do so determines the order in which they will appear. Menu items are simply push-button widgets attached to the pull-down menu container. Each of these push buttons is wired to call the **menuCB** function when the **activate** callback is triggered. Note that the **client_data** value passed to the callback function is a pointer to a string: You can pass just about anything in the **client_data** field as long as it is four bytes long. Generally, you pass an integer instead and trigger off of the integer with a switch statement. See Chapter 10 for an example.

The **menuCB** function prints the **client_data** string to stdout to demonstrate that the menus are working correctly. Then it checks the string to see if it contains the word "Quit." If it does, the program quits.

Once you have implemented this code, all of the widgets function together to look like menus on the screen. All of the buttons in the menu bar are cascade buttons that manage the appropriate pull-down menu widget. The pull-down menu widget is a container widget that holds the push buttons that make up the menu items. When a user clicks one of these push buttons, the **menuCB** callback function is triggered to handle the item selected.

6.2   CUSTOMIZING MENUS

6.2.1   ADDING LABELS AND SEPARATORS TO MENUS

A menu can contain separators and labels as well as push buttons. Users see but cannot select the label and separator items, and they often help to make the menu clearer and easier to use. You create labels and separators and add them to the menu in the same way you create a push-button menu item in the **make_menu_option** code. Again, the order in which you add these extra widgets to the menu determines the order of their appearance there. Listing 6.2 shows the functions to create labels and separators in a menu.

Listing 6.2 Adding Labels and Separators to Menus

```
void make_menu_label(item_name,menu)
    char *item_name;
    Widget menu;
```

```
/* adds a label into the menu. */
{
    int ac;
    Arg al[10];

    ac = 0;
    XtSetArg(al[ac], XmNlabelString,
    XmStringCreateLtoR(item_name,XmSTRING_DEFAULT_CHARSET)); ac++;
    XtManageChild(XmCreateLabel(menu,item_name,al,ac));
}


void make_menu_separator(menu)
    Widget menu;
/* adds a separator into the menu. */
{
    XtManageChild(XmCreateSeparator(menu,"sep",NULL,0));
}
```

To try out labels and separators in a menu, add these two functions to the
original code in Listing 6.1. Add an include statement for the separator widget
and then change the **create_menus** function to look like this:

```
void create_menus(menu_bar)
    Widget menu_bar;
/* creates all the menus for this program */
{
    /* create the file menu */
    file_menu=make_menu("File",menu_bar);
    open_item=make_menu_item("Open","Open selected",file_menu);
    close_item=make_menu_item("Close","Close selected",file_menu);
    quit_item=make_menu_item("Quit","Quit",file_menu);

    /* create the edit menu */
    edit_menu=make_menu("Edit",menu_bar);
    make_menu_label("This is a sample label",edit_menu);
    make_menu_separator(edit_menu);
    copy_item=make_menu_item("Copy","Copy selected",edit_menu);
    cut_item=make_menu_item("Cut","Cut Selected",edit_menu);
    paste_item=make_menu_item("Paste","Paste Selected",edit_menu);
}
```

When you run the code, you should see a label and a separator at the top
of the Edit menu. Note when you run the program that the label and the
separator cannot be selected.

6.2.2   CHANGING THE SENSITIVITY OF MENU ITEMS

You can use the **sensitive** resource to turn menu options on and off. This resource disables menu items whose use would be inappropriate at some point in the program. For example, imagine that the Open and Close menu items demonstrated in the code above are part of an editor program that lets you edit only one file at a time. If no file is currently open, the program should enable Open and disable Close. Once a file is open, Close should be enabled and Open disabled. A disabled menu item appears "grayed out" so the user knows it is disabled and cannot select it. The following code makes the Open option insensitive:

```
XtSetSensitive(open_item,False);
```

The following code makes it sensitive again:

```
XtSetSensitive(open_item,True);
```

The call to **XtSetSensitive** is a convenience function for setting the **sensitive** resource in the core widget. You can set the sensitivity of something to true or false repeatedly without hurting anything.

XtSetSensitive   *Sets a widget's sensitive resource.*

```
Boolean XtSetSensitive(
    Widget w,
    Boolean value);
```

w   The widget that generated the callback.
value   The Boolean value to which you want to set the
             widget's sensitive resource.

6.2.3   HIERARCHICAL MENUS

Using the **make_menu** and **make_menu_item** functions shown above, you can easily create hierarchical menus (that is, menus that contain submenus). For example, you can change the **create_menus** function to demonstrate hierarchical menus by adding several lines at the end of the function, as shown in Listing 6.3.

Listing 6.3   Creating Hierarchical Menus

```
void create_menus(Widget menu_bar)
/* creates all the menus for this program */
{
        /* create the file menu */
        file_menu=make_menu("File",menu_bar);
        open_item=make_menu_item("Open","Open selected",file_menu);
        close_item=make_menu_item("Close","Close selected",file_menu);
        quit_item=make_menu_item("Quit","Quit",file_menu);

        /* create the edit menu */
        edit_menu=make_menu("Edit",menu_bar);
        copy_item=make_menu_item("Copy","Copy selected",edit_menu);
        cut_item=make_menu_item("Cut","Cut Selected",edit_menu);
        paste_item=make_menu_item("Paste","Paste Selected",edit_menu);
        /* add an "extra" sub-menu to the edit menu */
        extra_menu=make_menu("Extra",edit_menu);
        extra1_item=make_menu_item("Extra1","Extra1 Selected",
            extra_menu);
        extra2_item=make_menu_item("Extra2","Extra2 Selected",
            extra_menu);
}
```

You should declare the widget variables **extra_menu**, **extra1_item**, and **extra2_item** at the top of the program.

When you run this code, a new menu item named Extra appears at the bottom of the Edit menu. When you select Extra, another submenu pops up containing the items Extra1 and Extra2. The callback structure for the submenu items is the same as for an ordinary menu item, so the use of these submenu items is extremely easy.

6.2.4   ADDING ACCELERATORS

Many programs assign special key sequences to frequently used menu items to improve user access. For example, META-O might trigger File Open, META-C might trigger Edit Copy, and so on. The META key is different on different keyboards. On some it is the ALT key, on others it is the COMPOSE CHARACTER key. The name of the key is machine-dependent.

Accelerators are easy to set up. The function shown in Listing 6.4 demonstrates the process.

Listing 6.4   Function for Adding an Accelerator to a Menu Item

```
void add_accelerator(w, acc_text, key)
    Widget w;
    char *acc_text;
    char *key;
/* adds an accelerator to a menu option. */
{
    int ac;
    Arg al[10];

    ac=0;
    XtSetArg(al[ac],XmNacceleratorText,
        XmStringCreate(acc_text,XmSTRING_DEFAULT_CHARSET)); ac++;
    XtSetArg(al[ac],XmNaccelerator,key); ac++;
    XtSetValues(w,al,ac);
}
```

Add the following line to the **create_menus** function to use the function in Listing 6.4:

```
add_accelerator(open_item,"meta+o","Meta<Key>o:");
```

This code sets up the menus so that the appropriate callback function for the **open_item** widget is activated when a user presses META-O. The **accelerator-Text** resource is an **XmString** that appears in the menu next to the Open item. The **accelerator** resource accepts a normal C string that represents the accelerator character.

You can set up function keys and control keys as accelerators as well. For example, `Ctrl<Key>o:` creates a CTRL-O accelerator, and `<Key>F1:` sets up the F1 key as an accelerator. Be careful to capitalize properly: You *must* spell the accelerator `Ctrl<Key>o:`, not `ctrl<Key>o:` or `Ctrl<key>o:`. Motif will compile the improperly capitalized versions, but the code won't run correctly. Also, be sure to include the colon.

6.2.5   ADDING MNEMONIC TRAVERSAL

A menu mnemonic offers users a way to traverse menus without using the mouse. To create a mnemonic, a character is passed into the **mnemonic** resource (inherited from the label widget) of either a cascade button in the menu bar or a push button in the menu pane. Motif shows the user the mnemonic chosen by underlining the first character in the button's name that matches the mnemonic character.

If a menu pane is visible and the program uses mnemonics in the menu, the user can choose a specific menu item by pressing the appropriate key for the mnemonic character on the keyboard. To select a menu from the menu bar, the user first holds down the META key and then presses the mnemonic character.

Adding the code shown in Listing 6.5 to Listing 6.1 demonstrates the use of mnemonic characters. Replace same-named functions with the functions shown in Listing 6.5.

Listing 6.5 Using Menu Mnemonics

```
Widget make_menu_item(item_name,client_data,mnemonic,menu)
    char *item_name;
    caddr_t client_data;
    char mnemonic;
    Widget menu;
/* adds an item into a menu. */
{
    int ac;
    Arg al[10];
    Widget item;

    ac = 0;
    XtSetArg(al[ac],XmNlabelString,
        XmStringCreateLtoR(item_name,char_set)); ac++;
    XtSetArg (al[ac],XmNmnemonic,mnemonic); ac++;
    item=XmCreatePushButton(menu,item_name,al,ac);
    XtManageChild(item);
    XtAddCallback(item,XmNactivateCallback,menuCB,client_data);
    XtSetSensitive(item,True);
    return(item);
}


Widget make_menu(menu_name,mnemonic,menu_bar)
    char *menu_name;
    char mnemonic;
    Widget menu_bar;
/* creates a menu on the menu bar */
{
    int ac;
    Arg al[10];
    Widget menu, cascade;

    menu=XmCreatePulldownMenu(menu_bar,menu_name,NULL,0);
```

```
        ac=0;
        XtSetArg (al[ac],XmNsubMenuId, menu); ac++;
        XtSetArg (al[ac],XmNmnemonic,mnemonic); ac++;
        XtSetArg(al[ac],XmNlabelString,
            XmStringCreateLtoR(menu_name,char_set)); ac++;
        cascade=XmCreateCascadeButton(menu_bar,menu_name,al,ac);
        XtManageChild(cascade);
        return(menu);
}


void create_menus(menu_bar)
    Widget menu_bar;
/* creates all the menus for this program */
{
    /* create the file menu */
    file_menu=make_menu("File",'F',menu_bar);
    open_item=make_menu_item("Open","Open selected",'O',file_menu);
    close_item=make_menu_item("Close","Close selected",'C',file_menu);
    quit_item=make_menu_item("Quit","Quit",'Q',file_menu);

    /* create the edit menu */
    edit_menu=make_menu("Edit",'E',menu_bar);
    copy_item=make_menu_item("Copy","Copy selected",'o',edit_menu);
    cut_item=make_menu_item("Cut","Cut Selected",'u',edit_menu);
    paste_item=make_menu_item("Paste","Paste Selected",'P',edit_menu);
}
```

Mnemonics traverse menu structures without a mouse and therefore might require several keystrokes to invoke a menu option. Accelerators, on the other hand, invoke a menu item with a single keystroke no matter where the item is in the menu structure.

Make sure that none of the mnemonic characters in a single menu pane or in the menu bar conflict, and that no META keystroke needed to activate a mnemonic in the menu bar conflicts with an accelerator keystroke that uses the META key.

6.3   MENU BAR HELP

When you use a RowColumn widget as a menu bar, you can also use the **menuHelpWidget** resource to display a Help menu in a special place on the menu bar. To use this feature, create a cascade button and its menu pane as usual with the **make_menu** and **make_menu_item** functions. Then pass the cascade button widget in an argument list to the **menuHelpWidget** using an **XtSetArg/XtSetValues** call. The Help cascade button appears on the far right of the menu bar. Traditionally, this menu contains specific items. See the sidebar for details. Listing 6.6 shows how to add a Help menu.

Listing 6.6   Creating a Help Menu

```
Widget make_help_menu(menu_name, menu_bar)
    char *menu_name;
    Widget menu_bar;
/* Creates a new menu on the menu bar. */
{
    int ac;
    Arg al[10];
    Widget menu, cascade;

    ac = 0;
    menu = XmCreatePulldownMenu (menu_bar, menu_name, al, ac);

    ac = 0;
    XtSetArg (al[ac], XmNsubMenuId, menu); ac++;
    XtSetArg(al[ac], XmNlabelString,
        XmStringCreateLtoR(menu_name, XmSTRING_DEFAULT_CHARSET)); ac++;
    cascade = XmCreateCascadeButton (menu_bar, menu_name, al, ac);
    XtManageChild (cascade);

    /* Wire the help menu into the rowcol widget's help menu resource. */
    ac=0;
    XtSetArg(al[ac],XmNmenuHelpWidget,cascade); ac++;
    XtSetValues(menu_bar,al,ac);

    return(menu);
}

void create_menus(menu_bar)
    Widget menu_bar;
/* creates all the menus for this program */
{
    /* create the File menu, Edit menu, etc. */

    /* Create the help menu. */
    help_menu=make_help_menu("Help",menu_bar);
    about_item=make_menu_item("About","About selected",help_menu);
    help_item=make_menu_item("Help","Help selected",help_menu);
}
```

Menu Style

Menus in a Motif program should comply with the style guidelines laid out in the Motif style guide (Appendix C). All programs that use menus should have a menu bar at the top of the application window. The menu bar should contain only cascade buttons, and these cascade buttons should always manage menu panes. Although you can wire a cascade button so that it has no menu pane and therefore acts like a push button, doing so is considered improper. The style guide states that all programs should have the following menus in the menu bar when appropriate: File, Edit, View, Options, and Help, with the mnemonics F, E, V, O, and H.

The File menu should contain file options, such as opening and closing files, saving files, and including files. By convention, the File menu also contains the Exit option at the bottom. The Edit menu should contain activities that the user can perform on the current data: Undo, Selection, Clipboard functions, and so on. The View menu should contain options that change the user's view of the data. And the Options menu should let the user customize the application. Finally, the Help menu should provide on-line help with the following options: On Context (context-sensitive help), On Help (help on using the Help menu), On Window (help on the current window), On Keys (help on function keys and accelerators), Index (an index of all help topics), Tutorial (a tutorial for the application), and On Version (version information such as the author and release date). The mnemonics for these items are C, H, W, K, I, T, and V, respectively. The Help menu should appear in a specific place on the menu bar (see Section 6.7). See the style guide for specific menu items and accelerators for these menus.

The application can supply additional menus to meet the specific needs of the application.

Motif supports hierarchical menus. Hierarchical menus can increase the number of menu items available in a limited space.

Pop-up menus can make an application much easier to use. Instead of being forced to keep returning to the menu bar, the user can pop up a menu at the current location. Pop-up menu items should always have equivalents in the main menu structure. That is, the user should always be able to activate any pop-up menu item from the main menu bar. Although pop-up menus could duplicate the entire menu bar structure, they generally do not. They contain only frequently used options.

6.4   OTHER MENU STYLES

The standard menu bar/menu pane format is the most common configuration for menus. However, Motif also supports two other menu formats: pop-up menus and option menus.

Chapter 17 discusses pop-up menus with the drawing area widget. Pop-up menus are useful in programs in which constant mouse movement between the work area and the menu bar is distracting.

Option menus allow users to select one of several options. The current option appears on a button; when the user clicks the button, other options pop up in a menu pane. Chapter 11 covers option menus.

The *Motif Style Guide* (see Appendix C) defines behavior and appearance guidelines for menu bars and panes. These guidelines include such issues as the definition of File and Edit menus, the placement and contents of the Help menu, and restrictions on items in the menu bar. When you build a complete application, it is important to consult the style guide so that your menus meet the normal expectations of the Motif user community.

7 DIALOGS

Dialog boxes provide an easy and friendly way to acquire information from and display messages to the user. In graphical user interfaces, they replace the standard "prompt-read" sequence commonly found in text-based programs.

You can create custom dialog boxes to do anything you want (see Chapter 13). However, Motif provides a set of canned dialog boxes that handle the vast majority of user interaction situations. They are very easy to use once you have seen a few examples.

The simplest form of canned dialog box is the *message dialog box*. It contains a statement or a question and up to three buttons with which a user can respond or reply (see Figure 7.1). The *prompt dialog box* displays a message or a question and allows the user to type in a string in reply. The user enters text and then clicks a button or presses the RETURN key (see Figure 7.2). A *selection dialog box* lets the user choose one item from a list of items. The user can scroll through the list and then click the desired item to select it (see Figure 7.3). A *file selection dialog* box lets the user specify the name of a file. The user can switch directories and select from a list of file names in the current directory (see Figure 7.4).

In this chapter, we will look at example code that creates each of these four dialog box types. In all of these examples, we create the dialog box widget, manage the dialog box when it needs to appear on the screen, and then handle the callbacks generated by the dialog box so that the user's input can be retrieved.

7.1 MESSAGE DIALOG BOXES

As a programmer, you will frequently want to ask a user yes-or-no questions or send messages of various types. Motif provides a message dialog box that you can use to handle these situations. The code in Listing 7.1 demonstrates the process. When you run this code, a push button with the words "Push Me" appears in the application window. When this button is pushed, the message

Figure 7.1   A Message Dialog Box

Figure 7.2   A Prompt Dialog Box

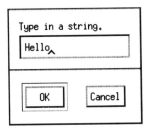

dialog box shown in Figure 7.1 appears. The result of the user's interaction with the dialog box is printed in stdout as the program is running.

Listing 7.1   Creating a Message Dialog Box

```
/* message.c*/

#include <Xm/Xm.h>
#include <Xm/PushB.h>
#include <Xm/MessageB.h>

#define OK        1
#define CANCEL    2

XtAppContext context;
XmStringCharSet char_set=XmSTRING_DEFAULT_CHARSET;

Widget toplevel, button, dialog;

void dialogCB(w,client_data,call_data)
    Widget w;
    int client_data;
    XmAnyCallbackStruct *call_data;
```

Figure 7.3   A Selection Dialog Box

```
/* callback function for the dialog box. */
{
    switch (client_data)
    {
        case OK:
            printf("OK selected\n");
            break;
        case CANCEL:
            printf("CANCEL selected\n");
            break;
    }
    /* make the dialog box invisible */
    XtUnmanageChild(w);
}

void buttonCB(w,client_data,call_data)
    Widget w;
    XtPointer client_data;
    XmPushButtonCallbackStruct *call_data;
/* callback function for the pushbutton */
{
    /* make the dialog box visible */
    XtManageChild(dialog);
}
```

Figure 7.4   A File Selection Dialog Box

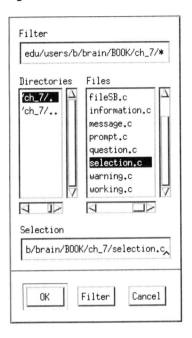

```
void main(argc,argv)
    int argc;
    char *argv[];
{
    Arg al[10];
    int ac;

    /* create the toplevel shell */
    toplevel = XtAppInitialize(&context,"",NULL,0,&argc,argv,
        NULL,NULL,0);

    /* create (but DO NOT manage) the message dialog */
    ac=0;
    XtSetArg(al[ac], XmNmessageString,
        XmStringCreateLtoR("Is everything OK?",char_set)); ac++;
    dialog=XmCreateMessageDialog(toplevel,"dialog",al,ac);
    XtAddCallback(dialog,XmNokCallback,dialogCB,OK);
    XtAddCallback(dialog,XmNcancelCallback,dialogCB,CANCEL);
    XtUnmanageChild(XmMessageBoxGetChild(dialog,XmDIALOG_HELP_BUTTON));

    /* create and manage pushbutton */
    ac=0;
```

```
XtSetArg(al[ac],XmNlabelString,
    XmStringCreate("Push Me",char_set)); ac++;
button=XmCreatePushButton(toplevel,"button",al,ac);
XtManageChild(button);
XtAddCallback (button, XmNactivateCallback, buttonCB, NULL);

XtRealizeWidget(toplevel);
XtAppMainLoop(context);
}
```

The code in Listing 7.1 has three parts: the **main** function to set everything up and two callback functions to handle the "Push Me" push button's **activate** callback and the callbacks generated by the buttons in the dialog box.

The **main** function starts normally, then creates the dialog box and the push buttons. It uses a convenience function for message dialogs to create the dialog box. Note that the dialog box is created but not managed: It will be managed when we want it to appear on the screen. The dialog box's **OK** and **cancel** callbacks return information to the **dialogCB** function, and constants are passed through the **client_data** parameter so that the callback function can tell which button the user pressed.

A message dialog box is built from a message box widget. The message box widget's resource list in Appendix J defines three buttons: OK, Cancel, and Help. A message box is like any other widget and can be incorporated into applications. A message box dialog is a message box put in a dialog shell so that it acts like a pop-up dialog box. (See Chapter 13 for details on dialog shells.)

The Help button is disabled and made invisible in the above program by a call that unmanages it in the **main** function:

```
XtUnmanageChild(XmMessageBoxGetChild(dialog, XmDIALOG_HELP_BUTTON));
```

XtUnmanageChild   *Unmanages the specified widget.*

```
void XtUnmanageChild(Widget widget);
```

widget   The widget.

XmMessageBoxGetChild, used in **main**, is a convenience function that extracts the widget variables of different children that make up the message dialog box. The entry for the message box in Appendix J lists the different child names you can extract, as shown below:

```
Widget XmMessageBoxGetChild(Widget widget, unsigned char child);
```

Valid values for child parameter:
```
    XmDIALOG_CANCEL_BUTTON
    XmDIALOG_DEFAULT_BUTTON
    XmDIALOG_HELP_BUTTON
    XmDIALOG_MESSAGE_LABEL
    XmDIALOG_OK_BUTTON
    XmDIALOG_SEPARATOR
    XmDIALOG_SYMBOL_LABEL
```

Once the desired child has been extracted from the dialog box with **XmMessageBoxGetChild**, it can be manipulated like any normal widget. In the code shown in Listing 7.1, the Help button is extracted and unmanaged to make it disappear.

When a user clicks the main push button, the **buttonCB** function is called. The act of managing the dialog box in **buttonCB** causes the dialog box to appear on the screen; unmanaging the dialog box in the **dialogCB** function makes it disappear again.

The **dialogCB** function gets called when a user clicks either the OK or cancel buttons in the dialog box. The integer in the **client_data** parameter tells it which button the user clicked. The **dialogCB** function writes the appropriate message to stdout and unmanages the dialog box so that it disappears. The dialog widget continues to exist (it was unmanaged, not deleted), but it must be remanaged to become visible and active again.

If you want to provide help, add a callback for the Help button instead of unmanaging it as shown in the code, or change the name used to display the Help button and use it for something else. To change the name, change the **helpLabelString** resource available in the message box widget. You can also change the names of the OK and Cancel buttons—for example, to read "Yes" and "No" instead—by changing the **okLabelString** or the **cancelLabelString** resources. To make a message dialog box that has only an OK button, unmanage the Cancel button as well as the Help button. The OK button will be centered automatically.

Note that the message box contains a **symbolPixmap** resource that lets you place an icon in it. Chapter 17 shows an example of how to place a pixmap in a label. You can use this same technique to place a pixmap in a message dialog box using the **symbolPixmap** resource.

Dialog Children

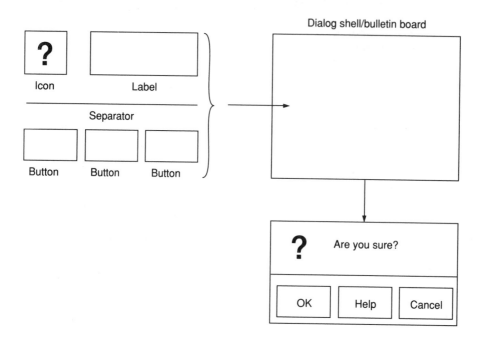

Dialog boxes are composed of a number of separate children bonded into a single widget. The children of a typical message dialog box are shown in the figure above.

There are two techniques for manipulating the children that make up the dialog box. The first technique uses several resources that exist in the resource list for the message box widget. These resources allow direct manipulation. For example, the labels on the three buttons have resources in the message box widget's resource list named

XmNcancelLabelString, XmNhelpLabelString, and **XmNokLabelString**. Changing these resources modifies the labels on the three buttons.

The second technique involves extracting the child's widget variable from the message box widget itself and then manipulating the child widget in the normal manner. For a message box widget, the extraction is done using a convenience function called **XmMessageBoxGetChild**. This function accepts as parameters the

Dialog Children (continued)

parent widget (which must be a message
box widget) and a constant to identify the
child (see Appendix J, which contains a
complete list of the message box widget's
children).

To retrieve the widget variable for the help
button, you can use the following code:

```
Widget help_button,message;
   :
   :
   :
```

```
message=XmCreateMessageBoxDialog
    (toplevel,"message",NULL,0);
   :
   :
help_button=XmMessageBoxGetChild
    (message,XmDIALOG_HELP_BUTTON);
```

Once you have extracted the help button,
you can manipulate it just as you would any
other push-button widget. You can change
its resources, add callbacks to it, unmanage
it to make it disappear, and so on.

In addition to the generic version shown here, you can create five specialized versions of the message dialog box. They are discussed at the end of this
chapter.

7.2   PROMPT DIALOG BOXES

Motif supports a prompt dialog box for getting strings from the user (see Figure
7.2). Prompt dialog boxes are almost identical to message dialog boxes—they
both have OK, Cancel, and Help buttons that the user accesses the same way—
but prompt dialog boxes allow the user to enter a string, and therefore require
an extra line of code to extract the string the user enters once the dialog box's
OK callback is activated. The code in Listing 7.2 shows how to use a prompt
dialog box.

Listing 7.2   Creating a Prompt Dialog Box

```
/* prompt.c*/

#include <Xm/Xm.h>
#include <Xm/PushB.h>
#include <Xm/SelectioB.h>
/* a prompt dialog is made from a stripped-down selection box. */
#define    OK       1
#define    CANCEL   2
```

```
XtAppContext context;
XmStringCharSet char_set = XmSTRING_DEFAULT_CHARSET;

Widget toplevel, button, dialog;

void dialogCB(w,client_data,call_data)
    Widget w;
    int client_data;
    XmSelectionBoxCallbackStruct *call_data;
/* callback function for the dialog box */
{
    char *s;

    switch (client_data)
    {
        case OK:
            /* get the string from the call_data parameter. */
            XmStringGetLtoR(call_data->value,char_set,&s);
            printf("string='%s'\n",s);
            XtFree(s);
            break;
        case CANCEL:
            printf("CANCEL selected\n");
            break;
    }
    /* make the dialog box invisible */
    XtUnmanageChild(w);
}

void buttonCB(w,client_data,call_data)
    Widget w;
    XtPointer client_data;
    XmPushButtonCallbackStruct *call_data;
/* callback function for the push button */
{
    /* make the dialog box visible */
    XtManageChild(dialog);
}

void main(argc,argv)
    int argc;
    char *argv[];
{
    Arg al[10];
    int ac;
```

```
    /* create the toplevel shell */
    toplevel = XtAppInitialize(&context,"",NULL,0,&argc,argv,
        NULL,NULL,0);

    /* create the dialog box. */
    ac=0;
    XtSetArg(al[ac], XmNselectionLabelString,
        XmStringCreateLtoR("Type in a string. ",char_set)); ac++;
    dialog = XmCreatePromptDialog(toplevel,"dialog",al,ac);
    XtAddCallback(dialog,XmNokCallback,dialogCB,OK);
    XtAddCallback(dialog,XmNcancelCallback,dialogCB,CANCEL);
    XtUnmanageChild(XmSelectionBoxGetChild(dialog,
        XmDIALOG_HELP_BUTTON));
    /* create the pushbutton */
    ac=0;
    XtSetArg(al[ac],XmNlabelString,
        XmStringCreate("Push Me",char_set)); ac++;
    button=XmCreatePushButton(toplevel,"label",al,ac);
    XtManageChild(button);
    XtAddCallback (button, XmNactivateCallback, buttonCB, NULL);

    XtRealizeWidget(toplevel);
    XtAppMainLoop(context);
}
```

In the case OK: portion of the **dialogCB** function the code extracts the string entered by the user. It gets this string from **call_data**. The **call_data** parameter is of the type **XmSelectionBoxCallbackStruct**:

```
typedef struct
{
  int reason;
  XEvent *event;
  XmString value;
  int length;
} XmSelectionBoxCallbackStruct;
```

Since the extracted string in the **value** field is an **XmString**, you must convert it to a normal C string to print it, as shown in Section 3.9. Once the string has been used, the block should be freed to prevent memory leaks. Except for the special string-extraction code and the different convenience function used to create the prompt dialog box, the rest of this program is identical to the code for the message dialog box in Listing 7.1.

Since a prompt dialog box is a selection dialog box without the scrolling list, you must include SelectioB.h when creating one. See Appendix J for a description of this widget's resources and callbacks.

7.3   SELECTION DIALOG BOXES

Motif provides a selection dialog box that lets users select items from a list. An example is shown in Figure 7.3. A selection dialog box is fairly complicated: It consists of several labels, four buttons, a text editing area, and a scrolling list of items from which the user can select.

The code for creating a selection dialog box, shown in Listing 7.3, is nearly identical to the code for creating a prompt dialog box, except for some extra code to set up the scrolling list.

Listing 7.3   Creating a Selection Dialog Box

```
/* selection.c */

#include <Xm/Xm.h>
#include <Xm/PushB.h>
#include <Xm/SelectioB.h>
#include <Xm/List.h>

#define OK       1
#define CANCEL   2

XtAppContext context;
XmStringCharSet char_set=XmSTRING_DEFAULT_CHARSET;

Widget toplevel, button, dialog;
char *animals[]={"cat","dog","cow","goat","horse","mouse","pig",
                 "sheep","rat","donkey","elephant","squirrel"};

void dialogCB(w,client_data,call_data)
    Widget w;
    int client_data;
    XmSelectionBoxCallbackStruct *call_data;
/* callback function for the dialog box. */
{
    char *s;

    switch (client_data)
```

```
    {
        case OK:
            /* get the string from the call_data parameter. */
            XmStringGetLtoR(call_data->value,char_set,&s);
            printf("string='%s'\n",s);
            XtFree(s);
            break;
        case CANCEL:
            printf("CANCEL selected\n");
            break;
    }
    XtUnmanageChild(w);
}


void buttonCB(w,client_data,call_data)
    Widget w;
    XtPointer client_data;
    XmPushButtonCallbackStruct *call_data;
/* callback function for the pushbutton */
{
    Arg al[10];
    int ac;
    Widget list;
    int list_cnt;
    XmString s;

    /* Add items to selection boxes list. */
    list=XmSelectionBoxGetChild(dialog, XmDIALOG_LIST);
    XmListDeleteAllItems(list);
    for (list_cnt=0; list_cnt<XtNumber(animals); list_cnt++)
    {
        s=XmStringCreate(animals[list_cnt],char_set);
        XmListAddItem(list,s,0);
        XmStringFree(s);
    }

    XtManageChild(dialog);
}
void main(argc,argv)
    int argc;
    char *argv[];
{
    Arg al[10];
    int ac;
```

```
/* create the toplevel shell */
toplevel = XtAppInitialize(&context,"",NULL,0,&argc,argv,
    NULL,NULL,0);

/* create the pushbutton */
ac=0;
XtSetArg(al[ac],XmNlabelString,
    XmStringCreate("Push Me",char_set)); ac++;
button=XmCreatePushButton(toplevel,"button",al,ac);
XtManageChild(button);
XtAddCallback (button, XmNactivateCallback, buttonCB, NULL);

/* create the selection box widget */
ac = 0;
/* the following line is commented out to make a point. Read
   more about it in the text description. */
/* XtSetArg(al[ac],XmNautoUnmanage,False); ac++; */
XtSetArg(al[ac],XmNmustMatch,True); ac++;
XtSetArg(al[ac],XmNselectionLabelString,
    XmStringCreateLtoR("Pick an animal. ",char_set)); ac++;
dialog=XmCreateSelectionDialog(toplevel,"dialog",al,ac);
XtAddCallback(dialog,XmNokCallback,dialogCB,OK);
XtAddCallback(dialog,XmNcancelCallback,dialogCB,CANCEL);
XtUnmanageChild(XmSelectionBoxGetChild(dialog,XmDIALOG_HELP_BUTTON));

XtRealizeWidget(toplevel);
XtAppMainLoop(context);
}
```

The animals array in Listing 7.3 represents a list of strings that you want to appear in the selection dialog box. The code to handle the push button's callback adds the items to the list by getting the list widget child from the selection dialog box and then using list widget convenience functions **Xm-ListDeleteAllItems** and **XmListAddItem** (see Chapter 11). Note the use of the **XtNumber** function, which returns the size of an array.

XtNumber   *Returns the number of elements in an array.*

```
Cardinal XtNumber(ArrayVariable array);
```

array   The array.

This code introduces you to the **mustMatch** resource, which is set in the **main** function. The selection box contains an editing area in which the user can type a selection. Theoretically, this selection can be anything. However, the strings in the scrolling list are often the only valid strings, and the user should be allowed to enter only valid strings. The **mustMatch** resource forces the user to enter a string that matches an item in the list. Try running the code as is, then enter some garbage into the string area of the selection box. The selection box will close, but the callback will not be triggered. Now change the code and set **mustMatch** to false. When you enter garbage, the program returns garbage.

When **mustMatch** is true, the selection box closes even if the user enters an invalid string. This can be rather disconcerting. The program receives no notification through the callback and the user receives no message. It is better for the selection box to remain on screen until it receives a valid response. To achieve this, use the **autoUnmanage** resource of the bulletin board widget (the selection box is made up of separate widgets attached to a bulletin board). When set to true, the **autoUnmanage** resource makes the bulletin board automatically disappear whenever the user clicks OK, Cancel, or Help. Such behavior is undesirable here. To change the behavior, uncomment the line that sets the **autoUnmanage** resource to false and rerun the program, making sure that **mustMatch** is true. Now when you enter garbage into the text editing area, the dialog box remains on the screen until the user enters a valid string. Note that the **autoUnmanage** resource works only if it is set to false *at the time of widget creation*.

You can create an even more user-friendly interface by using **noMatchCallback**, which is specially designed for this purpose. This callback is triggered when the user enters a nonmatching text string in the text editing region. You can use **noMatchCallback** to display a message dialog box containing an error message when the user enters a nonmatching string.

The selection box widget contains an Apply button that this code does not use. Use it as you please in your own applications, or unmanage it. Generally, an Apply button allows the user to see the effect of a change on-screen without unmanaging the dialog.

7.4   FILE SELECTION DIALOG BOXES

A file selection dialog box (Figure 7.1) lets users select from a list of files available in the current directory. It also gives the user an intuitive way of traversing the directory structure. Although it looks very different from the selection box shown in Figure 7.3, the code for creating a file selection dialog box (Listing 7.4) is nearly identical to the code for normal selection boxes.

Listing 7.4   Creating a File Selection Dialog Box

```
/* fileSB.c */

#include <Xm/Xm.h>
#include <Xm/PushB.h>
#include <Xm/FileSB.h>

#define OK        1
#define CANCEL    2

XtAppContext context;
XmStringCharSet char_set=XmSTRING_DEFAULT_CHARSET;

Widget toplevel, button, dialog;

void dialogCB(w,client_data,call_data)
    Widget w;
    int client_data;
    XmSelectionBoxCallbackStruct *call_data;
/* callback function for the dialog box */
{
    char *s;

    switch (client_data)
    {
        case OK:
            XmStringGetLtoR(call_data->value,char_set,&s);
            printf("string='%s'\n",s);
            XtFree(s);
            break;
        case CANCEL:
            printf("CANCEL selected\n");
            break;
    }
    XtUnmanageChild(w);
}

void buttonCB(w,client_data,call_data)
    Widget w;
    XtPointer client_data;
    XmPushButtonCallbackStruct *call_data;
/* callback function for the pushbutton */
```

```
{
    /* make the dialog box visible */
    XtManageChild(dialog);
}

void main(argc,argv)
    int argc;
    char *argv[];
{
    Arg al[10];
    int ac;

    /* create the toplevel shell */
    toplevel = XtAppInitialize(&context,"",NULL,0,&argc,argv,
        NULL,NULL,0);

    /* create and manage the pushbutton */
    ac=0;
    XtSetArg(al[ac],XmNlabelString,
        XmStringCreate("Push Me",char_set)); ac++;
    button=XmCreatePushButton(toplevel,"button",al,ac);
    XtManageChild(button);
    XtAddCallback(button,XmNactivateCallback,
        buttonCB,NULL);

    /* create the dialog box */
    ac = 0;
    dialog=XmCreateFileSelectionDialog(toplevel,
        "dialog",al,ac);
    XtAddCallback(dialog,XmNokCallback,dialogCB,OK);
    XtAddCallback(dialog,XmNcancelCallback,
        dialogCB,CANCEL);
    XtUnmanageChild(XmSelectionBoxGetChild(dialog,
        XmDIALOG_HELP_BUTTON));

    XtRealizeWidget(toplevel);
    XtAppMainLoop(context);
}
```

The file selection dialog box is extremely powerful and provides a number of resources that contain such data as the current directory, the list of files, and the filter string. Much of this data is also returned in the callback structure. See Appendix J for more information.

Figure 7.5   An Error Dialog Box

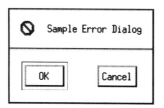

Figure 7.6   An Information Dialog Box

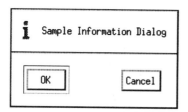

7.5   OTHER CANNED DIALOG BOXES IN MOTIF

Motif provides five other canned dialog boxes, all of which use the message dialog box as a foundation: error dialog boxes, information dialog boxes, question dialog boxes, warning dialog boxes, and working dialog boxes (see Figures 7.5 through 7.9). Each is simply a message dialog box with an icon supplied through the **symbolPixmap** resource. The code in Listing 7.5 produced the error dialog box shown in Figure 7.5.

Listing 7.5   Creating an Error Message Dialog Box

```
/* error.c */

#include <Xm/Xm.h>
#include <Xm/PushB.h>
#include <Xm/MessageB.h>

#define OK      1
#define CANCEL  2

Widget toplevel, button, dialog;

XtAppContext context;
XmStringCharSet char_set=XmSTRING_DEFAULT_CHARSET;

void dialogCB(w,client_data,call_data)
```

```
    Widget w;
    int client_data;
    XmSelectionBoxCallbackStruct *call_data;
/* callback function for the dialog box. */
{
    switch (client_data)
    {
    case OK:
        printf("OK selected\n");
        break;
    case CANCEL:
        printf("CANCEL selected\n");
        break;
    }
    /* make the dialog box invisible */
    XtUnmanageChild(w);
}
void buttonCB(w,client_data,call_data)
    Widget w;
    XtPointer client_data;
    XmPushButtonCallbackStruct *call_data;
/* callback function for the pushbutton */
{
    /* make the dialog box visible */
    XtManageChild(dialog);
}

void main(argc,argv)
    int argc;
    char *argv[];
{
    Arg al[10];
    int ac;

    /* create the toplevel shell */
    toplevel = XtAppInitialize(&context,"",NULL,0,&argc,argv,
        NULL,NULL,0);

    /* create (but DO NOT manage) the message dialog */
    ac=0;
    XtSetArg(al[ac], XmNmessageString,
        XmStringCreateLtoR("Sample Error Dialog",char_set));  ac++;
    dialog = XmCreateErrorDialog(toplevel,"dialog", al, ac);
    XtAddCallback(dialog,XmNokCallback,dialogCB,OK);
    XtAddCallback(dialog,XmNcancelCallback,dialogCB,CANCEL);
```

```
XtUnmanageChild(XmMessageBoxGetChild(dialog,
    XmDIALOG_HELP_BUTTON));

/* create and manage pushbutton */
ac=0;
XtSetArg(al[ac],XmNlabelString,
    XmStringCreate("Push Me",char_set)); ac++;
button=XmCreatePushButton(toplevel,"button",al,ac);
XtManageChild(button);
XtAddCallback(button,XmNactivateCallback,
    buttonCB,NULL);

XtRealizeWidget(toplevel);
XtAppMainLoop(context);
}
```

Note that code in Listing 7.5 is almost the same as the sample code for creating a message dialog box, except that the message string has been changed, and the following line creates the error dialog box:

```
dialog = XmCreateErrorDialog(toplevel, "dialog", al, ac);
```

You can replace the word "Error" in this line with "Information," "Question," "Warning," or "Working" to create the other four dialog boxes.

Figure 7.7   A Question Dialog Box

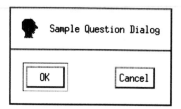

Figure 7.8   A Warning Dialog Box

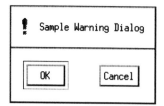

Figure 7.9   A Working Dialog Box

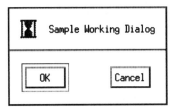

8 TIC-TAC-TOE APPLICATION

At this point you have all of the tools you need to create applications. Now we will combine these tools to form a simple application that plays a game of tic-tac-toe. This application uses label and push-button widgets along with their resources and callbacks, a form widget, a menu, and a dialog box. When we are done, we will have created a complete graphical application with a very small amount of code, all of which is fairly simple and straightforward to understand.

8.1 DESIGNING AN APPLICATION

Whenever you are about to start building an application using Motif, spend some time working on the user interface design. Ask yourself two important questions: What functionality does the user interface need to provide? And what combination of widgets will best produce a user interface that is easy to use, visually appealing, and intuitive?

In a program that plays a tic-tac-toe game, the user needs to be able to accomplish certain tasks. The user must be able to quit the application and restart it, enter a move, see the game's current state, and know when the game is over. What combination of widgets best implements these capabilities? Often, the only way to answer such a question is to code an interface and see how it feels. If the interface seems to be getting in your way, or if new users have trouble learning how to use it quickly, then you probably need to change it.

In the the tic-tac-toe program, you can most likely handle quitting and restarting with a menu, since the user will expect the program to work that way. Quit and Restart push buttons are also a possibility, however. A three-by-three grid of push buttons can handle the user's moves, and the labels or pixmaps on these buttons can also show the current state of the game. A label widget will prompt the user to make his or her move, and a message dialog box can announce the winner at the end of each game.

Figure 8.1   A Rough Sketch of a Tic-Tac-Toe User Interface

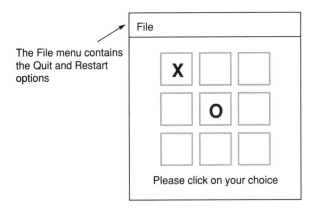

In the process of designing the tic-tac-toe interface, you might get out a piece of scratch paper and sketch out what the interface will look like. Figure 8.1 shows a drawing of one possibility. In larger applications, rough sketches like this can give you a good feel for user interface options quickly.

8.2   CODING THE TIC-TAC-TOE PROGRAM

When you look at the rough sketch for the tic-tac-toe application, you can easily see which widgets you need to use. You need a form widget to hold the other widgets (because it resizes buttons automatically) and nine push buttons for the grid. You also need a label widget to display the "Please click your choice" message, a menu bar widget and appropriate menu items, and a message dialog box to announce the winner.

The **main** function (Listing 8.1) consists of the code needed to create all of these widgets and attach them to the form. It creates nine buttons in a loop that spaces each appropriately on the form based on the value of the loop variables.

Listing 8.1   Code for the main Function and Declarations for the Tic-Tac-Toe Application

```
/* tictactoe.c */

#include <Xm/Xm.h>
#include <Xm/PushB.h>
#include <Xm/Form.h>
```

```
#include <Xm/Label.h>
#include <Xm/MessageB.h>
#include <Xm/RowColumn.h>
#include <Xm/CascadeB.h>

#define OK        1
#define CANCEL    2

#define RESTART   1
#define QUIT      2

XtAppContext context;
XmStringCharSet char_set=XmSTRING_DEFAULT_CHARSET;

Widget file_menu;
Widget restart_item;
Widget quit_item;
Widget menu_bar;
Widget toplevel;
Widget dialog;
Widget button[3][3];
Widget form;
Widget label;

int board[3][3]={0,0,0,0,0,0,0,0,0};
int rand_seed=10;

Widget make_menu_item();    /* Adds an item into the menu.        */
Widget make_menu();         /* Creates a menu on the menu bar.    */
void create_menus();        /* Creates all menus for this program. */
void init_board();          /* Resets the state of the game to    */
                            /* the beginning.                     */
void menuCB();              /* Callback routine used for all menus. */
void dialogCB();            /* Callback function for the dialog box */
                            /* called whenever the user clicks on */
                            /* the OK or Cancel buttons in the    */
                            /* dialog box.                        */
Boolean check_win();        /* Checks for a winner or a draw. If a */
                            /* win or a draw is detected, the     */
                            /* dialog box is activated.           */
int rand();                 /* Random number generator from K&R.  */
void do_computers_move();   /* Determines the computer's next move */
                            /* and places it on the grid.         */
```

```
void buttonCB();            /* Callback function for the 9 grid    */
                            /* buttons called when one of the grid */
                            /* buttons is clicked.                 */

void main(argc,argv)
    int argc;
    char *argv[];
{
    Arg al[10];
    int ac;
    int x,y;

    /* create the toplevel shell */
    toplevel = XtAppInitialize(&context,"",NULL,0,&argc,argv,
        NULL,NULL,0);
    /* set the default size of the window. */
    ac=0;
    XtSetArg(al[ac],XmNwidth,200); ac++;
    XtSetArg(al[ac],XmNheight,200); ac++;
    XtSetValues(toplevel,al,ac);

    /* create a form widget */
    ac=0;
    form=XmCreateForm(toplevel,"form",al,ac);
    XtManageChild(form);

    /* create the menu bar and attach it to the form. */
    ac=0;
    XtSetArg(al[ac],XmNtopAttachment,XmATTACH_FORM); ac++;
    XtSetArg(al[ac],XmNrightAttachment,XmATTACH_FORM); ac++;
    XtSetArg(al[ac],XmNleftAttachment,XmATTACH_FORM); ac++;
    menu_bar=XmCreateMenuBar(form,"menu_bar",al,ac);
    XtManageChild(menu_bar);

    /* set up the buttons for the board. Attach them to the form. */
    for (x=0; x<3; x++)
    {
        for (y=0; y<3; y++)
        {
            ac=0;
            XtSetArg(al[ac],XmNlabelString,
                XmStringCreate("-",char_set)); ac++;
            XtSetArg(al[ac],XmNleftAttachment,
```

```
                    XmATTACH_POSITION); ac++;
            XtSetArg(al[ac],XmNleftPosition,20+x*20); ac++;
            XtSetArg(al[ac],XmNrightAttachment,
                XmATTACH_POSITION); ac++;
            XtSetArg(al[ac],XmNrightPosition,40+x*20); ac++;
            XtSetArg(al[ac],XmNtopAttachment,
                XmATTACH_POSITION); ac++;
            XtSetArg(al[ac],XmNtopPosition,20+y*20); ac++;
            XtSetArg(al[ac],XmNbottomAttachment,
                XmATTACH_POSITION); ac++;
            XtSetArg(al[ac],XmNbottomPosition, 40+y*20); ac++;
            button[x][y]=XmCreatePushButton(form,"label",al,ac);
            XtManageChild(button[x][y]);
            XtAddCallback(button[x][y],XmNactivateCallback,
                buttonCB,x*3+y);
        }
    }


    /* create a label widget and attach it to the form. */
    ac=0;
    XtSetArg(al[ac],XmNlabelString,
        XmStringCreate("Please click on your choice",char_set)); ac++;
    XtSetArg(al[ac],XmNrightAttachment,XmATTACH_FORM); ac++;
    XtSetArg(al[ac],XmNleftAttachment,XmATTACH_FORM); ac++;
    XtSetArg(al[ac],XmNtopAttachment,XmATTACH_POSITION); ac++;
    XtSetArg(al[ac],XmNtopPosition,85); ac++;
    label=XmCreateLabel(form,"label",al,ac);
    XtManageChild(label);

    /* create a dialog that will announce the winner. */
    ac=0;
    dialog=XmCreateMessageDialog(toplevel,"dialog",al,ac);
    XtAddCallback(dialog, XmNokCallback,dialogCB,OK);
    XtUnmanageChild(XmMessageBoxGetChild(dialog,
        XmDIALOG_CANCEL_BUTTON));
    XtUnmanageChild(XmMessageBoxGetChild(dialog,
        XmDIALOG_HELP_BUTTON));

    create_menus(menu_bar);

    XtRealizeWidget(toplevel);
    XtAppMainLoop(context);
}
```

You can copy the code that handles the menus from Chapter 6. The **make_menu**, **make_menu_item** and **create_menus** code requires only minor modifications, including a change to the **client_data** parameter to make it accept integers rather than strings. Other changes include modifying **create_menus** so that the correct menu structure is built for this application (Listing 8.2).

**Listing 8.2 The Menu-Handling Code for the
Tic-Tac-Toe Application**

```
Widget make_menu_item(item_name,client_data,menu)
    char *item_name;
    int client_data;
    Widget menu;
/* adds an item into the menu. */
{
    int ac;
    Arg al[10];
    Widget item;

    ac = 0;
    XtSetArg(al[ac], XmNlabelString,
        XmStringCreateLtoR(item_name,char_set)); ac++;
    item=XmCreatePushButton(menu,item_name,al,ac);
    XtManageChild(item);
    XtAddCallback (item,XmNactivateCallback,menuCB,client_data);
    XtSetSensitive(item,True);
    return(item);
}
Widget make_menu(menu_name,menu_bar)
    char *menu_name;
    Widget menu_bar;
/* creates a menu on the menu bar */
{
    int ac;
    Arg al[10];
    Widget menu, cascade;

    menu=XmCreatePulldownMenu(menu_bar,menu_name,NULL,0);
    ac=0;
    XtSetArg(al[ac],XmNsubMenuId,menu);  ac++;
    XtSetArg(al[ac],XmNlabelString,
        XmStringCreateLtoR(menu_name,char_set)); ac++;
    cascade=XmCreateCascadeButton(menu_bar,menu_name,al,ac);
    XtManageChild (cascade);
    return(menu);
}
```

```
void create_menus(menu_bar)
    Widget menu_bar;
/* creates all the menus for this program */
{
    /* create the file menu */
    file_menu=make_menu("File",menu_bar);
    restart_item=make_menu_item("Restart",
        RESTART,file_menu);
    quit_item=make_menu_item("Quit",QUIT,file_menu);
}
```

When the game begins, all of the buttons will display a "–" label to show
that they are available. The **init_board** routine reinitializes the button widgets
to contain the "–" label and initializes the **board** variable to all zeros. The
menuCB routine either quits the program or reinitializes the board with **init_
board** when a user selects one of the menu items (see Listing 8.3).

Listing 8.3   The Menu Callback Code for the
Tic-Tac-Toe Application

```
void init_board()
/* Resets the state of the game to the beginning. */
{
    int x,y;
    int ac;
    Arg al[10];

    for(x=0; x<3; x++)
        for (y=0; y<3; y++)
        {
            board[x][y]=0;
            ac=0;
            XtSetArg(al[ac],XmNlabelString,
                XmStringCreate("-",char_set)); ac++;
            XtSetValues(button[x][y],al,ac);
        }
}


void menuCB(w,client_data,call_data)
    Widget w;
    int client_data;
    XmAnyCallbackStruct *call_data;
```

```
/* callback routine used for all menus */
{
    if (client_data==QUIT) /* if quit seen, then exit */
        exit(0);
    if (client_data==RESTART)
        init_board();
}
```

The dialog box appears whenever anyone wins or the game ends in a draw. Its OK button triggers the callback function **dialogCB**, which closes the dialog box and restarts the game (see Listing 8.4).

Listing 8.4 The Dialog Box Callback Code for the Tic-Tac-Toe Application

```
void dialogCB(w,client_data,call_data)
    Widget w;
    int client_data;
    XmAnyCallbackStruct *call_data;
/* callback function for the dialog box. Called whenever the
    user clicks on the OK or Cancel buttons on the dialog box. */
{
    /* after someone wins, restart. */
    XtUnmanageChild(w);
    init_board();
}
```

The remainder of the code, shown in Listing 8.5, handles the moves of the user and the computer and recognizes and announces winners. When the user clicks the button of his or her choice, the button's **activate** callback triggers the code for **buttonCB**, which checks to make sure that the user clicked on an empty button.

If the user did so, the button's label changes to show that the user holds the position. The program then calls the function that handles the computer's move, which checks to see if the user has won. If not, it chooses a random position for the computer's move (you can add an AI move calculation function here if you like). The program checks the board again to see if the computer has won. If someone wins, the code displays the dialog box. If not, the code falls back to the main event loop to await events.

Listing 8.5   The Button Callback and Win-Checking Code for the Tic-Tac-Toe Application

```
Boolean check_win()
/* checks for a winner or a draw. If a win or a draw is detected,
   the dialog box is activated. */
{
    Arg al[10];
    int ac;
    char *s=NULL;
    int x,y;
    int sum1,sum2,tot=0;

    /* check all rows and columns for a win */
    for (x=0; x<3; x++)
    {
        sum1=sum2=0;
        for (y=0; y<3; y++)
        {
            sum1 += board[x][y];
            sum2 += board[y][x];
        }
        if (sum1 == 3 || sum2 == 3) s="You won.";
        else if (sum1 == -3 || sum2 == -3) s="I won!";
    }

    /* check diagonals for a win */
    sum1=sum2=0;
    for (x=0; x<3; x++)
    {
        sum1 += board[x][x];
        sum2 += board[2-x][x];
    }
    if (sum1 == 3 || sum2 == 3) s="You won.";
    else if (sum1 == -3 || sum2 == -3) s="I won!";

    /* check for draw. */
    for (x=0; x<3; x++)
        for (y=0; y<3; y++)
            if (board[x][y] != 0) tot++;
                if (tot==9 && !s) s="It's a draw.";

    /* announce winner in dialog box */
    if (s)
```

```
    {
        ac=0;
        XtSetArg(al[ac], XmNmessageString,
            XmStringCreateLtoR(s,char_set));  ac++;
        XtSetValues(dialog,al,ac);
        XtManageChild(dialog);
        return(True);
    }
return(False);
}


int rand()
/* random number generator from K&R */
{
    rand_seed = rand_seed * 1103515245 +12345;
    return (unsigned int)(rand_seed / 65536) % 32768;
}


void do_computers_move()
/* determines the computers next move and places it on the grid. */
{
    Arg al[10];
    int ac;
    int x,y;

    if (!check_win())
    {
        /* computer move is random. Loop until valid move chosen.*/
        do { x=rand()%3; y=rand()%3; } while (board[x][y]!=0);
        board[x][y] = -1;

        /* update the screen. */
        ac=0;
        XtSetArg(al[ac],XmNlabelString,
            XmStringCreate("0",char_set)); ac++;
        XtSetValues(button[x][y],al,ac);
        check_win();
    }
}


void buttonCB(w,client_data,call_data)
    Widget w;
    int client_data;
```

```
    XmAnyCallbackStruct *call_data;
    /* callback function for the 9 grid buttons. Called when
    one of the grid buttons is clicked. */
{
    Arg al[10];
    int ac;
    int x,y;

    /* make sure the move is valid. If it is, update the screen. */
    x=client_data/3;
    y=client_data%3;
    if (board[x][y]==0)
    {
        board[x][y]=1;
        ac=0;
        XtSetArg(al[ac],XmNlabelString,
            XmStringCreate("X",char_set)); ac++;
        XtSetValues(button[x][y],al,ac);
        do_computers_move();
    }
}
```

Figure 8.2 shows a view of the tic-tac-toe game this program produces. When you run the code, try resizing the window; also try minimizing and then maximizing it. As you can see, this fairly small amount of code creates a full-blown graphical application. Motif handles almost all the ugly details; the

Figure 8.2   Output of the Tic-Tac-Toe Program

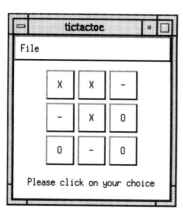

code simply sets up the widgets and makes the decisions needed to implement the game.

8.3   CALLBACK CHAINS

Callback chaining is a topic that many programmers find confusing at first. It represents a style of programming unique to Motif. When managed skillfully, callback chains work well and are easy to understand. To explain callback chaining, let's return to the push-button code we used in Chapter 4 and then look at the tic-tac-toe code, which contains several chains. Here is the push-button code from Chapter 4.

```
/* button.c*/

#include <Xm/Xm.h>
#include <Xm/PushB.h>

XtAppContext context;
XmStringCharSet char_set=XmSTRING_DEFAULT_CHARSET;

Widget toplevel, button;

void handle_button(w,client_data,call_data)
    Widget w;
    XtPointer client_data;
    XmPushButtonCallbackStruct *call_data;
/* handles the pushbutton's activate callback. */
{
    printf("button pushed\n");
}

void main(argc,argv)
    int argc;
    char *argv[];
{
    Arg al[10];
    int ac;

    /* create the toplevel shell */
    toplevel = XtAppInitialize(&context,"",NULL,0,&argc,argv,
        NULL,NULL,0);
```

```
    /* create the button widget */
    ac=0;
    XtSetArg(al[ac],XmNlabelString,
        XmStringCreate("Push Me",char_set)); ac++;
    button=XmCreatePushButton(toplevel,"button",al,ac);
    XtManageChild(button);
    XtAddCallback(button,XmNactivateCallback,handle_button,NULL);

    XtRealizeWidget(toplevel);
    XtAppMainLoop(context);
}
```

This code never calls **handle_button** directly. Although this fact may seem confusing, keep in mind that Motif promotes this style of programming: The function is called in response to a user event on a widget that Motif is managing because of the call to **XtAddCallback**. When a user clicks the push button, the push-button widget detects the click and handles it by calling the **handle_button** function (Figure 8.3).

The **handle_button** function performs like a normal C function and eventually returns, taking the program back into the main event loop.

In the tic-tac-toe program, the situation is a bit more complicated. The code never calls the **menuCB**, **dialogCB**, and **buttonCB** functions directly. Moreover, the callbacks in this program form chains among one another at several points, as shown in Figure 8.4.

The user's act of clicking on one of the grid buttons shown in Figure 8.4 sets off this chain. Clicking the button triggers the **buttonCB** function, which calls **do_computers_move**, which calls **check_win**. If the code detects a win-

Figure 8.3   The Main Event Loop and Widgets Managing the Callback Mechanism

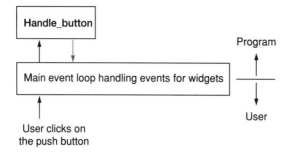

Figure 8.4 A Callback Chain in the Tic-Tac-Toe Program

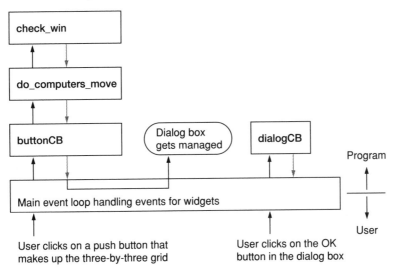

ner, the **check_win** function makes a call to **XtManageChild**, which manages the dialog box that announces a winner. The three functions then return to their callers and finally to the main event loop. The main event loop immediately maps the dialog box, which then appears. (The dialog box does not get mapped until the callback code returns to the main loop.) The user eventually clicks the OK button in the dialog box. The main event loop detects this click and activates the **dialogCB** callback function. The **dialogCB** function unmanages the dialog box, resets the board, and returns to the main loop. Keep in mind that this entire chain of events started with one button click.

In a large Motif program, callback chains can get fairly long and the number of callback functions in the code can get very large. It can become extremely hard to tell which callback function is being activated when and by whom unless your code is well documented. As your programs get larger, make sure you document your chains carefully. For example, you might enter a description of the callback chains similar to this one at the beginning of your program:

```
/* Callback chains found in this program:

The menuCB function is called by the Quit and Restart menu options.

When the user clicks on one of the buttons on the grid, buttonCB
```

```
is called. It calls do_computers_move and check_win, which
may manage the dialog box. The dialog box's buttons are handled
by dialogCB.

*/
```

In Chapter 10, you will create a program that implements a text editor. This code also documents its callback chains at the top of the program.

9 THE MKILL APPLICATION

For many new users, one of the most frustrating and difficult aspects of X workstations is the inconsistency of the user interface. For example, when someone wants to read news, he or she uses mxrn, the Motif version of the UNIX news reader. The mxrn application offers a very nice point-and-click user interface containing buttons, menus, scrolling text areas, selection dialog boxes, and so on, which makes news reading an easy and fairly intuitive task. On the other hand, if the user wants to copy a file from one deeply buried subdirectory to another, he or she has to type a long and hard-to-learn command at a command line prompt. Because of the inconsistencies in the user interface of a typical UNIX workstation, some applications are easy to use and others are not. These inconsistencies tend to intimidate users, giving them a bad first impression of their computing environment.

Even something as simple as a disk quota can get in a beginner's way. If a system has quotas, at some point the user runs out of disk space and programs begin to fail. Many programs fail quite ungracefully, and the user often has no idea why commands that worked fine yesterday are going wrong today. Of course, users learn about the quota command early on, but they usually forget about it as it is crushed under a huge mass of UNIX minutiae.

To solve the problem of disk quotas, I created a little program called the "quota dial," which is like a gas gauge for disk space. I built it on top of the quota command and a gauge widget from D.A. Young's book, *The X Window System* (see Appendix A). Figure 9.1 shows a typical quota dial. The gauge appears on screen at all times, providing the user with a constant and intuitive display of his or her disk usage.

The quota dial program is simple. Every 15 seconds it issues the quota command, looks at the returned text, and updates the dial widget accordingly. The program is called a wrapper because it wraps a graphical shell around an existing text application to make the application easier to use.

Figure 9.1   The Quota Dial
Keeps users informed of their current disk usage and
displays a warning when disk space begins to run
short.

X workstations commonly use many wrappers: xload graphically displays
the system's load average using a strip chart; xdbx puts a giant wrapper around
standard dbx; and xmh provides a wrapper around a set of mail commands.
NeXT machines have made wrapping a refined art and come close to providing
a completely wrapped UNIX system (although here most of the applications
and tools are completely rewritten rather than a text version simply being
wrapped).

In general, wrappers are easy to create because the text applications already
exist. All you have to do is create a Motif program that can receive data from
the text application, and then translate that data into a graphical form on the
screen. All of the difficult programming has already been done for you in the
text applications.

In this chapter, we will look at a simple wrapper called mkill that illustrates
the techniques of wrapper creation. You will also learn how to run and communicate with a separately executing text application from within a Motif
application.

9.1   THE IDEA BEHIND MKILL

The mkill program was born of my own frustration with the UNIX kill command. I tend to run many background jobs on my workstation and occasion-
ally I want to kill one. To do so, I have to perform the following steps:

1. Type ps -g.
2. Scan the process list for the program to kill.
3. Read off the process ID (1401, for example).
4. Type kill -9 1401.

I would prefer to click a button that pops up a selection dialog box containing

Figure 9.2   The mkill Application in the Quiescent State: A Small Push Button in a Corner of the Screen

Figure 9.3   The mkill Selection Box
Once the user clicks the push-to-kill button, the selection box appears so that the user can select the application to kill.

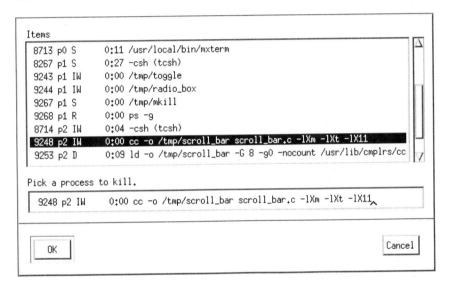

all of the jobs currently running, and simply double-click the jobs I want to kill. That's why I invented mkill. Figures 9.2 and 9.3 show the program in action. As you can see, mkill is nothing more than a wrapper around the **ps** and **kill** commands that greatly simplifies the act of killing a process.

9.2   THE LINK LIBRARY

The hardest part of creating a wrapper is establishing a communication link between the graphical application and the text application running simultaneously. Fortunately, this task is not particularly difficult under UNIX.

Forget for a moment about X, graphical user interfaces, and Motif, and concentrate on a simple task: getting two programs to run simultaneously and talk to one another under UNIX. To accomplish this, I created a library, called the link library, to form a textual communication link between two simultaneously running programs. Like all libraries, it comes in two parts. Listing 9.1 contains the library's header file, link.h.

**Listing 9.1   The Header File for the
Link Library, link.h**

```
/* link.h */

/* Link module, v1.0, 5/4/91 by Marshall Brain */

/* This module allows a program to form links to other separately
   executing programs and communicate with them. Links can be
   opened and closed, and the program using this library can
   write to and read from the other program over the link. */

/* Warning -
   This module will not link with all programs. If the program
   does anything weird with stdout, or if it fails to flush
   stdout correctly, then this module will fail. If you are creating
   a stand-alone program that you wish to link to another program
   with this library, then you MUST make sure that stdout is
   flushed correctly. Either call "fflush(stdout)" after every
   printf, or call "setbuf(stdout,NULL)" at the beginning of the
   program to eliminate buffering.                     */

#include <stdio.h>
#include <strings.h>
#include <signal.h>
#include <sys/ioctl.h>

struct link_handle  /* holds all info relevant to one link. */
{
  int pipefd1[2],pipefd2[2];
  int pid;
  FILE *fpin,*fpout;
};

extern link_open(struct link_handle *l, char name[], char param[]);
/* open a link to another program named name, passing a param
   to the program if desired. This routine will execute name
   in parallel and you can start communicating with it with
   link_read and link_write.*/
```

```
extern link_close(struct link_handle *l);
/* Close the link to a program that has terminated. Use link_kill
   if the program needs to be terminated as well.*/

extern int link_read(struct link_handle *l,char s[]);
/* read from the program started with link_open. Returns a 0 if
   there was stuff to read, or a 1 if the linked program terminated.*/

extern int link_input_waiting(struct link_handle *l);
/* Returns the number of bytes waiting in the input buffer. If
   0, then link_read will block if it is called. */

extern link_write_char(struct link_handle *l,char c);
/* write a char, without a newline, to the program.*/

extern link_write(struct link_handle *l,char s[]);
/* write a string to the program, with a newline.*/

extern link_kill(struct link_handle *l);
/*kill the program and close the link. If the program has terminated
   on its own use link_close instead.*/
```

When you use this library in an application, you call the function **link_open** to start up another program and to open up the read/write link with it. Then you can call the **link_read** function repeatedly to read information generated by the program to which you have made a link. You can use the **link_write** function to send text (such as commands) to the linked program.

When you no longer need the link, you can use either **link_close** or **link_kill** to terminate it. Use the **link_close** function when the linked program has already terminated. (For example, ls terminates on its own and tells you so by returning a 1 from **link_read**.) Use the **link_kill** function when you need to terminate the link and the linked program is still active.

The **link_read** function performs a blocking read. If the input buffer contains no data, **link_read** will block until it can read an entire line. You can call the **link_input_waiting** function to find out if the buffer contains information before **link_read** is called, and thereby avoid blocking when necessary.

Once you set up the link library, you can easily get a second program to run and communicate with a Motif application. Listing 9.2 uses the link library to demonstrate the process. This piece of code establishes a link to **ps** and then reads the data coming back from it. The code strips off the unnecessary information and displays the names of all of the active processes to stdout.

Listing 9.2   Test Code for the Link Library

```c
/* test.c */

#include "link.h"

void main()
{
    char s[1000], *p;
    struct link_handle l;

    link_open(&l,"ps","-g");
    link_read(&l,s);          /* throw away header line. */
    while (!link_read(&l,s)) /*read until ps terminates */
    {
        p=s+20;               /* point p to start of process names. */
        printf("%s\n",p);
    }
    link_close(&l);
}
```

The code you need to implement the link library is fairly short, but it is a little intricate if you have never seen the concepts before (a good reference book on pipes, forking, **dup**, **exec**, and the like, is *Topics in C Programming* by Stephen Kochan). The heart of the library is contained in the **link_open** function, which sets up a pair of pipes (which are coerced into being normal text streams, or files) hooked to stdin and stdout, and then forks and executes the requested program using these pipes in the **link_read** and **link_write** functions (see Listing 9.3).

Listing 9.3   link.c, the Implementation of the Link Library

```c
/* link.c */

/* Link module, v1.0, 5/4/91 Marshall Brain */

#include "link.h"

link_open(struct link_handle *l, char name[],char param[])
{
    pipe(l->pipefd1);
    pipe(l->pipefd2);
    if((l->pid=fork())==0)/*child*/
```

Fork, Exec, and Pipe

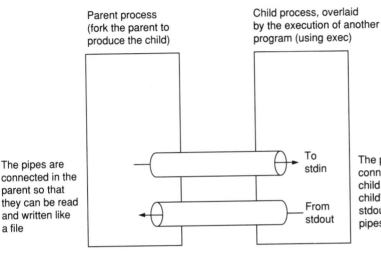

Parent process
(fork the parent to
produce the child)

Child process, overlaid
by the execution of another
program (using exec)

The pipes are
connected in the
parent so that
they can be read
and written like
a file

To
stdin

From
stdout

The pipes are
connected in the
child so that the
child's stdin and
stdout are the
pipes

UNIX lets a program split itself into two separately executing copies using the **fork** function. The traditional method for communicating between the two copies is called a *pipe*. The **exec** function lets a program overlay itself with another. A Motif program can thus use the **fork** function to split itself, then overlay its child with a text program using **exec**. The two programs then communicate using pipes. The process is shown in the figure.

The Motif program starts by calling the **fork** function, which makes a complete copy of the stack and variables of the current program and creates a new process so that two copies of the same program are running simultaneously. At the instant following the completion of the call to **fork**, both copies are identical except for their process IDs. The two copies can then go off on their own.

In order to communicate, the child must set up its pipes appropriately. In this case, the child starts by hooking one end of one pipe to stdin and one end of the other pipe to stdout. The child then calls the **exec** function: It is overlaid by the program specified in the call to **exec**, and that new program begins execution. Because of the pipe arrangement established before the call to **exec**, the new program's stdin and stdout are hooked to the pipes.

The parent can transfer data to and from the child through the pipes. When the parent writes data to the pipe connected to the child's stdin, the executing program in the child receives the data as though it came from stdin and processes it normally. When the child program writes to stdout, the data goes into the pipe and can be read by the parent.

```
  {
    close(l->pipefd1[0]);
    close(1);
    dup(l->pipefd1[1]);
    close(2);
    dup(l->pipefd1[1]);
    close(l->pipefd2[1]);
    close(0);
    dup(l->pipefd2[0]);
    execlp(name,name,param,(char*)0);
  }
  else
  {
    l->fpin=fdopen(l->pipefd1[0],"r");
    l->fpout=fdopen(l->pipefd2[1],"w");
    close(l->pipefd1[1]);
    close(l->pipefd2[0]);
  }
}


link_close(struct link_handle *l)
{
  wait((union wait*)0);
  close(l->pipefd1[1]);
  close(l->pipefd2[0]);
  fclose(l->fpin);
  fclose(l->fpout);
  l->pid=0;
}


int link_read(struct link_handle *l,char s[])
{
  int eof_flag;

  if (fgets(s,100,l->fpin)==NULL)
    eof_flag=1;   /* linked-to process has terminated on its own. */
  else
  {
    s[strlen(s)-1]='\0'; /* lose the newline character. */
    eof_flag=0;
  }
  return(eof_flag);
}


int link_input_waiting(struct link_handle *l)
```

```
{
  int num;

  ioctl(l->pipefd1[0],FIONREAD,&num); /* see how many chars in buffer. */
  return num;
}

link_write_char(struct link_handle *l,char c)
{
  fprintf(l->fpout,"%c",c);
  fflush(l->fpout);
}

link_write(struct link_handle *l,char s[])
{
  fprintf(l->fpout,"%s\n",s);
  fflush(l->fpout);
}

link_kill(struct link_handle *l)
{
  kill(l->pid,SIGKILL);
  link_close(l);
}
```

9.3   ## CREATING A WRAPPER

Once you have the link library, it is easy to create the mkill application. The code in Listing 9.4 is the same as the code that appeared in the selection box demonstration code in Chapter 7, with two additions. In the **buttonCB** routine, the link library function **link_open** creates a link to the **ps** command, and the **link_read** function reads the output of **ps** until **ps** terminates. The program uses the output of **ps** to create a list of items and displays them in the selection box. In the **dialogCB** function, the program reads the selected string out of the **call_data** parameter, extracts the process number, and kills the process with a system call.

Enter and run the code in Listing 9.4. If you encounter problems when running this program, try using the command **ps -g** at the UNIX command line on your machine. Because the **ps** command is slightly different between UNIX versions, you may have to change the **-g** parameter to something else, or else use no parameter.

**Listing 9.4   link.h, the Header File for the
Link Library**

```c
/* mkill.c */

#include <Xm/Xm.h>
#include <Xm/PushB.h>
#include <Xm/SelectioB.h>
#include "link.h"

#define    OK     1
#define CANCEL     2

XtAppContext context;
XmStringCharSet char_set=XmSTRING_DEFAULT_CHARSET;

Widget toplevel,button,dialog;


void dialogCB(w,client_data,call_data)
    Widget w;
    int client_data;
    XmSelectionBoxCallbackStruct *call_data;
/* callback function for the selection box */
{
    char *procstr,s[100];

    switch (client_data)
    {
        case OK:
            XmStringGetLtoR(call_data->value,char_set,&procstr);
            /* extract the process number from the line and
               kill that process number. */
            *(procstr+5)='\0';
            strcpy(s,"kill -9 ");
            strcat(s,procstr);
            system(s);

            XtFree(procstr);
            break;
        case CANCEL:
            break;
    }
    XtUnmanageChild(w);
}
```

```
void buttonCB(w,client_data,call_data)
    Widget w;
    int client_data;
    XmAnyCallbackStruct *call_data;
/* callback function for the push to kill button */
{
    Arg al[10];
    int ac;
    struct link_handle l;
    char s[200];
    XmString xs;
    Widget list;

    /* establish a link to ps with the link library, and place
       the strings from it into the selection box. */
    link_open(&l,"ps","-g");
    link_read(&l,s);  /*lose header line*/
    list=XmSelectionBoxGetChild(dialog,XmDIALOG_LIST);
    XmListDeleteAllItems(list);
    while (!link_read(&l,s))
    {
        xs=XmStringCreateLtoR(s,char_set);
        XmListAddItem(list,xs);
        XmStringFree(xs);
    }
    link_close(&l);

    XtManageChild(dialog);
}

void main(argc,argv)
    int argc;
    char *argv[];
{
    Arg al[10];
    int ac;

    /* create the toplevel shell */
    toplevel = XtAppInitialize(&context,"",NULL,0,&argc,argv,
        NULL,NULL,0);

    /* create the "push to kill" button */
    ac=0;
    XtSetArg(al[ac],XmNlabelString,
```

```
        XmStringCreate("Push to kill",char_set)); ac++;
    button=XmCreatePushButton(toplevel,"label",al,ac);
    XtManageChild(button);
    XtAddCallback(button, XmNactivateCallback, buttonCB, NULL);

    /* create the selection box dialog */
    ac = 0;
    XtSetArg(al[ac],XmNautoUnmanage,False); ac++;
    XtSetArg(al[ac],XmNmustMatch,True); ac++;
    XtSetArg(al[ac],XmNselectionLabelString,
        XmStringCreateLtoR("Pick a process to kill.",char_set)); ac++;
    dialog=XmCreateSelectionDialog(toplevel,"dialog",al,ac);
    XtAddCallback(dialog,XmNokCallback, dialogCB,OK);
    XtAddCallback(dialog,XmNcancelCallback,dialogCB,CANCEL);
    XtUnmanageChild(XmSelectionBoxGetChild(dialog,
        XmDIALOG_HELP_BUTTON));
    XtUnmanageChild(XmSelectionBoxGetChild(dialog,
        XmDIALOG_APPLY_BUTTON));

    XtRealizeWidget(toplevel);
    XtAppMainLoop(context);
}
```

Other techniques might be used to link to a separately running text program. Chapter 16 demonstrates the use of the **XtAddInput** function to produce X events on pending input for a pipe.

10 THE TEXT WIDGET

The text widget is the most complicated of the Motif widgets, but it is also the most interesting and the most useful. The text widget also gives you "the biggest bang for your buck": A tiny amount of code can produce amazing results. In this chapter, we will explore the text widget, its resources, and its numerous convenience functions. Then we will create a simple text editor.

10.1 A FIRST LOOK

To get an idea of the power of the text widget, enter and run the code shown in Listing 10.1.

Listing 10.1   A Multiline Text Widget

```
/* text1.c */

#include <Xm/Xm.h>
#include <Xm/Text.h>

XtAppContext context;

Widget toplevel, text;

void main(argc,argv)
    int argc;
    char *argv[];
{
    Arg al[20];
    int ac;

    /* create the toplevel shell */
    toplevel = XtAppInitialize(&context,"",NULL,0,&argc,argv,
        NULL,NULL,0);
```

```
       /* set the default size of the window. */
       ac=0;
       XtSetArg(al[ac],XmNwidth,200); ac++;
       XtSetArg(al[ac],XmNheight,200); ac++;
       XtSetValues(toplevel,al,ac);

       /* create a text widget */
       ac=0;
       XtSetArg(al[ac],XmNeditMode,XmMULTI_LINE_EDIT); ac++;
       text=XmCreateText(toplevel,"text",al,ac);
       XtManageChild(text);

       XtRealizeWidget(toplevel);
       XtAppMainLoop(context);
}
```

As you can see, this program creates a toplevel shell, resizes it, and then creates a text widget as the shell's child. Figure 10.1 shows a screen dump of this code during execution.

When you run the little program shown in Listing 10.1, you can do some amazing things. You can type characters, and the program accepts and displays them. You can press the RETURN key to begin a new line. You can use the arrow keys or the mouse to move the cursor around in the text. You can insert characters at any location in the text. You can delete characters at any location in the text, and even entire areas of text, using the BACKSPACE key. If you type more characters than the window can hold in either the horizontal or vertical

Figure 10.1   The Text Widget in Action

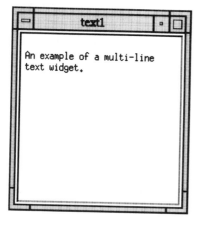

Figure 10.2 A Scrolling Text Widget in Action

direction, the text scrolls; you can scroll it back using the arrow keys. This is truly a startling amount of capability to get out of a 10-line program.

To create the same text widget adorned with scroll bars, you can replace the call to the **XmCreateText** function with a call to **XmCreateScrolledText**. Now if you type more characters than the window can hold, the scroll bars will tell you where you are in the text and give you a second way to move around. Figure 10.2 shows a screen dump of a scrolling text widget.

Now try running the code shown in Listing 10.2. This code creates a single-line text widget, which is the default. It provides the same general behavior as the multiline text widget, except that the RETURN key will not work. Figure 10.3 shows a screen dump of a single-line text widget.

As you might expect, the text widget has very large resource and callback lists. Take a minute to examine its description in Appendix J.

10.2   UNDERSTANDING THE TEXT WIDGET

In order to make full use of the text widget, it is important to understand all of its capabilities as well as the data structure it uses. You might expect a widget that carries as much functionality as this one to be complicated at the programming level, but this turns out not to be the case.

The text widget is based on an extremely simple data structure, and it provides a number of convenience functions to make a programmer's life easier. Figures 10.4 and 10.5 illustrate the data structure. Imagine that you have created code that displays a text widget on screen, and into that text widget the user has typed the text "Four score and seven," one word per line, as shown

Figure 10.3   A Single-Line Text Widget

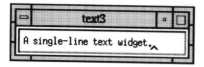

in Figure 10.4. If you execute a call to the **XtGetValues** function requesting the contents of the **value** resource (or better yet, use the **XmTextGetString** convenience function; see below and Appendix I), you get back a normal null-terminated C string containing a copy of the contents of the text widget, as shown in Figure 10.5. There, the normal \n convention represents line breaks and the normal \0 convention marks the end of the string.

Listing 10.2   A Single-Line Text Widget

```
/* text3.c */

#include <Xm/Xm.h>
#include <Xm/Text.h>

XtAppContext context;

Widget toplevel, text;

void main(argc,argv)
    int argc;
    char *argv[];
{
    Arg al[20];
    int ac;

    /* create the toplevel shell */
    toplevel = XtAppInitialize(&context,"",NULL,0,&argc,argv,
        NULL,NULL,0);

    /* create a text widget */
    text=XmCreateText(toplevel,"text",al,ac);
    XtManageChild(text);

    XtRealizeWidget(toplevel);
    XtAppMainLoop(context);
}
```

Figure 10.4 A Text Widget Holding the Words "Four score and seven"

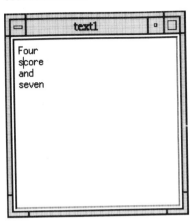

Figure 10.5 The Value Held by the Text Widget's Value Resource for Figure 10.4

0 1 2 3   etc.

F	o	u	r	\n	s	c	o	r	e	\n	a	n	d	\n	s	e	v	e	n	\0		

You can determine the cursor position with similar ease. If the cursor is currently positioned between the *s* and *c* of the word "score," and you use the **XtGetValues** function to get the value of the **cursorPosition** resource, you will receive the value 6 (better yet, use the **XmTextGetInsertionPosition** function; see below and Appendix I). The **cursorPosition** resource holds the current cursor position as an index into the C string held by the **value** resource. The value 6 is returned because, if the cursor is between the *s* and the *c*, it is immediately before character 6 in the string array shown in Figure 10.5.

A browse through the resource list shows that the text widget is extremely flexible. Following is a list of a few of the important and frequently used resources that tune the behavior of the text widget.

XmNautoShowCursorPosition. When this resource is true, a change to the **cursorPosition** resource causes the text to scroll automatically to keep the cursor visible.

XmNcursorPositionVisible. When this resource is true, a blinking I-bar cursor appears at the insertion point.

XmNeditable. If set to true, the user can edit; if set to false, the user cannot modify text held by the widget.

XmNeditMode. The **editMode** resource can have the values **XmSINGLE_ LINE_EDIT** or **XmMULTI_LINE_EDIT**. As demonstrated in Section 10.1, the SINGLE_LINE_EDIT mode restricts the text widget to a single, horizontally scrolling line.

XmNfontList. You can change the font used to display text in the text widget. However, since the **value** resource is a C string rather than an **XmString**, you can use only one font for the entire document.

XmNpendingDelete. When this resource is true, selected text is deleted when the user inserts new text. When it is false, selected text is not deleted.

XmNwordWrap. When this resource is true, inserted text wraps at word breaks as the lines approach the right edge of the widget.

Look through the text widget entry in Appendix J for other resources as well as for callback functions.

10.3   TEXT WIDGET CONVENIENCE FUNCTIONS

The text widget provides 30 convenience functions. Appendix I lists and describes each one. These convenience functions give you an easy way to access most of the resources you need to manipulate the text widget. Several of these functions also provide capabilities beyond the scope of the text widget itself—for example, **XmTextCut** manipulates the text widget as well as the clipboard.

Convenience functions exist for almost every action you will ever want to perform on a text widget. For example, instead of using **XtGetValues** to get the **value** resource, you can make the following call:

```
char *s;
    .
    .
    .
s = XmTextGetString(text);
```

where **text** is the name of the text widget variable. The variable **s** is simply a pointer to a string (which you should eventually free using **XtFree**).

Similarly, to get the current cursor position, you can use the following code:

```
XmTextPosition p;
    .
    .
    .
p = XmTextGetInsertionPosition(text);
```

Again, **text** is the text widget variable.

Several of the functions request a parameter of type **Time**. For all of the functions that require the time, you can extract a valid time value from the event record associated with the callback function. If you have a menu call-back function named **menuCB**, for example, you can use the following code fragment to extract the **time** field from the event record contained in the **call_data** parameter.

```
void menuCB(Widget w, int client_data,
   XmAnyCallbackStruct *call_data);
{
   Time time;
      .
      .
      .
   time = call_data->event->xbutton.time;
      .
      .
      .
}
```

The X Window System also defines a special constant named **CurrentTime** that you can use as a **Time** parameter if no event record value is handy (although its use is discouraged). The Xt layer defines a function named **XtLastTimestampProcessed**, which will accept a single parameter of type **Display** (pass in **XtDisplay(toplevel)**) and will return a value of type **Time**.

XtLastTimestampProcessed *Obtains a copy of the last time stamp processed.*

```
Time XtLastTimestampProcessed(Display d);
```

d   The display.

As you can see from the list of convenience functions in Appendix I, the text widget is extremely powerful. The best way to become familiar with its power is to try some of its functions using simple test programs. Listing 10.3 shows a test program that demonstrates the **XmTextGetCursorPosition** and **XmTextGetString** functions. The application consists of a form widget containing a text widget and a push button. When the user clicks the push button, the program performs actions specified in the **buttonCB** function. You can substitute other **XmText** functions in the push button's callback function to see what they do.

**Listing 10.3   Code for Experimenting with
the XmText Functions**

```c
/* text_test.c */

#include <Xm/Xm.h>
#include <Xm/Text.h>
#include <Xm/Form.h>
#include <Xm/PushB.h>

XtAppContext context;
XmStringCharSet char_set=XmSTRING_DEFAULT_CHARSET;

Widget toplevel;
Widget text;
Widget button;
Widget form;

void buttonCB(w,client_data,call_data)
    Widget w;
    XtPointer client_data;
    XmPushButtonCallbackStruct *call_data;
/* called whenever pushbutton is clicked. */
{
    char *s;

    /* Change the contents of this function to test different
       convenience functions. */

    /* print out cursorPosition and value string. */
    printf("%d\n",XmTextGetCursorPosition(text));
    s=XmTextGetString(text);
    printf("%s\n",s);
    XtFree(s);
}

void main(argc,argv)
    int argc;
    char *argv[];
{
    Arg al[10];
    int ac;

    /* create the toplevel shell */
    toplevel = XtAppInitialize(&context,"",NULL,0,&argc,argv,
        NULL,NULL,0);
```

```
/* set window size. */
ac=0;
XtSetArg(al[ac],XmNheight,300); ac++;
XtSetArg(al[ac],XmNwidth,300); ac++;
XtSetValues(toplevel,al,ac);

/* create a form to hold widgets */
ac=0;
form=XmCreateForm(toplevel,"form",al,ac);
XtManageChild(form);

/* create a push button */
ac=0;
XtSetArg(al[ac],XmNlabelString,
    XmStringCreate("Push to test",char_set)); ac++;
XtSetArg(al[ac], XmNtopAttachment,   XmATTACH_FORM); ac++;
XtSetArg(al[ac], XmNrightAttachment, XmATTACH_FORM); ac++;
XtSetArg(al[ac], XmNleftAttachment,  XmATTACH_FORM); ac++;
button=XmCreatePushButton(form,"button",al,ac);
XtManageChild(button);
XtAddCallback(button,XmNactivateCallback,buttonCB,NULL);

/* create a text widget. */
ac=0;
XtSetArg(al[ac], XmNtopAttachment,    XmATTACH_WIDGET); ac++;
XtSetArg(al[ac], XmNtopWidget, button); ac++;
XtSetArg(al[ac], XmNrightAttachment, XmATTACH_FORM); ac++;
XtSetArg(al[ac], XmNleftAttachment,   XmATTACH_FORM); ac++;
XtSetArg(al[ac], XmNbottomAttachment,  XmATTACH_FORM); ac++;
XtSetArg(al[ac],XmNeditMode,XmMULTI_LINE_EDIT); ac++;
text=XmCreateText(form,"text",al,ac);
XtManageChild(text);

XtRealizeWidget(toplevel);
XtAppMainLoop(context);
}
```

Once you become familiar with the convenience functions, you can create a complete text editor from the text widget fairly easily. To do so, you use a set of menu options to manipulate the text widget through its convenience functions in appropriate ways. For example, the text editor might contain an Open File menu option that uses a file selection box to get a file name from the user, opens and loads the file, and gives the file's text to the text widget with the **XmTextSetString** function. You can implement Clipboard functions such

as Cut, Copy, Paste, and Clear by creating menu options that call **XmTextCut,
XmTextCopy, XmTextPaste,** and **XmTextRemove.**

The **XmTextSetInsertionPosition** function can be used to create navigation
capabilities. A text editor might provide a Navigation menu that includes the
options Top (to jump to the top of the file), Bottom (to jump to the end of the
file), and Jump To Line (to jump to a specific line number). To implement the
Top option, you enter a single line of code:

```
XmTextSetInsertionPosition(text, (XmTextPosition) 0);
```

where **text** is a text widget. The convenience function positions the cursor at
the first character in the file. If the **autoShowCursorPosition** resource is true,
the widget scrolls as necessary to display the top of the file.

To implement the Bottom option, use the following lines of code:

```
XmTextPosition pos;
    .
    :
    .
pos = XmTextGetLastPosition(text);
XmTextSetInsertionPosition(text, pos);
```

The call to **XmTextGetLastPosition** retrieves the location of the last character
in the text widget's string. Setting the insertion position to that value displays
the bottom of the file.

To implement the Jump To Line option, use a prompt dialog box to get the
desired line number from the user. You can extract the text widget's **value**
string and count **\n** characters until you reach the desired line. You can then
set the insertion position to that location. The code in Listing 10.4 demonstrates the process.

**Listing 10.4   Jumping to a Line Number in the
Text Widget**

```
void jump_to_line(line_num)
    int line_num;
/* Counts '\n's so that cursor can be placed at correct line. */
{
    int x,l,curr;
    char *temp;
    Arg al[10];
    int ac;
```

```
/* get string from text widget */
temp=XmTextGetString(text);
x=0;
curr=1;
l=strlen(temp);

/* scan the string for '\n's, counting them. */
while ((x<l)&&(curr<line_num))
    if (temp[x++]=='\n') curr++;

/* set cursor position to beginning of the correct line. */
XmTextSetInsertionPosition(text,(XmTextPosition)x);

/* prevent memory leaks. */
if (temp != NULL)
    XtFree(temp);
}
```

The **XmTextGetString** function gets the string from the text widget. A **while** loop counts \n characters in the string. Then the **XmTextSetInsertion-Position** function sets the cursor position.

10.4   CREATING A SIMPLE EDITOR

Since the text widget does almost all of the work of creating a text editor for you, you can create a simple editor application fairly easily. In this section, we will look at the code necessary to create an editor capable of loading and saving files as well as supporting normal Clipboard functions. In creating this editor, you will use many of the techniques discussed in this and previous chapters.

The user interface design of a simple text editor is straightforward. We will use pull-down menus like those shown in Chapter 6. The File menu will contain Open, Close, and Quit, while the Edit menu will contain Cut, Copy, Paste, and Clear. The Open option manages a file selection dialog box that allows the user to select a file to open. The Close option displays a dialog box that asks the user whether or not to save the file if the user has made any changes to the text.

Listing 10.5 shows the code for the editor, interspersed with comments to help you to understand what is going on. A discussion of the code follows.

Listing 10.5   A Simple But Complete Text Editor

```
/* editor.c */

/* Editor program, ver 1.0, 5/30/91, by Marshall Brain */

/*    Callback chains found in this program -

      The menuCB function is called by any menu option.

      The Open menu option causes the file selection box (open_dialog) to
      be managed in menuCB. The buttons on this box are wired to the
      openCB function.

      The Save menu option causes the prompt dialog box (save dialog) to
      be managed in menuCB. The buttons on this box are wired to call the
      save_dialoCB function, which may call the handle_save function.

      The changedCB function is called whenever the text widget
      is changed.

*/

#include <stdio.h>
#include <sys/types.h>
#include <sys/stat.h>

#include <Xm/Xm.h>
#include <Xm/Text.h>
#include <Xm/Form.h>
#include <Xm/PushB.h>
#include <Xm/RowColumn.h>
#include <Xm/CascadeB.h>
#include <Xm/FileSB.h>
#include <Xm/MessageB.h>

/* integer values used to distinguish the call to menuCB. */
#define MENU_OPEN    1
#define MENU_CLOSE   2
#define MENU_QUIT    3

#define MENU_CUT     4
#define MENU_CLEAR   5
#define MENU_COPY    6
#define MENU_PASTE   7
```

```
/* integer values used to distinguish the call to dialogCB. */
#define OK          1
#define CANCEL      2


XtAppContext context;
XmStringCharSet char_set=XmSTRING_DEFAULT_CHARSET;


/* all widgets are global to make life easier. */
Widget toplevel, text, form, label, menu_bar;
Widget open_option, close_option, quit_option;
Widget cut_option, clear_option, copy_option, paste_option;
Widget open_dialog, save_dialog;


char *filename=NULL;
Boolean text_changed=False;


void change_sensitivity(open_state)
    Boolean open_state;
/* changes the menu sensitivities as needed for opened
   and closed states. */
{
    XtSetSensitive(open_option,open_state);
    XtSetSensitive(quit_option,open_state);
    XtSetSensitive(close_option,!open_state);
    XtSetSensitive(cut_option,!open_state);
    XtSetSensitive(copy_option,!open_state);
    XtSetSensitive(paste_option,!open_state);
    XtSetSensitive(clear_option,!open_state);
}


void changedCB(w,client_data,call_data)
    Widget w;
    XtPointer client_data;
    XmAnyCallbackStruct *call_data;
/* triggered everytime a character is inserted or deleted in
   the text widget. text_changed is used to decide if file needs
   saving or not. */
{
    text_changed=True;
}


void openCB(w,client_data,call_data)
    Widget w;
    int client_data;
    XmAnyCallbackStruct *call_data;
```

```
/* handles the file selection box callbacks. */
{
    XmFileSelectionBoxCallbackStruct *s =
        (XmFileSelectionBoxCallbackStruct *) call_data;
    FILE *f;
    char *file_contents;
    int file_length;
    struct stat stat_val;

    if (client_data==CANCEL) /* do nothing if cancel is selected. */
    {
        XtUnmanageChild(open_dialog);
        return;
    }

    if (filename != NULL) /* free up filename if it exists. */
    {
        XtFree(filename);
        filename = NULL;
    }

    /* get the filename from the file selection box */
    XmStringGetLtoR(s->value, char_set, &filename);

    /* open and read the file. */
    if (stat(filename, &stat_val) == 0)
    {
        file_length = stat_val.st_size;
        if ((f=fopen(filename,"r"))!=NULL)
        {
            /* malloc a place for the string to be read to. */
            file_contents = (char *) XtMalloc((unsigned)
                (file_length + 10));
            *file_contents = '\0';

            /* read the file string */
            fread(file_contents, sizeof(char), file_length, f);
            file_contents[file_length]='\0';
            fclose(f);

            /* give the string to the text widget. */
            XmTextSetString(text, file_contents);
            XtFree(file_contents);

            /* set up all resources as needed to make menus and
```

```
                    text widget sensitive. */
            change_sensitivity(False);
            XtSetSensitive(text,True);
            XmTextSetEditable(text,True);
            XmTextSetCursorPosition(text,0);
            text_changed=False;
        }
    }
    XtUnmanageChild(open_dialog);
}

void handle_save()
/* saves the text widget's string to a file. */
{
    FILE *f;
    char *s=NULL;

    if ((f=fopen(filename,"w"))!=NULL)
    {
        /* get the string from the text widget */
        s = (char *)XmTextGetString(text);

        if (s!=NULL)
        {
            /* write the file. */
            fwrite(s, sizeof(char), strlen(s), f);

            /* make sure the last line is terminated by '\n'
                so that vi, compilers, etc. like it. */
            if (s[strlen(s)-1]!='\n')
                fprintf(f,"\n");
            XtFree(s);
        }
        fflush(f);
        fclose(f);
    }
}

void save_dialogCB(w,client_data,call_data)
    Widget w;
    int client_data;
    XmAnyCallbackStruct *call_data;
/* handles save_dialog buttons. */
{
    switch (client_data)
```

```
    {
        case OK:
            handle_save();
            break;
        case CANCEL:
            break;
    }
    /* get rid of the text in the text widget and set it so it
        can't be used. */
    XtSetSensitive(text,False);
    XmTextSetEditable(text,False);
    XmTextSetString(text,"");

    /* change menu sensitivites and make the dialog invisible. */
    change_sensitivity(True);
    XtUnmanageChild(save_dialog);
}

void menuCB(w,client_data,call_data)
    Widget w;
    int client_data;
    XmAnyCallbackStruct *call_data;
/* handles menu options. */
{
    Time time;

    switch (client_data)
    {
        case MENU_OPEN:
            /* make the file selection box appear. */
            XtManageChild(open_dialog);
            break;
        case MENU_CLOSE:
            /* if the text was changed, ask the user about saving it.
                If not, lose the text and set the widget insensitve. */
            if (text_changed)
                XtManageChild(save_dialog);
            else
            {
                XtSetSensitive(text,False);
                XmTextSetEditable(text,False);
                XmTextSetString(text,"");
                change_sensitivity(True);
            }
            break;
```

```
            case MENU_QUIT:
                exit(0);
            case MENU_CUT:
                time=call_data->event->xbutton.time;
                XmTextCut(text,time);
                break;
            case MENU_CLEAR:
                XmTextRemove(text);
                break;
            case MENU_PASTE:
                XmTextPaste(text);
                break;
             case MENU_COPY:
                time=call_data->event->xbutton.time;
                XmTextCopy(text,time);
                break;
    }
}


Widget make_menu_option(option_name,client_data,menu)
    char *option_name;
    int client_data;
    Widget menu;
/* see Chapter 6. */
{
    int ac;
    Arg al[10];
    Widget b;

    ac = 0;
    XtSetArg(al[ac], XmNlabelString,
        XmStringCreateLtoR(option_name,char_set)); ac++;
    b=XmCreatePushButton(menu,option_name,al,ac);
    XtManageChild(b);

    XtAddCallback (b, XmNactivateCallback, menuCB, client_data);
    return(b);
}


Widget make_menu(menu_name,menu_bar)
    char *menu_name;
    Widget menu_bar;
/* see Chapter 6. */
{
    int ac;
```

```
    Arg al[10];
    Widget menu, cascade;

    ac = 0;
    menu = XmCreatePulldownMenu (menu_bar, menu_name, al, ac);

    ac = 0;
    XtSetArg (al[ac], XmNsubMenuId, menu);  ac++;
    XtSetArg(al[ac], XmNlabelString,
        XmStringCreateLtoR(menu_name, char_set)); ac++;
    cascade = XmCreateCascadeButton (menu_bar, menu_name, al, ac);
    XtManageChild (cascade);

    return(menu);
}

void create_menus(menu_bar)
    Widget menu_bar;
{
    int ac;
    Arg al[10];
    Widget menu;

    menu=make_menu("File",menu_bar);
    open_option = make_menu_option("Open",MENU_OPEN,menu);
    close_option = make_menu_option("Close",MENU_CLOSE,menu);
    XtSetSensitive(close_option,False);
    quit_option = make_menu_option("Quit",MENU_QUIT,menu);

    menu=make_menu("Edit",menu_bar);
    cut_option = make_menu_option("Cut",MENU_CUT,menu);
    copy_option = make_menu_option("Copy",MENU_COPY,menu);
    paste_option = make_menu_option("Paste",MENU_PASTE,menu);
    clear_option = make_menu_option("Clear",MENU_CLEAR,menu);
}

void main(argc,argv)
    int argc;
    char *argv[];
{
    Arg al[10];
    int ac;

    /* create the toplevel shell */
    toplevel = XtAppInitialize(&context,"",NULL,0,&argc,argv,
```

```
        NULL,NULL,0);

/* default window size. */
ac=0;
XtSetArg(al[ac],XmNheight,200); ac++;
XtSetArg(al[ac],XmNwidth,200); ac++;
XtSetValues(toplevel,al,ac);

/* create a form widget. */
ac=0;
form=XmCreateForm(toplevel,"form",al,ac);
XtManageChild(form);

/* create a menu bar and attach it to the form. */
ac=0;
XtSetArg(al[ac], XmNtopAttachment,    XmATTACH_FORM); ac++;
XtSetArg(al[ac], XmNrightAttachment, XmATTACH_FORM); ac++;
XtSetArg(al[ac], XmNleftAttachment,   XmATTACH_FORM); ac++;
menu_bar=XmCreateMenuBar(form,"menu_bar",al,ac);
XtManageChild(menu_bar);

/* create a text widget and attach it to the form. */
ac=0;
XtSetArg(al[ac], XmNtopAttachment,    XmATTACH_WIDGET); ac++;
XtSetArg(al[ac], XmNtopWidget, menu_bar); ac++;
XtSetArg(al[ac], XmNrightAttachment, XmATTACH_FORM); ac++;
XtSetArg(al[ac], XmNleftAttachment,   XmATTACH_FORM); ac++;
XtSetArg(al[ac], XmNbottomAttachment,   XmATTACH_FORM); ac++;
XtSetArg(al[ac],XmNeditMode,XmMULTI_LINE_EDIT); ac++;
text=XmCreateScrolledText(form, "text", al, ac);
XtAddCallback (text, XmNvalueChangedCallback, changedCB, NULL);
XtManageChild(text);
XtSetSensitive(text,False);
XmTextSetEditable(text,False);

create_menus(menu_bar);

/* create the file selection box used by open option. */
ac=0;
XtSetArg(al[ac],XmNmustMatch,True); ac++;
XtSetArg(al[ac],XmNautoUnmanage,False); ac++;
open_dialog=XmCreateFileSelectionDialog(toplevel,
    "open_dialog",al,ac);
XtAddCallback (open_dialog, XmNokCallback,openCB, OK);
XtAddCallback (open_dialog, XmNcancelCallback, openCB, CANCEL);
```

```
XtUnmanageChild(XmSelectionBoxGetChild(open_dialog,
    XmDIALOG_HELP_BUTTON));

/* create the file saving dialog. */
ac=0;
XtSetArg(al[ac], XmNmessageString,
    XmStringCreateLtoR("The text was changed. Save it?",
        char_set));  ac++;
save_dialog=XmCreateMessageDialog(toplevel,
    "ok_dialog",al,ac);
XtAddCallback(save_dialog,XmNokCallback,save_dialogCB,OK);
XtAddCallback(save_dialog,XmNcancelCallback,
    save_dialogCB,CANCEL);
XtUnmanageChild(XmMessageBoxGetChild(save_dialog,
    XmDIALOG_HELP_BUTTON));

XtRealizeWidget(toplevel);
XtAppMainLoop(context);
}
```

The **main** routine is simple: It creates a form widget and attaches the menu bar and text widget to it. In addition, it creates the dialog boxes that the program uses.

The menu-handling code has been copied almost verbatim from Chapter 6. The **menuCB** function uses an integer **client_data** parameter and a switch statement to distinguish among the seven possible menu choices. The Open and Close menu options manage the two dialog boxes as needed. The items in the Edit menu call the appropriate convenience functions to handle the clipboard.

The two dialog boxes talk to their own callback functions. The **save_dialogCB** function decides if the user wishes to save the text and clears out the text widget, making it insensitive after saving it. The **openCB** function gets the name of the file to open and reads that file in.

The **changedCB** function works off the **valueChanged** callback of the text widget. Whenever a user changes anything in the text widget, the **valueChanged** callback is triggered. The **changedCB** callback function sets a variable that remembers if the text has changed. This **text_changed** variable decides if saving the text is necessary inside the **save_dialogCB** function.

The **change_sensitivity** function enables and disables menu options as appropriate to the state of the program.

10.5   ENHANCEMENTS

You can make several enhancements to the code in Listing 10.5 to create a more functional editor. For example, you can add a New option to the File menu to allow the user to create new files directly rather than using Open and entering a new file name (which is unintuitive). You can also detect if the file being opened is read-only and set the **editable** resource to false so that the user can read the file but not alter it.

You can add an Insert File option using the file-loading code that already exists along with an **XmTextInsert** function. Using the techniques discussed in Section 10.3, you can also add a Navigation menu that might contain Jump To Top, Jump To Bottom, and Jump To Line Number options. You might also try experimenting with the **wordWrap** resource to see how it affects the behavior of the editor.

In Chapter 13, we will look at code that adds a customized find dialog box to the editor. Appendix F contains a listing of a complete text editor that contains the navigation commands discussed above as well as the find dialog code from Chapter 13.

11 OTHER MOTIF WIDGETS

Depending on how you count them, we have so far discussed 26 different widgets:

bulletin board, bulletin board dialog	menu bar
	message box
cascade button	pull-down menu
dialogs: error, file selection box, information, message, prompt, question, selection box, warning, working	push button
	RowColumn
	scale
file selection box	selection box
form, form dialog	separator
label	text, scrolled text

In this chapter, we will look at widgets we have not yet discussed, with the exception of the drawing area widget (which is discussed in detail in Chapter 17). We will also look at example code to better understand each widget's uses.

11.1   TOGGLE BUTTON WIDGETS

A toggle button lets the user change the state of a two-state variable. The user clicks on a toggle button to change the state. A visual indicator lets the user see the toggle's current state. Figures 11.1 and 11.2 show examples of a toggle button in its on and off states. When the user clicks the toggle, the **set** resource (a Boolean) inverts and the visual indicator turns on or off accordingly.

The code in Listing 11.1 shows how to use a toggle button widget in a program. When the toggle button changes state, it activates its **valueChanged** callback. The code can then examine the **set** resource (or the value of the **set** field in the **call_data** parameter) of the toggle widget to find the widget's current state.

Figure 11.1   A Single Toggle Button in the Off State

Figure 11.2   A Single Toggle Button in the On State

Listing 11.1   Creating a Single Toggle Button

```
/*toggle.c*/

#include <Xm/Xm.h>
#include <Xm/ToggleB.h>

XtAppContext context;
XmStringCharSet char_set=XmSTRING_DEFAULT_CHARSET;

void toggleCB(w,client_data,call_data)
    Widget w;
    XtPointer client_data;
    XmAnyCallbackStruct *call_data;
/* handle state changes in the toggle. */
{
    Boolean set;
    Arg al[10];
    int ac;

    /* get the value of the set resource. */
    ac=0;
    XtSetArg(al[ac], XmNset, &set); ac++;
    XtGetValues(w,al,ac);

    if (set)
        printf("Toggle turned on\n");
    else
        printf("Toggle turned off\n");
}
```

```
void main(argc,argv)
    int argc;
    char *argv[];
{
    Widget toplevel, toggle;
    Arg al[10];
    int ac;

    /* create the toplevel shell */
    toplevel = XtAppInitialize(&context,"",NULL,0,&argc,argv,
        NULL,NULL,0);

    /* Create the toggle button. */
    ac=0;
    XtSetArg(al[ac],XmNlabelString,
        XmStringCreateLtoR("Toggle Button",char_set)); ac++;
    toggle=XmCreateToggleButton(toplevel,"toggle",al,ac);
    XtManageChild(toggle);
    XtAddCallback (toggle, XmNvalueChangedCallback, toggleCB, NULL);

    XtRealizeWidget(toplevel);
    XtAppMainLoop(context);
}
```

Programmers often arrange toggle button widgets into groups in two ways. One way is a check box, a group of normal toggle buttons arranged in a manager widget, usually a RowColumn widget. You might see a check box in a compiler in which users can turn a number of two-state compiler options on or off (range checking on/off, short-circuit evaluation on/off, and so on). The RowColumn widget makes placing the toggles easier for the programmer.

The other way to group toggle buttons is with a *radio box*, which lets users make one-of-many choices among a number of options. This arrangement takes its name from the buttons on a car radio, which allow you to make one-of-many choices among the programmed stations. For example, by clicking one of four time-zone toggles arranged in a radio box, a user can choose a time zone from the four possible time zones in the United States. Figure 11.3 shows an example of a radio box.

A radio box is made from a RowColumn widget and is created with a convenience function, as shown below:

```
Widget radio_box;
    .
    .
    .
radio_box=XmCreateRadioBoxWidget(toplevel, "radio_box", al, ac);
```

When toggle buttons have a radio box as their parent, only one of the toggles
can be set on at any one time. The code in Listing 11.2 demonstrates how to
use a radio box. When you click a toggle, that toggle turns on and all the other
toggles turn off.

**Listing 11.2 Creating Several Toggle Buttons in a
Radio Box Container**

```
/*radio_box.c*/

#include <Xm/Xm.h>
#include <Xm/ToggleB.h>
#include <Xm/RowColumn.h>

XtAppContext context;
XmStringCharSet char_set=XmSTRING_DEFAULT_CHARSET;

Widget toplevel, radio_box, toggles[5];

void changeCB(w,client_data,call_data)
    Widget w;
    int client_data;
    XmAnyCallbackStruct *call_data;
/* called when any toggle changes */
{
    Boolean set;
    Arg al[10];
    int ac;

    /* find out if toggle has been set or unset */
    ac=0;
    XtSetArg(al[ac], XmNset, &set); ac++;
    XtGetValues(w,al,ac);

    if (set)
        printf("%d turned on\n",client_data);
    else
        printf("%d turned off\n",client_data);
}

void main(argc,argv)
    int argc;
    char *argv[];
{
    Arg al[10];
```

Toggles in Menus

You can add toggle buttons to menus in the same way you add push buttons and labels. You insert the toggle in the appropriate menu pane when it is created. The order of its insertion determines its position.

Toggles in menus function in one of two ways. You can add one to a menu to turn an individual option on or off. A text editor, for example, might have a toggle in its Edit menu to start and stop wrapping. Or a compiler might have a menu of toggles that handle certain compiler options.

The second way toggles function in a menu is in a radio box fashion. In this case, the menu contains a set of toggles. For example, a text editor might allow the user to select one of several fonts from a font list. Since the menu pane is a form of RowColumn widget, its **radioBehavior** resource can be set to true. This resource causes all of the toggles in the menu to behave as in a radio box. The following code fragment demonstrates this process.

```
Widget make_menu_toggle(
    item_name,
    client_data,menu)
    char *item_name;
    caddr_t client_data;
    Widget menu;
/* adds a toggle item into a menu. */
{
    int ac;
    Arg al[10];
    Widget item;

    ac = 0;
    XtSetArg(al[ac],XmNlabelString,
        XmStringCreateLtoR(item_name,char_set)); ac++;
    item=XmCreateToggleButton(menu,item_name,al,ac);
    XtManageChild(item);
    XtAddCallback(item,XmNvalueChangedCallback,
        menuCB,client_data);
    XtSetSensitive(item,True);
    return(item);
}
```

Toggles in Menus (continued)

Inside create_menus:

```
font_menu=make_menu("Font",menu_bar);
font1_item=make_menu_toggle("Font 1","Font 1 selected",font_menu);
font2_item=make_menu_toggle("Font 2","Font 2 selected",font_menu);
font3_item=make_menu_toggle("Font 3","Font 3 selected",font_menu);
ac=0;
XtSetArg(al[ac],XmNradioBehavior,True); ac++;
XtSetValues(font_menu,al,ac);
```

```
    int ac;
    int x;

    /* create the toplevel shell */
    toplevel = XtAppInitialize(&context,"",NULL,0,&argc,argv,
        NULL,NULL,0);

    /* create a Radio Box container to hold the toggles */
    ac=0;
    radio_box=XmCreateRadioBox(toplevel,"radio_box",al,ac);
    XtManageChild(radio_box);

    /* create 5 toggles */
    for (x=0; x<5; x++)
    {
        ac=0;
        XtSetArg(al[ac],XmNlabelString,
            XmStringCreate("I'm a toggle",char_set)); ac++;
        toggles[x]=XmCreateToggleButton(radio_box,"toggle",al,ac);
        XtManageChild(toggles[x]);
        XtAddCallback (toggles[x], XmNvalueChangedCallback,
            changeCB, x);
    }

    XtRealizeWidget(toplevel);
    XtAppMainLoop(context);
}
```

**Figure 11.3   A Radio Box Containing Five
Toggle Buttons, Only One of Which Can Be Chosen**

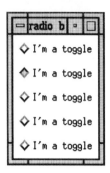

Figure 11.4   A Scroll Bar Widget

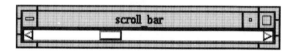

The default behavior for the radio box requires that at least one of the buttons always be on (after the initial selection). For example, if a radio box displays the selection of a time zone, then one of the time zones should always be on. However, the RowColumn widget, and therefore the radio box widget in this code, has a **radioAlwaysOne** resource that, when set to false, allows the selected option to be selected again to turn it off, so that none of the options are selected.

11.2   SCROLL BAR WIDGETS

The scroll bar widget closely resembles the scale widget discussed in Chapter 4. You use the **minimum** and **maximum** resources to set up the scroll bar's range. Each time the user manipulates the scroll bar, a **valueChanged** callback is activated to make the code aware of the change.

The resource list for the scroll bar widget in Appendix J shows that scroll bars are highly customizable, and that you can wire them to return a great deal of information through their callbacks. In their most simple form, however, scroll bar widgets behave like scale widgets. Figure 11.4 illustrates a scroll bar widget.

The code in Listing 11.3 demonstrates how to use a scroll bar widget. This code creates a scroll bar, sets up its **valueChanged** callback, and prints the new value each time the callback is triggered.

Listing 11.3   Creating a Scroll Bar Widget

```
/*scroll_bar.c*/

#include <Xm/Xm.h>
#include <Xm/ScrollBar.h>

XtAppContext context;

Widget toplevel, scroll;

void scrollCB(w,client_data,call_data)
    Widget w;
    XtPointer client_data;
    XmAnyCallbackStruct *call_data;
/* called every time the scroll bar changes. */
{
    int value;
    Arg al[10];
    int ac;

    /* get the value of the scroll bar. */
    ac=0;
    XtSetArg(al[ac], XmNvalue, &value); ac++;
    XtGetValues(w,al,ac);

    printf("value = %d\n",value);
}

void main(argc,argv)
    int argc;
    char *argv[];
{
    Arg al[10];
    int ac;

    /* create the toplevel shell */
    toplevel = XtAppInitialize(&context,"",NULL,0,&argc,argv,
        NULL,NULL,0);

    /* create the scroll bar. */
    ac=0;
```

```
        XtSetArg(al[ac],XmNminimum,0); ac++;
        XtSetArg(al[ac],XmNmaximum,1000); ac++;
        XtSetArg(al[ac],XmNorientation,XmHORIZONTAL); ac++;
        scroll=XmCreateScrollBar(toplevel,"scroll",al,ac);
        XtManageChild(scroll);
        XtAddCallback (scroll, XmNvalueChangedCallback,
            scrollCB, NULL);

        XtRealizeWidget(toplevel);
        XtAppMainLoop(context);
}
```

Section 17.4.6 contains a sample application of a scroll bar. See also the *Motif PRM* or Appendix J for a complete description of this highly functional and useful widget, as well as the scrolled window widget, which is discussed in Section 11.9.

11.3   SHELL WIDGETS

At times, you might want to create an entirely new shell from within an application—that is, you might want to call some code and have it create an entirely new and separate shell into which you can add widgets. For example, in a text editor, you might want to have two documents open at once, each in its own window. Creating new shells is easy in Motif. Listing 11.4 demonstrates the process.

Listing 11.4   Creating a Separate Shell Widget from Within an Application

```
/* new_shell.c*/

#include <Xm/Xm.h>
#include <Xm/Text.h>
#include <Xm/PushB.h>
#include <X11/Shell.h>

XtAppContext context;

Widget toplevel, button, text, shell;

void buttonCB(w,client_data,call_data)
    Widget w;
    caddr_t client_data;
```

```
        caddr_t call_data;
/* called when pushbutton is clicked. */
{
        Arg al[10];
        int ac;

        /* turn the button off. */
        XtSetSensitive(button,False);

        /* create a new shell */
        ac=0;
        XtSetArg(al[ac], XmNheight, 300);     ac++;
        XtSetArg(al[ac], XmNwidth, 300);      ac++;
        shell=XtAppCreateShell("Shell","Shell", applicationShellWidgetClass,
            XtDisplay(toplevel), al, ac);

        /* create a text widget in the new shell. */
        ac=0;
        XtSetArg(al[ac],XmNeditMode,XmMULTI_LINE_EDIT); ac++;
        text=XmCreateText(shell,"text",al,ac);
        XtManageChild(text);

        XtRealizeWidget(shell); /* the new shell must be realized. */
}

void main(argc,argv)
        int argc;
        char *argv[];
{
        Arg al[10];
        int ac;

        /* create the toplevel shell */
        toplevel = XtAppInitialize(&context,"",NULL,0,&argc,argv,
            NULL,NULL,0);

        /* create a pushbutton widget. */
        ac=0;
        button=XmCreatePushButton(toplevel,"button",al,ac);
        XtManageChild(button);
        XtAddCallback(button, XmNactivateCallback, buttonCB, NULL);

        XtRealizeWidget(toplevel);
        XtAppMainLoop(context);
}
```

In Listing 11.4, the **main** function creates a push button. When a user clicks this button, the **buttonCB** function is called. The code creates a completely new and separate shell widget containing a text widget in **buttonCB** using a call to **XtAppCreateShell**. The text widget, in its independent shell, behaves like any other text widget.

XtAppCreateShell   *Creates a new shell.*

```
Widget XtAppCreateShell(
    String application_name,
    String application_class,
    WidgetClass widget_class,
    Display *display,
    ArgList args,
    Cardinal num_args);
```

application_name	Name of the application.
application_class	The class name for the application.
widget_class	Widget class for the new shell.
Display	Display for the new shell (determines resource source).
args	An argument list for the shell.
num_args	Number of arguments in the argument list.

Note that this new shell has all of the attributes of the toplevel shell and fulfills the same function. It can contain anything you would normally put in a toplevel shell: any widget, form, bulletin board, and so on. The new shell is a complete window, and you can resize it, minimize it, and maximize it just like any other window.

11.4   ARROW BUTTON WIDGETS

An arrow button widget is a push-button widget with special properties that make it appropriate for the arrow portion of a scroll bar. The code in Listing 11.5 demonstrates how to use an arrow button widget and Figure 11.5 illustrates one.

Listing 11.5   Creating an Arrow Button Widget

```
/*arrow.c*/

#include <Xm/Xm.h>
#include <Xm/ArrowB.h>

XtAppContext context;

Widget toplevel, arrow;

void arrowCB(w,client_data,call_data)
    Widget w;
    XtPointer client_data;
    XmArrowButtonCallbackStruct *call_data;
{
    printf("click_count = %d \n",call_data->click_count);
}

void main(argc,argv)
    int argc;
    char *argv[];
{
    Arg al[10];
    int ac;

    /* create the toplevel shell */
    toplevel = XtAppInitialize(&context,"",NULL,0,&argc,argv,
        NULL,NULL,0);

    /* create the arrow button. */
    ac=0;
    XtSetArg (al[ac], XmNmultiClick, XmMULTICLICK_KEEP);  ac++;
    arrow=XmCreateArrowButton(toplevel,"arrow",al,ac);
    XtManageChild(arrow);
    XtAddCallback (arrow, XmNactivateCallback, arrowCB, NULL);

    XtRealizeWidget(toplevel);
    XtAppMainLoop(context);
}
```

Try entering and running the code shown in Listing 11.5. It takes advantage of
the **click_count** capability unique to Motif's button widgets. If the user clicks

Figure 11.5   An Arrow Button Widget

an arrow button multiple times within the multiclick time defined in your window manager, the **click_count** variable is incremented. You can use this capability to avoid repeating an action when a user accidentally clicks on the arrow button more than once. You can turn this capability off by setting the **multiClick** resource to **XmMULTICLICK_DISCARD**.

11.5   FRAME WIDGETS

A frame widget places a frame around widgets that otherwise lack frames (such as labels and toggle buttons). A frame is a very simple manager widget. The child of the frame widget is encased in the frame. The code in Listing 11.6 demonstrates how to place a frame widget around a label widget. It creates the frame with a label as its child.

Listing 11.6   Creating a Frame Widget Surrounding a Label

```
/*frame.c*/

#include <Xm/Xm.h>
#include <Xm/Label.h>
#include <Xm/Frame.h>

XtAppContext context;
XmStringCharSet char_set=XmSTRING_DEFAULT_CHARSET;

Widget toplevel, label, frame;

void main(argc,argv)
    int argc;
    char *argv[];
{
    Arg al[10];
    int ac;
```

```
        /* create the toplevel shell */
        toplevel = XtAppInitialize(&context,"",NULL,0,&argc,argv,
            NULL,NULL,0);

        /* Create the frame widget. */
        frame=XmCreateFrame(toplevel,"frame",NULL,0);
        XtManageChild(frame);

        /* Create the label widget as a child of the frame. */
        ac=0;
        XtSetArg(al[ac],XmNlabelString,
            XmStringCreate("Hello World",char_set)); ac++;
        label=XmCreateLabel(frame,"label",al,ac);
        XtManageChild(label);

        XtRealizeWidget(toplevel);
        XtAppMainLoop(context);
}
```

11.6   LIST WIDGETS

We have already seen the list widget once, embedded in the selection dialog
box. We saw several list widget convenience functions in Chapter 7 during the
introduction to the selection box. You can also use the list widget by itself in
your code.

Like the text widget, the list widget is large and fairly complicated, with
many capabilities. It provides 25 convenience functions, listed and described
briefly in Appendix I.

The list widget manages a list of **XmString** items on screen. The user can
select items from the list using one of four selection policies:

1. Single Select. User can select one item at a time.
2. Browse Select. User can select one item at a time and can drag the cursor to
   change selections.
3. Multiple Select. User can select multiple items at once.
4. Extended Select. User can select multiple items at once and drag the cursor
   to select groups of items.

You can control the selection policy with the aptly named **selectionPolicy**
resource. When the user selects an item, one of the following callbacks is generated depending on the value of **selectionPolicy**: **browseSelectionCallback**,

Figure 11.6   A Scrolling List Widget

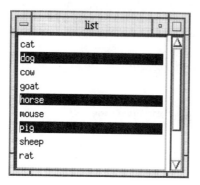

extendedSelectionCallback, multipleSelectionCallback, or **singleSelection-Callback.**

You can use three different techniques in the callback routine to extract the list of selected items: You can retrieve the selected items from the normal resource list using **XtGetValues**; you can retrieve the selected items from the **call_data** parameter structure; or you can retrieve positions of the selected items using the **XmListGetSelectedPos** convenience function.

Listing 11.7 demonstrates a list widget in multiple select mode, using the third technique for extracting the selected item list. Figure 11.6 shows the list widget in action with several items selected at once.

Listing 11.7   Creating and Using a List Widget

```
/*list.c*/

#include <Xm/Xm.h>
#include <Xm/List.h>

XtAppContext context;
XmStringCharSet char_set=XmSTRING_DEFAULT_CHARSET;

Widget toplevel, list;
char *animals[]={"cat","dog","cow","goat","horse","mouse","pig",
        "sheep","rat","donkey","elephant","squirrel"};

void selectCB(w,client_data,call_data)
    Widget w;
    XtPointer client_data;
    XmAnyCallbackStruct *call_data;
/* called when an item in the list is selected */
```

```
{
    int *pos_list;
    int pos_list_length;
    int x, *p;
    int mem_allocated;

    mem_allocated = XmListGetSelectedPos(list,&pos_list,
        &pos_list_length);
    p=pos_list;
    for (x=0; x<pos_list_length; x++)
        printf("%d ",*p++);
    printf("\n");
    if (mem_allocated)
        XtFree(pos_list);
}

void add_items()
/* add items to the list */
{
    XmString s;
    int list_cnt;

    for (list_cnt=0; list_cnt<XtNumber(animals); list_cnt++)
    {
        s = XmStringCreate(animals[list_cnt], char_set);
        XmListAddItem(list,s,0);
        XmStringFree(s);
    }
}

void main(argc,argv)
    int argc;
    char *argv[];
{
    Arg al[20];
    int ac;

    /* create the toplevel shell */
    toplevel = XtAppInitialize(&context,"",NULL,0,&argc,argv,
        NULL,NULL,0);

    /* set the default size of the window. */
    ac=0;
    XtSetArg(al[ac],XmNwidth,200); ac++;
    XtSetArg(al[ac],XmNheight,200); ac++;
```

```
XtSetValues(toplevel,al,ac);

/* create a list widget */
ac=0;
XtSetArg(al[ac],XmNselectionPolicy,XmMULTIPLE_SELECT); ac++;
list=XmCreateScrolledList(toplevel,"list",al,ac);
XtManageChild(list);
XtAddCallback (list, XmNmultipleSelectionCallback, selectCB, NULL);

add_items();

XtRealizeWidget(toplevel);
XtAppMainLoop(context);
}
```

In this code, the **main** routine creates the list widget and calls the **add_ items** function to add the items that will appear in the list, using the **Xm- ListAddItem** convenience function. Whenever a user selects any item, the **selectCB** function is triggered. It gets the list of selected item positions using the **XmListGetSelectedPos** function and displays the list to stdout. **XmListGetSelectedPos** returns an array of values in **pos_list**, and each value is an integer that indicates the position of a selected item. The value returned in **pos_list_length** indicates the number of values in the array. The function result **mem_allocated** will be true whenever **XmListGetSelectedPos** has allocated memory for the list in **pos_list**.

The list widget provides a great deal of functionality. The best way to learn about it is to experiment with the convenience functions, callbacks, and resources listed in Appendix J.

11.7   PANED WINDOW WIDGETS

A paned window, like the form widget, is a constraint widget. It holds other widgets and imparts several new resources to its children. Paned windows let users resize different panes of a window using a draggable control called a *sash*.

The code in Listing 11.8 demonstrates a simple use of a paned window by placing two scrolling text widgets into a paned window container. When you run this code, you will see a display similar to Figure 11.7. With the code running, resize the window so that it is fairly large, then drag the small square on the line that separates the two text widgets. The text widgets automatically resize as the areas that hold them change.

**Listing 11.8 Creating a Paned Window Widget to
Hold Two Text Widgets**

```c
/*paned.c*/

#include <Xm/Xm.h>
#include <Xm/Text.h>
#include <Xm/PanedW.h>


XtAppContext context;

Widget toplevel, pane, text1, text2;

void main(argc,argv)
    int argc;
    char *argv[];
{
    Arg al[20];
    int ac;

    /* create the toplevel shell */
    toplevel = XtAppInitialize(&context,"",NULL,0,&argc,argv,
        NULL,NULL,0);

    /* create the paned window widget */
    ac=0;
    pane=XmCreatePanedWindow(toplevel,"pane",al,ac);
    XtManageChild(pane);

    /* create text1 widget */
    ac=0;
    XtSetArg(al[ac],XmNeditMode,XmMULTI_LINE_EDIT); ac++;
    text1=XmCreateScrolledText(pane,"text",al,ac);
    XtManageChild(text1);

    /* create text2 widget */
    ac=0;
    XtSetArg(al[ac],XmNeditMode,XmMULTI_LINE_EDIT); ac++;
    text2=XmCreateScrolledText(pane,"text",al,ac);
    XtManageChild(text2);

    XtRealizeWidget(toplevel);
    XtAppMainLoop(context);
}
```

Figure 11.7   A Paned Window Widget Holding Two Scrolling Text Widgets

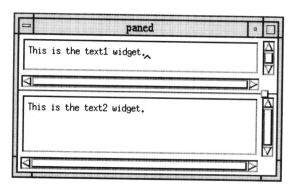

You can put almost any widget into a pane of a window. Programmers often place manager widgets like form or RowColumn widgets into panes and then place other widgets into these managers in the standard way.

Appendix J shows the resource and constraint resource list for a paned window widget. Remember that the constraint resource list augments the resource lists of all immediate children of the paned window.

The **paneMinimum** and **paneMaximum** resources let you determine the minimum and maximum size of a pane. For example, if a pane contains a RowColumn widget holding 20 push buttons, your code should set the minimum size of the pane such that the 20 buttons are always visible.

11.8   COMMAND WIDGETS

Command widgets provide an easy way to receive typed commands from the user. They accept commands as the user enters them. They also manage a scrolling list of previously entered commands, which allows users to see the command history at all times. Users can select and modify previously typed commands from the history list. Figure 11.8 shows a typical view of a command widget.

Command widgets are extremely straightforward, as shown in Listing 11.9. This code creates a command widget and wires in its callbacks. The **command-Entered** callback is the important one here. Each time the user enters a command, this callback is triggered so that the code can respond to the command. The **commandChanged** callback is called each time the user inserts or deletes a character from the current command. Both callback functions retrieve the command from the **value** field in the **call_data** parameter.

Figure 11.8   The Command Widget

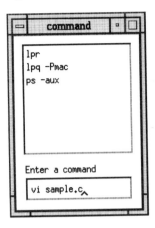

Listing 11.9   Creating a Command Widget

```
/*command.c*/

#include <Xm/Xm.h>
#include <Xm/Command.h>

XtAppContext context;
XmStringCharSet char_set=XmSTRING_DEFAULT_CHARSET;

Widget toplevel;
Widget command;
Widget button;

void command_enteredCB(w,client_data,call_data)
    Widget w;
    int client_data;
    XmCommandCallbackStruct *call_data;
/* handle callbacks generated when the command is entered. */
{
    char *s;

    XmStringGetLtoR(call_data->value,char_set,&s);
    printf("command entered='%s'\n",s);
    XtFree(s);
}

void command_changedCB(w,client_data,call_data)
    Widget w;
```

```
        int client_data;
        XmCommandCallbackStruct *call_data;
/* handle callbacks generated when the command is changed. */
{
        char *s;

        XmStringGetLtoR(call_data->value,char_set,&s);
        printf("command changed='%s'\n",s);
        XtFree(s);
}


void main(argc,argv)
        int argc;
        char *argv[];
{
        Arg al[10];
        int ac;

        /* create the toplevel shell */
        toplevel = XtAppInitialize(&context,"",NULL,0,&argc,argv,
            NULL,NULL,0);

        /* create the command widget. */
        ac = 0;
        XtSetArg(al[ac], XmNpromptString,
            XmStringCreateLtoR("Enter a command", char_set));  ac++;
        command = XmCreateCommand(toplevel, "command", al, ac);
        XtAddCallback (command, XmNcommandEnteredCallback,
            command_enteredCB, NULL);
        XtAddCallback (command, XmNcommandChangedCallback,
            command_changedCB, NULL);
        XtManageChild(command);

        XtRealizeWidget(toplevel);
        XtAppMainLoop(context);
}
```

11.9   SCROLLED WINDOW AND MAIN WINDOW WIDGETS

Scrolled window widgets are convenient: They let you set up a work area and two scroll bars more easily than do form widgets. The code in Listing 11.10 shows how to set up a drawing area and two scroll bars in a scrolled window widget (see Chapter 17 for a discussion of drawing area widgets).

Listing 11.10   Creating a Scrolled Window Widget

```
/*scrolled_window.c*/

#include <Xm/Xm.h>
#include <Xm/ScrollBar.h>
#include <Xm/DrawingA.h>
#include <Xm/ScrolledW.h>

XtAppContext context;

Widget toplevel, scroll1, scroll2, da, win;

void scrollCB(w,client_data,call_data)
    Widget w;
    int client_data;
    XmAnyCallbackStruct *call_data;
/* handle callbacks from either scrollbar. */
{
    int value;
    Arg al[10];
    int ac;

    ac=0;
    XtSetArg(al[ac], XmNvalue, &value); ac++;
    XtGetValues(w,al,ac);

    printf("bar=%d value = %d\n",client_data,value);
}

handle_click(w,client_data,event)
    Widget w;
    XtPointer client_data;
    XEvent *event;
/* handle a click in the drawing area. */
{
    printf("%d %d\n",event->xbutton.x,event->xbutton.y);
}

void main(argc,argv)
    int argc;
    char *argv[];
{
    Arg al[10];
    int ac;
```

```
    /* create the toplevel shell */
    toplevel = XtAppInitialize(&context,"",NULL,0,&argc,argv,
        NULL,NULL,0);

    /* create scrolled window. */
    ac=0;
    XtSetArg(al[ac],XmNscrollingPolicy,XmAPPLICATION_DEFINED); ac++;
    XtSetArg(al[ac],XmNscrollBarDisplayPolicy,XmSTATIC); ac++;
    XtSetArg(al[ac],XmNscrollBarPlacement,XmBOTTOM_RIGHT); ac++;
    win=XmCreateScrolledWindow(toplevel,"win",al,ac);
    XtManageChild(win);

    /* create scroll bars and drawing area. */
    ac=0;
    XtSetArg(al[ac],XmNminimum,0); ac++;
    XtSetArg(al[ac],XmNmaximum,1000); ac++;
    XtSetArg(al[ac],XmNorientation,XmHORIZONTAL); ac++;
    scroll1=XmCreateScrollBar(win,"scroll1",al,ac);
    XtManageChild(scroll1);
    XtAddCallback (scroll1, XmNvalueChangedCallback, scrollCB, 1);

    ac=0;
    XtSetArg(al[ac],XmNminimum,0); ac++;
    XtSetArg(al[ac],XmNmaximum,1000); ac++;
    scroll2=XmCreateScrollBar(win,"scroll2",al,ac);
    XtManageChild(scroll2);
    XtAddCallback (scroll2, XmNvalueChangedCallback, scrollCB, 2);

    ac=0;
    da=XmCreateDrawingArea(win,"da",al,ac);
    XtManageChild(da);
    XtAddEventHandler(da, ButtonPressMask, FALSE,
        handle_click, NULL);

    /* link scroll bars and drawing area into scrolled window. */
    XmScrolledWindowSetAreas(win,scroll1,scroll2,da);

    XtRealizeWidget(toplevel);
    XtAppMainLoop(context);
}
```

Listing 11.10 produces the window shown in Figure 11.9. It draws nothing in the drawing area, but when you click in the drawing area, it prints the mouse coordinates of the clicked point to stdout.

**Figure 11.9 A Scrolled Window Widget Containing
Two Scroll Bars and a Drawing Area**

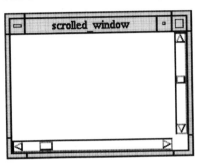

The **main** function creates a scrolled window widget, then two scroll bars and a drawing area *as the scrolled window's children*; it won't work otherwise. A call to **XmScrolledWindowSetAreas** combines these four widgets. Once combined, the scroll bars and drawing area work as you would expect. You wire in whatever callbacks you need, manipulate their resources, draw, and so on, in exactly the same way you would otherwise. The scrolled window widget simply saves you the trouble of having to create a form widget and its attachments.

The main window widget works the same way. It lets you combine a command window, a horizontal scroll bar, a vertical scroll bar, a work area, and a menu bar in a single window. Use the same techniques demonstrated in Listing 11.10, making the parent a main window widget instead.

If you are creating something this advanced, you probably need more control over placement than the main window widget affords, and you will likely end up placing the widgets yourself on a form. However, main windows are useful when you need to create standard applications quickly. See Appendix J for more information.

11.10 OPTION MENUS

An Option menu provides radio-box-style functionality in a space smaller than that required by a radio box. A button shows the currently selected option, and a click of the button pops up a menu from which the user can select another option. Figure 11.10 shows a typical Option menu when inactive. Clicking the label pops up the menu. The code in Listing 11.11 demonstrates how to create an Option menu.

Figure 11.10   An Option Menu Showing the Currently Selected Option

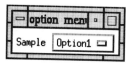

Listing 11.11   Creating an Option Menu

```
/* option_menu.c */

#include <Xm/Xm.h>
#include <Xm/PushB.h>
#include <Xm/RowColumn.h>

XtAppContext context;
XmStringCharSet char_set=XmSTRING_DEFAULT_CHARSET;

Widget toplevel;
Widget option_menu;
Widget option1_item;
Widget option2_item;
Widget option3_item;

void menuCB(w,client_data,call_data)
    Widget w;
    char *client_data;
    XmAnyCallbackStruct *call_data;
/* callback routine used for all menus */
{
    printf("%s\n",client_data);
}


Widget make_menu_item(item_name,client_data,menu)
    char *item_name;
    XtPointer client_data;
    Widget menu;
/* Adds an item into a menu. See Chapter 6. */
{
    int ac;
    Arg al[10];
    Widget item;

    ac = 0;
    XtSetArg(al[ac],XmNlabelString,
```

```
                XmStringCreateLtoR(item_name,char_set)); ac++;
        item=XmCreatePushButton(menu,item_name,al,ac);
        XtManageChild(item);
        XtAddCallback(item,XmNactivateCallback,menuCB,client_data);
        XtSetSensitive(item,True);
        return(item);
}

void main(argc,argv)
    int argc;
    char *argv[];
{

    Arg al[10];
    int ac;
    Widget menu;

    /* create the toplevel shell */
    toplevel = XtAppInitialize(&context,"",NULL,0,&argc,argv,
        NULL,NULL,0);

    /* create the option menu */
    menu=XmCreatePulldownMenu(toplevel,"menu",NULL,0);
    ac=0;
    XtSetArg (al[ac],XmNsubMenuId, menu); ac++;
    XtSetArg(al[ac],XmNlabelString,
        XmStringCreateLtoR("Sample",char_set)); ac++;
    option_menu=XmCreateOptionMenu(toplevel,"option_menu",al,ac);
    XtManageChild(option_menu);
    option1_item=make_menu_item("Option1","Option1 selected",menu);
    option2_item=make_menu_item("Option2","Option2 selected",menu);
    option3_item=make_menu_item("Option3","Option3 selected",menu);

    XtRealizeWidget(toplevel);
    XtAppMainLoop(context);
}
```

The **main** function creates a pull-down menu pane. The parent of this menu pane *must* be the same as the parent of the Option menu itself. The code then sets the **subMenuId** resource of the Option menu to this pane and creates the Option menu. The **make_menu_item** function adds items to the Option menu, as first seen in Chapter 6.

An Option menu is not a widget itself but an adaptation of a RowColumn widget. See the RowColumn widget's resource list in Appendix J for resources that control the Option menu.

Figure 11.11   A Drawn Button Widget

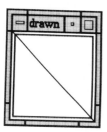

11.11   DRAWN BUTTONS

A drawn button widget is a push-button widget with a drawing area on its face. The drawing area behaves like a normal drawing area and generates expose and resize events (see Chapter 17 for a description of drawing areas). Figure 11.11 shows an example of a drawn button, and the code in Listing 11.12 demonstrates how to use one.

Listing 11.12   Creating a Drawn Button Widget

```
/*drawn_button.c*/

#include <Xm/Xm.h>
#include <Xm/DrawnB.h>

XtAppContext context;

Widget toplevel, button;
GC gc;

void buttonCB(w,client_data,call_data)
    Widget w;
    XtPointer client_data;
    XmDrawnButtonCallbackStruct *call_data;
/* called when button is clicked */
{
    printf("click_count = %d \n",call_data->click_count);
}

void exposeCB(w,client_data,call_data)
    Widget w;
    XtPointer client_data;
    XmDrawnButtonCallbackStruct *call_data;
/* Called when button is exposed. See Chapter 17. */
```

```
{
    XDrawLine(XtDisplay(w),XtWindow(w),gc,0,0,100,100);
}


void setup_gc()
/* set up the graphics context. See Chapter 17. */
{
    int foreground,background;
    Arg al[10];
    int ac;
    XGCValues vals;

    /* get the current fg and bg colors. */
    ac=0;
    XtSetArg(al[ac], XmNforeground, &foreground); ac++;
    XtSetArg(al[ac], XmNbackground, &background); ac++;
    XtGetValues(button, al, ac);

    /* create the copy gc. */
    vals.foreground = foreground;
    vals.background = background;
    gc= XtGetGC(button, GCForeground | GCBackground, &vals);
}

void main(argc,argv)
    int argc;
    char *argv[];
{
    Arg al[10];
    int ac;

    /* create the toplevel shell */
    toplevel = XtAppInitialize(&context,"",NULL,0,&argc,argv,
        NULL,NULL,0);

    /* create the drawn button. */
    ac=0;
    XtSetArg (al[ac], XmNmultiClick, XmMULTICLICK_KEEP);  ac++;
    XtSetArg (al[ac], XmNwidth, 100);  ac++;
    XtSetArg (al[ac], XmNheight, 100);  ac++;
    button=XmCreateDrawnButton(toplevel,"button",al,ac);
    XtManageChild(button);
    XtAddCallback (button, XmNactivateCallback, buttonCB, NULL);
    XtAddCallback (button, XmNexposeCallback, exposeCB, NULL);
```

```
    setup_gc();

    XtRealizeWidget(toplevel);
    XtAppMainLoop(context);
}
```

In Listing 11.12, the code sets up the drawn button and demonstrates its **expose** and **activate** callbacks. See Chapter 17 for more information on drawing area widgets and drawing commands.

12 RESOURCE OPTIONS

At this point in your training, you are well on your way to becoming a fully accomplished Motif programmer. You have seen and used almost every widget in the Motif widget set, you are familiar with their resources and callbacks, you have seen several different manager widgets and know their appropriate uses, you can handle menus and dialog boxes, and you have created several applications.

It is now time to add some depth to your knowledge. So far we have worked almost exclusively at the Motif widget level. In the remainder of the book, we will examine some of the capabilities available in the X and Xt layers, as well as investigate some of the other capabilities available in the Motif layer. You need this knowledge to make full use of the X environment. You now have enough knowledge and experience to explore these layers in some detail and begin to understand what they are doing.

We have so far ignored an important area of X and Motif programming: resource management. X and Motif provide several useful and important ways to manage resources. This chapter explores a variety of resource-setting options. The remaining chapters discuss in detail customized dialog boxes, Motif internals, the X layer, the Xt layer, and the X drawing model.

X, Xt, and Motif together form a vast landscape, a domain impossible to cover in a single book. The next six chapters will give you a taste of what is available and point you toward other sources of information. Also, Appendix A contains a list of reference books available to help you increase your knowledge of the terrain. The more you know, the more you can do.

12.1   A CLOSE EXAMINATION OF XTAPPINITIALIZE

We have been using the **XtAppInitialize** function to create the toplevel shell widget for each application. Following is a description of **XtAppInitialize**.

XtAppInitialize   *Creates the application's toplevel shell.*

```
Widget XtAppInitialize(
   XtAppContext *context,
   String application_class,
   XrmOptionDescRec options[],
   Cardinal num_options,
   Cardinal *argc,
   String *argv,
   String *fallback_resources,
   ArgList *args
   Cardinal num_args);
```

context	Returns the context value. Needed for calls to other **XtApp** functions.
application_class	The class name for the application.
options	Passed directly to the **XrmParseCommand** function.
num_options	Number of options.
argc	A pointer to the number of command line options (pass an address).
argv	The standard command line options array.
fallback_resources	A set of predefined resource strings.
args	An argument list for the toplevel shell.
num_args	Number of arguments in the argument list.

The call to **XtAppInitialize** used so far in this book has looked like this:

```
/* create the toplevel shell */
toplevel = XtAppInitialize(&context,"",NULL,0,&argc,argv,NULL,NULL,0);
```

Six of the parameters here are unused. All six have to do with resource setting in its various forms. An exploration of these six parameters provides an interesting introduction to the resource-setting techniques available to Motif programmers.

The last two parameters in the call to **XtAppInitialize** implement the normal, in-code method of resource setting, using an argument list and count. You can replace frequently used code such as this:

```
/* create the toplevel shell */
toplevel = XtAppInitialize(&context,"",NULL,0,&argc,argv,NULL,NULL,0);
```

```
/* resize toplevel */
ac=0;
XtSetArg(al[ac],XmNheight,200); ac++;
XtSetArg(al[ac],XmNwidth,200); ac++;
XtSetValues(toplevel,al,ac);
```

with the following code:

```
/* create the toplevel shell */
ac=0;
XtSetArg(al[ac],XmNheight,200); ac++;
XtSetArg(al[ac],XmNwidth,200); ac++;
toplevel = XtAppInitialize(&context,"",NULL,0,&argc,argv,NULL,al,ac);
```

We have used this technique frequently with the **XmCreate** series of convenience functions to set widget resource values during widget creation.

The **application_class** parameter is a normal C string that specifies the class name for the application. The class name determines a specific resource file that the application reads when you run it; it also specifies a set of resource values to be pulled in from other files at the same time. See Section 12.2 for a discussion of resource files.

The **options** and **num_options** parameters specify an array of strings you can use to parse command line options that can set resource values. X automatically supports its own set of options, and the application can augment this set. See Section 12.4.

The **fallback_options** parameter points to an array of strings that contain fallback resources. The application uses fallback resources in case the resource files the application needs at startup are not available. See Section 12.5.

12.2   RESOURCE FILES

In all of the programs presented so far, we have explicitly set all of the widget resource values directly in the code, using the **XtSetArg** and **XtSetValues** functions. Motif and X support a second mechanism for setting resources using resource files. Resource files allow the programmer to set up resource values in a text file external to the program. The resource values in the file are read in when the program begins running, and these values change the behavior of the specified widgets.

Resource files allow users to customize an application's appearance and behavior when running the program and thereby avoid the need to recompile the code. Users can customize an application simply by editing the resource file. For example, all of the **labelString** resources associated with all buttons and labels in a program might reside in a resource file. You could create several different resource files to supply the same labels in different languages. The user can simply install the appropriate resource file to translate the application into the desired language.

To experiment with a resource file, enter the code shown in Listing 12.1 which resembles that used in Chapter 4 to create a push-button widget. Note that this code does not change any resource values: It simply creates a button. Compile and run the program. You will see that the button behaves according to the default settings of the push-button widget resources.

Listing 12.1   Example Code to Demonstrate the Use of Resource Files with a Push Button

```
/* buttonR.c */

#include <Xm/Xm.h>
#include <Xm/PushB.h>

XtAppContext context;

Widget toplevel, button;

main(argc,argv)
    int argc;
    char *argv[];
{
    Arg al[10];
    int ac;

    /* create the toplevel shell */
    toplevel = XtAppInitialize(&context,"Sample",NULL,0,&argc,argv,
        NULL,NULL,0);

    /* create the pushbutton button */
    ac=0;
    button=XmCreatePushButton(toplevel,"button",al,ac);
    XtManageChild(button);

    XtRealizeWidget(toplevel);
    XtAppMainLoop(context);
}
```

Now, using a text editor, create a second text file containing the following lines. This file will function as a resource file. Call the file Sample.

```
Sample.height:300
Sample.width:300
Sample*button*labelString:Resource file label
```

Align the text in this file flush to the left margin. Case matters, but the number of spaces following each colon does not.

At the UNIX command line, type `setenv XENVIRONMENT filename`, where `filename` is the complete path to the resource file (for instance, `/usr/users/smith/motif/Sample`, or whatever the correct path to the resource file is on your own machine).

Run the program again *without recompiling*. Now the application creates a 300-by-300 pixel window and a button with the label "Resource file label." Edit `Sample` again to change the window size and label string. Then re-run the program, noting how the button's behavior changes even though you have not modified or recompiled the actual code.

To make the `Sample` resource file work correctly, the **XtAppInitialize** call has been changed to include the string `"Sample"`. The `"Sample"` parameter is a class name, which identifies resources intended for this application. When the program runs, the system looks in a variety of places for the appropriate resource values. For example, the system looks for a file specified with the **XENVIRONMENT** variable. If **XENVIRONMENT** has been set and the specified file exists, the system scans the file for resources that have the class name **Sample**.

Inside the resource file itself, you specify resource values by creating individual lines for each resource you intend to change. The first word of each line in the resource file is the class name **Sample**. Following the class name are widget names and a resource name, delimited with a . (period) or a * (asterisk). Use the period when you know the explicit path through the widget hierarchy to the resource and the asterisk when you do not. For example, the first two lines of the file `Sample` specify an explicit path to the **height** and **width** resources of the application: **Sample** is the class name for the application (the toplevel shell), and **width** and **height** are resources belonging to **toplevel**. In the third line, "button" is the name we gave to the button widget when we created it (the second parameter to the **XmCreatePushButton** call). The resource name **labelString** is the name usually given to the widget resource, without the **XmN** prefix. Since we do not really care about specifying the path down to button's **labelString** resource, we use the * delimiter.

X searches in several places and in a specific order for resource values pertinent to the application. These values create a resource database, which the application consults each time it creates a widget. If you do not explicitly set a value for a resource in your code, and if a value for a given resource exists in the database, Motif modifies the resource value according to the database value as it creates the widget. Note that if you specify a value for a resource in your code, that value will override any value in the database.

The loading of the resource database starts with a app-defaults directory. You usually find this directory at /usr/lib/X11/app-defaults. Inside this directory is a set of files, the names of which are class names. If the example program above found a file in the app-defaults directory named Sample, the program would open this file and read each line into the resource database. Typically, if you set resource values in a resource file, any application you build and distribute will include a second file that goes in the app-defaults directory on all systems running your code.

As you can see from the above discussion, you have to make a choice. You either set resource values internally, and therefore have a single executable file, or you set resource values externally and include a second app-defaults file with the executable. The latter approach gives both the user and the programmer more control over the application.

Once the system checks and loads an app-defaults file, it tries to load resources from a file named .Xdefaults located in your home directory. This is a resource file that the user maintains to customize the window manager and different X applications. The system only loads values in the .Xdefaults file that have the appropriate class name. Once it loads .Xdefaults, it loads the file specified in the **XENVIRONMENT** variable into the database. Again, it loads only those values with the appropriate class name. Note that the file loaded last has precedence, since it overrides identical values from earlier files. Also, if you set a resource explicitly in your code, that setting overrides any setting in any external resource file.

There are some minor quirks in this loading sequence. First, if you incorrectly specify a resource name or value, the program ignores it. Second, a resource that you set explicitly in your code cannot be set by an external resource file. Third, the .Xdefaults file is generally cached, or read into memory at log-in time, where it resides to improve performance. Thus, any changes to the .Xdefaults file have no effect unless you log in again. Alternatively, you can issue the command

```
xrdb -merge .Xdefaults
```

from the home directory to reload the file into the database. You can also use xrdb to explicitly load other resource files into the database.

12.3   AN EXAMPLE

There is a whole little science associated with resources and resource files, and an entire book could be dedicated to this topic alone. For example, you can define your own application-specific resources and use them as the application is running. You can also create your own resource databases. You can find in-depth discussions of these topics in *X Window System* by Scheifler and Gettys, *X Window System Toolkit* by Asente and Swick, and *The X Window System* by Young (see Appendix A).

For simple tasks, however, resource files are straightforward. They can greatly help the programmer in creating applications and dialog boxes containing many widgets attached to forms or bulletin boards. In creating a dialog box, for example, the correct positioning of the widgets within the dialog can take several iterations. If the positioning resources reside in a resource file instead of within the actual source code, these iterations can occur without the code being recompiled (see Chapter 13 for an example).

Listing 12.2 shows the bulletin board widget demonstration code from Chapter 5, with all of the resource setting code in the **main** function removed. Note that the code is now somewhat shorter.

**Listing 12.2   A Celsius-to-Fahrenheit Conversion
Program Using a Bulletin Board**

```
/* c2f.bbR.c */

#include <Xm/Xm.h>
#include <Xm/PushB.h>
#include <Xm/Label.h>
#include <Xm/Scale.h>
#include <Xm/BulletinB.h>

XtAppContext context;
XmStringCharSet char_set=XmSTRING_DEFAULT_CHARSET;

Widget toplevel, button, bb, label, scale;

void buttonCB(Widget w,
    int client_data,
    XmPushButtonCallbackStruct *call_data)
/* handles the pushbutton's activate callback. */
{
    exit(0);
}
```

```
void scaleCB(Widget w,
    int client_data,
    XmScaleCallbackStruct *call_data)
/* handles the scale's ValueChanged callback. */
{
    char s[100];
    Arg al[10];
    int ac;

    sprintf(s,"farenheit=%d",call_data->value*9/5+32);
    ac=0;
    XtSetArg(al[ac],XmNlabelString,
        XmStringCreate(s,char_set)); ac++;
    XtSetValues(label,al,ac);
}

void main(argc,argv)
    int argc;
    char *argv[];
{
    Arg al[10];
    int ac;

    /* create the toplevel shell */
    toplevel=XtAppInitialize(&context,"Example",NULL,0,&argc,argv,
        NULL,NULL,0);

    /* create a bulletin board to hold the three widgets */
    bb=XmCreateBulletinBoard(toplevel,"bb",NULL,0);
    XtManageChild(bb);

    /* create a push button */
    button=XmCreatePushButton(bb,"button",NULL,0);
    XtManageChild(button);
    XtAddCallback(button,XmNactivateCallback,buttonCB,NULL);

    /* create a scale */
    scale=XmCreateScale(bb,"scale",NULL,0);
    XtManageChild(scale);
    XtAddCallback(scale,XmNdragCallback,scaleCB,NULL);

    /* create a label */
    label=XmCreateLabel(bb,"label",NULL,0);
```

```
    XtManageChild(label);

    XtRealizeWidget(toplevel);
    XtAppMainLoop(context);
}
```

You can place the attachment resources in a resource file named Example (the class name in the **XtAppInitialize** call is Example). A typical Example resource file appears below.

```
Example.width:200
Example.height:200

Example*button*x:10
Example*button*y:10
Example*button*labelString:Quit

Example*scale*x:1
Example*scale*y:100
Example*scale*titleString:Celsius Temperature
Example*scale*orientation:XmHORIZONTAL
Example*scale*showValue:True

Example*label*x:10
Example*label*y:200
Example*label*labelString:Farenheit = 32
```

You can put the Example file in the app-defaults directory if you have the privileges to do so, or you can place it in your own directory and use the **XENVIRONMENT** variable as shown previously. If you do not want to create an explicit resource file named Example, you can incorporate these values into the .Xdefaults file instead. No matter which technique you use, the label, button, and separator widgets will appear in positions on the bulletin board specified in the resource file.

When you attach widgets to a form using a resource file, it is similar to that shown for the bulletin board. The resource file contains the attachment resource values for the widgets on the form. You cannot use the **XmATTACH_WIDGET** option because you cannot use widget names in a resource file. You must therefore specify all widget attachments to other widgets in the code.

If your program requires many labels and buttons, place all of their **label-String** values in a resource file so that you can change them easily after compiling the program.

Generally, color information is highly user-specific and therefore is almost always determined in a resource file rather than in the code. In fact, it is considered good practice to specify in your code only those resources needed for correct program execution, and all other resource values externally so that the user can modify them.

12.4   USING COMMAND LINE OPTIONS TO MODIFY RESOURCES

All X and Motif applications automatically support a set of command line options to control colors, geometry, fonts, and so on. The following options are available:

-background	-foreground
-bd	-geometry
-bg	-iconic
-borderwidth	-name
-bordercolor	-reverse
-bw	-rv
-display	-synchronous
-fg	-title
-fn	-xrm
-font	

These options will work on the command line in any of the programs created so far in this book. The program passes command line arguments to **XtAppInitialize**, which extracts the known arguments and handles them automatically. As an example, you can execute the editor created in Chapter 10 with the following command line:

```
ed -iconic -foreground white -background black -geometry 200x200+50+500
```

This starts the editor as an icon. Once expanded, the editor will have a black background and a white foreground. The window will be 200 × 200 pixels and will appear on the screen with the upper-left corner at the point 50, 500.

You can create customized command line options for an application as well. Listing 12.3 shows how.

Listing 12.3   Command Line Argument Processing

```
/* options.c */

#include <Xm/Xm.h>
#include <Xm/Label.h>

XtAppContext context;
XmStringCharSet char_set=XmSTRING_DEFAULT_CHARSET;

Widget toplevel, label;

static XrmOptionDescRec options[]={
{"-label", "*label*labelString",XrmoptionSepArg,(caddr_t)NULL},
{"-width", "*label*width",       XrmoptionSepArg,(caddr_t)NULL},
{"-height","*label*height",      XrmoptionSepArg,(caddr_t)NULL},
};

main(argc,argv)
    int argc;
    char *argv[];
{
    Arg al[10];
    int ac;

    /* create the toplevel shell */
    toplevel=XtAppInitialize(&context,"",options,XtNumber(options),
        &argc,argv,NULL,NULL,0);

    /* create the label widget */
    ac=0;
    label=XmCreateLabel(toplevel,"label",al,ac);
    XtManageChild(label);

    XtRealizeWidget(toplevel);
    XtAppMainLoop(context);
}
```

The **options** array contains the specification for the new command line
options. In this case, the code specifies three options: **-label**, **-width**, and
-height. If you compile this code to an executable file named `options`, you
can use the following command line to invoke the program:

```
options -width 200 -height 300 -label sample
```

The label widget will be 200 × 300 pixels and will display a label string containing the word `sample`.

To find out more about command line parsing and resource databases in general, see Scheifler and Getty's *X Window System*. *The X Window System* by Young is also informative.

12.5   USING FALLBACK RESOURCES

The **XtAppInitialize** function accepts as a parameter an array of fallback resource strings. The function merges these strings into the resource database and uses them if it cannot find the specified resources in an app-defaults or other resource file as the program is being loaded. The code in Listing 12.4 demonstrates how to use fallback resources.

Listing 12.4   Fallback Resources

```
/* fallback.c */

#include <Xm/Xm.h>
#include <Xm/Label.h>

XtAppContext context;
XmStringCharSet char_set=XmSTRING_DEFAULT_CHARSET;

Widget toplevel, label;

String fallbacks [] =
{
  "*label.width:500",
  "*label.height:500",
  "*label.labelString:sample of using fallback resources",
  NULL
};

main(argc,argv)
    int argc;
    char *argv[];
{
    Arg al[10];
    int ac;

    /* create the toplevel shell */
    toplevel = XtAppInitialize(&context,"",NULL,0,&argc,argv,
        fallbacks,NULL,0);
```

```
/* create the label widget */
ac=0;
label=XmCreateLabel(toplevel,"label",al,ac);
XtManageChild(label);

XtRealizeWidget(toplevel);
XtAppMainLoop(context);
}
```

You can place any resource string in the **fallbacks** array, using the same format as for a resource file. The strings are merged into the resource database if necessary, and the application uses them normally.

13 CUSTOMIZED DIALOG BOXES

Although Motif provides a number of predefined dialog boxes, you sometimes need to create your own. Designed to address a certain problem, customized dialog boxes can provide the user with a very simple and intuitive way to accomplish the assigned task. This chapter will provide insight into the process of creating customized dialog boxes by showing you how to create a find dialog for the editor discussed in Chapter 10.

13.1   CREATING A CUSTOMIZED DIALOG

Creating a customized dialog box is similar to creating an application. When you build an application, you usually create, as a child of the toplevel shell, a bulletin board widget or form widget that acts as a manager for other user interface widgets. To create a customized dialog box, you either create a bulletin board *dialog* widget or form *dialog* widget, and attach the user interface widgets you need to the dialog box. The bulletin board dialog widget and form dialog widget are simply the manager widgets we saw in Chapter 5, hooked into a dialog shell widget. The dialog shell allows the managers to act like dialog boxes when they appear on-screen.

Motif provides two convenience functions to create these manager dialogs, as shown in the following examples

```
bb_dialog = XmCreateBulletinBoardDialog(toplevel, "bb_dialog", al, ac);

form_dialog = XmCreateFormDialog(toplevel, "form_dialog", al, ac);
```

where **bb_dialog** and **form_dialog** are declared normally as type **Widget**. The code should not manage the dialog until you want it to appear on screen.

Once you have created the container dialog, you create and *manage* all the user interface widgets that will make up the dialog. Create them as children of the manager dialog, so that the dialog box will appear with all of the children

**Figure 13.1 A Find Dialog for the Editor Presented
in Chapter 10**

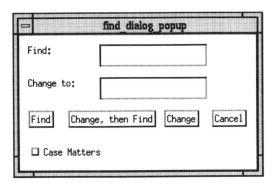

in the correct places when the dialog is managed. The children's callbacks,
resources, and so on, are all completely standard.

13.2 CREATING A FIND DIALOG

Most editors provide find and replace capabilities that let users search for and
modify strings in a document. You can implement such a capability at the user
interface level in many ways. One intuitive and consistent method of dealing
with all of the editor's find and replace capabilities is through a customized
Find dialog box.

Figure 13.1 shows the Find dialog box we will examine in this chapter. The
box consists of two label widgets (Find and Change To), along with associated
text widgets that let the user enter strings. Four push buttons let the user
find, change, change and then find the next match, or cancel. Finally, a Case
Matters toggle button lets the user toggle between case-sensitive and case-
insensitive search modes.

Creating this dialog box is straightforward. You can make several additions
to the editor code shown in Chapter 10 so that the find/replace capability
becomes available to the program. At the top of the editor program, you need
to declare several constants and widget variables required by the dialog:

```
#include <Xm/Text.h>
#include <Xm/BulletinB.h>
#include <Xm/ToggleB.h>

#define MENU_FIND        8
```

```
#define FIND_FIND              1
#define FIND_FIND_CHANGE       2
#define FIND_CHANGE            3
#define FIND_CANCEL            4
#define FIND_CASE              5
```

```
/* widgets having to do with find dialog */
Widget find_dialog;
Widget find_label1, find_label2;
Widget find_edit1, find_edit2;
Widget find_button, find_change_button, change_button, cancel_button;
Widget case_toggle;
```

In the **main** function, add a single line to call the function that sets up the dialog box:

```
setup_find_dialog();
```

The **setup_find_dialog** function creates a bulletin board dialog widget and attaches two labels, two text widgets, four push buttons, and one toggle button. This function is shown in Listing 13.1.

Listing 13.1   Creating the Find Dialog Box

```
void setup_find_dialog()
{
    Arg al[10];
    int ac;

    /* create but do NOT manage the container dialog. */
    ac=0;
    XtSetArg(al[ac],XmNheight,200); ac++;
    XtSetArg(al[ac],XmNwidth,400); ac++;
    XtSetArg(al[ac],XmNautoUnmanage,False); ac++;
    find_dialog=XmCreateBulletinBoardDialog(toplevel,
        "find_dialog",al,ac);

    /* create and manage the two labels. */
    ac=0;
    XtSetArg(al[ac],XmNx,10); ac++;
    XtSetArg(al[ac],XmNy,10); ac++;
    XtSetArg(al[ac], XmNlabelString,
        XmStringCreateLtoR("Find:", char_set));     ac++;
    find_label1=XmCreateLabel(find_dialog,"find_label1",al,ac);
    XtManageChild(find_label1);
```

```
ac=0;
XtSetArg(al[ac],XmNx,10); ac++;
XtSetArg(al[ac],XmNy,50); ac++;
XtSetArg(al[ac], XmNlabelString,
    XmStringCreateLtoR("Change To:", char_set));    ac++;
find_label2 = XmCreateLabel(find_dialog,"find_label2",al,ac);
XtManageChild(find_label2);

/* create and manage the two text widgets. */
ac=0;
XtSetArg(al[ac],XmNx,100); ac++;
XtSetArg(al[ac],XmNy,10); ac++;
find_edit1 = XmCreateText(find_dialog,"find_edit1",al,ac);
XtManageChild(find_edit1);

ac=0;
XtSetArg(al[ac],XmNx,100); ac++;
XtSetArg(al[ac],XmNy,50); ac++;
find_edit2 = XmCreateText(find_dialog,"find_edit2",al,ac);
XtManageChild(find_edit2);

/* create and manage the four pushbuttons. */
ac=0;
XtSetArg(al[ac],XmNx,10); ac++;
XtSetArg(al[ac],XmNy,90); ac++;
XtSetArg(al[ac], XmNlabelString,
    XmStringCreateLtoR("Find", char_set));    ac++;
find_button = XmCreatePushButton(find_dialog,
    "find_button",al,ac);
XtManageChild(find_button);
XtAddCallback (find_button, XmNactivateCallback, findCB, FIND_FIND);

ac=0;
XtSetArg(al[ac],XmNx,60); ac++;
XtSetArg(al[ac],XmNy,90); ac++;
XtSetArg(al[ac], XmNlabelString,
    XmStringCreateLtoR("Change, Then Find", char_set));    ac++;
find_change_button = XmCreatePushButton(find_dialog,
    "find_change_button",al,ac);
XtManageChild(find_change_button);
XtAddCallback (find_change_button, XmNactivateCallback, findCB,
    FIND_FIND_CHANGE);

ac=0;
XtSetArg(al[ac],XmNx,180); ac++;
```

```
XtSetArg(al[ac],XmNy,90); ac++;
XtSetArg(al[ac], XmNlabelString,
    XmStringCreateLtoR("Change", char_set));    ac++;
change_button = XmCreatePushButton(find_dialog,
    "change_button",al,ac);
XtManageChild(change_button);
XtAddCallback (change_button, XmNactivateCallback, findCB,
    FIND_CHANGE);


ac=0;
XtSetArg(al[ac],XmNx,240); ac++;
XtSetArg(al[ac],XmNy,90); ac++;
XtSetArg(al[ac], XmNlabelString,
    XmStringCreateLtoR("Cancel", char_set));    ac++;
cancel_button = XmCreatePushButton(find_dialog,
    "cancel_button",al,ac);
XtManageChild(cancel_button);
XtAddCallback (cancel_button, XmNactivateCallback, findCB,
    FIND_CANCEL);

/* create and manage the toggle button. */
ac=0;
XtSetArg(al[ac],XmNx,10); ac++;
XtSetArg(al[ac],XmNy,130); ac++;
XtSetArg(al[ac], XmNlabelString,
    XmStringCreateLtoR("Case Matters", char_set));    ac++;
case_toggle = XmCreateToggleButton(find_dialog,
    "case_toggle",al,ac);
XtManageChild(case_toggle);
XtAddCallback (case_toggle, XmNvalueChangedCallback, findCB,
    FIND_CASE);
}
```

In the **setup_find_dialog** function, the first step is to create the **find_dialog** widget as a bulletin board dialog. Note that it is created but not managed and that its parent is **toplevel**. Also note that the **autoUnmanage** resource is set to false so that the dialog will stay on-screen until explicitly told to go away. The other widgets are created normally as children of the bulletin board and attached to it with their x and y resources.

As an alternative, you could place the four push buttons in a RowColumn widget and let the RowColumn manage their locations automatically. The code for creating the four push buttons is shown in Listing 13.2.

**Listing 13.2   Alternative Code to Create the Find
Dialog Buttons as Children of a RowColumn Widget**

```
/* create a rowcolumn widget to hold the four pushbuttons. */
ac=0;
XtSetArg(al[ac],XmNx,10); ac++;
XtSetArg(al[ac],XmNy,90); ac++;
XtSetArg(al[ac],XmNorientation, XmHORIZONTAL); ac++;
XtSetArg(al[ac],XmNpacking,XmPACK_TIGHT); ac++;
XtSetArg(al[ac],XmNadjustLast,False); ac++;
find_rc=XmCreateRowColumn(find_dialog,"find_rc",al,ac);
XtManageChild(find_rc);

/* create and manage the four pushbuttons as children of the rc. */
ac=0;
XtSetArg(al[ac], XmNlabelString,
    XmStringCreateLtoR("Find", char_set));    ac++;
find_button=XmCreatePushButton(find_rc,"find_button",al,ac);
XtManageChild(find_button);
XtAddCallback (find_button, XmNactivateCallback, findCB, FIND_FIND);

ac=0;
XtSetArg(al[ac], XmNlabelString,
    XmStringCreateLtoR("Change, Then Find", char_set));    ac++;
find_change_button=XmCreatePushButton(find_rc,"find_change_button",
    al,ac);
XtManageChild(find_change_button);
XtAddCallback (find_change_button, XmNactivateCallback, findCB,
    FIND_FIND_CHANGE);

ac=0;
XtSetArg(al[ac], XmNlabelString,
    XmStringCreateLtoR("Change", char_set));    ac++;
change_button=XmCreatePushButton(find_rc,"change_button",al,ac);
XtManageChild(change_button);
XtAddCallback (change_button, XmNactivateCallback, findCB,
    FIND_CHANGE);

ac=0;
XtSetArg(al[ac], XmNlabelString,
    XmStringCreateLtoR("Cancel", char_set));    ac++;
cancel_button=XmCreatePushButton(find_rc,"cancel_button",al,ac);
XtManageChild(cancel_button);
XtAddCallback (cancel_button, XmNactivateCallback, findCB,
    FIND_CANCEL);
```

The code creates the **find_rc** widget and the four buttons as its children. You need no positioning code for the buttons because the RowColumn widget handles the positioning itself.

To activate the find dialog, you need a new menu option. The following code (which should be added at the end of the **create_menus** function) adds a Utilities menu containing a Find item to the application and wires in a **MENU_FIND client_data** parameter. This constant allows the **menuCB** function to distinguish the new menu option.

```
menu = make_menu("Utilities",menu_bar);
find_option = make_menu_option("Find",MENU_FIND,menu);
```

The **menuCB** function receives a new case statement that can manage the **find_dialog** widget when necessary:

```
case MENU_FIND:
    XtManageChild(find_dialog);
    break;
```

The **findCB** function itself handles callbacks from the four push buttons and the toggle button. The function dispatches each to an appropriate handling routine. The Cancel button simply unmanages the dialog to make it disappear.

```
void do_find()
{
}

void do_find_change()
{
}

void do_change()
{
}

void do_case_sensitivity()
{
}

void findCB(w,client_data,call_data)
    Widget w;
    int client_data;
    XmAnyCallbackStruct *call_data;
```

```
{
    switch (client_data)
    {
        case FIND_FIND:
            do_find();
            break;
        case FIND_FIND_CHANGE:
            do_find_change();
            break;
        case FIND_CHANGE:
            do_change();
            break;
        case FIND_CANCEL:
            XtUnmanageChild(find_dialog);
            break;
        case FIND_CASE:
            do_case_sensitivity();
            break;
    }
}
```

As the above code shows, there is nothing magic about creating a customized dialog box. You simply use a special dialog box form of the usual manager widgets and attach other widgets to these managers using standard techniques.

13.3   USING A RESOURCE FILE FOR CUSTOMIZED DIALOGS

You might have noticed that the **setup_find_dialog** function devotes a great deal of code to the setting of resources. Moreover, it usually takes several tries to position widgets inside a dialog box such as this correctly, which can be time-consuming if you have to recompile the code after every attempt. Resource files (Chapter 12) are very appropriate in this situation.

You can use the code in Listing 13.3 for the **setup_find_dialog** function when using a resource file. This is the same code we used above, but with all the resource information removed.

Listing 13.3   Creating the Find Dialog Box Using a Resource File

```
void setup_find_dialog()
{
    Arg al[10];
```

```
    int ac;

    ac=0;
    XtSetArg(al[ac],XmNautoUnmanage,False); ac++;
    find_dialog=XmCreateBulletinBoardDialog(toplevel,
        "find_dialog",al,ac);

    find_label1=XmCreateLabel(find_dialog,"find_label1",NULL,0);
    XtManageChild(find_label1);

    find_label2=XmCreateLabel(find_dialog,"find_label2",NULL,0);
    XtManageChild(find_label2);

    find_edit1=XmCreateText(find_dialog,"find_edit1",NULL,0);
    XtManageChild(find_edit1);

    find_edit2=XmCreateText(find_dialog,"find_edit2",NULL,0);
    XtManageChild(find_edit2);

    find_button=XmCreatePushButton(find_dialog,"find_button",NULL,0);
    XtManageChild(find_button);
    XtAddCallback (find_button, XmNactivateCallback, findCB, FIND_FIND);

    find_change_button=XmCreatePushButton(find_dialog,
        "find_change_button",NULL,0);
    XtManageChild(find_change_button);
    XtAddCallback (find_change_button, XmNactivateCallback, findCB,
        FIND_FIND_CHANGE);

    change_button=XmCreatePushButton(find_dialog,"change_button",NULL,0);
    XtManageChild(change_button);
    XtAddCallback (change_button, XmNactivateCallback, findCB,
        FIND_CHANGE);

    cancel_button=XmCreatePushButton(find_dialog,"cancel_button",NULL,0);
    XtManageChild(cancel_button);
    XtAddCallback (cancel_button, XmNactivateCallback, findCB,
        FIND_CANCEL);

    case_toggle=XmCreateToggleButton(find_dialog,"case_toggle",NULL,0);
    XtManageChild(case_toggle);
    XtAddCallback (case_toggle, XmNvalueChangedCallback, findCB,
        FIND_CASE);
}
```

You should change the call to **XtAppInitialize** in the editor code to include an appropriate class name. The following example uses the class named **Editor**.

```
toplevel = XtAppInitialize(&context,"Editor",NULL,0,&argc,argv,
    NULL,NULL,0);
```

Finally, you can create a resource file named Editor as a normal, separate text file. It should contain something like the resource list shown in Listing 13.4.

Listing 13.4 Contents of the Editor Resource File

```
Editor*find_dialog.height:200
Editor*find_dialog.width:400

Editor*find_dialog*find_label1*x:10
Editor*find_dialog*find_label1*y:10
Editor*find_dialog*find_label1*labelString:Find:

Editor*find_dialog*find_label2*x:10
Editor*find_dialog*find_label2*y:50
Editor*find_dialog*find_label2*labelString:Change To:

Editor*find_dialog*find_edit1*x:100
Editor*find_dialog*find_edit1*y:10

Editor*find_dialog*find_edit2*x:100
Editor*find_dialog*find_edit2*y:50

Editor*find_dialog*find_button*x:10
Editor*find_dialog*find_button*y:90
Editor*find_dialog*find_button*labelString:Find

Editor*find_dialog*find_change_button*x:60
Editor*find_dialog*find_change_button*y:90
Editor*find_dialog*find_change_button*labelString:Change, Then find

Editor*find_dialog*change_button*x:180
Editor*find_dialog*change_button*y:90
Editor*find_dialog*change_button*labelString:Change

Editor*find_dialog*cancel_button*x:240
Editor*find_dialog*cancel_button*y:90
Editor*find_dialog*cancel_button*labelString:Cancel
```

```
Editor*find_dialog*case_toggle*x:10
Editor*find_dialog*case_toggle*y:130
Editor*find_dialog*case_toggle*labelString:Case Matters
```

You can make the resource file known to the program by placing it in the app-defaults directory (if you have permission); by typing setenv XENVIRON-MENT filename, where filename is the complete path to the Editor resource file; or by adding the resources into the .Xdefaults file and remerging, as shown in Chapter 12.

Rather subtle bugs can arise in the creation of this resource file. For example, when I first created the resource file, the first two lines looked like this:

```
Editor*find_dialog*height:200
Editor*find_dialog*width:400
```

Using the * delimiter in place of the . delimiter had an interesting effect: The code set the width and height of *all* of the children of **find_dialog**, which made quite a mess on-screen. The correct form sets the height and width of the dialog box only:

```
Editor*find_dialog.height:200
Editor*find_dialog.width:400
```

13.4   RESOURCES PERTINENT TO DIALOG BOXES

When creating a customized dialog box, you can modify several resources to make the dialog more appropriate to the application.

If you run an application that uses dialog boxes and do not see decorations around the dialogs, you are missing out. Dialogs with decorations can be moved and resized easily and are therefore more useful. In the Motif window manager, you can remedy this situation by adding the following line to your .Xdefaults file:

```
Mwm*transientDecoration:all
```

This resource will add title bars to the dialog boxes and make them resizable.

Dialogs with decorations have default titles that are not very informative. To change the title of a dialog box, use code such as the following:

```
XtSetArg(al[ac],XmNdialogTitle,XmStringCreateLtoR(
    "Editor: Find",XmSTRING_DEFAULT_CHARSET)); ac++;
```

By convention, you should include the name of the application as well as the dialog's name in the dialog title.

Decorations provide the ability to resize. In the case of our find dialog, we are using a bulletin board widget and resizing is not desirable. You can remove the resizing capability by changing the bulletin board's **noResize** resource:

```
XtSetArg(al[ac],XmNnoResize,True); ac++;
```

The bulletin board widget also has an **autoUnmanage** resource that automatically unmanages the dialog when a user clicks a button. In a find dialog, this behavior is inappropriate. Use the following code:

```
XtSetArg(al[ac],XmNautoUnmanage,False); ac++;
```

When using a dialog such as the Prompt dialog (Chapter 7), you might have noticed that you can use the RETURN key to activate the OK button. This behavior is controlled by the bulletin board's **defaultButton** resource. The bulletin board also has a **cancelButton** resource. In our find dialog, we want the RETURN key to activate the Find button. We can also cause recognition of the Cancel button. The following lines accomplish this:

```
ac=0;
XtSetArg(al[ac],XmNdefaultButton,find_button); ac++;
XtSetArg(al[ac],XmNcancelButton,cancel_button); ac++;
XtSetValues(find_dialog,al,ac);
```

Note that this code must follow the code that creates all three of the widgets it references, hence the call to **XtSetValues**.

Finally, the **dialogStyle** resource of the bulletin board widget controls the behavior of the dialog with respect to the application. You can define six styles:

XmDIALOG_SYSTEM_MODAL. The user must respond to this dialog before anything else can happen in any application on the system.

XmDIALOG_PRIMARY_APPLICATION_MODAL. The user must respond to this dialog before anything else can happen in the ancestors of this dialog.

XmDIALOG_APPLICATION_MODAL. Same as above.

XmDIALOG_FULL_APPLICATION_MODAL. The user must respond to this dialog before anything else can happen in this application.

XmDIALOG_MODELESS. The user may use the dialog simultaneously with the application.

XmDIALOG_WORK_AREA. The default value for bulletin boards not in a dialog shell.

We want our find dialog to be available at all times, and we do not want it to interfere with the application. We therefore want modeless operation, which the following code sets:

```
XtSetArg(al[ac],XmNdialogStyle,XmDIALOG_MODELESS); ac++;
```

When we combine all of these features, we can use the following code to create the desired find dialog box behavior:

```
ac=0;
XtSetArg(al[ac],XmNheight,200); ac++;
XtSetArg(al[ac],XmNwidth,400); ac++;
XtSetArg(al[ac],XmNautoUnmanage,False); ac++;
XtSetArg(al[ac],XmNnoResize,True); ac++;
XtSetArg(al[ac],XmNdialogStyle,XmDIALOG_MODELESS); ac++;
XtSetArg(al[ac],XmNdialogTitle,XmStringCreateLtoR(
    "Editor: Find",XmSTRING_DEFAULT_CHARSET)); ac++;
find_dialog=XmCreateBulletinBoardDialog(toplevel,
    "find_dialog",al,ac);
```

See the bulletin board description in Appendix J for other available resources. A form widget inherits its behavior from the bulletin board, so the resources described above work as well when used with a form dialog widget.

13.5   IMPLEMENTING THE FIND DIALOG

You can use the code in Listing 13.5 to implement the four functions called by the **findCB** function. They use the text widget's convenience functions fairly heavily. See Appendix I for descriptions of these functions.

Listing 13.5   Implementing the Find and Change Operations

```
char *string_search(cs,ct)
    char *cs;
    char *ct;
/* searches for ct in cs. Returns a pointer to the beginning of the
   first instance of ct. */
{
    int done;
    char *ct2,*cs2;

    /* check for "no work" situations */
    if (cs==NULL || ct==NULL)
        return NULL;
```

Enhancing Dialog Boxes

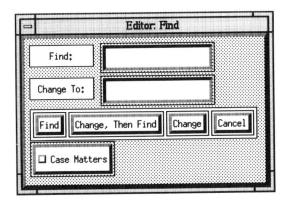

You can do several things to make your dialog boxes look good. The figure above shows the results of several techniques applied to the editor's find dialog box.

This dialog box consists of two labels, two text widgets, a RowColumn widget containing four buttons, and a toggle, all residing in a bulletin board. The background of the entire dialog displays the standard gray3 bitmap, which is done by setting the **background-Pixmap** resource for the bulletin board to /usr/include/X11/bitmaps/gray3. Try other bitmaps in this directory to see different effects. Note that the background of the RowColumn widget has been left white so that it stands out.

The widths of the labels are set to 80 to make sure they are the same.

The **borderWidth** resource of all of the widgets has been set to 1 to place a one-pixel-wide border around all of the widgets. This makes the labels and the RowColumn widget stand out better in the dialog.

The **shadowThickness** resource for the entire dialog has also been set to 4 to make the three-dimensional appearance of the button and text widgets more pronounced.

If the class name for the editor is "Editor," the resource specifications for this dialog box will look like those shown below.

```
Editor*find_dialog.backgroundPixmap:  /usr/include/X11/bitmaps/gray3
Editor*find_dialog*shadowThickness:   4
Editor*find_dialog*borderWidth:       1
Editor*find_dialog*borderColor:       Black
```

```
    if (*cs=='\0' || *ct=='\0')
        return NULL;

    /* loop through each character of cs. */
    done=False;
    while ((!done)&&(*cs!='\0'))
    {
        /* check to see if the first char of ct is in *cs. If it
           is proceed to check the rest of the letters in ct against
           cs. */
        if (*cs!=*ct)
            cs++;
        else
        {
            cs2=cs;
            ct2=ct;
            do
            {
                ct2++;
                cs2++;
            } while ((*cs2==*ct2) && (*ct2!='\0') && (*cs2!='\0'));
            if (*ct2=='\0')
            {
                done=True;
                return cs;
            }
            else
                cs++;
        }
    }
    if (!done)
        return NULL;
}

void lowercase(s)
    char *s;
/* converts s to lower case. */
{
    int x,y;

    y=strlen(s);
    for (x=0; x<y; x++)
    {
        if (s[x]>='A' && s[x]<='Z')
```

```
                s[x]=s[x]+32;
    }
}


void do_find()
/* finds the string in find_edit1 in the text starting at the current
   cursor position. */
{
    Arg al[10];
    int ac;
    XmTextPosition cursor_pos;
    char *find_string,*start,*temp,*p;
    Boolean found=False;
    int i;

    /* get the strings from the dialog box and the main text widget. */
    find_string=XmTextGetString(find_edit1);
    cursor_pos=XmTextGetInsertionPosition(text);
    start=XmTextGetString(text);
    temp=start+cursor_pos+1;
    if (!case_matters)
    {
      lowercase(temp);
      lowercase(find_string);
    }
    p=string_search(temp,find_string);
    /* if not found, display an error. */
    if (p==NULL)
    {
        ac=0;
        XtSetArg(al[ac], XmNmessageString, XmStringCreateLtoR(
            "String not found between current\ncursor location and end.",
            XmSTRING_DEFAULT_CHARSET));  ac++;
        XtSetValues(finderror_dialog,al,ac);
        XtManageChild(finderror_dialog);
    }
    /* if found, select the found string and scroll it to the top of
       the window. */
    else if (p!=NULL)
    {
        i=p-start;
        XmTextSetSelection(text,(XmTextPosition)i,
            (XmTextPosition)(i+strlen(find_string)),CurrentTime);
        XmTextSetInsertionPosition(text,(XmTextPosition)i);
```

```
            XmTextSetTopCharacter(text,(XmTextPosition)i);
            found=True;
        }
        XtFree(start);
        XtFree(find_string);
    }


    void do_change()
    /* changes the found string to the new value. */
    {
        Arg al[10];
        int ac;
        XmTextPosition cursor_pos;
        char *start,*temp,*p,*find_string,*replace_string;

        find_string=XmTextGetString(find_edit1);
        replace_string=XmTextGetString(find_edit2);
        cursor_pos=XmTextGetInsertionPosition(text);
        start=XmTextGetString(text);
        temp=start+cursor_pos;
        if (!case_matters)
        {
            lowercase(temp);
            lowercase(find_string);
        }
        /* Make sure selected text is same as find_string. */
        if ((find_string==NULL)||
            (strncmp(temp,find_string,strlen(find_string))!=0))
        {
            ac = 0;
            XtSetArg(al[ac], XmNmessageString, XmStringCreateLtoR(
                "Change must be preceeded by a find.",
                XmSTRING_DEFAULT_CHARSET));  ac++;
            XtSetValues(finderror_dialog, al, ac);
            XtManageChild(finderror_dialog);
        }
        else
        {
            XmTextReplace(text,cursor_pos,cursor_pos+
                (XmTextPosition)strlen(find_string),replace_string);
            XmTextSetSelection(text,cursor_pos,
                cursor_pos+(XmTextPosition)strlen(replace_string),
                CurrentTime);
            XmTextSetInsertionPosition(text,(XmTextPosition)(cursor_pos+
                strlen(replace_string)));
```

```
    }
    XtFree(find_string);
    XtFree(replace_string);
}

void do_find_change()
{
    do_change();
    do_find();
}

void do_case_sensitivity()
/* get the new value of the case toggle button. */
{
    Arg al[10];
    int ac;

    ac=0;
    XtSetArg(al[ac],XmNset,&case_matters); ac++;
    XtGetValues(case_toggle,al,ac);
}
```

Listing 13.5 assumes the existence of a **finderror_dialog** dialog box. Create it as an error message dialog. Make its parent the **find_dialog** widget.

The **do_find** code searches for the entered string starting at the current cursor position. If the program finds the string, it selects the found segment in the main text widget, scrolls the line that contains it to the top of the window, and sets the insertion position at the beginning of the segment. If the program does not find the string, an error dialog appears.

The **do_change** code first gets the strings it will need, then checks to make sure that the change operation was preceded by a find operation. If it was, the program replaces the selected string in the text widget with the string that the user entered.

The **do_case_sensitivity** function retrieves the current value from the toggle button and sets a global variable to remember the current state.

14 MOTIF INTERNALS

Chapters 1 through 11 focused on individual widgets in the Motif widget set, but there are other aspects to Motif besides the widgets. For example, Motif contains its own string and font types, as well as Clipboard functions. This chapter introduces you to the **XmString** type and commands, the **XmFontList** type and commands, the Motif Clipboard, Motif gadgets, and shell widgets.

14.1   MOTIF STRINGS

Motif supports its own string type, **XmString**, also known as a *compound string*. This type offers more functionality than a standard null-terminated C string. The *OSF Motif Programmer's Reference Manual* says that "**XmString** is the data type for a compound string. Compound strings include one or more components, each of which contains text, character set, and string direction. When a compound string is displayed, the character set and direction are used to determine how to display the text."

A compound string contains different text segments kept apart by separators. Each segment consists of two parts: the text of the string and a character set. The character set is a string that determines how characters in the compound string map to a given font in a font list. As a result, the **XmString** and **XmFontList** types are intimately intertwined. When a compound string is displayed using **XmStringDraw**, **XmStringDrawImage**, or **XmStringDrawUnderline**, the character set of each segment is matched with the corresponding character set in the supplied font list, which controls how the drawn characters appear on the screen. Section 14.2 contains example code that shows how to tie strings and font lists together.

The **XmString** type provides a number of convenience functions. Appendix I lists and describes each briefly. The table lists the functions alphabetically, but you might want to start with the creation functions and fan out from there.

Figure 14.1 The Structure of an XmString Created by XmStringCreateLtoR

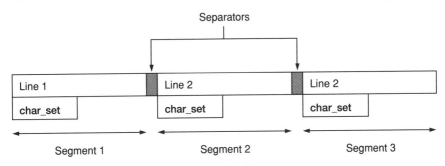

The simplest functions are **XmStringCreate** and **XmStringCreateLtoR**, which we have used throughout the book. Each accepts a normal null-terminated C string and a character set as parameters and uses these to create an **XmString**. The **XmStringCreate** function creates an **XmString** with a single segment using the specified character set. The **XmStringCreateLtoR** function creates an **XmString** with multiple segments isolated by separators; all segments have the same character set. Figure 14.1 shows the structure of such an **XmString** created with the following code:

```
XmString s;
     .
     .
     .
s=XmStringCreateLtoR("line 1\nline 2\nline3",char_set);
```

Figure 14.1 is a simplification, because each segment also contains direction information. In English, however, the direction is always left to right.

You can also map each segment to a different character set in a font list, as shown in the following section.

All the other **XmString** functions listed in Appendix I are self-explanatory. The set includes functions that concatenate strings, copy strings, free strings, and so on. Many of the functions require a font list as well. The relationship between **XmString** functions and font lists is clarified in the following section.

14.2 MOTIF FONT LISTS

The X Window System supports multiple fonts. Motif builds on the X font model with the **XmFontList** type. A Motif font list stores a collection of X fonts that are tagged by character set labels.

To create a Motif font list, you must start with one font and then add others. You must load the fonts first using the X font loading function. In general,

**Figure 14.2   The Relationship Between the XmString
and XmFontlist Used in Listing 14.1**

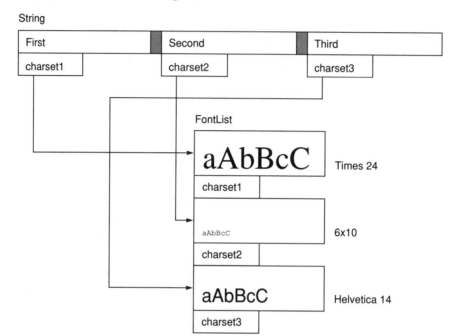

XLoadQueryFont provides the easiest way to do this: It loads the specified font into the designated display (or X server, as discussed in Chapter 15) and returns a result of the type **XFontStruct**. You can use this value to add the font to a Motif font list. Motif provides several convenience functions for manipulating font lists, described in Appendix I.

When adding a font to a font list, you must specify a *character set*, which is simply a string that names the font in the font list. You map the segments in an **XmString** to different fonts in the font list by specifying corresponding character set strings. **XmString**s and **XmFontList**s are closely related by the character sets: The font list determines how the string will look when drawn. The code in Listing 14.1 illustrates this relationship. It uses a drawing area widget and so the drawing portion may be easier to understand once you have finished Chapter 17. The code isolates font and string manipulations in the function **setup_string_and_fontlist**.

In Listing 14.1 the code creates an **XmString** containing three segments, kept apart by separators. Each segment specifies a different character set. The code then creates a font list containing three fonts (Times 24, a fixed font

Figure 14.3   A Single XmString Using Multiple Fonts

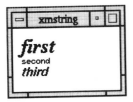

named 6x10, and Helvetica 14), each of which uses a character set name that corresponds to one of the character sets used in the string. In Listing 14.1, the character sets are called **charset1**, **charset2**, and **charset3**. However, you may wish to use the name of each font as the character set string (for example, Times24, 6x10, and Helvetica14 could be used as the character set names). Figure 14.2 illustrates the relationship between the **XmString** and the **XmFontList** created in Listing 14.1.

Figure 14.3 shows the output of Listing 14.1. As you can see, the character set names reference the different fonts in the font list so that the string displays as expected.

Listing 14.1   A Multifont XmString

```
/* xmstring.c */

#include <Xm/Xm.h>
#include <Xm/DrawingA.h>
#include <Xm/Form.h>
#include <Xm/PushB.h>

#define SIZE      100

XtAppContext context;

GC gc;
Widget toplevel;
Widget drawing_area;
XmString string;
XmFontList fontlist=NULL;

void setup_gc()
/* set up the graphics context. */
{
    int foreground,background;
    XGCValues vals;
```

```
    XFontStruct *font=NULL;
    Arg al[10];
    int ac;

    /* Set the default font in the GC--a necessary step. */
    font=XLoadQueryFont(XtDisplay(drawing_area),"fixed");

    /* get the current fg and bg colors. */
    ac=0;
    XtSetArg(al[ac],XmNforeground,&foreground); ac++;
    XtSetArg(al[ac],XmNbackground,&background); ac++;
    XtGetValues(drawing_area,al,ac);

    /* create the gc. */
    vals.foreground = foreground;
    vals.background = background;
    vals.font=font->fid; /* The XFontStruct contains a field named
                            "fid" of type Font, as expected by the GC. */
    gc=XtGetGC(drawing_area,GCForeground | GCBackground | GCFont,&vals);
}


void exposeCB(w,client_data,call_data)
    Widget w;
    XtPointer client_data;
    XtPointer call_data;
/* called whenever drawing area is exposed. */
{
    XmStringDraw(XtDisplay(drawing_area),XtWindow(drawing_area),
        fontlist,string,gc,10,10,1000,XmALIGNMENT_BEGINNING,
        XmSTRING_DIRECTION_L_TO_R,NULL);
}


void setup_string_and_fontlist()
/* create the XmString and the associated fontlist. */
{
    XFontStruct *font=NULL;
    char *namestring=NULL;
    XmString s1,s2,s3,sep,t1,t2,t3;

    /* Place three different fonts in the fontlist. */
    namestring="*times*24*";          /* you may need to change this */
    font=XLoadQueryFont(XtDisplay(toplevel),namestring);
    fontlist = XmFontListCreate(font,(XmStringCharSet)"charset1");

    namestring="6x10";                /* you may need to change this */
```

```
        font=XLoadQueryFont(XtDisplay(toplevel),namestring);
        fontlist = XmFontListAdd(fontlist,font,(XmStringCharSet)"charset2");

        namestring="*helvetica*14*";    /* you may need to change this */
        font=XLoadQueryFont(XtDisplay(toplevel),namestring);
        fontlist = XmFontListAdd(fontlist,font,(XmStringCharSet)"charset3");

        /* create three segments in an XmString and tie them to different
           fonts in the fontlists with corresponding charsets. */
        s1=XmStringCreate("first",(XmStringCharSet)"charset1");
        s2=XmStringCreate("second",(XmStringCharSet)"charset2");
        s3=XmStringCreate("third",(XmStringCharSet)"charset3");
        sep=XmStringSeparatorCreate();

        /* build the XmString. */
        t1=XmStringConcat(s1,sep);
        t2=XmStringConcat(t1,s2);
        t3=XmStringConcat(t2,sep);
        string=XmStringConcat(t3,s3);

        /* deallocate memory. */
        XmStringFree(s1);
        XmStringFree(s2);
        XmStringFree(s3);
        XmStringFree(sep);
        XmStringFree(t1);
        XmStringFree(t2);
        XmStringFree(t3);
}

main(argc,argv)
    int argc;
    char *argv[];
{
    Arg al[10];
    int ac;

    /* create the toplevel shell */
    toplevel = XtAppInitialize(&context,"",NULL,0,&argc,argv,
        NULL,NULL,0);

    /* set window size. */
    ac=0;
    XtSetArg(al[ac],XmNheight,SIZE); ac++;
    XtSetArg(al[ac],XmNwidth,SIZE); ac++;
```

```
    XtSetValues(toplevel,al,ac);

    /* create a drawing area widget. */
    ac=0;
    drawing_area=XmCreateDrawingArea(toplevel,"drawing_area",al,ac);
    XtManageChild(drawing_area);
    XtAddCallback(drawing_area,XmNexposeCallback,exposeCB,NULL);

    setup_gc();

    setup_string_and_fontlist();

    XtRealizeWidget(toplevel);
    XtAppMainLoop(context);
}
```

The **XmString** type imposes certain limits. For example, each segment can have only one character set, and each is displayed on a separate line. It is not easy, therefore, to display multiple fonts on a single line. As a result, programmers often place only one font in a font list and display all **XmString**s with that single font.

Motif widgets that have a font list resource use a default font list. Throughout the book, we have used **XmSTRING_DEFAULT_CHARSET** to access the default font in that font list. This specification simply tells Motif to choose the first font in the widget's font list. The *Motif PRM* calls the default character set in the default font list ISO8859-1. You can see this by extracting the default character set name from the default font list, using the code in Listing 14.2.

Listing 14.2   Extracting the Default Font String from the Default Font List for a Label Widget

```
/* default_font.c */

#include <Xm/Xm.h>
#include <Xm/Label.h>

XtAppContext context;
XmStringCharSet char_set=XmSTRING_DEFAULT_CHARSET;

Widget toplevel, label;

void main(argc,argv)
```

```
    int argc;
    char *argv[];
{
    Arg al[10];
    int ac;
    XmFontList fl;
    XFontStruct *font;
    XmFontContext font_context;

    /* create the toplevel shell */
    toplevel = XtAppInitialize(&context,"",NULL,0,&argc,argv,
        NULL,NULL,0);

    /* create the label widget */
    ac=0;
    label=XmCreateLabel(toplevel,"label",al,ac);
    XtManageChild(label);

    /* get the default font list */
    ac=0;
    XtSetArg(al[ac],XmNfontList,&fl); ac++;
    XtGetValues(label,al,ac);

    /* print out the charset name of the first font */
    XmFontListInitFontContext(&font_context,fl);
    XmFontListGetNextFont(font_context,&char_set,&font);
    printf("%s\n",char_set);
}
```

Listing 14.2 creates a label widget, then retrieves the font list from it and uses the **XmFontListGetNextFont** convenience function (Appendix I) to extract the name of the first character set. When you run this code, it outputs the string ISO8859-1, as expected.

One of the problems with using **XmSTRING_DEFAULT_CHARSET** is that it is defined as an empty string. Several synonyms for ISO8859-1 exist in Xm.h, however, including **XmSTRING_ISO8895_1**, **XmSTRING_OS_CHARSET**, and **XmFALLBACK_CHARSET**. Using these, or the literal string "ISO8859-1", yields the default character set, and therefore can be used in place of **Xm-STRING_DEFAULT_CHARSET**.

If you do not like the default character set, define a new font list and use any font and character set you choose.

14.3   THE MOTIF CLIPBOARD

You can use the Motif Clipboard to transfer information within or between Motif applications. Appendix I lists and describes in some detail the functions available for manipulating the Clipboard. You can access these functions by including the file <Xm/CutPaste.h>. The Clipboard has three unique features:

1. It has a locking facility which prevents more than one application from accessing the Clipboard at any one time when multiple applications run together.

2. It can store a single item of data in multiple formats, each of which has a unique name. For example, an advanced word processor might store an item on the Clipboard in the word processor's native format, in a standard format for transferring to other word processing programs, and in raw text format (STRING format) for copying to simple editors. A program pasting from the Clipboard can examine these different formats and choose the most appropriate one.

3. You can copy data onto it directly or by name. A direct copy moves a block of data directly from a buffer onto the Clipboard. A copy by name passes a callback function to the Clipboard. The callback function is called and the data is transferred to the Clipboard only if the item is pasted. Thus, the application can defer copying large data items until it needs to do so.

You can use the program in Listing 14.3 to examine the contents of the Clipboard at any time. This piece of code creates a push button that dumps the Clipboard's contents to stdout when clicked.

Listing 14.3   Retrieving the Contents of the Clipboard and Dumping Them to Stdout

```
/* clipboard_test.c */

#include <Xm/Xm.h>
#include <Xm/PushB.h>
#include <Xm/CutPaste.h>

XtAppContext context;
XmStringCharSet char_set=XmSTRING_DEFAULT_CHARSET;

Widget toplevel;
Widget button;

void show_status(status,s)
```

```
        int status;
        char *s;
{

    switch (status)
    {
        case ClipboardSuccess:
            printf("%s successful\n",s);
            break;
        case ClipboardLocked:
            printf("%s found locked clipboard\n",s);
            break;
        case ClipboardFail:
            printf("%s failed\n",s);
            break;
        case ClipboardTruncate:
            printf("%s truncated data\n",s);
            break;
        case ClipboardNoData:
            printf("%s found no data\n",s);
            break;
    }
}


void buttonCB(w,client_data,call_data)
    Widget w;
    XtPointer client_data;
    XmPushButtonCallbackStruct *call_data;
/* called whenever pushbutton is clicked. */
/* gets the contents of the clipboard and dumps it to stdout. */
{
    char format[1000];
    char buffer[10000];
    int status, private_id;
    unsigned long num_bytes;

    /* get the first format of the clipboard. */
    status=XmClipboardInquireFormat(XtDisplay(toplevel), XtWindow(w),
        1, format, 999, &num_bytes);
    format[num_bytes]='\0';
    show_status(status,"XmClipboardInquireFormat");
    printf("Format=%s\n",format);

    /* start the retrieve. */
    status=XmClipboardStartRetrieve(XtDisplay(toplevel), XtWindow(w),
        call_data->event->xbutton.time);
```

```
        show_status(status,"XmClipboardStartRetrieve");

        /* get the data and dump it. */
        status=XmClipboardRetrieve(XtDisplay(toplevel), XtWindow(w),
            format, buffer, 9999, &num_bytes, &private_id);
        buffer[num_bytes]='\0';
        show_status(status,"XmClipboardRetrieve");
        printf("format=%s\n",format);
        printf("Private ID=%d\n",private_id);
        printf("num of bytes=%d\n",num_bytes);
        printf("data=%s\n",buffer);

        /* end the retrieve. */
        status=XmClipboardEndRetrieve(XtDisplay(toplevel), XtWindow(w));
        show_status(status,"XmClipboardEndRetrieve");
        printf("---------------------------------------\n");
}

void main(argc,argv)
    int argc;
    char *argv[];
{
    Arg al[10];
    int ac;

    /* create the toplevel shell */
    toplevel = XtAppInitialize(&context,"",NULL,0,&argc,argv,
        NULL,NULL,0);

    /* create a push button */
    ac=0;
    XtSetArg(al[ac],XmNlabelString,XmStringCreate
        ("Push to dump clipboard contents",char_set)); ac++;
    button=XmCreatePushButton(toplevel,"button",al,ac);
    XtManageChild(button);
    XtAddCallback(button,XmNactivateCallback,buttonCB,NULL);

    XtRealizeWidget(toplevel);
    XtAppMainLoop(context);
}
```

To use the code in Listing 14.3, compile and execute the editor shown in Chapter 10. Cut or copy some text from the editor onto the Clipboard using the Edit menu, then click the push button created when Listing 14.3

is executed. A copy of the Clipboard's contents will be dumped to stdout. To retrieve the data from the Clipboard, the code extracts the name of the first format on the Clipboard. Since this item came from the text widget in the editor, we know that it will be stored in the STRING format. The code then retrieves the material using the format name and prints it to stdout.

14.4   MOTIF GADGETS

A gadget is virtually the same as a widget from both the programmer's and the user's point of view. The advantage of using a gadget, however, is that it takes less time and memory to create, manage, and update on the screen, thereby making an application smaller and faster.

The main difference between a gadget and a widget is that a gadget does not possess its own window. This means you must attach gadgets to a parent that has a window (almost always some type of manager widget). Note that you cannot attach gadgets to **toplevel**, because **toplevel** does not have a window that gadgets can use.

Listing 14.4 demonstrates how to use a gadget by creating a radio box filled with five toggle gadgets. Chapter 11 described the same process, but with toggle-button widgets instead.

Listing 14.4   Using Toggle Button Gadgets in a Radio Box

```
/* radio_gadget.c */

#include <Xm/Xm.h>
#include <Xm/ToggleBG.h>
#include <Xm/RowColumn.h>

XtAppContext context;
XmStringCharSet char_set=XmSTRING_DEFAULT_CHARSET;

Widget toplevel, radio_box, toggles[5];

void changeCB(w,client_data,call_data)
    Widget w;
    int client_data;
    XmAnyCallbackStruct *call_data;
/* called whenever one of the toggles changes state */
{
    Boolean set;
```

```
    Arg al[10];
    int ac;

    ac=0;
    XtSetArg(al[ac], XmNset, &set); ac++;
    XtGetValues(w,al,ac);

    if (set)
        printf("%d turned on\n",client_data);
    else
        printf("%d turned off\n",client_data);
}


void main(argc,argv)
    int argc;
    char *argv[];
{
    Arg al[10];
    int ac;
    int x;

    /* create the toplevel shell */
    toplevel = XtAppInitialize(&context,"",NULL,0,&argc,argv,
        NULL,NULL,0);

    /* create a Radio Box container to hold the toggles */
    ac=0;
    radio_box=XmCreateRadioBox(toplevel,"radio_box",al,ac);
    XtManageChild(radio_box);

    /* create 5 toggles */
    for (x=0; x<5; x++)
    {
        ac=0;
        XtSetArg(al[ac],XmNlabelString,
            XmStringCreate("I'm a toggle", char_set)); ac++;
        toggles[x]=XmCreateToggleButtonGadget(radio_box,"toggle",al,ac);
        XtManageChild(toggles[x]);
        XtAddCallback (toggles[x], XmNvalueChangedCallback, changeCB, x);
    }

    XtRealizeWidget(toplevel);
    XtAppMainLoop(context);
}
```

Listing 14.4's code differs from the radio box code shown in Chapter 11 in only two respects: The **#include** line includes `<Xm/ToggleBG.h>` instead of `<Xm/ToggleB.h>`, and it calls **XmCreateToggleButtonGadget** instead of **XmCreateToggleButton**. The toggle buttons look exactly the same whether they're implemented with widgets or gadgets.

Gadgets are available for labels, push buttons, toggles, separators, arrow buttons, and cascade buttons. To improve efficiency, you can create all menu buttons, button arrays in RowColumn widgets, separators attached to forms and bulletin boards, and all appropriate widgets in dialog boxes as gadgets instead of widgets.

14.5 SHELLS

The toplevel shell widget returned by **XtAppInitialize** possesses an impressive inheritance hierarchy. It is of the class **ApplicationShell**, and it inherits resources from **ToplevelShell**, **VendorShell**, **WMShell**, **Shell**, **Composite**, and **Core**. The toplevel widget thus provides 68 resource values that you can use to customize its appearance. The resource lists for all of these widgets appear at the end of Appendix J.

The toplevel widget inherits many resources important for its on-screen behavior from the **WMShell** widget. You can customize many aspects of an application's window, including the window's title, its icon pixmap, its minimum and maximum size, and so on. The code in Listing 14.5 shows how.

Listing 14.5 Manipulating the Toplevel Shell's Resources

```
/* shell.c */

#include <Xm/Xm.h>

#include "folder.xbm"

XtAppContext context;

Widget toplevel;

void main(argc,argv)
    int argc;
    char *argv[];
```

```
{
    Arg al[20];
    int ac;
    int foreground,background;
    Pixmap pix;
    unsigned int depth;

    /* create the toplevel shell */
    toplevel = XtAppInitialize(&context,"",NULL,0,&argc,argv,
        NULL,NULL,0);

    /* create the bitmap for the icon pixmap. */
    pix=XCreateBitmapFromData(XtDisplay(toplevel),
        RootWindowOfScreen(XtScreen(toplevel)),
        folder_bits,folder_width,folder_height);

    /* modify toplevel. */
    ac=0;
    XtSetArg(al[ac], XmNtitle, "Sample Title"); ac++;
    XtSetArg(al[ac], XmNminWidth, 200); ac++;
    XtSetArg(al[ac], XmNmaxWidth, 400); ac++;
    XtSetArg(al[ac], XmNminHeight, 200); ac++;
    XtSetArg(al[ac], XmNmaxHeight, 400); ac++;
    XtSetArg(al[ac], XmNiconPixmap, pix); ac++;
    XtSetArg(al[ac], XmNheight, 300); ac++;
    XtSetArg(al[ac], XmNwidth, 300); ac++;
    XtSetValues(toplevel,al,ac);

    XtRealizeWidget(toplevel);
    XtAppMainLoop(context);
}
```

The argument list passed to **toplevel** sets the window title, the minimum and maximum size of the window, the initial width and height of the window, and the icon pixmap that appears when you iconify the window (see Chapter 17 for information on pixmaps). Run the code and try resizing the window. Iconify the window to see the icon pixmap.

Refer to the end of Appendix J, or to the *Motif PRM*, for more information on the available resources.

15 THE X LAYER

The X Window System is a basic windowing system. It provides the fundamental resources and capabilities you need to create graphical applications. Sitting on top of X is the X Toolkit, on top of which sits Motif, as shown in Figure 15.1. A Motif application can use any of the four libraries in this stack: UNIX, X, Xt, or Motif.

In order fully to understand and use Motif, you need a basic understanding of X. As your knowledge of Motif grows, your knowledge of X should grow as well, because X contains functionality that can significantly enhance Motif applications or handle areas that Motif alone cannot handle (for example, resource databases, inter-client communication, drawing, and changing cursors). This chapter introduces you to some of the basics of X. Chapter 17 covers the X drawing model in detail and shows you how to use it to support graphics in a Motif program. A book such as Scheifler and Gettys's, or Jones's, provides detailed information on the X layer.

15.1   CAPABILITIES OF THE X WINDOW SYSTEM

The X Window System provides a number of different capabilities. The two most basic and frequently used are window creation and drawing. Each Motif widget that appears on the screen consists of a window and the drawing that represents the widget's contents. Other capabilities that X provides are less easy to see, but are nonetheless very important to the application. These capabilities include event and event loop handling, cursor management, resource management, color mapping, inter-client communication (the ability of different X applications to communicate with one another), input and output buffering, and so on. X provides its capabilities in a general way and does not specify what you should do with them. It does not say where windows should appear or how they should look. It simply provides the tools you need to create them. A widget set like Motif enforces a specific "look and feel" in user interfaces that you create.

243

Figure 15.1   The Motif/Xt/X/UNIX Hierarchy

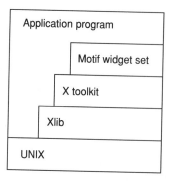

Application program — Accesses any layer in the hierarchy

Motif widget set — Implements a specific set of widgets that gives applications a certain look and feel

X toolkit — Allows the creation and management of object-oriented user interface widget sets

Xlib — Handles low-level window creation, drawing, and events

UNIX

One of the most interesting features of X is its handling of networks. Its fundamental design assumes the existence of networks, so using X over a network is completely transparent. The desire for this transparency drove many of the design decisions that led to X's structure and functionality.

15.2   THE X SERVER/CLIENT MODEL

A concrete example can help you understand the design of X as well as the server/client model. Assume that you have an X terminal on your desk, connected to a network. It is extremely important to understand the difference between an X terminal and a workstation. Unlike a workstation, an X terminal contains no general processing capabilities of its own, but like a normal dumb terminal depends on another machine somewhere on the network to perform the computations that update its display.

An X terminal consists of one or more screens (X supports multiple screens, but a single screen is the most common configuration), a keyboard, a mouse or other pointing device, a CPU, some RAM (typically 4 MB or so), and a network connection. Its CPU executes a single program, typically in ROM, that causes it to act like an *X server*, or a server of X for client programs running on other machines on the network. The *X server/client model* enforces a total separation of the X server and client programs: Clients generate commands that cause the X server to update its display, and the X server accepts actions from the user and sends them back to client programs as events.

Most of the time the X terminal is doing two things. First, when the user uses the keyboard or the mouse, the terminal packages the action as an event and sends it over the network to the client. The client responds to events by sending commands to the X server (the terminal). Second, the terminal interprets these commands to create windows, draw in them, and so on. The configuration is shown in Figure 15.2.

Figure 15.2   The X Server/Client Model

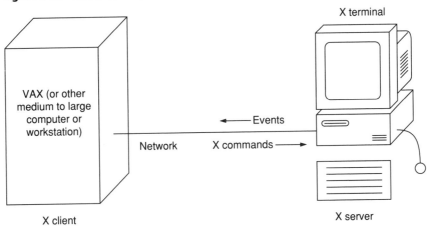

Together, the X terminal's screen, keyboard, and mouse are called a *display*. In order for an X client to do anything on the X terminal, it must use a function to open a communication path to a display. In a pure server/client situation, where the server is an X terminal and the client is running on another computer, the communication path is the network.

On a workstation, the situation is no different: The server and client remain completely separate, although they both happen to run on the same machine. A background process running on the workstation's CPU implements the X server as an independent entity. Client programs also run on the workstation (or client programs on other machines can use the workstation's X server over the network). In general, the client programs running on the workstation itself talk to the X server on the workstation through some relatively efficient mechanism such as shared memory. But keep in mind that there is still complete separation between the X server and its clients. As you might expect, this separation entails a performance penalty. By accepting X, the marketplace has decided that network transparency is more important than peak performance.

The *X protocol* controls the communication between the client program and the X server, specifying the format of bits and bytes in the network packets flowing between the two. The client program and its programmer do not have to worry about the actual format of the packets because Xlib.h—the library of functions, types, constants, and variables that provide the C programming interface to X—imposes a layer of abstraction between the protocol and the program. X can talk to any language, provided that a programming interface exists between the language and the protocol.

15.3   INSIDE AN X SERVER

An X server is an interesting device. For efficiency's sake, all of the basic resources provided by X are stored in the X server rather than in the client machine. These resources include windows, pixmaps, fonts, colormaps, cursors, and graphics contexts. Definitions of each of these resources follow. Scheifler and Gettys, in various chapters of *X Window System*, provide further details.

Window

A *window* is a rectangular area on the screen that you can draw in using X drawing commands. Windows in X can be nested and overlapped. They are specific to a given screen and have a strict ownership hierarchy. The Root window is the entire screen. Each window on the screen is owned by the root or another window on the screen. The tree that derives from this ownership hierarchy is called a *window tree*, and the entire tree resides in the X server.

Pixmap

A *pixmap* is a two-dimensional array of pixels, each of which consists of some number of bits known as the *depth* of the pixel. In general, all pixels on a given screen have the same depth. The depth determines the number of possible colors a single pixel can display. By convention, a pixmap of depth 1 is called a bitmap.

A pixmap is like a window, except that the window is on-screen and a pixmap is off-screen. You can perform all of the X drawing commands except **XClearArea** and **XClearWindow** in a pixmap as well as in a window. You can copy regions of pixels from pixmaps to windows and from windows to pixmaps, provided that the pixmap and the window are owned by the same screen and have the same depth. (See Chapter 17 for more information.)

Font

A *font* is a set of bitmaps, each of which determines how an individual character in the font appears on-screen. The font bitmaps are loaded from client to server when you first need them by using a font loading function such as **XLoadQueryFont**. (See Scheifler and Gettys.)

Colormap

On color systems, the *depth* of each screen pixel is often smaller than the full color range of the screen. For example, most screens can display 16.7 million colors per pixel. To save money, screen memory might consist of only one byte per pixel, giving each pixel a depth of 8 bits and a range of only 256 possible colors. A color map controls how the 256 possible colors map to the 16.7 million available colors. It controls the mapping of each 8-bit value to a specific 24-bit value. (See Scheifler and Gettys.)

Cursor

A *cursor* is a pointer on the screen whose movement follows the mouse. The appearance of the cursor is controlled by a pair of bitmaps, and it can change shape as it moves over different regions on the screen. (See Section 15.3.)

Graphics context

A *graphics context*, or GC, determines how a shape is drawn when one of the X drawing functions is invoked. A GC can control color, line width, pattern of pixels used during filling, and so on. (See Chapter 17 for more information.)

The fact that these resources exist in the server helps to make X more efficient. For example, a client program can create a pixmap, draw into it, and copy the contents of the pixmap to a window to provide smooth animation. Because the pixmap and window both reside in the X server, the copy operation takes place almost instantaneously. If the bits had to flow through the network during the copy operation, the usefulness of pixmaps would be severely diminished. On the other hand, the RAM available to the server can limit the space available for pixmaps.

The fact that these resources are allocated and stored in the server also requires that you use special functions to deallocate the space they occupy when you no longer need them. RAM limitations in many servers make the need for appropriate deallocation very important. The Xlib functions **XFreeColormap**, **XFreeCursor**, **XFreeFont**, **XFreeGC**, **XFreePixmap**, and **XDestroyWindow** provide appropriate ways to free each of the resources stored in an X server (see Appendix G for descriptions). You should use these deallocation functions as needed to avoid excessive consumption of RAM space in the X server.

Motif uses the X layer and the capabilities of the X server constantly. For example, each widget you see on-screen in an application consists of one or more windows created by X, as well as the contents of those windows created by X drawing commands. Because of the link between X and Motif, an interesting dichotomy occurs: The client program maintains a copy of the widget tree in the client's memory space, while the X server maintains the corresponding window tree for the application in the server's memory space.

15.4   X EVENTS

The X server is responsible for interpreting user events, packaging them, and sending them to the client so that it can respond to them appropriately. The concept of an event can best be explained with an example. The code in Listing 15.1 creates the simplest kind of X program: It contains no error checking and does no drawing. It simply creates one window, maps it to the screen, and starts processing its events.

Listing 15.1   A Very Simple X Program

```
/* xdemo.c */

#include <X11/Xlib.h>

Display *display;
Window window;
XEvent event;

void main()
{
    display=XOpenDisplay(NULL);
    window=XCreateSimpleWindow(display,XDefaultRootWindow(display),
        100,100,200,200,4,0,0);
    XMapWindow(display,window);
    XSelectInput(display,window,KeyPressMask | ButtonPressMask |
        ExposureMask);

    while (True)
    {
      XNextEvent(display,&event);
      printf("%d\n",event.type);
    }
}
```

To run the code in Listing 15.1, compile it using the following command:

```
cc -o xdemo xdemo.c -lX11
```

Then type xdemo to execute it. Now try clicking in the window, typing keys on the keyboard, and covering the window with another window and then uncovering it. Note that for each of these events, a number appears on the screen. This number is an integer that contains the event type for the event. The following code, which you can use to replace the bottom of Listing 15.1, provides another, slightly cleaner, way to handle the event loop:

```
while (True)
{
    XNextEvent(display,&event);
    if (event.type==ButtonPress)
        printf("ButtonPress event generated\n");
    else if (event.type==KeyPress)
        printf("KeyPress event generated\n");
    else if (event.type==Expose)
        printf("Expose event generated\n");
}
```

This code prints out appropriate messages instead of integers and is therefore easier to understand. **ButtonPress**, **KeyPress**, and **Expose** are constants defined in `Xlib.h` for each of the event types. These events are discussed below.

The program in Listing 15.1 starts by opening a connection to a display (an X server). The parameter **NULL** indicates that the contents of the environment's **DISPLAY** variable should be used for the display, but a connection to any display on the network can be formed by using the name of that display as the parameter. The program then creates a window on the display, using the root window of the specified display as its parent. The window's upper left corner is located at the point $100, 100$, and the window's size will be 200×200 pixels. The border width of the window is 4, and the border color and the background color are 0. The colors don't matter here, since the program does no drawing, but they would matter in a real application. The program then *maps* the window, making it visible.

Next, the program makes the window sensitive to certain user and system events using an event mask. This mask is a string of bits that specifies the events to which the window should be sensitive. The program in Listing 15.1 makes the window sensitive to three types of events: **KeyPress**, **ButtonPress**, and **Exposure**. If you omit this step, the window responds to no events of any type. You can use the following table of mask values to make any window in X sensitive to any of 25 possible event types. See Scheifler and Gettys for a detailed description of these event types and events in general.

KeyPressMask	ButtonMotionMask
KeyReleaseMask	KeymapStateMask

ButtonPressMask	ExposureMask
ButtonReleaseMask	VisibilityChangedMask
EnterWindowMask	StructureNotifyMask
LeaveWindowMask	ResizeRedirectMask
PointerMotionMask	SubstructureNotifyMask
PointerMotionHintsMask	SubstructureRedirectMask
Button1MotionMask	FocusChangeMask
Button2MotionMask	PropertyChangeMask
Button3MotionMask	ColormapChangeMask
Button4MotionMask	OwnerGrabButtonMask
Button5MotionMask	

The program now enters the event loop, duplicated below:

```
while (True)
{
    XNextEvent(display,&event);
    printf("%d\n",event.type);
}
```

The X server interprets events and stores them in an event queue. The event loop uses a call to **XNextEvent** to request an event from the event queue, and once the event has been extracted, a program generally parses it to determine which window it occurs in and what type of event it is. This parsing allows the program to handle the event correctly. Given that there are 25 different event types, and given that a typical large application has many nested windows on screen at once, the amount of code required to successfully parse the incoming events can be quite large. In Listing 15.1 the code does nothing but print out the event type as each event is received.

When you run the code, each keystroke, mouse click, and exposure generates an event. The code receives an **XEvent** structure returned by the call to **XNextEvent** and placed in the variable named **event**. The **XEvent** structure is a union of all of the possible event types, as shown below. This definition comes from Xlib.h.

```
typedef union _XEvent {
     int type;      /* must not be changed; first element */
     XAnyEvent xany;
     XKeyEvent xkey;
     XButtonEvent xbutton;
     XMotionEvent xmotion;
     XCrossingEvent xcrossing;
```

```
        XFocusChangeEvent xfocus;
        XExposeEvent xexpose;
        XGraphicsExposeEvent xgraphicsexpose;
        XNoExposeEvent xnoexpose;
        XVisibilityEvent xvisibility;
        XCreateWindowEvent xcreatewindow;
        XDestroyWindowEvent xdestroywindow;
        XUnmapEvent xunmap;
        XMapEvent xmap;
        XMapRequestEvent xmaprequest;
        XReparentEvent xreparent;
        XConfigureEvent xconfigure;
        XGravityEvent xgravity;
        XResizeRequestEvent xresizerequest;
        XConfigureRequestEvent xconfigurerequest;
        XCirculateEvent xcirculate;
        XCirculateRequestEvent xcirculaterequest;
        XPropertyEvent xproperty;
        XSelectionClearEvent xselectionclear;
        XSelectionRequestEvent xselectionrequest;
        XSelectionEvent xselection;
        XColormapEvent xcolormap;
        XClientMessageEvent xclient;
        XMappingEvent xmapping;
        XErrorEvent xerror;
        XKeymapEvent xkeymap;
        long pad[24];
} XEvent;
```

You can interrogate the **type** field to decide what type of event has occurred and then use the correct field of the union to access information in the event. The event structures for **KeyPress**, **ButtonPress**, and **Expose** events, for example, follow:

```
typedef struct {
        int type;                /* of event */
        unsigned long serial;    /* # of last request processed by server */
        Bool send_event;         /* true if this came from a SendEvent
                                        request */
        Display *display;        /* Display the event was read from */
        Window window;           /* "event" window it is reported
                                        relative to */
        Window root;             /* root window that the event occured on */
        Window subwindow;        /* child window */
```

```
        Time time;              /* milliseconds */
        int x, y;               /* pointer x, y coordinates in event
                                        window */
        int x_root, y_root;     /* coordinates relative to root */
        unsigned int state;     /* key or button mask */
        unsigned int keycode;   /* detail */
        Bool same_screen;       /* same screen flag */
} XKeyEvent;
typedef XKeyEvent XKeyPressedEvent;
typedef XKeyEvent XKeyReleasedEvent;

typedef struct {
        int type;               /* of event */
        unsigned long serial;   /* # of last request processed by server */
        Bool send_event;        /* true if this came from a SendEvent
                                        request */
        Display *display;       /* Display the event was read from */
        Window window;          /* "event" window it is reported
                                        relative to */
        Window root;            /* root window that the event occured on */
        Window subwindow;       /* child window */
        Time time;              /* milliseconds */
        int x, y;               /* pointer x, y coordinates in event
                                        window */
        int x_root, y_root;     /* coordinates relative to root */
        unsigned int state;     /* key or button mask */
        unsigned int button;    /* detail */
        Bool same_screen;       /* same screen flag */
} XButtonEvent;
typedef XButtonEvent XButtonPressedEvent;
typedef XButtonEvent XButtonReleasedEvent;

typedef struct {
        int type;
        unsigned long serial;   /* # of last request processed by server */
        Bool send_event;        /* true if this came from a SendEvent
                                        request */
        Display *display;       /* Display the event was read from */
        Window window;
        int x, y;               /* Upper left corner of expose rectangle */
        int width, height;      /* Width and height of expose rectangle */
        int count;              /* if non-zero, at least this many more */
} XExposeEvent;
```

In the **XKeyPressEvent** structure, the field of primary interest is **keycode**. In the **XButtonPressEvent** structure, the fields of interest are **x** and **y**. In The **XExposeEvent** structure, the fields **x**, **y**, **width**, and **height** specify the exposed rectangle.

The event loop also has another function: It flushes the output queue. X supports an event queue for incoming information as well as an output queue for requests to the X server. This output queue stores requests so that the program can send them to the server in bulk. The call to **XNextEvent** flushes this output queue, as does a call to **XFlush** (see Chapter 17).

From this simple example program you can begin to see Motif's advantages. Motif does almost all of the X interfacing for you. When you create and manage a widget, Motif is responsible for drawing the widget and creating its windows. When events arrive in a widget, Motif handles them for you and updates the screen as appropriate. Any events that interest you as the programmer are delivered to your code using the callback structure. With Motif, you avoid almost all of the event handling and drawing required in X.

15.5   USING X TO CHANGE CURSOR SHAPE AND MAKE NOISE

There are many reasons for using the X layer directly in your Motif programs. For example, since Motif has no drawing commands, you must use X to draw (see Chapter 17). You can also use X to change the cursor's shape. If your application is going to stall (stop processing events) for more than half a second or so, it is customary to change the cursor to a watch or an hourglass so that the user does not panic. The watch or hourglass frequently appears during file loading and saving, when a complicated figure is redrawn, and so on.

You can drop the code in Listing 15.2 into your program to make cursor changing easy.

Listing 15.2   X Code That Changes the Cursor

```
#include <X11/cursorfont.h>

void watch_cursor(Widget w)
/* change the cursor to a wrist watch shape. */
{
  Cursor c1;

  c1 = XCreateFontCursor(XtDisplay(w),XC_watch);
  XDefineCursor(XtDisplay(w),XtWindow(w),c1);
```

```
    XFlush(XtDisplay(w));
}

void normal_cursor(Widget w)
/* return the cursor to its normal shape. */
{
    XUndefineCursor(XtDisplay(w),XtWindow(w));
    XFlush(XtDisplay(w));
}
```

In general, you pass the toplevel widget to either of these functions so that the cursor shape applies to the entire application window. On the other hand, you can pass in a single widget from the application so that the new cursor shape applies only to that widget.

The code uses the X functions **XCreateFontCursor**, **XDefineCursor**, and **XUndefineCursor** to change the cursor's shape and return it to its previous shape (see Appendix G for descriptions). The **XCreateFontCursor** function loads the specified shape from the file /usr/include/X11/cursorfont.h. The **XDefineCursor** function defines the new shape in the specified widget, while the **XUndefineCursor** function returns the cursor to its prior shape. The call to **XFlush** changes the cursor immediately by flushing the X output buffer.

The file /usr/include/X11/cursorfont.h defines a large number of cursor shapes, any of which you can use by replacing the **XC_watch** parameter with the desired value. See the *OSF/Motif Style Guide* (Appendix C) for guidelines on cursor usage.

The X layer also provides access to available sound capabilities. Use the following call to **XBell** to cause the X server to beep.

```
XBell(display,percent);
```

display is the X display and **percent** controls the volume of the bell. If the display supports an adjustable volume on the bell, you can set the volume to any value between −100 and 100. The setting 100 provides maximum volume.

The X layer provides a wide range of capabilities, many of which can be used to add functionality to your Motif programs. You can learn a great deal by getting a book devoted to the X layer and studying the available features. (For example, Sheifler and Gettys or Jones, both cited in Appendix A.)

16 THE XT LAYER

Most of the abstraction offered by the Motif widget set comes from the layer below Motif: the X Toolkit layer, also known as Xt or "the Intrinsics." The X Toolkit makes the creation of widget sets possible. It also makes possible the object-oriented aspects of Motif programming—resources, callbacks, inheritance, and so on. *X Window System Toolkit*, by Asente and Swick, offers an in-depth look at the X toolkit and includes a great deal of material on how to create your own widgets and widget sets.

The Xt layer offers a number of capabilities that can be used to enhance Motif applications. The following sections offer some insight into this extended functionality by describing timeouts and work procs, event handlers, memory management functions, and so on.

16.1 TIME OUTS

A time out is like an alarm clock set to go off in a certain number of milliseconds. Once the alarm goes off, it is handled by a specified callback routine. Time outs are useful in any application that has to update itself periodically. For example, the xload application updates the load graph every specified number of seconds. The quota dial program discussed briefly in Chapter 9 updates its display every 15 seconds. You can use a time out to handle these updates and to perform other background processing.

To add a time out to a program, you have to make the event handler aware of it and create a callback function to respond to the callback it generates. Use the **XtAppAddTimeOut** function to add the time out.

XtAppAddTimeOut   *Add a timeout to the application.*

```
XtIntervalId XtAppAddTimeOut(
    XtAppContext context,
```

```
    unsigned long interval,
    XtTimerCallbackProc proc,
    XtPointer client_data);
```

context   The context value for this application.
interval   The time interval of the delay, in milliseconds.
proc   The callback function to call when the interval
               expires.
client_data   A four-byte piece of data passed to the callback
               function.

A typical call to this function might look like this:

```
id = XtAppAddTimeOut(context,1000,the_callback_function,client_data);
```

where **context** is the application's context variable, **1000** is the time delay
(in milliseconds), **the_callback_function** is the callback function, and **client_
data** is any four-byte value (as it is for any **client_data** parameter). The **id** result is of type **XtIntervalId** and uniquely identifies this time out. If necessary,
you can remove the time out before it goes off by calling **XtRemoveTimeOut**
and passing it **id**. Following is a typical callback function:

```
void the_callback_function(client_data, id)
    XtPointer client_data;
    XtIntervalId id;
/* function that is called when the timeout callback takes place. */
{
    do_whatever();
    XtAddTimeOut(context,1000,the_callback_function,client_data);
}
```

The callback function accepts the **client_data** and an **id** parameter. If you
need to trigger the time out again, you must add it again as shown here.

16.2   WORK PROCS

A work proc is similar to a time out, but you specify no time interval. Once
a work proc is registered, it calls its callback function as soon as there are no
other events pending in the event queue. The work proc is called repeatedly,
until a Boolean value of true returned by the work proc tells the system to stop
calling it. The following description identifies the work proc creation function.

XtAppAddWorkProc *Add a work proc to an application.*

```
XtWorkProcId XtAppAddWorkProc(
   XtAppContext context,
   XtWorkProc proc,
   XtPointer client_data);
```

context   The context value for the application.

proc   The callback function to be called.

client_data   A four-byte piece of data passed to the callback
               function.

You can register a work proc with the following code:

```
id = XtAppAddWorkProc(context,the_work_proc,client_data);
```

where **id** is of type **XtWorkProcId** and the parameters are the same as for a
time out. You can remove a work proc by calling **XtRemoveWorkProc** and
passing it **id**.

Following is a typical work proc callback function:

```
Boolean the_work_proc(client_data)
    XtPointer client_data;
/* work proc that is called when event loop is idle. */
{
    do_whatever();
    return False;
}
```

The callback receives the **client_data** parameter specified by **XtAppAddWork-
Proc**, does whatever it needs to do, and returns a Boolean value. If false, **the_
work_proc** remains registered and will be called again as soon as the event
loop is idle. If true, the work proc is removed.

The structure of the work proc lets you break up large tasks into small pieces
handled by multiple calls to the work proc function. The code in Listings
16.1 and 16.2 shows how to use work procs. The drawing area widget and the
drawing function **XDrawLine** are both discussed in Chapter 17.

In Listing 16.1, the code creates a drawing area and quit button, and draws
25,000 random line segments in the drawing area. On my machine, it takes
about 10 seconds for the drawing to complete. You should adjust the **NUM_**

LINES constant so that it takes approximately the same amount of time on your machine.

Listing 16.1   A Drawing Program That Does Not Use a Work Proc

```
/* noworkproc.c */

#include <Xm/Xm.h>
#include <Xm/DrawingA.h>
#include <Xm/Form.h>
#include <Xm/PushB.h>

#define NUM_LINES 25000
#define SIZE      500

XtAppContext context;
XmStringCharSet char_set=XmSTRING_DEFAULT_CHARSET;

GC gc;
Widget toplevel;
Widget drawing_area;
Widget button;
Widget form;
int rand_seed=10;
int line_index;

void setup_gc()
/* set up the graphics context. */
{
    int foreground,background;
    XGCValues vals;
    Arg al[10];
    int ac;

    /* get the current fg and bg colors. */
    ac=0;
    XtSetArg(al[ac],XmNforeground,&foreground); ac++;
    XtSetArg(al[ac],XmNbackground,&background); ac++;
    XtGetValues(drawing_area,al,ac);

    /* create the gc. */
    vals.foreground = foreground;
    vals.background = background;
```

```
        gc=XtGetGC(drawing_area,GCForeground | GCBackground,&vals);
}

int rand()
/* from K&R */
{
    rand_seed = rand_seed * 1103515245 +12345;
    return (unsigned int)(rand_seed / 65536) % 32768;
}

void exposeCB(w,client_data,call_data)
    Widget w;
    XtPointer client_data;
    XtPointer call_data;
/* called whenever drawing area is exposed. */
{
    int x;

    /* draw random line segments */
    for (x=1; x<=NUM_LINES; x++)
    {
        XDrawLine(XtDisplay(drawing_area),XtWindow(drawing_area),
            gc, rand()%SIZE,rand()%SIZE,rand()%SIZE,rand()%SIZE);
    }
}

void buttonCB(w,client_data,call_data)
    Widget w;
    XtPointer client_data;
    XtPointer call_data;
/* called whenever quit button is clicked. */
{
    printf("Quit button clicked\n");
    exit(0);
}

main(argc,argv)
    int argc;
    char *argv[];
{
    Arg al[10];
    int ac;

    /* create the toplevel shell */
    toplevel = XtAppInitialize(&context,"",NULL,0,&argc,argv,
```

```
        NULL,NULL,0);

    /* set window size. */
    ac=0;
    XtSetArg(al[ac],XmNheight,SIZE); ac++;
    XtSetArg(al[ac],XmNwidth,SIZE); ac++;
    XtSetValues(toplevel,al,ac);

    /* create a form to hold widgets */
    ac=0;
    form=XmCreateForm(toplevel,"form",al,ac);
    XtManageChild(form);

    /* create a push button */
    ac=0;
    XtSetArg(al[ac],XmNlabelString,
        XmStringCreate("Quit",char_set)); ac++;
    XtSetArg(al[ac], XmNtopAttachment, XmATTACH_FORM); ac++;
    XtSetArg(al[ac], XmNrightAttachment, XmATTACH_FORM); ac++;
    XtSetArg(al[ac], XmNleftAttachment, XmATTACH_FORM); ac++;
    button=XmCreatePushButton(form,"button",al,ac);
    XtManageChild(button);
    XtAddCallback(button,XmNactivateCallback,buttonCB,NULL);

    /* create a drawing area widget. */
    ac=0;
    XtSetArg(al[ac], XmNtopAttachment, XmATTACH_WIDGET); ac++;
    XtSetArg(al[ac], XmNtopWidget, button); ac++;
    XtSetArg(al[ac], XmNrightAttachment, XmATTACH_FORM); ac++;
    XtSetArg(al[ac], XmNleftAttachment, XmATTACH_FORM); ac++;
    XtSetArg(al[ac], XmNbottomAttachment, XmATTACH_FORM); ac++;
    drawing_area=XmCreateDrawingArea(form,"drawing_area",al,ac);
    XtManageChild(drawing_area);
    XtAddCallback(drawing_area,XmNexposeCallback,exposeCB,NULL);

    setup_gc();

    XtRealizeWidget(toplevel);
    XtAppMainLoop(context);
}
```

When you run this code, the expose event will cause the 25,000 segments
to be drawn. This causes a problem: Since it takes 10 seconds to draw 25,000
line segments, the user interface stalls for 10 seconds. Run the program, and

as soon as the window maps, click the quit button. The program does not
quit until after it draws all 25,000 segments. The delay occurs because the
main event loop is not processing events while the code is in the **exposeCB**
function.

A work proc can solve this problem. Replace the **exposeCB** function in
Listing 16.1 with that shown in Listing 16.2.

Listing 16.2 Adding a Work Proc to Listing 16.1

```
Boolean work_proc(client_data)
    XtPointer client_data;
/* The work proc divides the drawing of lines up into groups of 1000
   lines so that the event loop gets returned to regularly. */
{
    int x;

    for (x=0; x<=NUM_LINES/25 && line_index<NUM_LINES; x++)
    {
        XDrawLine(XtDisplay(drawing_area),XtWindow(drawing_area),
            gc, rand()%SIZE,rand()%SIZE,rand()%SIZE,rand()%SIZE);
        line_index++;
    }
    if (line_index<NUM_LINES)
        return False;
    else
        return True;
}


void exposeCB(w,client_data,call_data)
    Widget w;
    XtPointer client_data;
    XtPointer call_data;
/* called whenever drawing area is exposed. */
{
    XtWorkProcId id;

    line_index=0;
    id=XtAppAddWorkProc(context,work_proc,NULL);
}
```

In this code, **exposeCB** sets up a work proc, which divides the drawing task
into groups of 1,000 lines each. As each group completes, the work proc returns to the main loop so that it can process events before returning to the
work proc and the next 1,000 lines.

Now run the code again and click the quit button. The program quits almost immediately, because the quit button's events are processed during breaks in the work proc processing.

16.3   EVENT HANDLERS

At times, Motif gives you insufficient access to the events received by a widget. For example, as we will see in Chapter 17, you can access **ButtonPress**, **ButtonRelease**, and **ButtonMotion** events directly in a drawing area widget with the Xt function **XtAddEventHandler**. You can use this function on any widget in the Motif widget set to receive raw X events intended for the widget.

XtAddEventHandler   *Adds an event handler to a widget.*

```
void XtAddEventHandler(
    Widget w,
    EventMask mask,
    Boolean nonmaskable,
    XtEventHandler proc,
    XtPointer client_data);
```

w	The widget to which to apply the event handler.
mask	An X event mask.
nonmaskable	If true, the handler is called when a nonmaskable event is received.
proc	The callback function to be called.
client_data	A four-byte piece of data passed to the event-handling function.

A typical call to the function follows. This statement adds an event handler to the **drawing_area** widget. Each time the widget receives a **ButtonRelease** event, the function **handle_click** is called. No **client_data** is specified.

```
XtAddEventHandler(drawing_area, ButtonReleaseMask, FALSE,
    handle_click, NULL);
```

The **handle_click** function looks very similar to a callback function:

```
void handle_click(w,client_data,event)
    Widget w;
```

```
        XtPointer client_data;
        XEvent *event;
{
        printf("%d %d\n",event->xbutton.x,event->xbutton.y);
}
```

The only difference between this event-handling function and a callback function is that an **XEvent** is passed directly rather than being embedded inside of a callback structure.

16.4   INPUT EVENTS

In Chapter 9, we used the link library to execute a standalone text application. The link library uses a polling system that waits for input: The Motif application must perform a **link_read**, which blocks if input is not available and thus stalls the user interface, or the application must wait for input by calling **link_input_waiting** repeatedly in a work proc. Xt avoids stalling by providing a way to implement input streams using the **XtAppAddInput** function. This function causes your application to receive a callback at any time input appears in a specified input buffer. Thus, your program services input requests only when input is available. The programs shown in Listing 16.3 and 16.4 demonstrate the process.

**Listing 16.3   A Motif Program That Uses
XtAppAddInput**

```
/* input.c */

#include <Xm/Xm.h>
#include <Xm/SelectioB.h>

#define    OK      1
#define CANCEL     2

XtAppContext context;
XmStringCharSet char_set=XmSTRING_DEFAULT_CHARSET;

Widget toplevel, dialog, list;
int pipefd1[2];
int pid;

void dialogCB(w,client_data,call_data)
    Widget w;
    int client_data;
```

```
    XmSelectionBoxCallbackStruct *call_data;
/* callback function for the selection box */
{
    char *s;

    switch (client_data)
    {
        case OK:
            /* get the string selected by the user */
            XmStringGetLtoR(call_data->value,char_set,&s);
            printf("%s\n",s);
            XtFree(s);
            break;
        case CANCEL:
            exit(0);
            break;
    }
}

void handle_input(client_data, source, id)
    XtPointer client_data;
    int *source;
    XtInputId *id;
{
    char *t,s[10000];
    XmString xs;
    int len;

    len=read(*source,s,10000);
    /* If the len==0, then the child has terminated so kill
       off the input event. Otherwise, parse the block into its
       separate lines and place them into the list widget. The
       parsing is necessary because the block will probably
       contain several lines rather than just one. */
    if (len==0)
    {
        XtRemoveInput(*id);
        printf("Exec-ed program done.\n");
    {
    else
    {
        s[len]='\0';
        t=strtok(s,"\n");
        while (t)
```

```
            {
                xs=XmStringCreateLtoR(t,char_set);
                XmListAddItem(list,xs);
                XmStringFree(xs);
                printf("%s\n",t);
                t=strtok(NULL,"\n");
            }
        }
}


void setup_input_event()
forks
/* Sets up pipes and executes a text application in the child. */
{
    Arg al[10];
    int ac;

    pipe(pipefd1);
    if((pid=fork())==0)/*child*/
    {
        close(pipefd1[0]);
        close(1);
        dup(pipefd1[1]);
        execlp("sample","sample",(char*)0);
    }
    else
    /* Creates an input event handler for the pipe. */
    {
        close(pipefd1[1]);
        XtAppAddInput(context,pipefd1[0],XtInputReadMask,
            handle_input,NULL);
    }
}


void main(argc,argv)
    int argc;
    char *argv[];
{
    Arg al[10];
    int ac;

    /* create the toplevel shell */
    toplevel = XtAppInitialize(&context,"",NULL,0,&argc,argv,
        NULL,NULL,0);
```

```
/* create the selection box */
ac = 0;
XtSetArg(al[ac],XmNautoUnmanage,False); ac++;
XtSetArg(al[ac],XmNmustMatch,True); ac++;
XtSetArg(al[ac],XmNselectionLabelString,
    XmStringCreateLtoR("Pick a process to kill.",char_set)); ac++;
dialog=XmCreateSelectionBox(toplevel,"dialog",al,ac);
XtManageChild(dialog);
XtAddCallback(dialog,XmNokCallback, dialogCB,OK);
XtAddCallback(dialog,XmNcancelCallback,dialogCB,CANCEL);
XtUnmanageChild(XmSelectionBoxGetChild(dialog,
    XmDIALOG_HELP_BUTTON));
XtUnmanageChild(XmSelectionBoxGetChild(dialog,
    XmDIALOG_APPLY_BUTTON));
list=XmSelectionBoxGetChild(dialog,XmDIALOG_LIST);

setup_input_event();

XtRealizeWidget(toplevel);
XtAppMainLoop(context);
}
```

Listing 16.4   Example Text Program

```
/* sample.c */

#include <stdio.h>

main()
{
    int x;

    for (x=0; x<20; x++)
    {
        sleep(1);
        printf("Line %d\n",x);
        fflush(stdout);
    }
}
```

The code Listing 16.3 sets up a selection box widget in a toplevel shell, then calls **setup_input_event**, which forks the application. The child fork routes its stdout into one end of a pipe and then executes a standalone text application, which in this case is the sample program shown in Listing 16.4 (although you can substitute any text application). At the same time, the parent establishes an input event sensitive to the other end of the pipe using **XtAppAddInput**. Now the parent program returns to the event loop. As soon as input appears in the pipe, the event loop senses the input event and triggers the **handle_input** callback function. The **handle_input** function responds by reading the input buffer, formatting the data found there, and then displaying it in the selection box.

The sample application in Listing 16.4 is a simple text program that produces one line of output each second for 20 seconds. You can compile it with the command cc -o sample sample.c before running Listing 16.3.

When you run the program in Listing 16.3, the selection box slowly fills as the sample text program generates its output. The Motif application never stalls: While the selection box fills, you can still select items, click the OK button, and so on. The application receives events as input becomes available and responds to those events through a callback function.

The call to **XtAppAddInput** accepts five parameters, as shown below:

XtAppAddInput   *Specifies a callback function to be called when data becomes available.*

```
XtInputId XtAppAddInput(
    XtAppContext context,
    int source,
    XtPointer condition,
    XtInputCallbackProc proc,
    XtPointer client_data);
```

context	The application context.
source	The input stream.
condition	The condition for which to wait. Valid values are **XtInputReadMask**, **XtInputWriteMask**, and **XtInputExceptMask**.
proc	The callback function to call.
client_data	User-defined data.

In Listing 16.3, **XtAppAddInput** receives the application's context, the parent's end of the pipe, the input mask condition, the name of the callback function, and NULL for the client data.

Note that this technique will not work properly with many text programs, because those programs do not flush their output correctly when used with a pipe. Unfortunately, the same is true for most UNIX commands (`ls`, `find`, and so on). You can simulate the problem by removing the **fflush** call in Listing 16.4. If you recompile the code and run Listing 16.3, the selection box remains empty for 20 seconds until the application terminates, then suddenly fills with 20 lines.

16.5   XT MEMORY MANAGEMENT

The Xt layer provides its own versions of **malloc**, **calloc**, **realloc**, and **free**, called **XtMalloc**, **XtCalloc**, **XtRealloc**, and **XtFree**. The Xt versions are functionally equivalent to and interchangeable with the standard UNIX versions.

Xt also provides two convenience macros for memory allocation: **XtNew** (which accepts a type as a parameter) and **XtNewString** (which accepts a string as a parameter). **XtNew** calls **XtMalloc** and requests enough memory to hold an item of the type specified. **XtNewString** calls **XtMalloc** to allocate a block large enough to hold the string passed and performs a **strcpy** to copy the string into the new block.

Xt memory allocation functions have problems with error handling. For example, the **malloc** function returns a NULL pointer when it runs out of memory to allocate. The **XtMalloc** function, on the other hand, kills the application. I often use **malloc** instead of **XtMalloc** to avoid such problems.

XtMalloc   *Allocates memory.*

```
char *XtMalloc(Cardinal size);
```

size   Number of bytes to allocate.

XtCalloc   *Allocates an array of the specified size.*

```
char *XtCalloc(
    Cardinal num,
    Cardinal size);
```

num   Number of elements to allocate.
size   Size of each element.

XtRealloc   *Reallocates memory, copying old block to new.*

```
char *XtRealloc(
    char *ptr,
    Cardinal size);
```

ptr   Pointer to a block previously allocated.
size   New number of bytes to allocate.

XtFree   *Frees memory.*

```
void XtFree(char *ptr);
```

ptr   Pointer to block previously allocated.

XtNew   *Allocates enough memory for the type specified.*

```
type *XtNew(type);
```

type   Type of block required.

XtNewString   *Allocates enough memory for the string specified.*

```
String XtNewString(String s);
```

s   The string.

16.6   WARNING AND ERROR MESSAGES

Xt provides standard mechanisms for generating warning and error messages. You can use these mechanisms to create message databases, provide your own error handlers, and so on. Two routines for generating warning and error messages follow.

XtAppErrorMsg   *Generates an error message and exits the program.*

```
void XtAppErrorMsg(
    XtAppContext context,
    String name,
    String type,
    String class,
    String default,
    String *params,
    Cardinal *num_params);
```

context	The application's context.
name	The name of the error.
type	The type of the error.
class	The class of the error (e.g., the application's name).
default	The error message, possibly containing **%s** identifiers.
params	Substitution strings for **%s** identifiers.
num_params	The number of parameters in params.

XtAppWarningMsg   *Generates a warning message.*

```
void XtAppWarningMsg(
    XtAppContext context,
    String name,
    String type,
    String class,
    String default,
    String *params,
    Cardinal *num_params);
```

context	The application's context.
name	The name of the warning.
type	The type of the warning.
class	The class of the warning (e.g., the application's name).
default	The warning message, possibly containing **%s** identifiers.
params	Substitution strings for **%s** identifiers.
num_params	The number of parameters in params.

Do not worry about the name, type, and class parameters when you create a simple error or warning message. The code for creating a simple warning message appears in Listing 16.5.

Listing 16.5   Creating a Simple Warning Message

```
/* warning.c */

#include <Xm/Xm.h>
#include <Xm/PushB.h>
#include <Xm/CutPaste.h>

XtAppContext context;
XmStringCharSet char_set=XmSTRING_DEFAULT_CHARSET;

Widget toplevel;
Widget button;

void buttonCB(w,client_data,call_data)
    Widget w;
    XtPointer client_data;
    XmPushButtonCallbackStruct *call_data;
/* called whenever pushbutton is clicked. */
{
    XtAppWarningMsg(context,"","","",
        "You have clicked the push button.", NULL,0);
}

void main(argc,argv)
    int argc;
    char *argv[];
{
    Arg al[10];
    int ac;

    /* create the toplevel shell */
    toplevel = XtAppInitialize(&context,"",NULL,0,&argc,argv,
        NULL,NULL,0);

    /* create a push button */
    ac=0;
    XtSetArg(al[ac],XmNlabelString,
        XmStringCreate("Push for warning",char_set)); ac++;
    button=XmCreatePushButton(toplevel,"button",al,ac);
    XtManageChild(button);
```

```
XtAddCallback(button,XmNactivateCallback,buttonCB,NULL);

XtRealizeWidget(toplevel);
XtAppMainLoop(context);
}
```

When you click the button, the specified warning message is printed to stdout. If you replace the call to **XtAppWarningMsg** with a call to **XtAppErrorMsg**, the application will exit after generating the message.

16.7   XT FUNCTIONS FOR DEALING WITH WIDGETS

We have frequently used the Xt function **XtManageChild** to manage widgets. The Xt layer provides several additional functions you can use for widget creation and management.

XtCreateWidget   *Creates a widget. Use in place of **XmCreate** functions.*

```
Widget XtCreateWidget(
    String name,
    Widget_class class,
    Widget parent,
    ArgList args,
    Cardinal num_args);
```

name	The name of the widget.
class	The class of the widget. Get the class name of a widget from Appendix J.
parent	The parent widget of this widget.
args	A normal **al** argument list.
num_args	**ac**.

You can use the **XtCreateWidget** function in place of an **XmCreate** function call. Although there is no substantive reason to do this, you will sometimes see it in other programmers' code.

XtManageChild   *Manages the widget specified.*

```
void XtManageChild(Widget widget);
```

widget   The widget to manage.

The **XtManageChild** function manages a widget so that it can be mapped to
the screen. We have used this function throughout the book.

XtManageChildren   *Manage the widgets specified.*

```
void XtManageChildren(
    WidgetList children,
    Cardinal num_children);
```

children   A list of widgets to manage, in an array.
num_children   The number of widgets in the list.

The **XtManageChildren** function manages groups of children simultaneously.
In general, this is faster than managing children individually because it requires less geometry negotiation.

XtCreateManagedWidget   *Creates and manages a widget. Use in place of **XmCreate** func-*
tions.

```
Widget XtCreateWidget(
    String name,
    WidgetClass class,
    Widget parent,
    ArgList args,
    Cardinal num_args);
```

name   The name of the widget.
class   The class of the widget. Get the class name of a widget
              from Appendix J.

parent   The parent widget of this widget.

args   A normal **al** argument list.

num_args   **ac.**

The **XtCreateManagedWidget** function creates and manages the widget specified.

XtUnmanageChild   *Unmanages the widget specified.*

```
void XtManageChild(Widget widget);
```

widget   The widget to unmanage.

The **XtUnmanageChild** function unmanages a widget so that it can be unmapped. We have used this function throughout the book.

XtUnmanageChildren   *Unmanages the widgets specified.*

```
void XtManageChildren(
    WidgetList children,
    Cardinal num_children);
```

children   A list of widgets to unmanage, in an array.

num_children   The number of widgets in the list.

The **XtUnmanageChildren** function unmanages groups of children simultaneously. In general, this is faster than unmanaging children individually because it requires less geometry negotiation.

XtDestroyWidget   *Destroys the widget specified.*

```
void XtDestroyChild(Widget widget);
```

widget   The widget to destroy.

The **XtDestroyWidget** function destroys a widget and frees up its memory.

XtDisplay, XtWindow, XtScreen, XtParent, XtIsManaged, XtIsRealized, XtIsSensitive   *Return the specified information for a widget.*

```
Display XtDisplay(Widget widget);
Window XtWindow(Widget widget);
Screen XtScreen(Widget widget);
Widget XtParent(Widget widget);
Boolean XtIsManaged(Widget widget);
Boolean XtIsRealized(Widget widget);
Boolean XtIsSensitive(Widget widget);
```

widget   The widget.

All of these functions return information about a widget that you can use when calling X functions or when determining a widget's state.

17 DRAWING

Graphical user interfaces exist for two reasons: They make application programs more intuitive and easier to use, and they allow applications to produce graphical output on the screen. Pictures are often far easier to understand than words.

Up to this point, we have focused on the first of these two reasons: the creation of user interfaces with Motif. In this chapter, we will examine the second reason by looking at the X drawing model and learning how to use it.

One of the more interesting ironies of Motif programming is that Motif, a tool designed for implementing graphical user interfaces, has no drawing commands. It is nothing more than a set of user interface widgets and convenience functions. If you want to create computer graphics in a Motif program, you have to drop down two levels and talk directly to the X libraries. Figure 17.1 shows a diagram of how all of the libraries involved in Motif programming relate to one another.

In Figure 17.1, the UNIX libraries are the standard, such as `stdio`, `strings`, and `math`. The X libraries are those with which you access X functions and variables. The Xt libraries provide access to the X Toolkit functions and variables. And the Motif libraries provide access to the Motif widget set. The arrows show a strict hierarchy: The Motif libraries use the Xt, X, and UNIX libraries; the Xt libraries use the X and UNIX libraries; and the X libraries use the UNIX libraries. Any Motif application you write can access any of these libraries at any time. This accessibility allows Motif to omit drawing commands.

In this chapter, we will discuss the basics of drawing under X. This chapter also examines the Motif drawing area widget and its resize and exposure events, as well as pop-up menus because they are frequently used in drawing applications.

Figure 17.1 Relationships Between All of the Libraries Used in Motif Programming

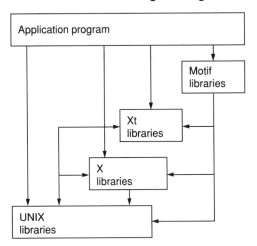

17.1 BASIC COMPUTER GRAPHICS CONCEPTS

A computer display is made up of a set of dots, called *pixels*, arranged in a two-dimensional array. Although the number of pixels on a given screen varies, a typical workstation might have a $1,024 \times 864$-pixel screen.

The pixels on a given screen have a *depth*, which is usually the same for all. A pure black-and-white screen—the cheapest and therefore the most common—can have either black or white pixels; No other colors are possible. The depth of such a screen is 1: that is, it takes one bit to determine the value, or color, of any one pixel. This type of display is often called a bitmap display, a bitmap being a black or white image. A pixmap, on the other hand, is an image with any depth greater than or equal to 1. A typical color display might have a depth of 8 bits, or 256 colors per pixel. An advanced color display might have 16.7 million colors per pixel and a depth of 24 bits or 32 bits, in which case the extra 8 bits provide customized graphics functions.

Graphics displays usually have at least two coordinate systems: screen coordinates and window coordinates, as shown in Figure 17.2. Screen coordinates start in the upper left corner of the screen itself. More often, you need to refer to the coordinate system of the window in which you are currently drawing. Each window has its own coordinate system, starting at 0, 0 in the upper left corner. This point is called the *origin*. From the origin, the positive X direction extends to the right, while the positive Y direction extends down. When you move a window on the screen, its window coordinate system moves with it.

Figure 17.2   The Screen and Window Coordinate Systems

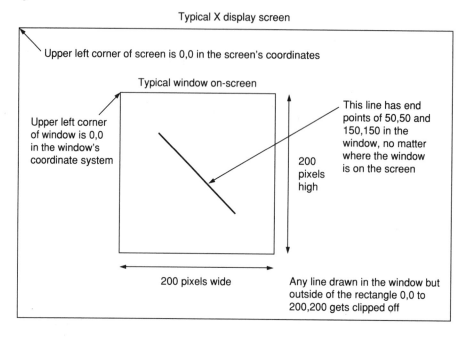

Typical X display screen

Upper left corner of screen is 0,0 in the screen's coordinates

Typical window on-screen

Upper left corner of window is 0,0 in the window's coordinate system

This line has end points of 50,50 and 150,150 in the window, no matter where the window is on the screen

200 pixels high

200 pixels wide

Any line drawn in the window but outside of the rectangle 0,0 to 200,200 gets clipped off

The upper left corner of the window is still 0, 0 no matter where the window appears on the screen.

All windows have a finite size that appears on the screen, but they are essentially infinite when you draw in them. For example, imagine a window 200 pixels wide by 200 pixels high. Anything you draw in the square extending from 0, 0 to 200, 200 will appear on the screen. You can draw anywhere, but the window automatically clips off anything outside of the square. In other words, if you draw a line from −500, −500 to −100, −100, from 100, 100 to 300, 300, or from 10000, 10000 to 11000, 11000, nothing evil will happen. The user simply will not see anything that falls outside of the 0, 0 to 200, 200 square established by the window. In the case of the −500, −500 to −100, −100 and 10000, 10000 to 11000, 11000 lines, nothing will appear on the screen. In the case of the 100, 100 to 300, 300 line, the unclipped half of the line will appear and the clipped half will not.

You can draw into either a window on the screen or a pixmap in memory. For example, when trying to create smooth animation, it is common to draw into a pixmap until you have completed a frame of the animation, and then

Figure 17.3 A Drawing Area Widget Displaying a Single Diagonal Line

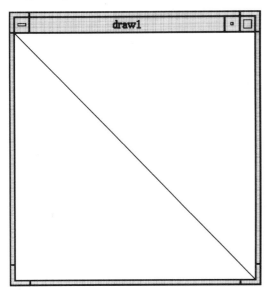

copy the completed image into a window for display. The pixmap or window in which drawing occurs is called a *drawable*.

17.1.1 DRAWING AREA WIDGETS

Let's start the discussion of X drawing commands by looking at a piece of code that draws a single diagonal line in a window, as shown in Figure 17.3. Enter the code shown in Listing 17.1 and run it. When the program is running, you should see on screen a window containing a single diagonal line. You should also see the message "Exposure event generated" in stdout whenever you expose part of the window: In other words, whenever you cover it with another window and then uncover it, or iconify and then expand it.

Listing 17.1 Drawing a Single Diagonal Line in a Drawing Area Widget

```
/* draw1.c*/

#include <Xm/Xm.h>
#include <Xm/DrawingA.h>

XtAppContext context;
```

```
GC gc;
Widget toplevel;
Widget drawing_area;

void setup_gc()
/* set up the graphics context. */
{
    int foreground,background;
    XGCValues vals;
    Arg al[10];
    int ac;

    /* get the current fg and bg colors. */
    ac=0;
    XtSetArg(al[ac],XmNforeground,&foreground); ac++;
    XtSetArg(al[ac],XmNbackground,&background); ac++;
    XtGetValues(drawing_area,al,ac);

    /* create the gc. */
    vals.foreground = foreground;
    vals.background = background;
    gc=XtGetGC(drawing_area,GCForeground | GCBackground,&vals);
}

void exposureCB(w,client_data,call_data)
    Widget w;
    XtPointer client_data;
    XtPointer call_data;
/* called whenever drawing area is exposed. */
{
    printf("exposure event generated\n");
    XDrawLine(XtDisplay(drawing_area),XtWindow(drawing_area),
        gc, 0, 0, 300, 300);
}

void main(argc,argv)
    int argc;
    char *argv[];
{
    Arg al[10];
    int ac;

    /* create the toplevel shell */
    toplevel = XtAppInitialize(&context,"",NULL,0,&argc,argv,
        NULL,NULL,0);
```

```
/* set window size. */
ac=0;
XtSetArg(al[ac],XmNheight,300); ac++;
XtSetArg(al[ac],XmNwidth,300); ac++;
XtSetValues(toplevel,al,ac);

/* create a drawing area widget. */
ac=0;
drawing_area=XmCreateDrawingArea(toplevel,"drawing_area",al,ac);
XtManageChild(drawing_area);
XtAddCallback(drawing_area,XmNexposeCallback,exposureCB,NULL);

setup_gc();

XtRealizeWidget(toplevel);
XtAppMainLoop(context);
}
```

The **main** function starts off normally by calling **XtAppInitialize** and resizing the window. It then creates a *drawing area* widget using the normal widget creation technique. A drawing area widget behaves like a drawing surface for X: Once you have established a drawing area, you can use any of the X drawing functions to draw in it. The X drawing functions allow you to draw points, lines, rectangles, arcs, and so on. As with any other widget, you can attach a drawing area widget to a form, make it sensitive and insensitive, resize it, and so on.

After the **main** function creates the drawing area, the drawing area's exposure callback is wired to the **exposeCB** function using a call to **XtAddCallback**, and a function is called that creates a graphics context. Note that the **main** function contains no code for drawing a line.

17.1.2   A DRAWING FAILURE

It might help you understand the code in Listing 17.1 if you look at a similar piece of code that does not work and then compare the two. Listing 17.2 is a program that is supposed to draw a line, but doesn't.

Listing 17.2   A Program That Does Not Draw a Single Diagonal Line

```
/* draw2.c*/

#include <Xm/Xm.h>
```

```
#include <Xm/DrawingA.h>

XtAppContext context;

GC gc;
Widget toplevel;
Widget drawing_area;

void setup_gc()
/* set up the graphics context. */
{
    int foreground,background;
    XGCValues vals;
    Arg al[10];
    int ac;

    /* get the current fg and bg colors. */
    ac=0;
    XtSetArg(al[ac],XmNforeground,&foreground); ac++;
    XtSetArg(al[ac],XmNbackground,&background); ac++;
    XtGetValues(drawing_area,al,ac);

    /* create the gc. */
    vals.foreground = foreground;
    vals.background = background;
    gc=XtGetGC(drawing_area,GCForeground | GCBackground,&vals);
}

void main(argc,argv)
    int argc;
    char *argv[];
{
    Arg al[10];
    int ac;

    /* create the toplevel shell */
    toplevel = XtAppInitialize(&context,"",NULL,0,&argc,argv,
        NULL,NULL,0);

    /* set window size. */
    ac=0;
    XtSetArg(al[ac],XmNheight,300); ac++;
    XtSetArg(al[ac],XmNwidth,300); ac++;
    XtSetValues(toplevel,al,ac);
```

```
      /* create a drawing area widget. */
      ac=0;
      drawing_area=XmCreateDrawingArea(toplevel,"drawing_area",al,ac);
      XtManageChild(drawing_area);

      setup_gc();
      /* Draw a line */

      XDrawLine(XtDisplay(drawing_area),XtWindow(drawing_area),
          gc, 0, 0, 300, 300);

      XtRealizeWidget(toplevel);
      XtAppMainLoop(context);
}
```

Listing 17.2 is very similar to Listing 17.1, except that it has no **exposeCB**
function. Instead, the command to draw the line appears in the **main** function. When you run this code, you should receive a message similar to the
following:

```
X Error of failed request:  BadDrawable (invalid Pixmap or
    Window parameter)
  Major opcode of failed request:  66 (X_PolySegment)
  Minor opcode of failed request:  0
  Resource id in failed request:  0x0
  Serial number of failed request:  26
  Current serial number in output stream:  40
```

This error message is generated by the **XDrawLine** call. The call to **XDrawLine**
is passed seven parameters, as shown below.

```
XDrawLine(XtDisplay(drawing_area), XtWindow(drawing_area), gc,
    0,0,300,300);
```

You must pass the first two parameters to every X drawing function. X supports multiple windows on multiple screens. Therefore, every time you want
to draw something, you have to tell X which X server and which drawable
(that is, which window or pixmap) you want to draw in. However, when you
use Motif widgets, you do not really care about such things. You simply use
the **XtDisplay** and **XtWindow** functions to extract the necessary information
from the drawing area widget into which you want to draw.

The third parameter is the graphics context. This code is correct and is not causing a problem, so we will come back to it later.

The final four parameters are the x and y coordinates of the two end points of the line, which in this case are 0, 0 and 300, 300.

Everything looks fine here, so why doesn't it work? At the time the call to **XDrawLine** is made, the drawable has not yet been mapped to the screen. It will not be mapped until the toplevel shell is realized and the event loop has been entered. When the program tries to draw at this point in the **main** function, the fact that the drawable does not exist causes the **XDrawLine** function call to fail and generates a **BadDrawable** error to tell you about it.

17.1.3   USING THE EXPOSE CALLBACK

How do you get around this problem? You need a piece of line-drawing code that is activated after the drawing area widget has been mapped to the screen. One possible solution is to create a form widget and attach a push button and a drawing area to it. This push button and a blank drawing area are what the user will see when the application starts. You can place the call to **XDrawLine** in the push button's callback function so that the application draws the line in the drawing area when the user clicks the push button. Listing 17.3 contains the code that produces this solution.

Listing 17.3   Drawing a Single Diagonal Line When the User Clicks a Push Button

```
/* draw3.c*/

#include <Xm/Xm.h>
#include <Xm/DrawingA.h>
#include <Xm/Form.h>
#include <Xm/PushB.h>

XtAppContext context;
XmStringCharSet char_set=XmSTRING_DEFAULT_CHARSET;

GC gc;
Widget toplevel;
Widget drawing_area;
Widget button;
Widget form;
```

```
void setup_gc()
/* set up the graphics context. */
{
    int foreground,background;
    XGCValues vals;
    Arg al[10];
    int ac;

    /* get the current fg and bg colors. */
    ac=0;
    XtSetArg(al[ac],XmNforeground,&foreground); ac++;
    XtSetArg(al[ac],XmNbackground,&background); ac++;
    XtGetValues(drawing_area,al,ac);

    /* create the gc. */
    vals.foreground = foreground;
    vals.background = background;
    gc=XtGetGC(drawing_area,GCForeground | GCBackground,&vals);
}

void buttonCB(w,client_data,call_data)
    Widget w;
    XtPointer client_data;
    XtPointer call_data;
/* called whenever drawing area is exposed. */
{
    printf("button clicked\n");
    XDrawLine(XtDisplay(drawing_area),XtWindow(drawing_area),
        gc, 0, 0, 300, 300);
}

void main(argc,argv)
    int argc;
    char *argv[];
{
    Arg al[10];
    int ac;

    /* create the toplevel shell */
    toplevel = XtAppInitialize(&context,"",NULL,0,&argc,argv,
        NULL,NULL,0);

    /* set window size. */
    ac=0;
    XtSetArg(al[ac],XmNheight,300); ac++;
```

```
XtSetArg(al[ac],XmNwidth,300); ac++;
XtSetValues(toplevel,al,ac);

/* create a form to hold widgets */
ac=0;
form=XmCreateForm(toplevel,"form",al,ac);
XtManageChild(form);

/* create a push button */
ac=0;
XtSetArg(al[ac],XmNlabelString,
    XmStringCreate("Push to draw line",char_set)); ac++;
XtSetArg(al[ac], XmNtopAttachment, XmATTACH_FORM); ac++;
XtSetArg(al[ac], XmNrightAttachment, XmATTACH_FORM); ac++;
XtSetArg(al[ac], XmNleftAttachment, XmATTACH_FORM); ac++;
button=XmCreatePushButton(form,"button",al,ac);
XtManageChild(button);
XtAddCallback(button,XmNactivateCallback,buttonCB,NULL);

/* create a drawing area widget. */
ac=0;
XtSetArg(al[ac], XmNtopAttachment, XmATTACH_WIDGET); ac++;
XtSetArg(al[ac], XmNtopWidget, button); ac++;
XtSetArg(al[ac], XmNrightAttachment, XmATTACH_FORM); ac++;
XtSetArg(al[ac], XmNleftAttachment, XmATTACH_FORM); ac++;
XtSetArg(al[ac], XmNbottomAttachment, XmATTACH_FORM); ac++;
drawing_area=XmCreateDrawingArea(form,"drawing_area",al,ac);
XtManageChild(drawing_area);

setup_gc();

XtRealizeWidget(toplevel);
XtAppMainLoop(context);
}
```

Run Listing 17.3 and click the push button. Note that the line no longer lines up with the bottom right corner any more, because the drawing area widget is no longer 300 × 300 pixels, since the push button is taking up some space. Even though the code draws a line that extends beyond the window's boundaries, nothing "bad" happens; the window simply clips off the part that falls outside.

Now move another window so that it overlaps part of the diagonal line, and then move it back out of the way. Figures 17.4 and 17.5 show what happens: Once the window moves away, the part of the line that the window over-

**Figure 17.4   A View of the Application Showing the
Push Button and an Intact Diagonal Line**

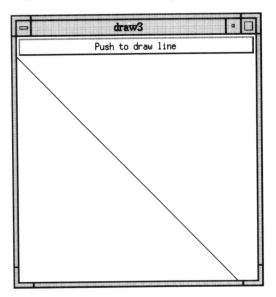

lapped is erased. (The application may behave differently on your machine. If your version of X supports a backing store, it restores the line when you move the overlapping window.)

Exposure events come into play here. Whenever part of a drawing area is exposed and needs to be redrawn, the X server generates an expose event and Motif passes it to the drawing area widget. This event tells your code to redraw part or all of the drawing area. By hooking in the drawing area's **expose** callback, your code can handle exposure automatically.

The code in Listing 17.1 demonstrated this process. When the drawing area appears on-screen initially, it generates a callback to the **exposeCB** function, which tells the code to draw a diagonal line. Subsequently, any time the window is exposed and must be redrawn, the callback function is called and the code draws the line again. Thus, the window displays the line continuously and correctly.

17.2   UNDERSTANDING THE GRAPHICS CONTEXT

Now that you have seen the correct way to draw a line in a drawing area widget using the drawing area's **expose** callback, we will turn to the topic of graphics contexts. A graphics context, or GC, is a structure that contains all of the information necessary to control the appearance of any object drawn with

Figure 17.5 A View of the Application After an Overlapping Window Has Been Removed

Note that the area previously occupied by the window is now blank.

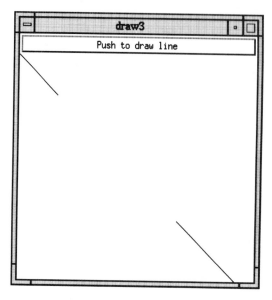

X. This section only scratches the surface. For complete information, refer to Scheifler and Gettys.

Say you want to draw a line. The line has two end points as well as a number of attributes that control its appearance, such as its colors, width, pattern, and style. When you draw a line, you call the **XDrawLine** function and pass it a GC variable along with the coordinates of the two end points. The GC variable contains all of the appearance information.

The following structure definition shows you the values that are held by a GC variable.

```
/*
 * Data structure for setting graphics context.
 */
typedef struct {
        int function;              /* logical operation (copy,
                                         xor, etc.) */
        unsigned long plane_mask; /* plane mask */
        unsigned long foreground; /* foreground pixel color */
        unsigned long background; /* background pixel color*/
        int line_width;           /* line width */
```

```
        int line_style;              /* LineSolid, LineOnOffDash,
                                            LineDoubleDash */
        int cap_style;               /* CapNotLast, CapButt,
                                            CapRound, CapProjecting */
        int join_style;              /* JoinMiter, JoinRound, JoinBevel */
        int fill_style;              /* FillSolid, FillTiled, FillStippled,
                                            FillOpaqueStippled */
        int fill_rule;               /* EvenOddRule, WindingRule */
        int arc_mode;                /* ArcChord, ArcPieSlice */
        Pixmap tile;                 /* tile pixmap for tiling
                                            operations */
        Pixmap stipple;              /* stipple 1 plane pixmap for
                                            stippling */
        int ts_x_origin;             /* offset for tile or stipple
                                            operations */
        int ts_y_origin;
        Font font;                   /* default text font for text
                                            operations */
        int subwindow_mode;          /* ClipByChildren,
                                            IncludeInferiors */
        Bool graphics_exposures;     /* boolean, should exposures be
                                            generated */
        int clip_x_origin;           /* origin for clipping */
        int clip_y_origin;
        Pixmap clip_mask;            /* bitmap clipping mask */
        int dash_offset;             /* patterned/dashed line
                                            information */
        char dashes;
} XGCValues;
```

This structure definition comes from the Xlib.h include file. Each of the variables has a default value, as shown below:

function	**GXcopy**
plane_mask	All ones
foreground	0
background	1
line_width	0
line_style	**LineSolid**
cap_style	**CapButt**
join_style	**JoinMiter**
fill_style	**FillSolid**
fill_rule	**EvenOddRule**

arc_mode	**ArcPieSlice**
tile	Pixmap filled with foreground pixel color
stipple	Pixmap filled with ones
ts_x_origin	0
ts_y_origin	0
font	Implementation dependent, probably Fixed
subwindow_mode	**ClipByChildren**
graphics_exposures	True
clip_x_origin	0
clip_y_origin	0
clip_mask	None
dash_offset	0
dashes	4

Note that the foreground and background colors default to 1 and 0 automatically. On almost any color system, the user will want to change these. The line width defaults to 0, which does not make much sense unless you know that zero is a special value that means "Let any graphics acceleration hardware available on the system generate the line." A line width of 0 therefore produces the same line that a line width of 1 does, but any available graphics hardware accelerates the drawing of the line.

In Listing 17.1, the **setup_gc** function sets up a graphics context in the following way:

```
void setup_gc()
/* set up the graphics context. */
{
  int foreground,background;
  XGCValues vals;
  Arg al[10];
  int ac;

  /* get the current fg and bg colors. */
  ac=0;
  XtSetArg(al[ac], XmNforeground, &foreground); ac++;
  XtSetArg(al[ac], XmNbackground, &background); ac++;
  XtGetValues(drawing_area, al, ac);

  /* create the gc. */
  vals.foreground = foreground;
  vals.background = background;
  gc= XtGetGC(drawing_area, GCForeground | GCBackground, &vals);
}
```

This function declares an **XGCValues** structure, called **vals** here. It makes a standard **XtGetValues** call to extract the foreground and background colors of the drawing area widget. It is likely that some resource file has set these colors, especially if the code is running on a color system. The function then sets the `foreground` and `background` fields of the **vals** structure appropriately.

Finally, a call to **XtGetGC** is made. The parameters for **XtGetGC** are as follows:

XtGetGC *Returns a shareable, read-only GC.*

```
GC XtGetGC(
    Widget w,
    XtGCMask value_mask,
    XGCValues *values)
```

w	The widget.
value_mask	Specifies fields in the GC that will be modified.
values	Specifies the values with which to modify the GC defaults.

The call to **XtGetGC** creates a **GC**, sets all of its values to the default values, and then modifies the specified fields to the values held in the **vals** structure. Note that you must pass the *address* of the **vals** structure.

The **value_mask** parameter is a bit string formed by joining bit values with Boolean OR statements. You create the names of these mask bit values by taking the field names found in the **XGCValues** structure, capitalizing the first character, adding "GC" to them, removing any underscore characters, and converting to uppercase any characters that immediately followed an underscore. For example, the mask bit for the `clip_x_origin` field is **GCClipX-Origin**. In the **setup_gc** function shown here, only the foreground and background colors change from their default values. Suppose you also want to change the line width. The following fragment shows what changes to make:

```
/* create the gc. */
vals.foreground = foreground;
vals.background = background;
vals.line_width = 5;
gc= XtGetGC(drawing_area, GCForeground | GCBackground | GCLineWidth,
    &vals);
```

Change other fields in a similar manner.

The **XtGetGC** function returns a value of type GC. All of the X drawing functions expect this type of value. Note that a variable of type **GC** is an X server resource (Chapter 15): **GC**s consume X server memory space. To free up a **GC**, use the **XtReleaseGC** function and pass it the GC variable.

It is common to have many GCs associated with an application. For example, if you want to draw some lines one pixel wide and other lines five pixels wide, you typically create two different **GC** variables and use each when appropriate. Because **GC**s are cached in the X server, this method provides the fastest performance. When you change a **GC**, the information about the change must travel over the network to the server, which can be time-consuming.

In some cases, you may need to change a GC. For example, you may want to draw in 4,000 different colors, thus making GCs for each color impractical. X therefore provides a number of functions, such as **XSetForeground**, **XSetBackground**, and **XSetClipOrigin**. Since **XtGetGC** returns a read-only GC, you should use **XCreateGC** to create a GC that you plan to change.

XCreateGC   *Returns a new GC.*

```
GC XtGetGC(
    Display *disp,
    Drawable draw,
    unsigned long value_mask,
    XGCValues *values)
```

disp, draw	The display and drawable.
value_mask	Specifies fields in the GC that will be modified.
values	Specifies the values with which to modify the GC defaults.

The choice of whether to create multiple GCs with **XtGetGC** or to create one GC and then modify it must be made on an application-by-application basis. If an application needs only ten or twenty GCs, you should create multiple GCs. On the other hand, if you will use numerous colors or will frequently change the clip origin, a single changeable GC is called for.

Below is a brief discussion of what each field in **XGCValues** does and the values it can hold.

function

The drawing function determines the logical operation that places the source pixels—what you are drawing, such as a line or an arc—into the destination: the window or pixmap in which the drawing occurs. The default drawing function, **GXcopy**, by far the most common drawing function, copies the source pixels into the destination pixmap without regard for the destination pixmap's existing contents; however, there are many other possibilities. The entire set of drawing functions follows. In this list, "src" represents the source pixels being drawn, while "dst" represents the destination pixmap or window in which the drawing occurs.

GXclear	0 (0 is copied into dst for all points in src)
GXand	src AND dst
GXandReverse	src AND NOT dst
GXcopy	src (pixels in src replace those in dst)
GXandInverted	(NOT src) AND dst
GXnoop	dst (do nothing)
GXxor	src XOR dst
GXor	src OR dst
GXnor	(NOT src) AND (NOT dst)
GXequiv	(NOT src) XOR dst
GXinvert	NOT dst (the inverse of dst for all points in src)
GXorReverse	src OR (NOT dst)
GXcopyInverted	NOT src
GXorInverted	(NOT src) OR dst
GXnand	(NOT src) OR (NOT dst)
GXset	1 (1 is copied into dst for all points in src)

plane_mask

The `plane_mask` field controls which planes of the destination pixmap the drawing operation affects. If the bit in the plane mask is 1, that plane is modified. If the bit is 0, the drawing operation does not affect that plane.

foreground, background

These fields contain the foreground and background colors for drawing. The background color is irrelevant when drawing points, lines, rectangles, and so on, but applies to such things as text and tiling. Both fields accept integer values. On a bitmap screen (depth 1), only the values 0 and 1 are valid. On a screen with depth 8, values between 0 and 255 are valid, and on a screen with depth 24, values between 0 and 16,777,215 are valid.

line_width

The line_width field controls the width of the line in the drawing of a line, rectangle, or arc. Zero is a special value meaning "Draw a line 1 pixel wide using any available graphics acceleration hardware." Values greater than zero indicate that a line width of the specified number of pixels should be used.

line_style

This field determines the type of dashed line. **LineSolid** draws a solid line. **LineDoubleDash** draws odd dashes using the current **fill_style**, and even dashes as in **LineSolid**. **LineOnOffDash** draws even dashes as in **LineSolid**, but draws nothing for odd dashes.

cap_style

This field affects the drawing of ends of lines and arcs. **CapButt** draws square ends on lines and arcs. **CapRound** draws the ends of lines and arcs rounded off (effective only if the **line_width** is greater than 2). **CapProjecting** extends the end point of the line a distance equal to one-half of the line's width. **CapNotLast**, on lines with width 0, does not draw the end-point pixel.

join_miter

This field affects how the corners look where lines with widths greater than 1 join. **JoinMiter** joins lines normally, **joinRound** joins lines with rounded corners, and **joinBevel** joins lines with beveled edges.

fill_style

The fill_style field determines the drawing of filled and dashed objects. **Fill-Solid** fills using the foreground color. **FillTiled** uses the fill tile. **FillStippled** fills using the foreground color masked by the stipple bitmap. **FillOpaqueStippled** fills like **FillTiled**, but uses the stipple values to create the tile.

fill_rule

When drawing filled polygons, the fill_rule field determines which parts to fill. The **WindingRulevalue**, for example, fills the polygon solid. The **EvenOddRule** value is somewhat esoteric; try it on a filled polygon with intersecting sides and see what happens. As different parts of a complex polygon are drawn, the **EvenOddRule** specifies which parts are "inside" the polygon and therefore filled. See Scheifler and Gettys for a complete description.

arc_mode

The `arc_mode` field determines how the undrawn portion of a filled arc is handled. **ArcPieSlice** causes the part of an arc that is not filled to be treated as a pie slice, while **ArcChord** causes it to be treated as a straight edge of the chord drawn between the starting and ending angles of the arc, as shown here:

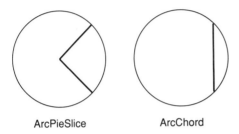

ArcPieSlice   ArcChord

tile

The `tile` field is a pixmap of the same depth as the drawable. You can use `tile` to draw tiled patterns in filled objects: The pixmap pattern it holds is repeated across the object being filled. See `fill_style`.

stipple

The `stipple` field is a bitmap that determines which bits are drawn and not drawn. See `fill_style`.

ts_x_origin, ts_y_origin

This is the origin that controls tiling and stippling.

font

This is the font used for any text operation. See the section on text drawing below for an example of changing the `font` field.

clip_mask, clip_x_origin, clip_y_origin

The **clip_mask** field is a bitmap that can control where drawing takes place. If a **clip_mask** is defined, only pixels where the mask contains the value 1 are drawn. The origin of the **clip_mask** is the position for the upper left corner of the masking bitmap.

17.3   DRAWING COMMANDS IN X

At this point, you should have a general feel for drawing in Motif. You should understand how to create a drawing area widget; how to draw a line in it; how to set up, customize, and use a GC; and how and why a drawing area's exposure event is important in maintaining the drawing on-screen. In this section, we will look at the X functions for drawing different shapes in a drawing area. All of them follow the model of **XDrawLine**.

Almost all of the commands below come in two versions: "draw one" and "draw many at once." If you have to draw 100 lines, for example, the drawing takes place more quickly when you use the "draw many" version.

17.3.1   DRAWING POINTS

The **XDrawPoint** function lets you set the color of an individual pixel in a drawing area. A typical call to this function looks like this:

```
XDrawPoint(XtDisplay(da),XtWindow(da),gc,x,y);
```

The **da** variable is a drawing area widget. The parameters **x** and **y** are the coordinates of the pixel you want to change. The pixel is colored according to the contents of the GC parameter.

If you want to draw many points at once, use **XDrawPoints**. A typical call looks like this:

```
XDrawPoints(XtDisplay(da),XtWindow(da),gc,points,num,CoordModeOrigin);
```

where **points** and **num** have been declared as follows:

```
XPoint points[100];
int num;
```

The **points** parameter can be either an array of **XPoints**, as shown here, or a pointer to such an array (which you have allocated or acquired in a similar manner). The **num** parameter indicates the number of values in the array. The declaration of **XPoint** is defined by Xlib.h as follows:

```
typedef struct {
    short x,y;
} XPoint;
```

The function shown in Listing 17.4 demonstrates how to use **XDrawPoints** by drawing a 10 × 10 square of pixels. Assume that **da** and **gc** are global and valid.

Listing 17.4 Drawing a Block of Points

```
void draw_points()
{
    int x,y;
    XPoint points[100];
    int num=100;

    for (x=0; x<10; x++)
        for (y=0; y<10; y++)
        {
            points[x*10+y].x=x;
            points[x*10+y].y=y;
        }
    XDrawPoints(XtDisplay(da),XtWindow(da),gc,
        points,num,CoordModeOrigin);
}
```

The **CoordModeOrigin** parameter specifies that all point coordinates in the point array are referenced from the origin. You can also use **CoordModePrevious**, which adds the coordinates of a point in the point array to the coordinates of the previous point to determine its position.

17.3.2 DRAWING LINES

XDrawLine draws a single line

```
XDrawLine(XtDisplay(da), XtWindow(da), gc, x1, y1, x2, y2);
```

where **x1,y1** and **x2,y2** specify the end points of the line to be drawn.

You can draw groups of lines in either of two ways. You can use **XDrawLines** to draw a set of lines with contiguous end points (that is, the end of one line acts as the beginning of the next). Or you can use **XDrawSegments** to draw groups of independent lines. A call to **XDrawLines** looks exactly like **XDrawPoints**:

```
XDrawLines(XtDisplay(da), XtWindow(da), gc,
    points, num, CoordModeOrigin);
```

Contiguous pairs of points in the array act as the end points of the lines; for example **points[0]** to **points[1]** are a line, and **points[1]** to **points[2]** are a line, and so on. The points array and mode work exactly as in **XDrawPoints**. If the last point in the array is identical to the first point, **XDrawLines** draws a polygon.

To draw groups of lines that are independent of one another, use **XDrawSegments**, as shown below:

```
XDrawSegments(XtDisplay(da), XtWindow(da), gc, segments, num);
```

Declare the **segments** parameter as follows, or as a pointer to such an array:

```
XSegment segments[100];
```

X defines the **XSegment** type as follows:

```
typedef struct {
    short x1,y1,x2,y2;
} XSegment;
```

Set up an **XSegment** array similar to the **points** array for **XDrawPoints**, but supply four coordinates instead of two.

17.3.3   DRAWING RECTANGLES

Creating rectangles is nearly identical to creating lines. You can draw one rectangle using the **XDrawRectangle** function:

```
XDrawRectangle(XtDisplay(da), XtWindow(da), gc, x, y, w, h);
```

where **x** and **y** are the coordinates of the upper left corner of the rectangle and **w** and **h** are the width and height of the rectangle.

To draw multiple rectangles, use **XDrawRectangles**:

```
XDrawRectangles(XtDisplay(da), XtWindow(da), gc, rectangles, num);
```

Declare the **rectangles** parameter as follows, or as a pointer to such an array:

```
XRectangle rectangles[100];
```

X defines the **XRectangle** type as follows:

```
typedef struct {
    short x,y;
    unsigned short width,height;
} XRectangle;
```

Set up an **XRectangle** array similar to the points array for **XDrawPoints**, but supply four coordinates instead of two.

17.3.4 DRAWING ARCS, CIRCLES, AND ELLIPSES

You draw arcs like you draw rectangles, specifying a rectangle that controls the size and shape of the circle or ellipse, and also specifying the angles between which an arc will be drawn. A typical call looks like this:

```
XDrawArc(XtDisplay(da), XtWindow(da), gc, x, y, w, h, a1, a2);
```

where **x** and **y** are the coordinates of the upper left corner of the rectangle and **w** and **h** are the width and height of the rectangle that controls the size and shape of the ellipse. The **a1** and **a2** parameters determine where the arc starts and stops. For example, if the arc starts at 90 degrees and stops at 180 degrees, **a1** is $5,760$ (or 90×64) and **a2** is $11,520$ (or 180×64). To draw a complete circle or ellipse, set **a1** to 0 and **a2** to $23,040$ (or 360×64). You must multiply all angles by 64 as shown to make them work correctly. Figure 17.6 shows the result of drawing an arc in a 200×200 pixel rectangle between angles $5,760$ and $11,520$.

To draw multiple arcs, use **XDrawArcs**:

```
XDrawArcs(XtDisplay(da), XtWindow(da), gc, arcs, num);
```

Declare the arcs parameter as follows, or as a pointer to such an array:

```
XArc arcs[100];
```

X defines the **XArc** type as follows:

```
typedef struct {
   short x,y;
   unsigned short width,height;
   short angle1,angle2;
} XArc;
```

Set up an **XArc** array similar to the points array for **XDrawPoints**, but supply six coordinates instead of two.

17.3.5 DRAWING FILLED RECTANGLES

The functions **XFillRectangle** and **XFillRectangles** use the same parameters as **XDrawRectangle** and **XDrawRectangles**, but they draw filled rectangles. The `fill_style` field in the GC controls how the rectangle will be filled.

Figure 17.6   An Example Arc

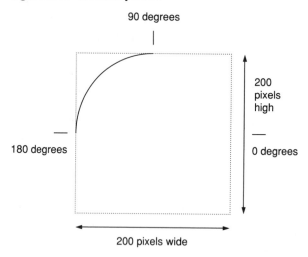

17.3.6   DRAWING FILLED ARCS AND CIRCLES

The functions **XFillArc** and **XFillArcs** use the same parameters as **XDrawArc** and **XDrawArcs**, but draw filled arcs. The `fill_style` and `arc_mode` fields in the GC control how the arc will be filled.

17.3.7   DRAWING FILLED POLYGONS

You draw filled polygons using the same technique you use to draw lines with contiguous end points (see **XDrawLines**): setting up an array of points that determine the vertices of the polygon. The resulting polygon is filled according to the `fill_rule` and the `fill_style` fields in the GC. A typical call looks like this:

```
XFillPolygon(XtDisplay(da), XtWindow(da), gc,
    points, num, Complex, CoordModeOrigin);
```

The **points**, **num**, and **CoordModeOrigin** parameters are the same as for **XDrawLines**.

The **Complex** parameter improves the efficiency of the X server in drawing the polygon. Three values are possible for this parameter: **Complex**, **Convex**, and **Nonconvex**. If you know that the shape of the polygon is convex, specify **Convex**. If lines in the polygon intersect at any point, specify **Complex**. If the polygon is neither convex nor complex, specify **Noncomplex**. If you don't know, use **Complex**. If the first and last point in the point array are the same, then the polygon is closed. If not, X closes it for you.

Figure 17.7 Origin of X and Y Coordinates for a Drawn String

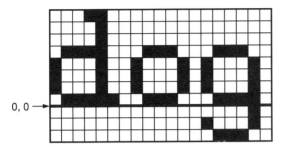

17.3.8 DRAWING STRINGS

You can draw text in a drawing area using the **XDrawString** and **XDrawImageString** functions. These two functions are identical, except that **XDrawString** draws only foreground pixels, while **XDrawImageString** draws foreground and background pixels to fill in the square cell bounding each character. A typical call looks like this:

```
XDrawString(XtDisplay(da), XtWindow(da), gc, x, y, s, strlen(s));
```

The **x** and **y** parameters control the position of the string. Note that **x** and **y** do not specify the string's upper left corner. Instead, the y coordinate is determined by the baseline of the characters in the string, as is shown in Figure 17.7.

The **s** parameter is a standard array of characters containing the string to be drawn. The **XDrawString** function also accepts a parameter indicating the number of characters to be drawn. Since the string passed in **s** is usually a standard C null-terminated string, I have used the **strlen** function here for the **length** parameter. If the array of characters is not null-terminated, specify the length explicitly.

XDrawImageString takes the same parameters as **XDrawString**.

The font for the string is controlled by the font field in the GC. Listing 17.5 shows how to change the font field. Note the similarity to the process of changing the font discussed in Chapter 3. We do not need the step that translates the **XFontList** to a Motif font list (as seen in Chapter 3) here because we are working at the raw X level. The code in the **exposureCB** function draws the string. The code in the **setup_gc** function sets the font at the same time it sets up the foreground and background colors.

Listing 17.5   Drawing a Text String

```
/* draw_string.c */

#include <Xm/Xm.h>
#include <Xm/DrawingA.h>

XtAppContext context;

GC gc;
Widget drawing_area;
Widget toplevel;

void setup_gc()
/* set up the graphics context. */
{
    int foreground,background;
    XGCValues vals;
    Arg al[10];
    int ac;
    XFontStruct *font=NULL;
    char *namestring=NULL;

    /* load the font */
    namestring = "*times*-24-*";
    font=XLoadQueryFont(XtDisplay(drawing_area),namestring);

     /* get the current fg and bg colors. */
    ac=0;
    XtSetArg(al[ac], XmNforeground, &foreground); ac++;
    XtSetArg(al[ac], XmNbackground, &background); ac++;
    XtGetValues(drawing_area, al, ac);

    /* create the gc. */
    vals.foreground = foreground;
    vals.background = background;
    vals.font=font->fid; /* The XFontStruct contains a field named
                             "fid" of type Font, as expect by the GC. */
    gc = XtGetGC(drawing_area, GCForeground | GCBackground | GCFont,
        &vals);
}


void exposureCB(w,client_data,call_data)
    Widget w;
    XtPointer client_data;
```

```
    XtPointer call_data;
/* called whenever drawing area is exposed. */
{
    printf("exposure event generated\n");
    XDrawString(XtDisplay(drawing_area), XtWindow(drawing_area),
        gc, 100, 100, "hello", 5);
}

void main(argc,argv)
    int argc;
    char *argv[];
{
    Arg al[10];
    int ac;

    /* create the toplevel shell */
    toplevel = XtAppInitialize(&context,"",NULL,0,&argc,argv,
        NULL,NULL,0);

    /* set window size. */
    ac=0;
    XtSetArg(al[ac],XmNheight,200); ac++;
    XtSetArg(al[ac],XmNwidth,200); ac++;
    XtSetValues(toplevel,al,ac);

    /* create a drawing area widget. */
    ac=0;
    drawing_area=XmCreateDrawingArea(toplevel,
        "drawing_area",al,ac);
    XtManageChild(drawing_area);
    XtAddCallback(drawing_area,XmNexposeCallback,
        exposureCB,NULL);

    setup_gc();

    XtRealizeWidget(toplevel);
    XtAppMainLoop(context);
}
```

In addition, Motif provides three other string drawing functions: **XmString-Draw**, **XmStringDrawImage**, and **XmStringDrawUnderline** (see Chapter 14 for further information). You can use these functions to draw **XmString** objects directly.

17.3.9   DRAWING BITMAPS AND PIXMAPS

A pixmap is an off-screen area of memory that you can use as a drawable for all X drawing commands except **XClearArea** and **XClearWindow**. The only difference between an X window and an X pixmap is that the window, unlike the pixmap, appears on the screen (see Chapter 15 for more information).

You can create a blank pixmap of any size, provided the X server has enough memory, with the **XCreatePixmap** function.

XCreatePixmap   *Create a blank pixmap.*

```
Pixmap XCreatePixmap(
    Display *display,
    Drawable drawable,
    unsigned int width,
    unsigned int height,
    unsigned int depth)
```

display	The X display.
drawable	The drawable.
width, height	The width and height of the pixmap.
depth	The depth of the pixels in the pixmap.

Once you have created a pixmap, you can use it as the drawable for a drawing command.

Typically, you use a pixmap to copy groups of pixels to and from a window. The window and pixmap must belong to the same screen and must have the same depth. You use the **XCopyArea** function to do the copying.

XCopyArea   *Copy a group of pixels.*

```
void XCopyArea(
    Display *display,
    Drawable src,
    Drawable dst,
    GC gc,
    int src_x,
    int src_y,
```

```
unsigned int width,
unsigned int height,
int dest_x,
int dest_y)
```

display	The X display.
src,dst	Source and destination drawables.
gc	The graphics parameter.
src_x,src_y	Starting coordinates of rectangle to copy.
width, height	The width and height of the rectangle to copy.
dest_x, dest_y	Coordinates of destination rectangle.

You can use a program named Bitmap to create small or large bitmap images written to disk in the X bitmap format. Once the image exists on disk, you can read it into a Motif program and draw it in a drawing area widget fairly easily. Figure 17.8 shows the Bitmap program at work creating a 30 × 30 pixel icon that represents a file folder. The program was invoked with the command `bitmap folder.xbm 30x30`.

The output of the Bitmap program is an X bitmap file, a text file containing the bitmap's description. The contents of bitmap file for the folder icon, called `folder.xbm`, look like this:

```
#define folder_width 30
#define folder_height 30
static char folder_bits[] = {
0x00, 0x00, 0x00, 0x00, 0x00, 0x00, 0x80, 0x3f, 0x00, 0x00, 0xc0, 0x20,
0x00, 0x00, 0x60, 0x20, 0xfe, 0xff, 0x3f, 0x20, 0x02, 0x00, 0x00, 0x20,
0x02, 0x00, 0x00, 0x20, 0x02, 0x00, 0x00, 0x20, 0x02, 0x00, 0x00, 0x20,
0x02, 0x00, 0x00, 0x20, 0x02, 0x00, 0x00, 0x20, 0x02, 0x00, 0x00, 0x20,
0x02, 0x00, 0x00, 0x20, 0x02, 0x00, 0x00, 0x20, 0x02, 0x00, 0x00, 0x20,
0x02, 0x00, 0x00, 0x20, 0x02, 0x00, 0x00, 0x20, 0x02, 0x00, 0x00, 0x20,
0x02, 0x00, 0x00, 0x20, 0x02, 0x00, 0x00, 0x20, 0x02, 0x00, 0x00, 0x20,
0x02, 0x00, 0x00, 0x20, 0x02, 0x00, 0x00, 0x20, 0x02, 0x00, 0x00, 0x20,
0x02, 0x00, 0x00, 0x20, 0x02, 0x00, 0x00, 0x20, 0x02, 0x00, 0x00, 0x20,
0xfe, 0xff, 0xff, 0x3f, 0x00, 0x00, 0x00, 0x00, 0x00, 0x00, 0x00, 0x00};
```

As you can see, `folder.xbm` is simply a text file, conveniently set up in a format so that you can include it in a C program. The code in Listing 17.6 shows how to display this bitmap in a drawing area.

Figure 17.8 Creating a Folder Icon with the Bitmap Program

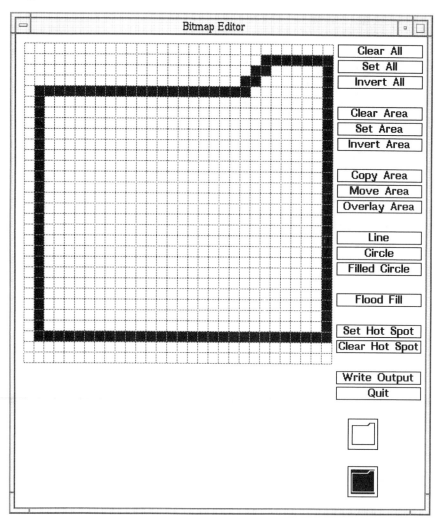

Listing 17.6   Drawing a Bitmap in a Drawing Area

```
/* bitmap.c */

#include <Xm/Xm.h>
#include <Xm/DrawingA.h>
#include "folder.xbm"

XtAppContext context;

GC gc;
Widget drawing_area;
Widget toplevel;

unsigned int get_depth(w)
    Widget w;
/* gets the depth of the display holding w. */
{
    Window r;
    unsigned int x,y,wd,ht,bw,depth;

    XGetGeometry(XtDisplay(w),XtWindow(w),
        &r,&x,&y,&wd,&ht,&bw,&depth);
    return depth;
}

void setup_gc()
/* set up the graphics context. */
{
    int foreground,background;
    XGCValues vals;
    Arg al[10];
    int ac;

    /* get the current fg and bg colors. */
    ac=0;
    XtSetArg(al[ac], XmNforeground, &foreground); ac++;
    XtSetArg(al[ac], XmNbackground, &background); ac++;
    XtGetValues(drawing_area, al, ac);

    /* create the gc. */
    vals.foreground = foreground;
    vals.background = background;
    gc=XtGetGC(drawing_area, GCForeground | GCBackground ,&vals);
}
```

```
void draw_icon(w,client_data,call_data)
    Widget w;
    XtPointer client_data;
    XtPointer call_data;
{

    Pixmap p;
    int fc,bc,depth;
    Arg al[10];
    int ac;

    /* get the current fg and bg colors. */
    ac=0;
    XtSetArg(al[ac], XmNforeground, &fc); ac++;
    XtSetArg(al[ac], XmNbackground, &bc); ac++;
    XtGetValues(drawing_area, al, ac);

    depth=get_depth(drawing_area);

    /* create the pixmap and display it. */
    p=XCreatePixmapFromBitmapData(XtDisplay(drawing_area),
        XtWindow(drawing_area),folder_bits,folder_width,folder_height,
        fc, bc, depth);
    XCopyArea(XtDisplay(drawing_area),p,XtWindow(drawing_area),gc,0,0,
        folder_width, folder_height, 100,100 );
    XFreePixmap(XtDisplay(drawing_area),p);
}

void main(argc,argv)
    int argc;
    char *argv[];
{
    Arg al[10];
    int ac;

    /* create the toplevel shell */
    toplevel = XtAppInitialize(&context,"",NULL,0,&argc,argv,
        NULL,NULL,0);

    /* set window size. */
    ac=0;
    XtSetArg(al[ac],XmNheight,200); ac++;
    XtSetArg(al[ac],XmNwidth,200); ac++;
    XtSetValues(toplevel,al,ac);
```

```
/* create a drawing area widget. */
ac=0;
drawing_area=XmCreateDrawingArea(toplevel,"drawing_area",al,ac);
XtManageChild(drawing_area);
XtAddCallback(drawing_area,XmNexposeCallback,draw_icon,NULL);

setup_gc();

XtRealizeWidget(toplevel);
XtAppMainLoop(context);
}
```

Figure 17.9 shows the output of Listing 17.6. The folder icon appears at position $100, 100$ in a 200×200 drawing area.

Most of the code in this program is the standard drawing code we have used since the beginning of the chapter. The **main** routine opens and resizes the toplevel shell, creates a drawing area, routes the exposure event to the **draw_icon** function, and forms a standard GC.

The **draw_icon** function contains several sections, duplicated below:

```
/* get the current fg and bg colors. */
ac=0;
XtSetArg(al[ac], XmNforeground, &fc); ac++;
XtSetArg(al[ac], XmNbackground, &bc); ac++;
XtGetValues(drawing_area, al, ac);

depth=get_depth(drawing_area);

/* create the pixmap and display it. */
p=XCreatePixmapFromBitmapData(XtDisplay(drawing_area),
    XtWindow(drawing_area),folder_bits,folder_width,folder_height,
    fc, bc, depth);
XCopyArea(XtDisplay(drawing_area),p,XtWindow(drawing_area),gc,0,0,
    folder_width, folder_height, 100,100 );
XFreePixmap(XtDisplay(drawing_area),p);
```

The first section gets the foreground and background color information from the **drawing_area** widget using a standard **XtGetValues** call.

The next section consists of a single line that makes a call to the **get_depth** function. It uses **XGetGeometry** to get the depth of the screen. This step is extremely important. A bitmap file contains picture information that has a depth of 1. However, the window that displays the picture can have a depth of

Figure 17.9   Output of Listing 17.6

between 1 and 32 bits, depending on the system. You must know the depth of the window so that when the program converts the bitmap data to a pixmap, the pixmap has the same depth as the window that will display it.

You can extract the depth value easily using the **XGetGeometry** function, which returns a variety of information about a drawable. A call to this function looks like this:

```
XGetGeometry(XtDisplay(da), XtWindow(da),
    &root, &x, &y, &w, &h, &bw, &depth);
```

Note that the *address* of the variables is passed so that values can be returned. The **root** parameter is of type **Window** and returns a pointer to the root window; the **x** and **y** parameters return the offset of the drawable from its parent window; the **w** and **h** parameters return the width and height of the drawable; and the **bw** parameter returns the border width.

The **depth** parameter—the value we actually care about here—returns the depth of the window. Do not make assumptions about the depth. For example, if you are working on a display of depth 1, it is tempting simply to pass a 1 as the depth parameter to **XCreatePixmapFromBitmap**. This value will crash the program if you ever run it on a color display. Note that the **depth** resource in the core widget also contains the depth. This resource has the advantage of avoiding a query on the X server.

The last section creates a pixmap from the bitmap information using the **XCreatePixmapFromBitmapData** function. The parameters tell this function the source of the bitmap data, the width and height of the bitmap, and the

colors and depth to use when creating the pixmap. The pixmap is copied onto
the screen using the **XCopyArea** function, which copies an area of pixels from
a source pixmap (in this case, the pixmap returned by **XCreatePixmapFrom-**
BitmapData) to a destination pixmap (in this case, the window in which we
want to display the bitmap). The parameters include the display, the source,
the destination, a GC, the x and y coordinates and width and height of the
rectangular area to be copied, and the x and y coordinates of the destination
location. In this case, we want to copy the entire pixmap, so we select a rectangular area starting at 0, 0 and extending for the pixmap's full width and
height (**folder_width** and **folder_height**). We want to copy the area to the
point 100, 100 in the destination window.

The pixmap variable **p** is a resource stored in the X server (see Chapter 15),
so you should use **XFreePixmap** to free the block of memory it points to when
you are done with it.

Remember that a label widget, as well as other widgets inheriting a label
widget (such as the push-button widget), can display a pixmap instead of a
text label. The code to get the pixmap data for a label widget is identical to the
pixmap code we saw above, as shown in Listing 17.7.

Listing 17.7   Displaying a Pixmap on a Label Widget

```
/* label_pixmap.c */

#include <Xm/Xm.h>
#include <Xm/Label.h>
#include "folder.xbm"

XtAppContext context;

Widget toplevel, label;

unsigned int get_depth(w)
    Widget w;
/* gets the depth of the display holding w. */
{
    Window r;
    unsigned int x,y,wd,ht,bw,depth;

    XGetGeometry(XtDisplay(w), RootWindowOfScreen(XtScreen(toplevel)),
        &r, &x, &y, &wd, &ht, &bw, &depth);
    return depth;
}

main(argc,argv)
```

```
    int argc;
    char *argv[];
{
    Arg al[10];
    int ac;
    int foreground,background;
    Pixmap pix;
    unsigned int depth;

    /* create the toplevel shell */
    toplevel = XtAppInitialize(&context,"",NULL,0,&argc,argv,
        NULL,NULL,0);

    /* create the label */
    ac=0;
    label=XmCreateLabel(toplevel,"label",al,ac);
    XtManageChild(label);

    /* get colors of label */
    ac=0;
    XtSetArg(al[ac], XmNforeground, &foreground); ac++;
    XtSetArg(al[ac], XmNbackground, &background); ac++;
    XtGetValues(label, al, ac);

    /* get the depth so pixmap can be created. */
    depth=get_depth(toplevel);

    /* create the pixmap */
    pix=XCreatePixmapFromBitmapData(XtDisplay(toplevel),
        RootWindowOfScreen(XtScreen(toplevel)),
        folder_bits,folder_width,folder_height,
        foreground,background,depth);

    /* set appropriate label resources. */
    ac=0;
    XtSetArg(al[ac], XmNlabelType, XmPIXMAP); ac++;
    XtSetArg(al[ac], XmNlabelPixmap, pix); ac++;
    XtSetValues(label, al, ac);

    XtRealizeWidget(toplevel);
    XtAppMainLoop(context);
}
```

The **main** routine gets the depth of the display and the foreground and background colors of the label so that it can create the pixmap. It attaches the

Figure 17.10   A Label Displaying a Bitmap

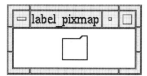

pixmap to the label using the label's **labelPixmap** and **labelType** resources. The code uses the folder bitmap file `folder.xbm` once again. Figure 17.10 shows the effect of mapping the bitmap onto the label.

In the code in Listing 17.7, note the following phrase:

```
RootWindowOfScreen(XtScreen(toplevel))
```

This phrase takes the place of **XtWindow(toplevel)** in Listing 17.7 to get around the **BadDrawable** error that occurs when the code asks for drawable information on the label before it has been realized. We use the root window (the background) of the screen containing the toplevel shell because it always exists and because all windows on a given screen by definition have the same depth.

17.4   ADVANCED DRAWING CONCEPTS

This section describes techniques needed to create drawing programs. It also demonstrates how to add sophisticated features such as pop-up menus to programs that use drawing area widgets.

17.4.1   CLEARING AREAS

You can use the **XClearArea** function to clear areas in windows. A call to this function looks like this:

```
XClearArea(XtDisplay(da), XtWindow(da), x, y, w, h, False);
```

The **x**, **y**, **w**, and **h** parameters specify the rectangular region to be cleared. If all four are set to 0, the function clears the entire drawing area.

The **False** parameter determines whether or not the **XClearArea** function should generate an exposure event. When set to false as shown above, **XClearArea** generates no exposure event. When set to true, it generates an exposure event for the cleared region. You can use this feature to clear the window and then allow your normal exposure-handling function to redraw the window for you. See the advanced drawing program in Section 17.4.6 for an example.

You cannot use **XClearArea** to clear an area on a pixmap. Instead, use **XFill-Rectangle**.

17.4.2   EXPOSURE REGIONS

When an exposure event is generated, often only a small part of the window is exposed. If your code redraws the entire window on every exposure event, it will waste a great deal of time. The **call_data** parameter passed to the exposure callback function contains information needed to determine the exact rectangle being exposed, so that only that portion of the window is redrawn. If you create the data structure for your program carefully enough to determine which parts of the drawing area fall within the exposure rectangle, you can take advantage of this capability to improve your program's performance.

The code in Listing 17.8 demonstrates the exposure rectangle by writing the coordinates of the rectangle to stdout each time an exposure event occurs.

Listing 17.8   Determining the Exposure Rectangle and Writing It to Stdout

```
/* exposure.c */

#include <Xm/Xm.h>
#include <Xm/DrawingA.h>

XtAppContext context;

Widget drawing_area;
Widget toplevel;

void exposeCB(w,client_data,call_data)
    Widget w;
    XtPointer client_data;
    XmAnyCallbackStruct *call_data;
/* called whenever an exposure occurs on the drawing area. */
{
    XExposeEvent *event;

    event=(XExposeEvent *) call_data->event;
    printf("Exposed rectangle: x=%d y=%d width=%d height=%d\n",
        event->x,event->y,event->width,event->height);
}

void main(argc,argv)
    int argc;
```

```
        char *argv[];
{
    Arg al[10];
    int ac;

    /* create the toplevel shell */
    toplevel = XtAppInitialize(&context,"",NULL,0,&argc,argv,
        NULL,NULL,0);

    /* default window size. */
    ac=0;
    XtSetArg(al[ac],XmNheight,400); ac++;
    XtSetArg(al[ac],XmNwidth,400); ac++;
    XtSetValues(toplevel,al,ac);

    /* create a drawing area widget. */
    ac=0;
    drawing_area=XmCreateDrawingArea(toplevel,
        "drawing_area",al,ac);
    XtManageChild(drawing_area);
    XtAddCallback(drawing_area,XmNexposeCallback,
        exposeCB,NULL);

    XtRealizeWidget(toplevel);
    XtAppMainLoop(context);
}
```

In the **exposeCB** procedure, the **call_data** parameter contains the event that generated the call to the callback. In this case, it is an exposure event. The code in **exposeCB** gets the x, y, width, and height fields in the exposure event structure and writes these values to stdout.

You may find that some actions generate multiple exposure rectangles. For example, bringing a window forward from behind several other windows generates several exposure events, each with its own rectangle. If you are using a redrawing technique that repaints the entire window for any exposure event, multiple exposure events can pose a problem, since the screen will be completely redrawn several times in a row. With complicated images, redrawing can take a great deal of time. To solve this problem the **XEvent** structure contains a field count that, when not 0, indicates how many exposure events in the same cluster will follow. Ignore all exposure events in which the count field does not equal 0 if you redraw the entire screen on each exposure.

17.4.3   HANDLING RESIZE EVENTS

A drawing area widget can generate resize callbacks as well as expose callbacks. Resize callbacks are quite useful if you are attempting to scale a figure to fill up a window. Each time you resize a window, your code can receive a resize callback that tells it to clear the drawing area and to redraw your figure at the new size.

To make use of the resize event, use the **XtAddCallback** function to activate the callback. In the callback function, use **XtGetValues** to extract the new **width** and **height** resource values from the drawing area widget. Rescale your figure accordingly.

The code in Listing 17.9 shows how to use the resize event. Figure 17.11 shows typical output of the program.

Listing 17.9   Demonstrating the Resize Event

```
/* resize.c */

#include <Xm/Xm.h>
#include <Xm/DrawingA.h>

XtAppContext context;

GC gc;
Widget drawing_area;
Widget toplevel;
XSegment lines[2];
int num_lines=2;

void setup_gc()
/* set up the graphics context. */
{
    int foreground,background;
    XGCValues vals;
    Arg al[10];
    int ac;

    /* get the current fg and bg colors. */
    ac=0;
    XtSetArg(al[ac], XmNforeground, &foreground); ac++;
    XtSetArg(al[ac], XmNbackground, &background); ac++;
    XtGetValues(drawing_area, al, ac);
```

```
    /* create the gc. */
    vals.foreground = foreground;
    vals.background = background;
    gc= XtGetGC(drawing_area, GCForeground | GCBackground, &vals);
}

void exposeCB(w,client_data,call_data)
    Widget w;
    XtPointer client_data;
    XtPointer call_data;
/* called whenever drawing area is exposed. */
{
    printf("exposure event generated\n");
    XDrawSegments(XtDisplay(w),XtWindow(w),gc,lines,num_lines);
}

void resizeCB(w,client_data,call_data)
    Widget w;
    XtPointer client_data;
    XtPointer call_data;
/* called whenever drawing area is resized. */
{
    Dimension wdth,hght;
    Arg al[10];
    int ac;

    printf("resize event generated\n");

    /* get new window size. */
    ac=0;
    XtSetArg(al[ac],XmNheight,&(hght)); ac++;
    XtSetArg(al[ac],XmNwidth,&(wdth)); ac++;
    XtGetValues(w,al,ac);
    printf("%d %d \n",wdth,hght);

    lines[0].x1 = wdth/2;
    lines[0].y1 = 0;
    lines[0].x2 = wdth/2;
    lines[0].y2 = hght;

    lines[1].x1 = 0;
    lines[1].y1 = hght/2;
    lines[1].x2 = wdth;
    lines[1].y2 = hght/2;
```

```
    if (XtIsRealized(w))
        XClearArea(XtDisplay(w), XtWindow(w), 0, 0, 0, 0, True);
}

void main(argc,argv)
    int argc;
    char *argv[];
{
    Arg al[10];
    int ac;

    /* create the toplevel shell */
    toplevel = XtAppInitialize(&context,"",NULL,0,&argc,argv,
        NULL,NULL,0);

    /* set window size. */
    ac=0;
    XtSetArg(al[ac],XmNheight,500); ac++;
    XtSetArg(al[ac],XmNwidth,500); ac++;
    XtSetValues(toplevel,al,ac);

    /* create a drawing area widget. */
    ac=0;
    drawing_area=XmCreateDrawingArea(toplevel,"drawing_area",al,ac);
    XtManageChild(drawing_area);
    XtAddCallback(drawing_area, XmNexposeCallback, exposeCB, NULL);
    XtAddCallback(drawing_area, XmNresizeCallback, resizeCB, NULL);

    setup_gc();

    XtRealizeWidget(toplevel);
    XtAppMainLoop(context);
}
```

In Listing 17.9, the **resizeCB** callback function is triggered every time the user resizes the drawing area widget. This function checks the new size of the drawing area widget, then creates two lines that bisect the drawing area once it is redrawn. It also clears the drawing area widget, but only if it has been realized. The check for realization is necessary because one resize event will be generated very early in the code's execution—generally long before the widget has been realized—and if the check is not made, the **XClearArea** call fails on this initial resize event.

Note that the resize event does not actually need to redraw the lines. Since an exposure event follows any expansion of the window, the **exposeCB** func-

Figure 17.11   Two Lines Bisecting the Window
The lines adjust correctly as the window is resized.

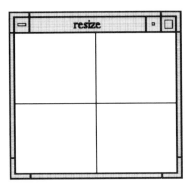

tion handles the redrawing. The **True** value in the **XClearArea** call handles shrinking windows. This parameter generates exposure events after each clear operation.

17.4.4   HANDLING CLICKS IN A WINDOW

You may want to draw in a drawing area widget and then let the user click on parts of the drawing. You can easily handle button clicks that occur in the drawing area widget by setting up an event handler.

The code in Listing 17.10 starts a drawing area widget and establishes a callback for mouse button releases using the **XtAddEventHandler** function. This function causes the specified function to be called each time the specified event occurs (see Chapter 16). If the user clicks in the drawing area, a callback is generated as the mouse button is released. In Listing 17.10, the callback is wired to display the x and y coordinates of the button click to stdout.

Listing 17.10   Handling Clicks in a Drawing Area

```
/* clicks.c */

#include <Xm/Xm.h>
#include <Xm/DrawingA.h>

#define size      400

XtAppContext context;

Widget toplevel, drawing_area;
```

```
void handle_click(w,client_data,event)
    Widget w;
    XtPointer client_data;
    XEvent *event;
/* event handler for mouse clicks */
{
    printf("%d %d\n",event->xbutton.x,event->xbutton.y);
}

void main(argc,argv)
    int argc;
    char *argv[];
{
    Arg al[10];
    int ac;

    /* create the toplevel shell */
    toplevel = XtAppInitialize(&context,"",NULL,0,&argc,argv,
        NULL,NULL,0);

    /* default window size. */
    ac=0;
    XtSetArg(al[ac],XmNheight,size); ac++;
    XtSetArg(al[ac],XmNwidth,size); ac++;
    XtSetValues(toplevel,al,ac);

    /* create drawing area */
    ac=0;
    drawing_area=XmCreateDrawingArea(toplevel,
        "drawing_area",al,ac);
    XtManageChild(drawing_area);
    /* add in event handler */
    XtAddEventHandler(drawing_area,ButtonReleaseMask,
        FALSE,handle_click,NULL);

    XtRealizeWidget(toplevel);
    XtAppMainLoop(context);
}
```

You can change the mask in **XtAddEventHandler** to **ButtonPressMask**, which calls the event handler as the user clicks the button. You can also change the mask to **ButtonMotionMask**, which generates callbacks when the user holds the button down and drags the mouse.

17.4.5 HANDLING RUBBER-BANDING

When creating any type of drawing or painting program, programmers often give the user a rubber-banding capability for drawing lines, boxes, circles, and so on. To rubber-band a line, the user clicks on the starting point of the line, then drags the cursor toward the line's ending point. On-screen, the user sees what looks like a rubber band stretching between the starting point and the cursor.

You can easily create the rubber-banding effect using **ButtonMotion** events to track cursor motion. In rubber-banding, the program must erase the old line each time the cursor moves and draw a new line to the new cursor position. However, if the program simply erases the old line, other lines that cross that line are erased as well at the crossing points. Instead, the old line must be "undrawn," leaving the original artwork untouched.

The undrawing effect is accomplished with the **GXxor** drawing function, which is a Boolean operation defined by the following truth table:

in1	in2	out
0	0	0
0	1	1
1	0	1
1	1	0

If you draw a black line using the **GXxor** function, all white areas under the line change to black and all black areas under the line change to white. If you draw the same line using **GXxor** again, the effect is reversed and the line is effectively undrawn.

The code in Listing 17.11 shows how to implement rubber-banding. To use this program, click on a starting point and drag to the ending point of the line that you wish to draw. You can easily modify the code to handle rubber-banded rectangles or ellipses. This code does not handle exposure events, because the drawn lines are not stored in a data structure. See the drawing program in Section 17.4.6 for more information on exposure handling.

Listing 17.11   Rubber-Banding

```
/* rubber_band.c */

#include <Xm/Xm.h>
#include <Xm/DrawingA.h>

XtAppContext context;
```

```
Widget toplevel;
Widget drawing_area;
GC gc_copy;
GC gc_xor;
int start_x,start_y;
int old_x,old_y;

void setup_gcs()
/* set up the graphics context. */
{
    int foreground,background;
    Arg al[10];
    int ac;
    XGCValues vals;

    /* get the current fg and bg colors. */
    ac=0;
    XtSetArg(al[ac], XmNforeground, &foreground); ac++;
    XtSetArg(al[ac], XmNbackground, &background); ac++;
    XtGetValues(drawing_area, al, ac);

    /* create the copy gc. */
    vals.foreground = foreground;
    vals.background = background;
    gc_copy= XtGetGC(drawing_area, GCForeground | GCBackground, &vals);

    /* create the xor gc. */
    vals.foreground = foreground ^ background;
    vals.function = GXxor;
    gc_xor= XtGetGC(drawing_area, GCForeground | GCBackground |
        GCFunction, &vals);
}


void handle_start(w,client_data,event)
    Widget w;
    XtPointer client_data;
    XEvent *event;
/* handles the ButtonPress event */
{
    old_x=start_x=event->xbutton.x;
    old_y=start_y=event->xbutton.y;
    XDrawLine(XtDisplay(w), XtWindow(w), gc_xor,
        start_x, start_y, old_x, old_y);
}
```

```
void handle_drag(w,client_data,event)
    Widget w;
    XtPointer client_data;
    XEvent *event;
/* handles the ButtonMotion event */
{
    XDrawLine(XtDisplay(w), XtWindow(w), gc_xor,
        start_x, start_y, old_x, old_y);
    old_x=event->xbutton.x;
    old_y=event->xbutton.y;
    XDrawLine(XtDisplay(w), XtWindow(w), gc_xor,
        start_x, start_y, old_x, old_y);
}

void handle_done(w,client_data,event)
    Widget w;
    XtPointer client_data;
    XEvent *event;
/* handles the ButtonRelease event */
{
    old_x=event->xbutton.x;
    old_y=event->xbutton.y;
    XDrawLine(XtDisplay(w), XtWindow(w), gc_copy,
        start_x, start_y, old_x, old_y);
}

void main(argc,argv)
    int argc;
    char *argv[];
{
    Arg al[10];
    int ac;

    /* create the toplevel shell */
    toplevel = XtAppInitialize(&context,"",NULL,0,&argc,argv,
        NULL,NULL,0);

    /* default window size. */
    ac=0;
    XtSetArg(al[ac],XmNheight,400); ac++;
    XtSetArg(al[ac],XmNwidth,400); ac++;
    XtSetValues(toplevel,al,ac);

    /* create drawing area */
    ac=0;
```

```
drawing_area=XmCreateDrawingArea(toplevel,
    "drawing_area",al,ac);
XtManageChild(drawing_area);

/* add in event handlers for drawing area */
XtAddEventHandler(drawing_area, ButtonPressMask, FALSE,
    handle_start, NULL);
XtAddEventHandler(drawing_area, ButtonReleaseMask, FALSE,
    handle_done, NULL);
XtAddEventHandler(drawing_area, ButtonMotionMask, FALSE,
    handle_drag, NULL);

setup_gcs();

XtRealizeWidget(toplevel);
XtAppMainLoop(context);
}
```

There are several interesting aspects to Listing 17.11. First, the **ButtonPress**, **ButtonMotion**, and **ButtonRelease** events are all wired to separate callback functions. When the user first presses the mouse button, **handle_start** is called, the starting and ending values of the new line are stored, and the line is drawn. As the user drags the mouse, **handle_drag** is called so that the old line is undrawn and a new line is drawn at the new position. When the user releases the mouse button, **handle_done** is called and the line is drawn one final time in **GXcopy** mode to make it a solid line.

The **setup_gcs** function creates two GCs here: One handles the normal **GX-copy** mode, and the other handles the **GXxor** mode. The **gc_xor** GC sets the drawing function to **GXxor**. It also uses an interesting foreground color:

```
vals.foreground = foreground ^ background;
```

The ^ operator in C is the **xor** operator, which you use for the following reason. Say you are working on an 8-bit color screen whose background color is 65 (01000001) and foreground color is 15 (00001111). **Xor**-ing these values together gives **vals.foreground** the value 01001110. When a pixel with this foreground color is **xor**-ed onto the background color as a line is drawn, you get 01001110^01000001 = 00001111, or the foreground color. If a pixel is **xor**-ed onto the foreground color, you get 01001110^00001111 = 01000001, or the background color. This is exactly the desired result.

Figure 17.12 Improved Drawing Program with Scroll Bar

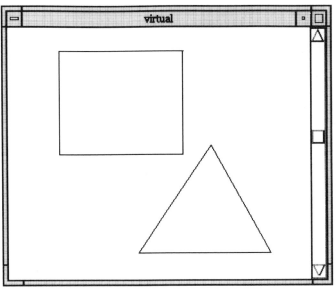

17.4.6 USING SCROLL BARS TO CREATE LARGE VIRTUAL SPACES

You can use scroll bars to create large virtual spaces for drawing or editing. To show the usefulness of scroll bars, we will create a large virtual drawing surface by adding a scroll bar to the rubber-banding code presented in Section 17.4.5.

The rubber-banding code in Section 17.4.5 is fairly simple: It allows the user to draw lines. This code cannot handle exposure events because it has no data structure to store the lines the user has drawn. Furthermore, the drawing can be no larger than the drawing area on the screen. We will improve this code by adding a data structure and a vertical scroll bar that allows the user to scroll through a drawing surface much longer than the height of one screen. Figure 17.12 shows a view of the improved program.

A virtual drawing surface creates the impression of a very large drawing area within a small window on-screen. The actual drawing area created by the program is only as big as the window. The user manipulates the scroll bar(s) to move around the larger drawing surface. The example code presented here adds vertical scrolling so the user will have the impression of a very long (5,000-pixel) drawing area. In order to create the large virtual area, the code

Figure 17.13 The Relationship Between the 5,000-Pixel-High Virtual Drawing Area and the Window That Appears on the Screen

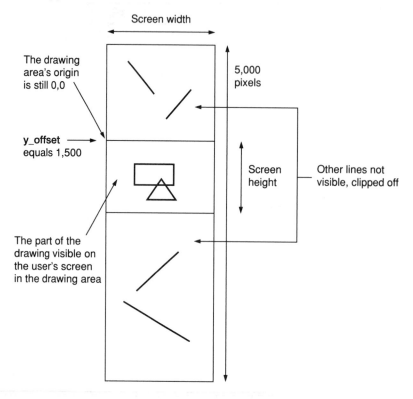

uses a **y_offset** variable and the natural clipping capabilities of a drawing area widget (see Figure 17.13).

All of the lines are stored in the data structure with their virtual coordinates. In other words, as far as the data structure is concerned, the drawing area really is 5,000 pixels high. In Figure 17.13, the user has scrolled the scroll bar so that the part of the drawing visible on the screen starts at the y coordinate of 1500 in the virtual drawing area. The **y_offset** variable keeps track of this offset.

Now, imagine that an exposure event occurs. If the lines in the data structure are drawn into the drawing area widget with the value in **y_offset** subtracted from all of the lines' y coordinates, then we will see exactly what we expect to see in the drawing area. If the **y_offset** value is adjusted each time the user manipulates the scroll bar, the user receives the impression of a large virtual drawing space.

The code for implementing a large virtual drawing area appears in Listing 17.12.

Listing 17.12   Creating a Virtual Drawing Area

```
/* virtual.c*/

#include <Xm/Xm.h>
#include <Xm/DrawingA.h>
#include <Xm/Form.h>
#include <Xm/ScrollBar.h>

#define MAX_Y 5000

XtAppContext context;

GC gc_copy;
GC gc_xor;
Widget toplevel, drawing_area, form, scroll;
int start_x,start_y;
int old_x,old_y;
int y_offset=0;

/* node for the single linked list contains the 4 line coordinates
     and a next pointer. */
struct node
{
    int x1,y1,x2,y2;
    struct node *next;
};

/* first points to the first node in the SLL. */
struct node *first=NULL;

void setup_gcs()
/* set up the graphics contexts */
{
    int foreground,background;
    Arg al[10];
    int ac;
    XGCValues vals;

    /* get the current fg and bg colors. */
    ac=0;
    XtSetArg(al[ac], XmNforeground, &foreground); ac++;
```

```
    XtSetArg(al[ac], XmNbackground, &background); ac++;
    XtGetValues(drawing_area, al, ac);

    /* create the copy gc. */
    vals.foreground = foreground;
    vals.background = background;
    gc_copy= XtGetGC(drawing_area, GCForeground | GCBackground, &vals);

    /* create the xor gc. */
    vals.foreground = foreground ^ background;
    vals.function = GXxor;
    gc_xor= XtGetGC(drawing_area, GCForeground | GCBackground |
            GCFunction, &vals);
}

void handle_start(w,client_data,event)
    Widget w;
    XtPointer client_data;
    XEvent *event;
/* See Section 17.4.5. */
{
    old_x=start_x=event->xbutton.x;
    old_y=start_y=event->xbutton.y;
    XDrawLine(XtDisplay(w), XtWindow(w), gc_xor,
        start_x, start_y, old_x, old_y);
}

void handle_drag(w,client_data,event)
    Widget w;
    XtPointer client_data;
    XEvent *event;
/* See Section 17.4.5. */
{
    XDrawLine(XtDisplay(w), XtWindow(w), gc_xor,
        start_x, start_y, old_x, old_y);
    old_x=event->xbutton.x;
    old_y=event->xbutton.y;
    XDrawLine(XtDisplay(w), XtWindow(w), gc_xor,
        start_x, start_y, old_x, old_y);
}

void handle_done(w,client_data,event)
    Widget w;
    XtPointer client_data;
    XEvent *event;
```

```
/* See Section 17.4.5. */
{
    struct node *temp;

    old_x=event->xbutton.x;
    old_y=event->xbutton.y;
    XDrawLine(XtDisplay(w), XtWindow(w), gc_copy,
        start_x, start_y, old_x, old_y);

    /* add the new line to the SLL. Add y_offset to y coords so that
        lines in the SLL are in virtual space coordinates. */
    temp=(struct node *) malloc(sizeof(struct node));
    temp->x1=start_x;
    temp->y1=start_y+y_offset;
    temp->x2=old_x;
    temp->y2=old_y+y_offset;
    temp->next=first;
    first=temp;
}

void exposeCB(w,client_data,call_data)
    Widget w;
    XtPointer client_data;
    XtPointer call_data;
/* called whenever drawing area is exposed. */
{
    struct node *temp;

    /* Traverse the SLL and draw all lines to the drawing area.
        Subtract off y_offset as each line is drawn so that virtual
        space is mapped correctly into the actual drawing area. */
    printf("expose event generated\n");
    temp=first;
    while (temp)
    {
        XDrawLine(XtDisplay(w), XtWindow(w), gc_copy,
            temp->x1, temp->y1-y_offset, temp->x2, temp->y2-y_offset );
        temp=temp->next;
    }
}

void scrollCB(w,client_data,call_data)
    Widget w;
    XtPointer client_data;
    XtPointer call_data;
```

```
    /* called whenever scrollbar moves. */
    {
        Arg al[10];
        int ac;
        int value;

        XClearArea(XtDisplay(drawing_area), XtWindow(drawing_area),
            0, 0, 0, 0, True); /* will generate a subsequent expose event. */

        /* get new scroll bar value and adjust y_offset. */
        ac=0;
        XtSetArg(al[ac],XmNvalue,&value); ac++;
        XtGetValues(w,al,ac);
        printf("scrollbar value = %d\n",value);

        y_offset=value;
    }


void resizeCB(w,client_data,call_data)
    Widget w;
    XtPointer client_data;
    XtPointer call_data;
/* called whenever drawing area is resized. */
{
    Dimension wdth,hght;
    Arg al[10];
    int ac;

    /* get new window size. */
    ac=0;
    XtSetArg(al[ac],XmNheight,&hght); ac++;
    XtSetArg(al[ac],XmNwidth,&wdth); ac++;
    XtGetValues(w,al,ac);
    printf("resized to %dx%d\n",wdth,hght);

    /* adjust scroll bar. */
    ac=0;
    XtSetArg(al[ac],XmNsliderSize,hght); ac++;
    XtSetArg(al[ac],XmNpageIncrement,hght/2); ac++;
    XtSetValues(scroll,al,ac);
}


void main(argc,argv)
    int argc;
    char *argv[];
```

```
{
    Arg al[10];
    int ac;

    /* create the toplevel shell */
    toplevel = XtAppInitialize(&context,"",NULL,0,&argc,argv,
        NULL,NULL,0);

    /* default window size. */
    ac=0;
    XtSetArg(al[ac],XmNheight,400); ac++;
    XtSetArg(al[ac],XmNwidth,400); ac++;
    XtSetValues(toplevel,al,ac);

    /* create a form to hold widgets */
    ac=0;
    form=XmCreateForm(toplevel,"form",al,ac);
    XtManageChild(form);

    /* create a scroll bar */
    ac=0;
    XtSetArg(al[ac], XmNtopAttachment, XmATTACH_FORM); ac++;
    XtSetArg(al[ac], XmNrightAttachment, XmATTACH_FORM); ac++;
    XtSetArg(al[ac], XmNleftAttachment, XmATTACH_NONE); ac++;
    XtSetArg(al[ac], XmNbottomAttachment, XmATTACH_FORM); ac++;
    XtSetArg(al[ac], XmNwidth, 20); ac++;
    XtSetArg(al[ac], XmNmaximum, MAX_Y); ac++;
    scroll=XmCreateScrollBar(form,"scroll",al,ac);
    XtManageChild(scroll);
    XtAddCallback(scroll,XmNvalueChangedCallback,scrollCB, NULL);

    /* create drawing area */
    ac=0;
    XtSetArg(al[ac], XmNtopAttachment, XmATTACH_FORM); ac++;
    XtSetArg(al[ac], XmNleftAttachment, XmATTACH_FORM); ac++;
    XtSetArg(al[ac], XmNrightAttachment, XmATTACH_WIDGET); ac++;
    XtSetArg(al[ac], XmNrightWidget, scroll); ac++;
    XtSetArg(al[ac], XmNbottomAttachment, XmATTACH_FORM); ac++;
    drawing_area=XmCreateDrawingArea(form,"drawing_area",al,ac);
    XtManageChild(drawing_area);
    /* add in event handlers */
    XtAddEventHandler(drawing_area, ButtonPressMask, FALSE,
        handle_start, NULL);
    XtAddEventHandler(drawing_area, ButtonReleaseMask, FALSE,
        handle_done, NULL);
```

```
XtAddEventHandler(drawing_area, ButtonMotionMask, FALSE,
    handle_drag, NULL);
XtAddCallback(drawing_area, XmNexposeCallback,
    exposeCB, NULL);
XtAddCallback(drawing_area, XmNresizeCallback,
    resizeCB, NULL);

setup_gcs();

XtRealizeWidget(toplevel);
XtAppMainLoop(context);
}
```

The **main** function in Listing 17.12 creates a form widget and attaches the scroll bar and drawing area. The **valueChanged** callback for the scroll bar is connected to the **scrollCB** callback function. The **expose** and **resize** callbacks for the drawing area are attached to appropriate callback functions as well. The event handlers for **ButtonMotion**, **ButtonPress**, and **ButtonRelease** are wired in; they use exactly the same code as in Section 17.4.5. The **ButtonRelease** function (**handle_done**) contains additional code that adds finished lines to the data structure, which is implemented as a simple single-linked list here. The **y_offset** value is added to the y coordinates of each line as it is stored in the data structure, so that all lines held there have virtual coordinates.

The **exposeCB** function is in charge of redrawing the screen after any exposure, or after any scroll bar manipulation: In the **scrollCB** function, the call to **XClearArea** generates an exposure event. The **exposeCB** function traverses the data structure and draws the lines, subtracting the **y_offset** value from all y coordinates to convert the virtual space coordinate system to the drawing area's coordinate system. All lines above **y_offset** in the virtual space have negative y coordinates and get clipped off, as do all lines below the drawing area's range. As a result, you see the correct portion of the virtual space in the drawing area.

The **resizeCB** function manipulates the scroll bar's **sliderSize** and **pageIncrement** resources to reflect the new window height. These resources allow the scroll bar to undertake some of the image alignment. For example, the code sets the **sliderSize** resource to the height of the drawing area. When the user drags the slider to the bottom of the scroll bar, the value held in the **value** resource exactly matches the value required to display the bottom of the virtual space.

The **scrollCB** function sets **y_offset** to reflect the change in the scroll bar's **value** resource. It also clears the drawing area, which in turn generates an exposure event to show the user the correct portion of the virtual space.

You can use a scrolled window widget as an alternative way of holding the drawing area and one or two scroll bars. See Chapter 11 for more information on the scrolled window widget.

17.4.7 POP-UP MENUS

Drawing programs like the one in Sections 17.4.5 and 17.4.6 often incorporate pop-up menus for frequently used options. Pop-ups allow the user to choose menu options without having to move the cursor up to the menu bar.

To demonstrate the use of pop-up menus, we will add one to the rubber-banding code presented in Section 17.4.5. This menu lets the user choose one of two different drawing shapes: lines or boxes. You could easily expand this menu to include choices for circles, polygons, filled shapes, and so on. Listing 17.13 contains the code for the pop-up menu.

Listing 17.13   Creating Pop-Up Menus

```
/*popup.c*/

#include <Xm/Xm.h>
#include <Xm/DrawingA.h>
#include <Xm/PushB.h>
#include <Xm/RowColumn.h>

#define LINE 1
#define BOX  2

XtAppContext context;
XmStringCharSet char_set=XmSTRING_DEFAULT_CHARSET;

Widget toplevel;
Widget drawing_area;
Widget menu;
Widget line_item;
Widget box_item;

GC gc_copy;
GC gc_xor;
int start_x,start_y;/* starting position of shape */
int old_x,old_y;/* previous cursor position    */
```

```
    int current_shape=LINE;
    Boolean shape_started=False;

    void setup_gcs()
    /* set up the graphics context. */
    {
        int foreground,background;
        Arg al[10];
        int ac;
        XGCValues vals;

        /* get the current fg and bg colors. */
        ac=0;
        XtSetArg(al[ac], XmNforeground, &foreground); ac++;
        XtSetArg(al[ac], XmNbackground, &background); ac++;
        XtGetValues(drawing_area, al, ac);

        /* create the copy gc. */
        vals.foreground = foreground;
        vals.background = background;
        gc_copy= XtGetGC(drawing_area, GCForeground | GCBackground, &vals);

        /* create the xor gc. */
        vals.foreground = foreground ^ background;
        vals.function = GXxor;
        gc_xor= XtGetGC(drawing_area, GCForeground | GCBackground |
            GCFunction, &vals);
    }

    void draw_shape(w,gc)
        Widget w;
        GC gc;
    {
        switch (current_shape)
        {
            case LINE:
                XDrawLine(XtDisplay(w), XtWindow(w), gc,
                    start_x, start_y, old_x, old_y);
                break;
            case BOX:
                XDrawRectangle(XtDisplay(w), XtWindow(w), gc,
                    start_x, start_y, old_x-start_x, old_y-start_y);
                break;
        }
    }
```

```
void handle_start(w,client_data,event)
    Widget w;
    XtPointer client_data;
    XEvent *event;
/* handles the ButtonPress event */
{
    shape_started=False;
    if (event->xbutton.button==Button1)
    {
        old_x=start_x=event->xbutton.x;
        old_y=start_y=event->xbutton.y;
        draw_shape(w,gc_xor);
        shape_started=True;
    }
    else if (event->xbutton.button==Button3)
    {
        XmMenuPosition(menu,(XButtonPressedEvent *)event);
        XtManageChild(menu);
    }
}


void handle_drag(w,client_data,event)
    Widget w;
    XtPointer client_data;
    XEvent *event;
/* handles the ButtonMotion event */
{
    if (shape_started)
    {
        draw_shape(w,gc_xor);
        old_x=event->xbutton.x;
        old_y=event->xbutton.y;
        draw_shape(w,gc_xor);
    }
}


void handle_done(w,client_data,event)
    Widget w;
    XtPointer client_data;
    XEvent *event;
/* handles the ButtonRelease event */
{
    if (event->xbutton.button==Button1)
    {
        old_x=event->xbutton.x;
```

```
            old_y=event->xbutton.y;
            draw_shape(w,gc_copy);
            shape_started=False;
        }
    }

    void menuCB(w,client_data,call_data)
        Widget w;
        int client_data;
        XmAnyCallbackStruct *call_data;
    /* callback routine used for all menus */
    {
        current_shape=client_data;
        XtUnmanageChild(menu);
    }

    Widget make_menu_item(item_name,client_data,menu)
        char *item_name;
        XtPointer client_data;
        Widget menu;
    /* adds an item into a menu. */
    {
        int ac;
        Arg al[10];
        Widget item;

        ac = 0;
        XtSetArg(al[ac],XmNlabelString,
            XmStringCreateLtoR(item_name,char_set)); ac++;
        item=XmCreatePushButton(menu,item_name,al,ac);
        XtManageChild(item);
        XtAddCallback(item,XmNactivateCallback,menuCB,client_data);
        XtSetSensitive(item,True);
        return(item);
    }

    void main(argc,argv)
        int argc;
        char *argv[];
    {
        Arg al[10];
        int ac;

        /* create the toplevel shell */
        toplevel = XtAppInitialize(&context,"",NULL,0,&argc,argv,
```

```
    NULL,NULL,0);

    /* default window size. */
    ac=0;
    XtSetArg(al[ac],XmNheight,400); ac++;
    XtSetArg(al[ac],XmNwidth,400); ac++;
    XtSetValues(toplevel,al,ac);

    /* create drawing area */
    ac=0;
    drawing_area=XmCreateDrawingArea(toplevel,"drawing_area",al,ac);
    XtManageChild(drawing_area);
    /* add in event handlers for drawing area */
    XtAddEventHandler(drawing_area, ButtonPressMask, FALSE,
        handle_start, NULL);
    XtAddEventHandler(drawing_area, ButtonReleaseMask, FALSE,
        handle_done, NULL);
    XtAddEventHandler(drawing_area, ButtonMotionMask, FALSE,
        handle_drag, NULL);

    /* create the popup menu */
    ac=0;
    menu=XmCreatePopupMenu(drawing_area,"menu",al,ac);
    line_item=make_menu_item("Line",LINE,menu);
    box_item=make_menu_item("Box",BOX,menu);

    setup_gcs();

    XtRealizeWidget(toplevel);
    XtAppMainLoop(context);
}
```

This program, for the most part identical to the code in Section 17.4.5, contains three significant changes. For one, the event-handling functions are button-sensitive. The rubber-banding code in Section 17.4.5 has no mouse button sensitivity: You can draw a line with any of the mouse's three buttons. For a pop-up menu to work, you must isolate the drawing activity to one mouse button so that you can use another for the menu. You assign buttons with an **if** statement in **handle_start** and **handle_done** that checks to see if the user has pressed **Button1**. If so, the program runs the normal rubber-banding code.

Button motion events do not return an indication of the button in use. Your code must set a Boolean variable to true when a shape is started and false when

Figure 17.14   Output of Listing 17.14

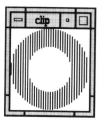

a shape is finished. The **handle_drag** function determines whether the button motion is tied to a drawing operation by examining this Boolean value.

The **handle_start** function has also been modified to recognize when the user presses the third menu button, so that it can manage the pop-up menu.

The second significant change is that the pop-up menu code has been added. The pop-up menu is created with a convenience function and filled with the **make_menu_item** function introduced in Chapter 6. The **menuCB** function sets the **current_shape** variable, so that the program knows the current shape, and unmanages the pop-up.

Third, the code now supports multiple shapes: lines and boxes. The **draw_shape** function handles the creation of the two shapes. The choice between the two is made with a **switch** statement triggered off of **current_shape**. You can easily extend this code to handle other shapes by adding menu options and augmenting the **draw_shape** function.

The program in Listing 17.13 does not handle exposure events, so if the menu pops up over part of the figure (and if your machine does not use a backing store), a blank patch remains when the menu closes. To solve this problem, add the code shown in Section 17.4.6 to handle exposure events and scrolling in a drawing area.

17.4.8   USING A CLIP MASK

The X drawing model supports a clip mask, which you can use to create some interesting drawing effects. A clip mask is a bitmap. When you use one in a GC, the program draws only those portions where the clip mask contains the value 1. Listing 17.14 shows how to use a clip mask. In this code, the clip mask is a bitmap that looks like a ring. Vertical lines extend through the mask, creating the effect shown in Figure 17.14.

Listing 17.14   Using a Clip Mask

```c
/* clip.c */

#include <Xm/Xm.h>
#include <Xm/DrawingA.h>
#include "circle.xbm"

XtAppContext context;

Widget toplevel;
Widget drawing_area;
GC gc;
int foreground,background;

void setup_gc()
/* set up the graphics context. */
{
    Arg al[10];
    int ac;
    XGCValues vals;
    Pixmap p;

    /* get the current fg and bg colors. */
    ac=0;
    XtSetArg(al[ac], XmNforeground, &foreground); ac++;
    XtSetArg(al[ac], XmNbackground, &background); ac++;
    XtGetValues(drawing_area, al, ac);

    /* create the mask. */
    p=XCreateBitmapFromData(XtDisplay(toplevel),
        RootWindowOfScreen(XtScreen(toplevel)),
        circle_bits,circle_width,circle_height);

    /* create the gc. */
    vals.foreground = foreground;
    vals.background = background;
    vals.clip_mask=p;
    vals.clip_x_origin=0;
    vals.clip_y_origin=0;
    gc= XCreateGC(XtDisplay(toplevel),
        RootWindowOfScreen(XtScreen(toplevel)),
        GCForeground | GCBackground | GCClipMask |
        GCClipXOrigin | GCClipYOrigin, &vals);
}
```

```
void exposeCB(w,client_data,call_data)
    Widget w;
    XtPointer client_data;
    XtPointer call_data;
/* handles the exposure event */
{
    int x;

    for (x=0; x<100; x+=3)
        XDrawLine(XtDisplay(drawing_area), XtWindow(drawing_area), gc,
            x,0,x,100);

}

void main(argc,argv)
    int argc;
    char *argv[];
{
    Arg al[10];
    int ac;

    /* create the toplevel shell */
    toplevel = XtAppInitialize(&context,"",NULL,0,&argc,argv,
        NULL,NULL,0);

    /* default window size. */
    ac=0;
    XtSetArg(al[ac],XmNheight,100); ac++;
    XtSetArg(al[ac],XmNwidth,100); ac++;
    XtSetValues(toplevel,al,ac);

    /* create drawing area */
    ac=0;
    drawing_area=XmCreateDrawingArea(toplevel,"drawing_area",al,ac);
    XtManageChild(drawing_area);
    /* add in event handlers for drawing area */
    XtAddCallback(drawing_area, XmNexposeCallback, exposeCB, NULL);

    setup_gc();

    XtRealizeWidget(toplevel);
    XtAppMainLoop(context);
}
```

The unique feature of the code in Listing 17.14 is the creation of a pixmap of depth 1 in the **setup_gc** function. This pixmap functions as the clip mask. When the user draws the lines, the mask automatically clips them.

The clip origin can be changed to move the clipping mask around in the drawing area. It is also possible to move the clip mask to follow the mouse. To do this, use **XCreateGC** to create a modifiable **GC**, and then use the **XSetClip-Origin** function to modify the clip origin in that **GC**.

17.4.9   USING XFLUSH

The X Window System stores drawing requests in an output buffer. If your program generates a large number of requests, the system stores them in the client until the buffer fills and then ships them to the X server all at once. In certain situations, this process creates a jerky display.

Imagine that you have created code that draws 1,000 shapes in a drawing area. Your program may take a while to generate all of those shapes. You will probably notice that the screen is blank for several seconds, then suddenly shows half the shapes, then shows the rest several seconds later. This visual effect of buffering can seriously detract from a program's overall appearance.

To flush the buffer, use the **XFlush** function, passing it the display as a parameter:

```
XFlush(XtDisplay(da));
```

Each time **XFlush** is called, the output buffer is flushed and its contents sent to the X server. By calling XFlush frequently during complicated redraws, display smoothness is improved.

18 CONCLUSION

In this book, I have tried to give you the essential knowledge you need to be a productive Motif programmer. Obviously you don't know everything, but you now know enough to create your own applications. You will learn more on your own as the need arises.

In conclusion, I would like to offer two suggestions. The first concerns design issues; the second concerns bad days.

18.1   DESIGNING A MOTIF APPLICATION

Whenever you design a complex Motif program, consider doing it in two parts: a user-interface part and a getting-the-work-done part. It does not matter if you use libraries to implement this separation, or if you build a text application that does the work and then put a Motif wrapper around it. Just try to keep these two parts separate. If you maintain this separation and if your program is successful, you can easily port it to other environments, such as the Macintosh and Microsoft Windows, by changing only the user-interface portion of your code.

There is a second reason for keeping the user interface separate, which the program Mathematica best illustrates. Mathematica, a FLOPS hog, is designed so that the user interface can run on one machine (say a Macintosh) while some number-crunching machine (say a Sun) does all the work. This arrangement greatly improves performance. By separating the work portion from the interface portion, you open the door to this sort of multiprocessing.

18.2   DEALING WITH BAD DAYS

If you do a lot of Motif programming, you will have occasional bad days. Almost all of the problems you encounter on these days will be "stupid C problems": bad addresses, missing or incorrect parameters, failures to increment

ac, forgetting to manage a widget, and so on. Motif and X seem to foster these mistakes. I will give you an example of a bad day from my own experience so that you will know one when you see it.

I was writing the code for the drawing program presented in Section 17.4.6. This program is not very long or complicated, and I figured that it would take me fifteen minutes, tops. To create it, I simply cut and pasted most of the code from other Motif programs. I compiled it and then ran it.

I had no drawing area. The scroll bar was there, but I could not draw anything. Staring at the code, I eventually noticed the following:

```
drawing_area=XmCreateDrawingArea(toplevel,"drawing_area", al, ac);
```

I was creating the drawing area and going through all of the correct attachment motions to hook it into the form, but the parent of the drawing area was not the form but **toplevel**. This does not work in Motif: The code accepts but ignores all of the attachment code. I changed the word **toplevel** to **form** and recompiled.

Now I could draw, but the program was sucking up a huge amount of CPU time, it would not resize, and the scroll bar had no effect. Not good. Into the program I went. I found the following code in the main function where the callbacks for the drawing area are wired in:

```
XtAddCallback(drawing_area, XmNexposeCallback,exposeCB, NULL);
XtAddCallback(drawing_area, XmNresizeCallback,exposeCB, NULL);
```

This is not the sort of thing I can usually see in five seconds: It took some staring, scrolling around, and muttering. Eventually I saw that both the **resize** and **expose** callbacks were wired into **exposeCB**. So I changed the **resize** callback to get it talking to **resizeCB**, recompiled, and ran the program.

I got a segmentation fault immediately. Segmentation faults are obnoxious. I recompiled with the **-g** option and used **dbx** to see where the crash was occurring. I started up **dbx**, typed run, let it crash, and then typed where. I found that in the **resizeCB** function, I had used **XtGetValues** instead of **XtSetValues** to set the value of the **pageIncrement** and **sliderSize**—a stupid mistake. I corrected the error, recompiled, and ran the program again. The segmentation fault was gone.

The scroll bar still did not work, however, so I decided to try something else. The program was still sucking up huge quantities of CPU time: The machine would fall to its knees as soon as I drew a line. I decided to check exposure events. I drew two lines, iconified the window, and then expanded it. Only the first line redrew. I killed the program and scanned **exposeCB**. Where else could the problem be?

```
void exposeCB(Widget w, caddr_t client_data, caddr_t call_data)
/* called whenever drawing area is exposed. */
{
  struct node *temp;

  printf("expose event generated\n");
  temp=first;
  while (temp)
  {
    XDrawLine(XtDisplay(w), XtWindow(w), gc_copy,
      temp->x1, temp->y1-y_offset, temp->x2, temp->y2-y_offset);
  }
}
```

This code looked all right to me. I looked in a few other places and came back. It still looked all right. The phone rang, and after a few more distractions I noticed that something was missing: `temp=temp->next` in the `while` loop was noticeable by its absence, and I had an infinite loop. The infinite loop was using up all of the CPU time drawing a single line over and over again. I fixed that, recompiled, and re-ran the program.

Exposure now worked, but the scroll bar still did not. I stared at the code. I added in a **printf** statement to confirm that **scrollCB** was getting called, but then I noticed that the exposure event that **XClearArea** should have triggered was not occurring. I stared at the **XClearArea** call:

```
XClearArea(XtDisplay(w), XtWindow(w), 0, 0, 0, 0, True);
```

At this point, I was getting very annoyed. What could possibly be wrong with such a simple line? The exposure parameter was set to **true**, and I knew that exposure events were working correctly. Eventually I noticed the problem: I had pasted this line from somewhere else, where the **w** variable was a drawing area. But here, **w** was the scroll bar, and **XClearArea**, of course, was having no effect on it. "Sheesh!" is not what I said, but this is a family publication so imagine that I said it. I then changed **w** to **drawing_area** and recompiled.

It finally worked! "Cheese and crackers got all muddy!" as my father used to say. A task that should have taken ten minutes ended up taking an hour and a half.

I will make a prediction: You will have days like this, too. And when they happen, don't let them get you down. Even the best and the brightest have bad days on occasion, so get used to them. Go take a shower, play raquetball, or do *something*, and then go back the next day and get on with it.

Fortunately, the bad days are rare. On the good days, you can create some great applications with Motif. I hope you have fun creating your own programs.

A SOURCES OF INFORMATION

Downloading the Code

The code contained in this book can be downloaded from several FTP sites, as listed below:

ftp.uu.net
Look for the file `brain.motif.tar.Z` in `published`.

osl.csc.ncsu.edu
Look for the file `brain.motif.tar.Z` in `pub/ncsu_motif`.

ftp.eos.ncsu.edu
Look for the file `brain.motif.tar.Z` in `pub`.

Here is an example of how to get the file. First, type

```
ftp ftp.uu.net
```

When asked for the name, type

```
anonymous
```

When asked for the password, type

```
guest
```

On some systems, your email address is also acceptable as the password, and its use is encouraged.

Now, type `binary` to switch to binary mode, which is necessary to download compressed files. Then change to the appropriate directory with a normal `cd` command. For example, type `cd published`. Once you are in the correct directory, download the file by typing

```
get brain.motif.tar.Z
```

Now type `quit` to exit the FTP command.

On your own system, type

```
uncompress brain.motif.tar.Z
```

Then type

```
tar -xvf brain.motif.tar
```

This will build a new directory called `brain.motif`, which will contain all of the code found in the book.

If you have problems, or if you are unable to use FTP from your machine, please send me mail at one of the two following addresses:

brain@adm.csc.ncsu.edu

brain@eos.ncsu.edu

If you have problems sending email to me, you can send regular mail to:

Marshall Brain
P.O. Box 841
Zebulon, NC 27597

For further information about Appendix D, Lance Lovette can be reached via email at: ltlovett@eos.ncsu.edu.

Further Reading

All Motif programmers I know use two or more of the following references on a regular basis. There's so much in X, Xt, and Motif that it's impossible to remember it all.

Adobe Systems, Inc. *PostScript Language Program Design*. Reading, Mass.: Addison-Wesley, 1989.

Adobe Systems, Inc. *PostScript Language Reference Manual*. Reading, Mass.: Addison-Wesley, 1986.

Adobe Systems, Inc. *PostScript Language Tutorial and Cookbook*. Reading, Mass.: Addison-Wesley, 1985.

Asente, P., and R. Swick. *X Window System Toolkit: The Complete Programmer's Guide and Specification*. Bedford, Mass.: Digital Press, 1990.

Barkakati, N. *X Window System Programming*. Carmel, Ind.: Sams, a division of Macmillan Computer Publishing, 1991.

comp.windows.x.motif

This news group deals with Motif questions and answers. Get on the news reader, and watch and learn. Be sure to download the Frequently Asked Questions (FAQ) file for answers to basic questions.

Jones, O. *Introduction to the X Window System*. Englewood Cliffs, N.J.: Prentice-Hall, 1989.

Kernighan, B., and D. Ritchie. *The C Programming Language*. 2d ed. Englewood Cliffs, N.J.: Prentice-Hall, 1989.

Kochan, S. *Topics in C Programming*. New York: Wiley, 1991.

Man Pages, Section 3.
There are man pages for all X, XT, and Motif functions discussed in this book. If you do not have man pages on your system, get your system administrator to install them for you. They are extremely useful.

Nye, A. *The X Window System Series, Volume Zero: X Protocol Reference Manual for Version 11 of the X Window System*. Sebastapol, Calif.: O'Reilly and Associates, 1990.

Nye, A. *The X Window System Series, Volume One: Xlib Programming Manual for Version 11*. Sebastapol, Calif.: O'Reilly and Associates, 1990.

Nye, A. *The X Window System Series, Volume Two: Xlib Reference Manual for Version 11*. Sebastapol, Calif.: O'Reilly and Associates, 1990.

Nye, A., and T. O'Reilly. *The X Window System Series, Volume Four: X Toolkit Intrinsics Programming Manual*. Sebastapol, Calif.: O'Reilly and Associates, 1990.

Nye, A., and T. O'Reilly. *The X Window System Series, Volume Five: X Toolkit Intrinsics Reference Manual*. Sebastapol, Calif.: O'Reilly and Associates, 1990.

Open Software Foundation. *OSF/Motif Programmer's Reference*. Englewood Cliffs, N.J.: Prentice-Hall, 1990.

Open Software Foundation. *OSF/Motif Style Guide*. Englewood Cliffs, N.J.: Prentice-Hall, 1990.

O'Reilly, T. *The X Window System in a Nutshell*. Sebastapol, Calif.: O'Reilly and Associates, 1990.

Quercia, V., and T. O'Reilly. *The X Window System Series, Volume Three: X Window System User's Guide for X11 R3 and R4*. Sebastapol, Calif.: O'Reilly and Associates, 1990.

Rost, Randi J., *X and Motif Quick Reference Guide: X Window System 11 Release 4 and Motif 1.1*. Bedford, Mass.: Digital Press, 1990.

Scheifler, R. W., and J. Gettys. *X Window System: The Complete Reference to Xlib, X Protocol, ICCCM, XLFD—X Version 11 (Release 5)*. 3d ed. Bedford, Mass.: Digital Press, 1992.

Smith, R. *Learning PostScript: A Visual Approach*. Berkeley, Calif.: Peachpit Press, 1990.

Young, D. *The X Window System: Programming and Applications with Xt, OSF/ Motif Edition*. Englewood Cliffs, N.J.: Prentice-Hall, 1990.

B   DEBUGGING HINTS

Debugging Motif programs is not always easy. Many things can go wrong at many different levels, and it can be difficult to track the error to its point of origin. Even so, several common errors seem to occur quite frequently. In this appendix, I outline some common errors and their causes so that you can find them more easily when they occur.

Bug 1: Segmentation Faults (and Other Random Crashes)

One of the most disheartening errors possible is a segmentation fault. You can use dbx or a similar symbolic debugger to track them down quickly.

To use dbx, recompile the program with the -g option. Then, assuming you have compiled it to a.out for the sake of this example, type dbx a.out. Once dbx is started, type run and do whatever it takes to get the code to crash again. Once it crashes, type where. The where command dumps the contents of the program stack so that you can see the chain of function calls in effect at the time of the crash. Many of these calls will often be Motif internals. Look through the list until you find a function that you can call your own. Note its name, source file, and line number. You can also type print variable_name, where variable_name is the name of a variable in your program. If, for example, you get a crash on the line XtSetSensitive(cut_option,False), you should try typing print cut_option. If null or zero comes back, then you know that the program has not yet created the widget for some reason and this is causing the crash.

Once you have finished with dbx, type quit and then look at the offending line with an editor. You may not see *why* the line is offensive right away, but at least you can see the enemy. Some common causes of segmentation faults include uninitialized widgets, an incorrect number or type of parameters passed to a C function, a failure to initialize **ac**, and a failure to use the address operator (&).

Bug 2: "Toplevel shell has zero width and/or height" Error Message

For some reason, Motif novices see this message fairly often. As stated, the toplevel shell has no width or height and therefore cannot appear on the screen. This means that either the toplevel widget does not have a child, through omission or programming error, or it has a child but the child has not been managed. For example, the toplevel widget may be the parent of a form widget, and the form widget may have children, but you must manage the form widget with the **XtManageChild** function call so that **toplevel** has dimensions.

The cause of this error is easy to track down. Simply look at the parentage of the widgets, and make sure that you have managed all widgets properly.

Bug 3: One or More Widgets Do Not Appear On-Screen

A common error is to place an **XmCreate** function in a program but then forget the associated and necessary **XtManageChild** call. When you make this mistake, the code runs but the new widget does not appear on the screen. Make sure that you have given all widgets an **XtManageChild** call.

Bug 4: Setting a Resource Has No Effect

Here is the scenario: You entered a piece of code that places a new resource value in an argument list, but when you run the code, it seems to have no effect. You may have forgotten to increment **ac** or to call **XtSetValues**, or perhaps the resource name you specified is valid for some other widget but not for the widget you are using. For example, to change the name shown in the title bar of an application, you might use the following code:

```
XtSetArg(al[ac],XmNtitleString, "NMG Editor"); ac++;
```

The code compiles and runs, but the title will not change. The argument list is correct. Unfortunately, while **titleString** is a valid resource name in some widgets, it is not valid for a shell widget. The proper resource name for a shell widget is **title**. The code compiles because **titleString** is a known resource name, but when executed the shell widget simply ignores the improperly named resource.

Another possible cause is an invalid resource value. In many cases, if a resource value is of an invalid format or type, the widget will ignore it without complaining (although in other cases you get a segmentation fault). You should also use typecasting when necessary to convert integers to specific resource types such as **Dimension** or **XmTextPosition**.

Of course, the problem might be that resource interactions are nullifying the effect of the resource value change you are making. See Section 3.7 for more information on this problem.

Bug 5: A Resource Value Returned by XtGetValues Makes No Sense

The converse of being unable to set a resource value is being unable to get the value. Resource-getting problems frequently have one of these four causes: failure to increment **ac**; failure to use an **&** address operator for a scalar variable name; an invalid resource name for the widget; or a variable of the wrong type in which to place the resource value. If you wish to retrieve the width and height of a widget, for example, you should declare the variables as type **Dimension**. If you declare them as type **int**, you get back garbage values on many systems.

Bug 6: Failure to Return to the Main Event Loop in Time

Inside a callback function, you frequently want to cause something to happen on the screen. Perhaps you want to draw something or change the cursor or display a dialog box before returning to the event loop. In some cases, you can use **XFlush**. The cursor-changing code shown in Chapter 15, for example, uses **XFlush** to make the cursor change immediately.

In other cases, however, **XFlush** is ineffective. For example, you might want a dialog box to appear in the middle of a callback function. You can manage the dialog and call **XFlush**, but the dialog will not appear until Motif returns to the main event loop and brings up a pop-up shell, makes the child widgets of the dialog active, and so on.

Chapter 8 discusses callback chains. To make a dialog box appear, you must structure your code so that the program returns to the main event loop.

Bug 7: Bad Parentage Problems

A number of extremely subtle errors derive from parentage problems. When you give a widget the wrong parent, it often behaves in strange ways. For example, if a widget is supposed to be on a form widget but has toplevel as its parent, it either will not appear or will not attach correctly. Similarly, the pop-up menu code in Chapter 17 did not work correctly at first: Because of a parentage error, the menu simply would not appear on the screen. I had made toplevel the parent of the pop-up menu pane. Changing the parent to the drawing area widget instead solved the problem.

Bug 8: Forgetting Header Files

If you forget to include a header file for a widget you are using—for example, if you are using a label widget but forget to include `label.h`—your code will generate strange error messages as it compiles.

C   THE MOTIF STYLE GUIDE

If you have ever used a Macintosh for any length of time, you know that there is a definite look and feel that extends to all true Macintosh applications. One day, I walked into my sister's office in Atlanta and got a taste of how nice this look and feel is. She uses a Macintosh in her graphic design business and had created a business card for me. The card needed one correction. She was busy, so I found the document containing the card and opened it in the normal Macintosh way.

My heart sank when the document appeared in Aldus Pagemaker. I had never touched Pagemaker before, and I knew it to be a gigantic program. To my surprise, however, the File and Edit menus appeared as they do in all Macintosh programs, and I saw a tool palette that uses the standard tools found in most Macintosh drawing programs. I used the standard tools, modified the card, saved the document under a different name in case I had made any mistakes, and printed it. The whole process took less than two minutes. From a user-interface design perspective, this feat was amazing: I had used an enormous program successfully with no training and no experience.

Now imagine the same scenario in WordPerfect on a PC or in who-knows-what on a UNIX workstation. I could not have done anything. The point is that Apple expends an enormous amount of effort to ensure that Macintosh developers conform to one set of style guidelines, so that all applications perform similar tasks in similar ways. Furthermore, the Macintosh marketplace refuses to accept programs that do not conform. The result is a set of applications that work very well together.

In Motif, there is no central authority that influences all developers. Moreover, there are not enough users with voices loud enough to cause the demise of an application because it does not conform to established guidelines. However, the *OSF/Motif Style Guide* attempts to set down some standards. So far, it represents the only hope for establishing any consistency among Motif applications. Every Motif programmer should read through it at least once and follow its guidelines as closely as possible.

The first chapter of the style guide discusses user interface design principles. The section titles of this chapter provide a good checklist of objectives for successful user interface design, so I will repeat them here with my own annotations.

Adopt the user's perspective: Put yourself in the user's shoes.

Give the user control.

Keep interfaces flexible: Give the user several ways to do things.

Use progressive disclosure: Put common tasks within easy reach, obscure tasks out of the way.

Use real-world metaphors.

Allow direct manipulation: Use the mouse to manipulate directly.

Provide rapid response: Let the user know what is happening instantly.

Provide output as input: An application's output should work as input.

Keep interfaces natural.

Make navigation easy.

Provide natural shades and color.

Keep interfaces consistent.

Within the application itself:

Similar components operate similarly and have similar uses.

The same action should always have the same result.

The function components should not change based on context.

The position of components should not change based on context.

The position of the mouse pointer should not warp.

Between applications:

Components should look familiar.

Interaction should be familiar.

Components should be organized in a familiar manner.

Communicate application actions to the user.

Give the user feedback

Anticipate errors: Gray out or disable options that you know will cause errors.

Use explicit destruction: Get user confirmation before deleting files or data.

Avoid common design pitfalls.

Pay attention to details.

Do not finish prematurely.

Design iteratively: Build it, try it, see what does not work, change it, and so on.

Start with a fresh perspective.

Hide implementation details.

If you follow these guidelines, you will go a long way toward creating good programs on any system. This chapter provides a great deal of information.

Chapter 2 of the style guide discusses input and navigation models. Chapter 3 concerns selection and component activation. Chapter 4 discusses application design principles—an important subject. For example, it specifies standard menu bar entries, standard menu entries, and the principles of dialog box design (see also the "Menu Style" sidebar in Chapter 6). Chapter 5 covers window manager design principles. Chapter 6 discusses international design issues. Finally, Chapter 7 is a reference section of all Motif capabilities and how to use them.

Keep in mind the following principles when creating applications:

1. All applications should have File, Edit, and Help menus.
2. The menu bar should contain only cascade buttons that control menu panes.
3. Standard Motif dialogs (Chapter 7) should be used when possible. When creating customized dialogs, follow the pattern set by the standard dialogs.
4. Changing cursor shapes should be used to inform the user about what is happening. The *OSF/Motif Style Guide* provides a complete list of all available cursors and their appropriate uses.

D POSTSCRIPT PRINTING

by Lance Lovette

PostScript is a device-independent programming language for describing the appearance of text and graphics on a printed page. In this appendix, we will cover enough of the basics to allow you to incorporate PostScript graphics into your Motif applications.

D.1 SOME BASIC POSTSCRIPT TERMINOLOGY

D.1.1 STACKS

The PostScript interpreter manages: a dictionary stack, an operand stack, an execution stack, and a graphics state stack. Each is last-in, first-out (LIFO). Most PostScript operators use the operand stack—for example, the statement for adding two numbers is as follows:

```
2 3 add
```

This statement "pushes" a 2 and then a 3 onto the stack, and the **add** operator "pops" both numbers off and then pushes the result (5) back onto the stack (Figure D.1). PostScript uses postfix notation, where the operands (2 and 3) precede the operators (**add**).

D.1.2 THE GRAPHICS STATE AND PATHS

The graphics state is a data structure that contains the current values for the graphics operators (line width, color, font, and so on). One field of the graphics state is the path. Every object drawn in PostScript consists of one. When you draw a line, for example, the path is one straight line. When you draw a rectangle, it consists of four straight lines. The definition of characters in PostScript is nothing but a collection of paths made up of bezier curves and lines. When you want to "paint" something onto a page, you first have to define a path, then call a painting operator (**stroke**, **fill**, or **show**) that performs that function.

357

Figure D.1   PostScript Operand During an add Operation

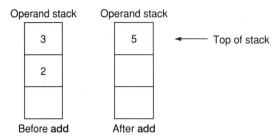

D.1.3   COORDINATE SYSTEM

The unit of measurement in PostScript is the *point*. There are 72 points per inch. Thus, a letter-size sheet of paper measures 612 × 792 points. The PostScript coordinate system resembles the Cartesian coordinate system, with the origin (0, 0) in the lower left corner of the page. PostScript operators allow you to manipulate the coordinate system if you want (**translate**, **scale**, **rotate**, and so on).

D.1.4   SYNTAX

PostScript is an interpreted language, which means that when a printer or other interpreter looks at the file, it executes the instructions on the fly—there is no compilation step. A PostScript file is an ordinary ASCII file that has a "magic cookie" at the beginning to let the interpreter know that this file is PostScript and to execute the instructions as PostScript. The first line of every PostScript file begins with %!, usually followed by the version identifier. The examples in this chapter use PS-Adobe 2.0 as the identifier. Comments begin with a % and end with a new line.

D.2   DRAWING WITH POSTSCRIPT

To introduce you to PostScript, I will show you pieces of example code. I will follow each piece with an explanation that discusses new operators and their use. First we will make a simple program that draws a diagonal line from the origin to the upper right corner of the page (Figure D.2).

Figure D.2 Output of Listing D.1

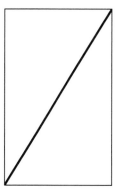

Listing D.1 A Simple PostScript Program

```
%!PS-Adobe-2.0
0 0 moveto
612 792 lineto
stroke
showpage
```

Line 1 contains the "magic cookie" and states the PostScript version. Line 2 establishes a new path and sets the current point to the origin. The statement pushes two zeros onto the stack; calls **moveto**, which requires two operands; and pops off both zeros, leaving the stack empty. Line 3 draws a line (extends the path) from the current point $0, 0$ to $612, 792$. The operator **lineto** draws a line from the current point to another point (x,y) where x and y are relative to the origin. The statement pushes 612 and 792 onto the stack, then **lineto** pops off both operands, leaving the stack empty. Line 4, the operator **stroke**, applies paint along the current path (renders the path). Paint is opaque, so if you paint a black line and then paint a white line over it, the white line will hide the black. Line 5 sends the page to the printer or other PostScript output device. The following C function produces the PostScript code above. It shows how easy it is to generate a PostScript file from within a C program.

Listing D.2 A C Program That Produces Listing D.1

```
void CreatePostScript(void)
{
    char *ps;
```

```
FILE *file;

ps=(char *) XtMalloc( 300 );

strcpy(ps, "!PS-Adobe-2.0  \n" );
strcat(ps, "0 0 moveto      \n" );
strcat(ps, "612 792 lineto \n" );
strcat(ps, "stroke          \n" );
strcat(ps, "showpage        \n" );

/*
 * After we open the file we want to make sure there
 * wasn't an error ( file != NULL ).
 * 'fprintf' is like 'printf' except that it prints
 * a string to a specified stream
 * (in this case 'file').
 */
    file=fopen("filename", "w");
    if( file != NULL )
      fprintf(file, "%s", ps);
    fclose( file );
    XtFree( ps );
}
```

D.3   CHARACTER STRINGS

In PostScript, a character's path is defined by a set of bezier curves and lines. This allows PostScript to manipulate a character or string like any other graphical object. Once you determine the path of a string using the **charpath** operator, you can use **stroke**, **fill**, **scale**, **rotate**, or any other path operator on the string. Alternatively, the **show** operator paints a character string onto the current page using the current graphics state without using the **charpath** operator. (See Figure D.3.)

**Listing D.3   A PostScript Program That Prints
a String**

```
%!PS-Adobe-2.0
100 200 moveto
/Times-BoldItalic findfont
72 scalefont
setfont
(Motif is neat.) show
showpage
```

Figure D.3   Output of Listing D.3

Motif is neat.

This code starts a new path with the current point at (100, 200). In line 2, the slash defines a literal name in PostScript. A literal name, as opposed to an executable name, is treated as data by the interpreter and pushed onto the operand stack to be used by an operator. The string `/Times-BoldItalic` pushes the font name "Times-BoldItalic" onto the stack. The **findfont** operator pops the font name off the stack and searches for it. If found, the font is pushed onto the top of the stack and becomes the current font. Since the **findfont** operator pushes a 1-point font on the stack, the code scales it 72 points (one inch) in both the x and y direction to make it more readable.

The **scalefont** operator has two operands, a font and a scale value. The font was pushed on the stack by **findfont**, and the scale value is 72. The **scale** operator pops both operands off the stack and returns the new font. The **scalefont** operator requires only one scale operand because it scales the font in both the x and y directions. You can use the **scale** operator to scale each axis separately. The **setfont** operator pops a font off the top of the stack and establishes it as the current font for subsequent character operations by changing the graphics state. The text to be printed is enclosed in parentheses unless the string is a literal. The **show** operator is used only with text, and does not use **charpath**. It fills the current string with the current color, rendering it as **stroke** did before, and moves the current point to the end of the string.

The following C code generates the PostScript code shown above.

Listing D.4   C Code That Generates Listing D.3

```
void CreatePostScript(void)
{
    char *ps, text[25];
```

```
    FILE *file;
/*
 * We use 'sprintf' with 'text' so that we can change
 * the string from within the program,
 * then include that string in the PostScript.
 * This comes in handy when you want to let the
 * user insert a title of his own or something.
 * 'sprintf' is like 'printf' except it prints a
 * string into another string.
 */
    ps=(char *) XtMalloc( 300 );
    sprintf(text, "(%s) show \n", "Motif is neat." );

    strcpy(ps, "!PS-Adobe-2.0                 \n" );
    strcat(ps, "100 200  moveto               \n" );
    strcat(ps, "/Times-BoldItalic findfont \n" );
    strcat(ps, "72 scalefont                  \n" );
    strcat(ps, "setfont                       \n" );
    strcat(ps, text );
    strcat(ps, "showpage                      \n" );

    file=fopen("filename", "w");
    if( file != NULL )
      fprintf(file, "%s", ps);
    fclose( file );
    XtFree( ps );
}
```

The **show** operator fills characters in a string with the current color. To *outline* an object instead (Figure D.4), you must use **stroke**, but to do so you must know the object's path. The **charpath** operator appends the paths of the characters in a string to the current path. To outline a string, get its path with **charpath**, and then use **stroke** as before, as shown in Listing D.5.

Listing D.5 PostScript Code That Demonstrates the Use of charpath

```
%!PS-Adobe-2.0
100 200 moveto
/Times-BoldItalic findfont
72 scalefont
setfont
(Motif is neat.) false charpath
stroke
showpage
```

Figure D.4   PostScript Characters Produced by Listing D.5

Motif is neat.

This listing is the same as the previous listing, except for line 6. The **charpath** operator has two operands, a string and a Boolean value. If the Boolean value is false, the path of the characters is appended to the current path unchanged, at which point you can only use stroke. If the Boolean value is true, then **charpath** applies the **strokepath** operator to the characters' path, yielding a new path that you can use for filling or clipping.

You can imitate the **show** operator if the Boolean value for **charpath** is set to true and you use **fill** instead of **stroke**. The **fill** operator can cause side-effects, so be cautious. It implicitly calls the **newpath** operator when it finishes filling. If you want to keep the current path while filling an object, you must save the current graphics state first (for example, with **gsave fill grestore**).

D.4   PROCEDURES

Procedures are handy if you have something you want to repeat more than once. You can dump a standard header containing %! and procedures into a file, then append the variable code (code that might change) to it. For example, if you want to draw 10 horizontal lines on a page, you can create a procedure that draws a line, then call that procedure 10 times. To create a procedure in PostScript, you define a literal name as the procedure name, then follow it with the body of the procedure, between curly braces.

Listing D.6   Demonstration of a PostScript Procedure

```
/drawHorizontalLine {
    gsave
```

```
      1 setlinewidth
      0 setgray
      moveto
      0 rlineto
      stroke
      grestore
} bind def
% arguments for drawHorizontalLine: width, starting x, starting y

612 0 10 drawHorizontalLine
```

First, you define the name of the procedure as a literal. The left bracket denotes where the procedure begins. The **gsave** operator pushes a copy of the current graphics state onto the graphics stack. Since you are going to edit some fields of the graphics state (the path, line width, and current color), and you want this procedure to leave the current graphics state alone, you make a copy of it, change the copy, then restore the original when you are done. The **setlinewidth** operator pops a number off the stack and sets it as the current line width. Here, the line width is 1. The line is stroked with equal amounts on each side of the path. The **setgray** operator pops a number off the stack and makes it the current color—0 is black and 1 is white. Any number between 0 and 1 is acceptable. For example, .99 is almost all white, .50 is medium gray, and .25 is dark gray. Here, the line is solid black.

Note that the **moveto** has no operands explicitly defined, since the caller will pass the procedure the operands using the stack. The **rlineto** operator means "relative line to." It takes the same operands as **lineto**, but x and y are relative to the current point, not the origin. For example, 0 10 moveto 10 0 rlineto sets the current point at (0, 10), then draws a line over (10 + the current x) and up (0 + the current y): a horizontal line 10 points wide, starting at (0, 10). Only 0 is set explicitly; the second argument is passed on the stack from the caller.

The **grestore** operator pops the top graphics state off the stack, leaving the current graphics state as it was when the procedure was called. The **bind** and **def** operators are separate. If the **bind** operator were left out of the declaration, the procedure would produce the same result. The **bind** operator binds all operator names in the procedure to the operators themselves, thus increasing the procedure's speed. The **def** operator pops two operands off the stack, the /literal and the procedure, and associates the two in the current dictionary, which defines the procedure for the rest of the program. You can also use **def** to create variables in PostScript.

**Figure D.5 How the drawHorizontalLine Procedure
Affects the Stack**

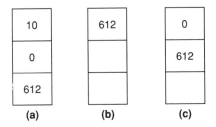

10	612	0
0		612
612		
(a)	(b)	(c)

The final line calls the procedure. The numbers preceding the call are the
arguments **drawHorizontalLine** requires. The first number is the width, the
second is x, and the third is y. First, 612 is pushed onto the stack, then 0 (x)
and 10 (y).

Figure D.5(a) shows how the operand stack looks when the procedure is
called. From within the procedure, the code pushes a 1, which **setlinewidth**
uses, then a 0 for **setgray**. Next, **moveto**, which has no explicitly set operands,
pops two numbers off the stack, that correspond to the last two arguments
pushed onto the stack with the call to **drawHorizontalLine**. One argument
remains on the stack: the 612 (Figure D.5(b)). The **rlineto** operator needs two
operands: an x offset and a y offset. The x offset is 612, since the line is to be
612 points wide. The code pushes a 0 onto the stack for the y offset (Figure
D.5(c)), and **rlineto** pops both operands off the stack, leaving the operand
stack empty.

The following C code creates a PostScript file that draws 10 horizontal lines
using the procedure defined above.

Listing D.7 A C Function That Generates Listing D.8

```
void CreatePostScript(void)
{
    char *ps, *temp;
    FILE *file;
    int i, width, x, y;

    ps=(char *) XtMalloc( 300 );
    temp=(char *) XtMalloc( 300 );

    strcpy(ps, "!PS-Adobe-2.0            \n");
    strcpy(ps, "/drawHorizontalLine  { \n");
    strcpy(ps, "   gsave 1 setlinewidth 0 setgray moveto 0 rlineto stroke
```

```
        grestore \n");
    strcpy(ps, "  } bind def              \n");

/*
 * First we dump the header into the file, which contains any
 * procedures used. Then we append the variable code on to it.
 * We will draw 10 horizontal lines starting
 * at 0,0 and going up the page, with 10 points
 * in between each line.  Each line will
 * be 50 points wide.
 */
    width=50;
    x=0;
    y=0;
    for( i=0; i < 10; i++ )
      {
        sprintf(temp,"%d %d %d drawHorizontalLine     \n", width, x, y);
        strcpy(ps, temp);
        y+=10;
      }
    strcpy(ps, "showpage \n");

    file=fopen("filename", "w");
    if( file != NULL )
      fprintf(file, "%s", ps);
    fclose( file );
    XtFree( ps );
    XtFree( temp );
}
```

This C code generates the following PostScript file.

Listing D.8 PostScript Code That Generates Ten Horizontal Lines

```
%!PS-Adobe-2.0
/drawHorizontalLine {
   gsave 1 setlinewidth 0 setgray moveto 0 rlineto stroke grestore
} bind def
50 0 0 drawHorizontalLine
50 0 10 drawHorizontalLine
50 0 20 drawHorizontalLine
50 0 30 drawHorizontalLine
50 0 40 drawHorizontalLine
50 0 50 drawHorizontalLine
```

```
50 0 60 drawHorizontalLine
50 0 70 drawHorizontalLine
50 0 80 drawHorizontalLine
50 0 90 drawHorizontalLine
showpage
```

D.5   LOOPS AND VARIABLES

Since PostScript is a programming language, it has control operators like **for**, **repeat**, **loop**, **if**, and **ifelse**. The last example drew 10 horizontal lines, and the C code generated a PostScript file containing 15 lines of code. What if you wanted to draw 10,000 lines? If you use the method above, with a for loop in the C code, the PostScript file will have a separate line of code for each line drawn. Thus, it will have over 10,000 lines of code! A more efficient way to draw multiple lines is to put a **for** loop within the PostScript code itself and let the PostScript interpreter do the work. The following PostScript file draws 10 lines more efficiently than the previous listing.

**Listing D.9   PostScript Code That Draws Ten
Horizontal Lines Using a for Loop**

```
%!PS-Adobe-2.0
/drawHorizontalLine {
    gsave 1 setlinewidth 0 setgray moveto 0 rlineto stroke grestore
} bind def
/width 50 def

0 10 90 {
    /y exch def
    width 0 y drawHorizontalLine
} for
showpage
```

Line 5 defines a PostScript variable. The **def** operator associates the name **width** with the value 50. Line 6 begins a **for** loop with initial value, increment value, limit, and a procedure enclosed in brackets. The **for** loop repeats the procedure with an initial value, increments that value by **increment**, and exits when **increment** equals **limit**. Each time the loop is performed, the control variable (the current value of the loop) is pushed onto the top of the stack (Figure D.6(a)). This code uses the control variable as the y value at which to draw, so it defines y as a variable to use later and gives it the current value of the control variable. The format of the operator is **key value def**, but /y (the

Figure D.6 Switching Values on the Stack with the Exch Operator

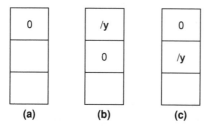

key) is on top of the value we want to assign to it on the stack (Figure D.6(b)). The **exch** operator switches the top two values on the stack. The next line calls the procedure **drawHorizontalLine**, and contains the necessary arguments. The width is always 50, x is always 0, and y depends on the control variable.

The following C code generates the preceding PostScript code.

Listing D.10   A C Function That Generates Listing D.9

```
void CreatePostScript(void)
{
    char *ps, *temp;
    FILE *file;
    int width, x, begin, limit, increment;

    ps=(char *) XtMalloc( 300 );
    temp=(char *) XtMalloc( 300 );

    strcpy(ps, "!PS-Adobe-2.0              \n");
    strcpy(ps, "/drawHorizontalLine  {  \n");
    strcpy(ps, "   gsave 1 setlinewidth 0 setgray  \n");
        strcpy(ps, " moveto 0 rlineto stroke grestore \n");
    strcpy(ps, "  } bind def            \n");

    width=50;
    sprintf(temp, "/width %d def \n", width);
    strcat(ps, temp);

/*
 * First we dump the header into the file, which contains any
 * procedures used. Then we append the variable code on to it.
 * We will draw 10 horizontal lines (begin -> limit by increments
```

```
* of increment), with a width of width, the starting x of 0
* and starting y of the current control variable.
*/
    x=0;
    begin=0;
    increment=10;
    limit=90;
    sprintf(temp, "%d %d %d { \n", begin, increment, limit);
    strcpy(ps, temp);
    strcpy(ps, "/y exch def \n");
    sprintf(temp,"width %d y drawHorizontalLine      \n",  x);
    strcpy(ps, temp);
    strcpy(ps, " } \n");

    strcpy(ps, "showpage \n");

    file=fopen("filename", "w");
    if( file != NULL )
      fprintf(file, "%s", ps);
    fclose( file );
    XtFree( ps );
    XtFree( temp );
}
```

D.6   DUMPING THE CONTENTS OF A DRAWING AREA TO THE PRINTER

You can use PostScript to create code that dumps the contents of a Motif drawing area widget to a printer. When you run the code in this section, you see a drawing area containing a circle, a square, a triangle, and three text labels. Above the drawing area is a push button: When you click it, the program dumps a PostScript file of the image to stdout.

In Listing D.11, **buttonCB** contains a set of calls to a series of **PSDraw** functions, which accept the same parameters as the equivalent **XDraw** functions. The goal is to create a series of function calls that closely duplicate the contents of the drawing area in a PostScript file with a minimum of effort. You can extend this example to draw almost anything.

The **PSInit** and **PSTerminate** function calls are important. **PSInit** dumps a standard header to the PostScript file. This header contains the magic cookie along with a set of PostScript procedures that draw lines, arcs, and text. The body of the PostScript file calls these procedures to draw the objects that appear in the drawing area widget. The **PSTerminate** function puts out a standard trailer.

Listing D.11   A Motif Program That Creates
a Drawing Area Widget and Its Equivalent
PostScript File

```
/* ps_demo.c*/
#include <Xm/Xm.h>
#include <Xm/DrawingA.h>
#include <Xm/Form.h>
#include <Xm/PushB.h>

#define OFFSET 612

XtAppContext context;

XmStringCharSet char_set=XmSTRING_DEFAULT_CHARSET;

GC gc;
Widget toplevel;
Widget drawing_area;
Widget button;
Widget form;

void setup_gc()
/* set up the graphics context. */
{
    int foreground,background;
    XGCValues vals;
    Arg al[10];
    int ac;

    /* get the current fg and bg colors. */
    ac=0;
    XtSetArg(al[ac],XmNforeground,&foreground); ac++;
    XtSetArg(al[ac],XmNbackground,&background); ac++;
    XtGetValues(drawing_area,al,ac);

    /* create the gc. */
    vals.foreground = foreground;
    vals.background = background;
    gc=XtGetGC(drawing_area,GCForeground | GCBackground,&vals);
}
```

```
void PSInit()
{
   printf("%%!PS-Adobe-2.0\n\n");
   printf("/DrawLine {\n");
   printf("   gsave 1 setlinewidth 0 setgray \n");
   printf("   moveto lineto stroke grestore\n");
   printf(" } bind def\n\n");
   printf("/DrawText {\n");
   printf("   gsave 1 setlinewidth 0 setgray moveto\n");
   printf("   /Courier findfont 12 scalefont setfont show grestore\n");
   printf(" } bind def\n\n");
   printf("/DrawArc {\n");
   printf("   gsave translate 1 setlinewidth 0 setgray\n");
   printf("   scale arc stroke grestore\n");
   printf(" } bind def\n\n");
   printf("612 0 translate\n");
   printf("90 rotate\n\n");
}

void PSDrawLine(x1,y1,x2,y2)
   int x1;
   int y1;
   int x2;
   int y2;
{
   printf("%d %d %d %d DrawLine\n",x1,OFFSET-y1,x2,OFFSET-y2);
}

void PSDrawRectangle(x,y,width,height)
   int x;
   int y;
   int width;
   int height;
{
   printf("%d %d %d %d DrawLine\n",x,OFFSET-y,x+width,OFFSET-y);
   printf("%d %d %d %d DrawLine\n",x+width,OFFSET-y,x+width,
      OFFSET-y-height);
   printf("%d %d %d %d DrawLine\n",
      x+width,OFFSET-y-height,x,OFFSET-y-height);
   printf("%d %d %d %d DrawLine\n",x,OFFSET-y-height,x,OFFSET-y);
}

void PSDrawArc(x,y,width,height,a1,a2)
   int x;
   int y;
```

```
   int width;
   int height;
   int a1;
   int a2;
{
    int radius, xrad, yrad, xscale, yscale;

    xrad=(int)width / 2;
    yrad=(int)height / 2;
    radius=(xrad < yrad) ? xrad : yrad;

    xscale=(int)(width > height) ? width/height : 1;
    yscale=(int)(height > width) ? height/width : 1;

    printf("0 0 %d %d %d %d %d %d %d DrawArc\n",
    radius,(int)a1/64,(int)a2/64,xscale,yscale,x+radius,OFFSET-y-radius);
}

void PSDrawString(x,y,s)
   int x;
   int y;
   char *s;
{
   printf("(%s) %d %d DrawText\n",s,x,OFFSET-y);
}

void PSTerminate()
{
   printf("\nshowpage\n");
   printf("%%%%Trailer\n");
}

void buttonCB(w,client_data,call_data)
   Widget w;
   caddr_t client_data;
   caddr_t call_data;
   /* called when the "Create PostScript" button is pushed */
{
   PSInit();
   PSDrawLine(20,150,70,50);
   PSDrawLine(70,50,120,150);
   PSDrawLine(120,150,20,150);
   PSDrawRectangle(140,50,100,100);
   PSDrawArc(260,50,100,100,0,23040);
   PSDrawString(20,170,"Triangle");
```

```
   PSDrawString(140,170,"Rectangle");
   PSDrawString(260,170,"Circle");
   PSTerminate();
}


void exposeCB(w,client_data,call_data)
   Widget w;
   caddr_t client_data;
   caddr_t call_data;
/* called whenever drawing area is exposed. */
{
   XDrawLine(XtDisplay(drawing_area),XtWindow(drawing_area),
      gc, 20,150,70,50);
   XDrawLine(XtDisplay(drawing_area),XtWindow(drawing_area),
      gc, 70,50,120,150);
   XDrawLine(XtDisplay(drawing_area),XtWindow(drawing_area),
      gc, 120,150,20,150);
   XDrawRectangle(XtDisplay(drawing_area),XtWindow(drawing_area),
      gc, 140,50,100,100);
   XDrawArc(XtDisplay(drawing_area),XtWindow(drawing_area),
      gc, 260,50,100,100,0,23040);
   XDrawString(XtDisplay(drawing_area),XtWindow(drawing_area),
      gc, 20,170,"Triangle",8);
   XDrawString(XtDisplay(drawing_area),XtWindow(drawing_area),
      gc, 140,170,"Rectangle",9);
   XDrawString(XtDisplay(drawing_area),XtWindow(drawing_area),
      gc, 260,170,"Circle",6);
}


void main(argc,argv)
   int argc;
   char *argv[];
{
   Arg al[10];
   int ac;

   /* create the toplevel shell */
   toplevel = XtAppInitialize(&context,"",NULL,0,&argc,argv,
      NULL,NULL,0);

   /* set window size. */
   ac=0;
   XtSetArg(al[ac],XmNheight,220); ac++;
   XtSetArg(al[ac],XmNwidth,380); ac++;
   XtSetValues(toplevel,al,ac);
```

```
/* create a form to hold widgets */
ac=0;
form=XmCreateForm(toplevel,"form",al,ac);
XtManageChild(form);

/* create a push button */
ac=0;
XtSetArg(al[ac],XmNlabelString,
    XmStringCreate("Push to generate PostScript",char_set)); ac++;
XtSetArg(al[ac], XmNtopAttachment, XmATTACH_FORM); ac++;
XtSetArg(al[ac], XmNrightAttachment, XmATTACH_FORM); ac++;
XtSetArg(al[ac], XmNleftAttachment, XmATTACH_FORM); ac++;
button=XmCreatePushButton(form,"button",al,ac);
XtManageChild(button);
XtAddCallback(button,XmNactivateCallback,buttonCB,NULL);

/* create a drawing area widget. */
ac=0;
XtSetArg(al[ac], XmNtopAttachment, XmATTACH_WIDGET); ac++;
XtSetArg(al[ac], XmNtopWidget, button); ac++;
XtSetArg(al[ac], XmNrightAttachment, XmATTACH_FORM); ac++;
XtSetArg(al[ac], XmNleftAttachment, XmATTACH_FORM); ac++;
XtSetArg(al[ac], XmNbottomAttachment, XmATTACH_FORM); ac++;
drawing_area=XmCreateDrawingArea(form,"drawing_area", al, ac);
XtAddCallback(drawing_area,XmNexposeCallback,exposeCB,NULL);
XtManageChild(drawing_area);

setup_gc();

XtRealizeWidget(toplevel);
XtAppMainLoop(context);
}
```

The code in Listing D.11 uses the **OFFSET** constant because in the X Window System, the origin is the upper left corner of the drawing area, but in PostScript the origin is the lower left corner of the page. **PSDrawArc** does some number-crunching to convert an X arc into a PostScript arc. The **radius** is the lesser of **width** and **height**. If **width** is greater than **height**, the circle must be scaled in the x direction by **width/height**. If **height** is greater than **width**, it must be scaled in the y direction by **height/width**. Scaling by a factor of 1 does nothing. The **scale** operator is enclosed by **gsave** and **grestore** because you want to scale the circle, not the whole user space. Without **gsave** and **grestore**, everything after **scale** would be scaled by x and y. To convert from an

X angle to a PostScript angle, the code divides the X angle by 64. Note that the header and procedures were dumped at once, then everything else was appended, and then a trailer was put at the end of the file.

Listing D.11 generates the following PostScript file.

**Listing D.12   PostScript Code Generated by
Listing D.11**

```
%!PS-Adobe-2.0

/DrawLine {
  gsave 1 setlinewidth 0 setgray moveto lineto stroke grestore
} bind def

/DrawText {
  gsave 1 setlinewidth 0 setgray moveto
  /Courier findfont 12 scalefont setfont show grestore
} bind def

/DrawArc {
  gsave translate 1 setlinewidth 0 setgray
  scale arc stroke grestore
} bind def

612 0 translate
90 rotate

20 462 70 562 DrawLine
70 562 120 462 DrawLine
120 462 20 462 DrawLine
140 562 240 562 DrawLine
240 562 240 462 DrawLine
240 462 140 462 DrawLine
140 462 140 562 DrawLine
0 0 50 0 360 1 1 310 512 DrawArc
(Triangle) 20 442 DrawText
(Rectangle) 140 442 DrawText
(Circle) 260 442 DrawText

showpage
%%Trailer
```

The first procedure, **DrawLine**, is **DrawHorizontalLine**, which we used above, altered to draw a line from (x1,y1) to (x2,y2). This procedure imitates the Motif **XDrawLine** function. The second procedure draws a string at (x,y) using the Courier font in black. The third procedure draws an arc 1 point wide in black.

The two lines following these procedures make the printer print in landscape, in which the longer dimension of a page is on top. The **translate** operator positions the new origin at the lower right corner of the page. The **rotate** operator flips the page 90 degrees counterclockwise.

The **DrawArc** procedure takes nine parameters: **x**, **y**, **radius**, **ang1**, **ang2**, **xscale**, **yscale**, **xcenter**, and **ycenter**. The first two are the coordinates of the center of the arc, which is (0, 0) because the procedure needs to center the user space at the origin of the original arc (**xcenter**, **ycenter**). The **scale** operator scales the entire user space. If you do not translate and then use a center of (0, 0) for the arc, the center gets scaled and does not show up on the page. The **radius**, **ang1**, and **ang2** parameters are normal arc parameters.

When you use PostScript files on different interpreters, you usually encapsulate them. Encapsulating provides them with a set of standardized comments such as who created the file, what fonts it uses, and how many pages it has. **%%Trailer** is an encapsulated PostScript (EPS) comment that some interpreters need when a file ends.

D.7   OPERATOR SUMMARY

This summary is a condensed and slightly modified version of the operator summary found in the *PostScript Language Reference Manual* from Adobe Systems.

Arguments	Operator	Return Values	Description
Stack Operators			
op1 op2	**exch**	op2 op1	Exchanges top two elements
op	**pop**	—	Removes element from stack
Control Operators			
Boolean proc	**if**	—	Executes **proc** if **Boolean** is true
Boolean proc1 proc2	**ifelse**	—	Executes **proc1** if **Boolean** is true, **proc2** if false

Control Operators, continued

init incr limit proc	**for**	—	Executes **proc** with values from **init** by steps of **incr** to **limit**
num proc	**repeat**	—	Executes **proc num** times
proc	**loop**	—	Executes **proc** an indefinite number of times

Graphics State Operators

—	**gsave**	—	Saves graphics state
—	**grestore**	—	Restores graphics state
num	**setlinewidth**	—	Sets line width to **num**
num	**setgray**	—	Sets color to gray **num** between 0 (black) and 1 (white)

Coordinate System Operators

x y	**scale**	—	Scales user space by **x** and **y**
angle	**rotate**	—	Rotates user space by **angle** degrees counterclockwise
x y	**translate**	—	Translates user space by **x** and **y**

Path Construction Operators

—	**newpath**	—	Initializes current path to be empty
x y	**moveto**	—	Sets current point to (**x**,**y**)
dx dy	**rmoveto**	—	Relative **moveto**
x y	**lineto**	—	Extends straight line to (**x**,**y**)

Path Construction Operators, continued

dx dy	**rlineto**	—	Relative **lineto**
x y r angle1 angle2	**arc**	—-	Extends arc counterclockwise with center (**x,y**) and radius **r**, from **angle1** to **angle2**
—	**closepath**	—	Extends path from current point to the starting point of the path
string Boolean	**charpath**	—	Extends character outline of **string** to current path

Painting Operators

—	**fill**	—	Fills current path with current color
—	**stroke**	—	Paints line along current path

Character and Font Operators

key	**findfont**	font	Returns font dictionary identified by **key**
font scale	**scalefont**	font2	Scales **font** by **scale** to produce new **font2**
font	**setfont**	—	Sets current font to **font**
string	**show**	—	Paints characters of **string** on page (solid)
string	**stringwidth**	x y	Returns width of **string**

Output Operators

—	**showpage**	—	Outputs and resets current page
—	**copypage**	—	Outputs current page

E   C REVIEW

E.1   INTRODUCTION

C is an easy language to learn, especially if you already know Pascal or some other procedural language. Every concept in Pascal maps directly to a concept in C: The ideas are exactly the same, but you use different words to express them. C sometimes seems difficult because it gives the programmer more freedom, and therefore makes it easier to make mistakes or create bugs that are hard to track down.

This appendix introduces you to C by showing you how Pascal maps to it. It also introduces several concepts not found in Pascal. Most of these new concepts deal with pointers.

I believe that the only way to learn C (or any language) is to write and read a lot of code in it. One very good way to get C programming experience is to take existing Pascal programs and convert them. This way, if the program does not work in C, you know that the translation is causing the problem and not the original code.

One major difference between Pascal and C causes problems: C does not allow nested procedures, so you must remove any in order to convert Pascal programs. You should avoid nested procedures in your Pascal programs altogether or remove nesting from programs in the Pascal version. That way, you can retest the program in the Pascal environment before you move it over to C.

Also watch case sensitivity in C. C compilers consider uppercase and lowercase characters to be different: XXX, xxx, and Xxx are three different names in C. By convention, constants in C are spelled with uppercase, while variables are spelled with lowercase, or an uppercase/lowercase combination. Keywords are always lowercase.

A good reference source for C programming is *The C Programming Language* by Kernighan and Ritchie. If you find it too terse, go to the library or bookstore and pick out a reference book that suits you.

In this appendix, all compilation instructions and references to man pages assume that you are working on a fairly normal UNIX workstation. If you are not, you will have to use the manuals for your system to map the instructions to your environment.

E.2   A SIMPLE FACTORIAL PROGRAM

Below is a very simple C program that finds the factorial of 6. Fire up your favorite editor and enter it. Do not copy the file or cut and paste: Actually type the code, because the act of typing will cause it to start entering your brain. Then save the program to a file named samp.c. If you leave off .c, you will get a "Bad Magic Number" error when you compile it, so make sure you remember it.

```
/* Program to find factorial of 6 */
#include <stdio.h>
#define VALUE 6
int i,j;

void main()
{
    j=1;
    for (i=1; i<=VALUE; i++)
        j=j*i;
    printf("The factorial of %d is %d\n",VALUE,j);
}
```

When you enter this program, position #include and #define so that the pound sign is in column 1. Otherwise, the spacing and indentation can be any way you like it. On most UNIX systems, you will find a program called cb, the C Beautifier, which will format code for you.

To compile this code, type cc samp.c. To run it, type a.out. If it does not compile or does not run correctly, edit it again and see where you went wrong.

Now let's look at the equivalent Pascal code:

```
{ Program to find factorial of 6 }

program samp;

const
    value=6;
var
    i,j:integer;
```

```
begin
    j:=1;
    for i:=1 to value do
        j:=j*i;
    writeln('The factorial of ',value,' is ',j);
end.
```

You can see an almost one-to-one correspondence. The only real difference is that the C code starts with #include <stdio.h>. This line includes the standard I/O library into your program so that you can read and write values, handle text files, and so on. C has a large number of standard libraries like stdio.

The #define line creates a constant. Two global variables are declared using the int i,j; line. Other common variable types are **float** (for real numbers) and **char** (for characters), both of which you can declare in the same way as **int**.

The line main() declares the **main** function. Every C program must have a function named **main** somewhere in the code. In C, { and } replace Pascal's begin and end. Also, = replaces Pascal's := assignment operator. The for loop and the **printf** statement are slightly strange, but they perform the same function as their Pascal counterparts. Note that C uses double quotes instead of single quotes for strings.

The **printf** statement in C is easier to use than the Pascal version once you get used to it. The portion in quotes is called the **format string** and describes how the data is to be formatted when printed. The format string contains string literals such as The factorial of and \n for carriage returns, and % operators as placeholders for variables. The two **%d** operators in the format string indicate that integer values found later in the parameter list are to be placed into the string at these points. Other operators include **%f** for floating point values, **%c** for characters, and **%s** for strings. You can type man printf to get the man page on formatting options.

In the **printf** statement, it is extremely important that the number of % operators in the format string corresponds exactly with the number and type of the variables following it. For example, if the format string contains the operators **%s**, **%d**, and **%f**, it must be followed by exactly three parameters, and they must have the same types in the same order as those specified by the % operators.

This program is good, but it would be better if it read in the value instead of using a constant. Edit the file, remove the **VALUE** constant, and declare a variable **value** instead as a global integer (changing all references to lower-case because **value** is now a variable). Then place the following two lines at the beginning of the program:

```
printf("Enter the value:");
scanf("%d",&value);
```

The equivalent code for this in Pascal is:

```
write('Enter a value:');
readln(value);
```

Make the changes, then compile and run the program to make sure it works. Note that **scanf** uses the same sort of format string as **printf** (type `man scanf` for more info). Also note the **&** sign in front of `value`. This is the *address operator* in C: It returns the address of the variable, and it will not make sense until we discuss pointers. You must use the & operator in **scanf** on any variable of type **char**, **int**, or **float**, as well as record types, which we will get to later. If you leave out the & operator, you will get a segmentation fault when you run the program.

C Errors to Avoid

1. Forgetting to use the **&** in **scanf**.
2. Too many or too few parameters following the format statement in **printf** or **scanf**.
3. Forgetting the */ at the end of a comment.

E.3   BRANCHING AND LOOPING

If statements and **while** loops in C both rely on the idea of *Boolean expressions*, as they do in Pascal. In C, however, there is no Boolean type: You use plain integers instead. The integer value 0 in C is false, while any other integer value is true.

Here is a simple translation from Pascal to C. First, the Pascal code:

```
if (x=y) and (j>k) then
    z:=1
else
    q:=10;
```

The C translation looks very similar, but there are some important differences, which we will discuss next.

```
if ((x==y) && (j>k))
    z=1;
else
    q=10;
```

Notice that = in Pascal became == in C. This is a very important difference, because C will accept a single = when you compile, but will behave differently when you run the program. The and in Pascal becomes && in C. Also note that z=1; in C has a semicolon, that C drops the then, and that the Boolean expression must be completely surrounded by parentheses.

The following chart shows the translation of all Boolean operators from Pascal to C.

Pascal	C
=	==
<	<
>	>
<=	<=
>=	>=
<>	!=
and	&&
or	||
not	!

The == sign is a problem because every now and then you may forget and type just =. Because integers replace Booleans, the following is legal in C:

```
void main()
{
    int a;

    printf("Enter a number:");
    scanf("%d",a);
    if (a)
    {
        blah blah blah
    }
}
```

If a is anything other than 0, the code that blah blah blah represents gets executed. Suppose you take the following Pascal statement:

```
if a=b then
```

and incorrectly convert it to C as:

```
if (a=b)   /* it SHOULD be "if (a==b)" */
```

In C, this statement means "Assign **b** to **a**, and then test **a** for its Boolean value." So if **a** becomes 0, the **if** statement is false; otherwise, it is true. The value of **a** changes as well. This is not the intended behavior (although this feature is useful when used correctly), so be careful with your = and == conversions.

While statements are just as easy to translate as **if** statements. For example, the following Pascal code:

```
while a<b do
begin
    blah blah blah
end;
```

in C becomes:

```
while (a<b)
{
    blah blah blah
}
```

C also provides a "do-while" structure to replace Pascal's "repeat-until," as shown below:

```
do
{
    blah blah blah
}
while (a<b);
```

The **for** loop in C is somewhat different from a Pascal **for** loop, because the C version is simply a shorthand way of expressing a **while** statement. For example, suppose you have the following code in C:

```
x=1;
while (x<10)
{
    blah blah blah
    x++; /* x++ is the same as saying x=x+1. It's an increment. */
}
```

You can convert this into a for loop as follows:

```
for(x=1; x<10; x++)
{
    blah blah blah
}
```

Note that the **while** loop contains an initialization step (x=1), a test step (x<10), and an increment step (x++). The **for** loop lets you put all three parts onto one line, but you can put anything into those three parts. For example, suppose you have the following loop:

```
a=1;
b=6;
while (a<b)
{
    a++;
    printf("%d\n",a);
}
```

You can place this into a **for** statement as well:

```
for (a=1,b=6; a<b; a++,printf("%d\n",a));
```

It is confusing, but it is possible. The comma operator lets you separate several different statements in the initialization and increment sections of the **for** loop (but not in the test section). Many C programmers like to pack a lot of information into a single line of C code. I think it makes the code harder to understand, so I break it up.

C Errors to Avoid

1. Putting = when you mean == in an **if** or **while** statement.
2. Accidentally putting a ; at the end of a **for** loop or if statement, so that the statement has no effect. For example,

   ```
   for (x=1; x<10; x++);
       printf(''%d\n'',x);
   ```

   only prints out one value because of the semicolon after the **for** statement.

E.4   ARRAYS AND THE BUBBLE SORT

In this section, you will create a small program that generates 10 random numbers and sorts them.

Start an editor and enter the following code:

```
#include <stdio.h>
#define MAX 10

int a[MAX];
int rand_seed=10;

int rand() /* from K&R - returns random number between 0 and 32767.*/
{
    rand_seed = rand_seed * 1103515245 +12345;
    return (unsigned int)(rand_seed / 65536) % 32768;
}


void main()
{
    int i,t,x,y;

    /* fill array */
    for (i=0; i<MAX; i++)
    {
        a[i]=rand();
        printf("%d\n",a[i]);
    }

        /* more stuff will go here in a minute */
}
```

This code contains several new concepts, although the lines #include and #define should be familiar to you. The line int a[MAX]; shows you how to declare an array of integers in C. As an example, the declaration int a[10]; is declared like this in Pascal:

```
a:array [0..9] of integer;
```

All arrays start at index zero and go to n-1 in C. Thus, int a[10]; contains 10 elements, and the largest valid index is 9. Unlike Pascal, C offers no way to change the range of index values. Also note that because of the position of the array **a**, it is global to the entire program.

The line int rand_seed=10; also declares a global variable, this time named **rand_seed**, that is initialized to 10 each time the program begins. This value is the starting seed for the random number code that follows. In a real random number generator, the seed should initialize as a random value, such as the system time. Here, the **rand** function will produce the same values each time you run the program.

The line int rand() is a function declaration. The equivalent function declaration looks like this in Pascal:

```
function rand:integer;
```

The **rand** function accepts no parameters and returns an integer value.

The four lines that follow implement the **rand** function. We will ignore them for now.

The **main** function is normal. Four local integers are declared, and the array is filled with 10 random values using a **for** loop. Note that arrays are indexed exactly as they are in Pascal.

Now add the following code in place of the more stuff ... comment:

```
/* bubble sort the array */
for (x=0; x<MAX-1; x++)
    for (y=0; y<MAX-x-1; y++)
        if (a[y]>a[y+1])
        {
            t=a[y];
            a[y]=a[y+1];
            a[y+1]=t;
        }

/* print sorted array */
printf("-------------------\n");
for (i=0; i<MAX; i++)
printf("%d\n",a[i]);
```

This code sorts the random values and prints them in sorted order.

Exercises

1. In the first piece of code, try changing the **for** loop that fills the array to a single line of code. Make sure that the result is the same as the original code.
2. Take the bubble sort code out and put it into its own function. (See E.6, if necessary.) The function header will be void bubble_sort(). Then move the variables used by the bubble sort to the function as well and make them local there. Because the array is global, you do not need to pass parameters.
3. Initialize the random number seed to different values.

C Errors to Avoid

1. C has no range checking, so if you index past the end of the array, it will not tell you about it. It will eventually crash or give you garbage data.
2. A function call must include (), even if no parameters are passed. For example, C will accept x=rand;, but the call will not work. The memory address of the **rand** function will be placed into x. You must say x=rand();.

E.5   DETAILS YOU NEED TO KNOW

E.5.1   OPERATORS AND OPERATOR PRECEDENCE

The operators in C are similar to the operators in Pascal, as shown below:

Pascal	C
+	+
-	-
/	/
*	*
div	/
mod	%

The / operator performs integer division if both operands are integers and floating point division otherwise. For example:

```
void main()
{
    float a;
    a=10/3;
    printf("%f\n",a);
}
```

This code prints out a floating point value since **a** is declared as type float, but **a** will be 3.0 because the code performed an integer division.

Operator precedence in C is also similar to that in Pascal. As in Pascal, parentheses control precedence. See E.14 for more information on precedence, which becomes somewhat complicated in C once pointers are introduced.

E.5.2   TYPECASTING

C allows you to perform type conversions on the fly. You do this especially often when using pointers. Typecasting also occurs during the assignment operation for certain types. For example, in the code above, the integer value was automatically converted to a float.

You do typecasting in C by placing the type name in parentheses and putting it in front of the value you want to change. Thus, in the above code, replacing the line a=10/3; with a=(float)10/3; produces 3.33333 in **a** because 10 is converted to a floating point value before the division.

E.5.3   TYPES

You declare named, user-defined types in C with the **typedef** statement. The following example shows a type that appears often in C code:

```
#define TRUE  1
#define FALSE 0

typedef int boolean;

void main()
{
    boolean b;

    b=FALSE;
    blah blah blah
}
```

This code allows you to declare Boolean types in C programs.

If you do not like the word "float" for real numbers, you can say:

```
typedef float real;
```

and then later say:

```
real r1,r2,r3;
```

You can place **typedef** statements anywhere in a C program as long as they come prior to their first use in the code. You do not have to group them together as in Pascal, and you need no special word to mark the beginning of the block as in Pascal.

E.5.4   RECORDS

Records in C and Pascal are very similar, as shown below. First, consider a Pascal record.

```
type
    rec=record
        a,b,c:integer;
        d,e,f:real;
    end;
var
    r:rec;
```

In C, the same code looks like:

```
struct rec
{
    int a,b,c;
    float d,e,f;
}; /* Note semicolon */

struct rec r;
```

As shown here, whenever you want to create records of the type **rec**, you have to say `struct rec`. This line is very easy to forget, and I get many compiler errors because I absent-mindedly leave out the `struct`. You can compress the code into the form

```
struct rec
{
    int a,b,c;
    float d,e,f;
} r;
```

where the type declaration for **rec** and the variable **r** are declared in the same statement.

You access fields of records exactly as in Pascal, using a period (.), for example, `r.a=5;`.

You can declare a **typedef** for a record. For example, if you do not like saying `struct rec r` every time you want to declare a record, you can say

```
typedef struct rec rec_type;
```

and then declare records of type **rec_type** by saying

```
rec_type r;
```

E.5.5   ARRAYS

You declare arrays by inserting an array size after a normal declaration, as shown below:

```
int a[10];        /* array of integers */
char s[100];      /* array of characters (a C string) */
float f[20];      /* array of reals */
struct rec r[50]; /* array of records */
```

E.5.6   INCREMENTING

We have seen that the statement i++ increments a variable. A few more of the C shorthand incrementing functions, and what they mean, follow:

Long Way	Short Way
i=i+1;	i++;
i=i-1;	i--;
i=i+3;	i += 3;
i=i*j;	i *= j;

Exercises

1. Try out different pieces of code to investigate typecasting and precedence. Try out int, char, float, and so on.
2. Create an array of records and write some code to sort that array on one integer field.

C Errors to Avoid

1. As described above, using the / operator with two integers will often produce an unexpected result, so think about it whenever you use it.

E.6   FUNCTIONS IN C

Most languages let you create procedures or functions, or both. C allows only functions, although you can create procedures by making functions that return nothing. C functions can accept an unlimited number of parameters. As mentioned in the introduction, they cannot be nested. In general, C does not care in what order you put your functions in the program.

We have already talked a little about functions. The **rand** function in E.4 is about as simple as a function can get. It accepts no parameters and returns an integer result:

```
int rand()
/* from K&R - produces a random number between 0 and 32767.*/
{
    rand_seed = rand_seed * 1103515245 +12345;
    return (unsigned int)(rand_seed / 65536) % 32768;
}
```

The `int rand()` line declares the function **rand** to the rest of the program and specifies that **rand** will accept no parameters and return an integer result. This function has no local variables, but if it needed locals, they would go right below the opening {. (C actually allows you to declare variables after any {. Those variables vanish as soon as the matching } is reached. While they exist, they are placed on the system stack.) Note that there is no ; after the () in the first line. If you accidentally put one in, you will get a huge cascade of error messages that make no sense. Also note that even though there are no parameters, you must use the (). They tell the compiler that you are declaring a function rather than simply declaring an **int**.

The **return** statement is important to any function that returns a result. It gives the function the value to return and causes it to exit immediately. This means that you can place multiple **return** statements in the function to give it multiple exit points. If you do not place a **return** statement in a function, it returns when it reaches } and gives you garbage. In C, a function can return values of any type.

There are several correct ways to call the **rand** function—for example; x=rand();. The x is assigned the value returned by **rand** in this statement. Note that you must use (), even though no parameter is passed. Otherwise, x is given the memory address of the **rand** function.

You might also call **rand** this way:

```
if (rand() > 100)
```

Or this way:

```
rand();
```

In the latter case, the value returned by **rand** is discarded. You may never want to do this with **rand**, but many functions return some kind of error code through the function name, and if you are not concerned with the error code (say you know that an error is impossible) you can discard it in this way.

You create procedures (in the Pascal sense) by giving the function a **void** return type. For example:

```
void print_header()
{
    printf("Program Number 1\n");
    printf("by Marshall Brain\n");
    printf("Version 1.0, released 12/26/91\n");
}
```

This function returns no value, so it is a procedure. You can call it with the following statement:

```
print_header();
```

You must include () in the call. If you do not, the function is not called, even though it will compile correctly on many systems.

C functions can accept parameters of any type. For example:

```
int fact(int i)
{
    int j,k;

    j=1;
    for (k=2; k<=i; k++)
        j=j*k;
    return j;
}
```

returns the factorial of i, which is passed in as an integer parameter. Separate multiple parameters with commas:

```
int add (int i, int j)
{
    return i+j;
}
```

C has evolved over the years. You will frequently see functions such as **add** written in the "old style," as shown below:

```
int add(i,j)
    int i;
    int j;
{
    return i+j;
}
```

It is important to be able to read code written in the older style. There is no difference in the way it executes; it is just a different notation. You should use the "new style," with the type declared as part of the parameter list, unless you know you will be shipping the code to someone who has access only to an "old style" compiler.

It is now considered good form to use *function prototypes* for all functions in your program. A prototype declares the function name, its parameters, and its return type to the rest of the program in a manner similar to a forward declaration in Pascal. To understand why function prototypes are useful, enter the following code and run it:

```
#include <stdio.h>

void main()
{
    printf("%d\n",add(3));
}

int add(int i, int j)
{
    return i+j;
}
```

This code compiles without giving you a warning, even though **add** expects two parameters but receives only one, because C does not check for parameter matching either in type or count. You can waste an enormous amount of time debugging code in which you are simply passing one too many or too few parameters. The above code compiles properly, but it produces the wrong answer.

To solve this problem, C lets you place function prototypes at the beginning of a program. If you do so, C checks the types and counts of all parameter lists. Try compiling the following:

```
#include <stdio.h>

int add (int,int); /* function prototype for add */

void main()
{
    printf("%d\n",add(3));
}

int add(int i, int j)
```

```
{
    return i+j;
}
```

The prototype causes the compiler to flag an error on the **printf** statement.

Place one prototype for each function at the beginning of your program. They can save you a great deal of debugging time, and they also solve the problem you get when you compile with functions that you use before they are declared. For example, the following code will not compile:

```
#include <stdio.h>

void main()
{
    printf("%d\n",add(3));
}

float add(int i, int j)
{
    return i+j;
}
```

Why, you might ask, will it compile when **add** returns **int** but not when it returns a **float**? Because C defaults to an **int** return value. Using a prototype will solve this problem. "Old style" compilers allow prototypes, but the parameter list for the prototype must be empty. Old style compilers do no error checking on parameter lists.

E.7 C LIBRARIES AND MAKEFILES

E.7.1 INTRODUCTION TO LIBRARIES

Libraries are very important in C because the C language supports only the most basic elements it needs. C does not even contain I/O functions to read from the keyboard and write to the screen. Anything that extends beyond the basic language must be written by a programmer. The resulting chunks of code are placed in libraries. We have seen the standard I/O, or `stdio`, library already: Libraries exist for math functions, string handling, time manipulation, and so on. Libraries also give you the ability to split up your programs into modules, which makes them easier to understand, test, and debug, and also makes it possible to reuse code from other programs that you write.

You can create your own libraries easily. As an example, we will take some code from E.4 and make a library out of two of its procedures.

```c
#include <stdio.h>
#define MAX 10

int a[MAX];
int rand_seed=10;

int rand()
/* from K&R - produces a random number between 0 and 32767.*/
{
    rand_seed = rand_seed * 1103515245 +12345;
    return (unsigned int)(rand_seed / 65536) % 32768;
}

void main()
{
    int i,t,x,y;

    /* fill array */
    for (i=0; i<MAX; i++)
    {
        a[i]=rand();
        printf("%d\n",a[i]);
    }

    /* bubble sort the array */
    for (x=0; x<MAX-1; x++)
        for (y=0; y<MAX-x-1; y++)
            if (a[y]>a[y+1])
            {
                t=a[y];
                a[y]=a[y+1];
                a[y+1]=t;
            }

    /* print sorted array */
    printf("--------------------\n");
    for (i=0; i<MAX; i++)
        printf("%d\n",a[i]);
}
```

This code fills an array with random numbers, sorts them using a bubble sort, and then displays the sorted list.

Take the bubble sort code, and use what you learned in E.6 to make a function from it. Since both the array **a** and the constant **MAX** are known

globally, the function you create needs no parameters, nor does it need to
return a result. However, you should use local variables for **x**, **y**, and **t**.

Once you have tested the function to make sure it is working, pass in the
number of elements as a parameter rather than using MAX. Do this first without looking at the code below and then compare the two only when you have
finished.

```c
#include <stdio.h>
#define MAX 10

int a[MAX];
int rand_seed=10;

int rand() /* from K&R - returns random number between 0 and 32767.*/
{
    rand_seed = rand_seed * 1103515245 +12345;
    return (unsigned int)(rand_seed / 65536) % 32768;
}

void bubble_sort(int m)
{
    int x,y,t;

    for (x=0; x<m-1; x++)
        for (y=0; y<m-x-1; y++)
            if (a[y]>a[y+1])
            {
                t=a[y];
                a[y]=a[y+1];
                a[y+1]=t;
            }
}

void main()
{
    int i,t,x,y;

    /* fill array */
    for (i=0; i<MAX; i++)
    {
        a[i]=rand();
        printf("%d\n",a[i]);
    }
```

```
    bubble_sort(MAX);

    /* print sorted array */
    printf("-------------------\n");
    for (i=0; i<MAX; i++)
        printf("%d\n",a[i]);
}
```

You can also generalize the **bubble_sort** function even more by passing in **a** and the size of **a** as parameters:

```
void bubble_sort(int m, int a[])
```

This line says, "Accept the integer array **a** of any size as a parameter." Nothing in the body of the **bubble_sort** function needs to change. To call **bubble_sort**, change the call to:

```
bubble_sort(MAX,a);
```

Note that &a has not been used even though the sort will change **a**. The reason for this will become clear in E.10.

E.7.2   MAKING A LIBRARY

Since the **rand** and **bubble_sort** functions in the program above are useful, you will probably want to reuse them in other programs you write. You can put them into a utility library to make their reuse easier.

Every library consists of two parts: a header file and the actual code file. The header file, normally denoted by a .h suffix, contains information about the library that programs using it need to know. In general, the header contains constants and types, along with headers for functions available in the library. Enter the following header file and save it to a file named util.h.

```
extern int rand();
extern void bubble_sort(int,int []);
```

These two lines should remind you of function prototypes. The word "extern" in C represents procedures that will be linked in later. In an old-style compiler, remove the parameters from the parameter list of **bubble_sort**.

Enter the following code into a file named util.c.

```
#include "util.h"

int rand_seed=10;
```

```
int rand()
/* from K&R - produces a random number between 0 and 32767.*/
{
    rand_seed = rand_seed * 1103515245 +12345;
    return (unsigned int)(rand_seed / 65536) % 32768;
}

void bubble_sort(int m,int a[])
{
    int x,y,t;

    for (x=0; x<m-1; x++)
        for (y=0; y<m-x-1; y++)
            if (a[y]>a[y+1])
            {
                t=a[y];
                a[y]=a[y+1];
                a[y+1]=t;
            }
}
```

Note that it includes its own header file (util.h) and that it uses quotes
instead of the symbols < and >, which are used only for system libraries. As
you can see, this looks like normal C code. Note that the variable **rand_seed**,
because it is not in the header file, cannot be seen or modified by a program
using this library. This is called **information hiding**. Adding the word static
in front of int enforces the hiding completely.

Enter the following **main** program in a file named main.c.

```
#include <stdio.h>
#include "util.h"

#define MAX 10

int a[MAX];

void main()
{
    int i,t,x,y;

    /* fill array */
    for (i=0; i<MAX; i++)
    {
        a[i]=rand();
```

```
        printf("%d\n",a[i]);
    }

    bubble_sort(MAX,a);

    /* print sorted array */
    printf("-------------------\n");
    for (i=0; i<MAX; i++)
        printf("%d\n",a[i]);
}
```

This code includes the utility library. The main benefit of using a library is that the code in the **main** program is much shorter.

E.7.3   COMPILING AND RUNNING WITH A LIBRARY

To compile the library, type the following:

```
cc -c -g util.c
```

The **-c** causes the compiler to produce an **object file** for the library. The object file contains the library's machine code. It cannot be executed until it is linked to a program file that contains a **main** function. The machine code resides in a separate file named util.o.

   To compile the main program, type the following:

```
cc -c -g main.c
```

This line creates a file named main.o that contains the machine code for the main program. To create the final executable that contains the machine code for both the main program and the library, link the two object files by typing the following:

```
cc -o main main.o util.o
```

which links main.o and util.o to form an executable named main. To run it, type main.

   It can be cumbersome to type all of the cc lines required to compile a large program, especially if you are making a lot of changes and it has several libraries. As an alternative, the **make** facility can be used. You can use the following makefile to replace the compilation sequence above:

```
main: main.o util.o
        cc -o main main.o util.o
```

```
main.o: main.c util.h
        cc -c -g main.c

util.o: util.c util.h
        cc -c -g util.c
```

Enter this into a file named `makefile`, and type `make` to build the executable. Note that you must precede all `cc` lines with a tab. (Eight spaces will not suffice—it must be a tab. All other lines must be flush left.)

This makefile contains two types of lines. The lines appearing flush left are **dependency lines**. The lines preceded by a tab are **executable lines**, which can contain any valid UNIX command. A dependency line says that some file is dependent on some other set of files. For example, `main.o: main.c util.h` says that the file `main.o` is dependent on the files `main.c` and `util.h`. If either of these two files changes, the following executable line(s) should be executed to recreate `main.o`.

Note that the final executable produced by the whole makefile is **main**, on line 1 in the makefile. The final result of the makefile should always go on line 1, which in this makefile says that the file `main` is dependent on `main.o` and `util.o`. If either of these changes, execute the line `cc -o main main.o util.o` to recreate `main`.

It is possible to put multiple lines to be executed below a dependency line— they must all start with a tab. A large program may have several libraries and a main program. The makefile automatically recompiles everything that needs to be recompiled because of a change.

E.8   TEXT FILES IN C

Text files in C are straightforward and easy to understand. They work the same way as Pascal text files. All text file functions and types in C come from the `stdio` library.

When you need text I/O in a C program, and you need only one source for input information and one sink for output information, you can rely on stdin (standard in) and stdout (standard out). You can then use input and output redirection at the command line to move different information streams through the program. There are six different I/O commands in `<stdio.h>` that you can use with stdin and stdout:

printf	prints formatted output to stdout
scanf	reads formatted input from stdin
puts	prints a string to stdout

gets	reads a string from stdin
putc	prints a character to stdout
getc, getchar	reads a character from stdin

The advantage of stdin and stdout is that they are easy to use. Likewise, the ability to redirect I/O is very powerful. For example, maybe you want to create a program that reads from stdin and counts the number of characters:

```c
#include <stdio.h>
#include <string.h>

void main()
{
    char s[1000];
    int count=0;

    while (gets(s))
        count += strlen(s);
    printf("%d\n",count);
}
```

Enter this code and run it. It waits for input from stdin, so type a few lines. When you are done, press CTRL-D to signal end-of-file (eof). **gets** reads a line until it detects eof, then returns a 0 so that the **while** loop ends. When you press CTRL-D, you see a count of the number of characters in stdout (the screen).

Now, suppose you want to count the characters in a file. If you compiled the program to a.out, you can type the following:

```
a.out <filename
```

Instead of accepting input from the keyboard, the contents of the file named filename will be used instead. You can achieve the same result using pipes:

```
cat <filename | a.out
```

You can also redirect stdout to a file:

```
a.out <filename >out
```

This code places the character count produced by the program in a text file named out.

Sometimes, you need to use a text file directly. For example, you might need to open a specific file name and read from or write to it. You might want to manage several streams of input or output or create a program like a text editor that can save and recall data or configuration files on command.

The commands that handle text files are similar to those for stdin and stdout. Again, they come from <stdio.h>

fopen   opens a text file
fclose   closes a text file
feof   detects end-of-file marker in a file
fprintf   prints formatted output to a file
fscanf   reads formatted input from a file
fputs   prints a string to a file
fgets   reads a string from a file
fputc   prints a character to a file
fgetc   reads a character from a file

You use **fopen** like **reset** and **rewrite** in Pascal. It opens a file for a specified mode (the three most common are **r**, **w**, and **a**, for read, write, and append). It then returns a file pointer that you use to access the file. For example, suppose you want to open a file and write the numbers 1 to 10 in it. You could use the following code:

```
#include<stdio.h>

#define MAX 10

void main()
{
    FILE *f;
    int x;

    f=fopen("out","w");
    for(x=1; x<=MAX; x++)
        fprintf(f,"%d\n",x);
    fclose(f);
}
```

The **fopen** statement here opens a file named out with the **w** mode. This is a destructive write mode, which means that if out does not exist it is created, but if it does exist it is destroyed and a new file is created in its place. The **fopen** command returns a pointer to the file, which is stored in the variable **f**. This variable is used to refer to the file. If the file cannot be opened for some reason, **f** will contain NULL.

The **fprintf** statement should look very familiar: It is just like **printf** but uses the file pointer as its first parameter. The **fclose** statement closes the file when you are done.

To read a file, open it with **r** mode. In general, it is not a good idea to use **fscanf** for reading: Unless the file is perfectly formatted, **fscanf** will not handle it correctly. Instead, use **fgets** to read in each line and then parse out the pieces you need.

The following code demonstrates the process of reading a file and dumping its contents to the screen:

```
#include<stdio.h>

void main()
{
    FILE *f;
    char s[1000];

    f=fopen("infile","r");
    while (fgets(s,1000,f)!=NULL)
        printf("%s",s);
    fclose(f);
}
```

The **fgets** statement returns a NULL value at the end-of-file marker. It reads a line (up to 1,000 characters in this case) and then prints it to stdout. Notice that the **printf** statement does not include \n in the format string, because **fgets** adds \n to the end of each line it reads. Thus, you can tell if a line is not complete in the event that it overflows the maximum line length specified in the second parameter to **fgets**.

C Errors to Avoid

1. Do not accidentally type `close` instead of `fclose`. The **close** function exists, so the compiler accepts it. It will even appear to work if the program only opens or closes a few files. However, if the program opens and closes a file in a loop, it will eventually run out of available file handles and/or memory space and crash, because **close** is not closing the files correctly.

E.9   INTRODUCTION TO POINTERS IN C

Pointers are used everywhere in C, and if you have a good understanding of them C should not pose a problem. If, however, you have never seen pointers before, or feel uncomfortable with them, you may want to read an extra book or two, or talk to someone who already understands them. C pointers are basically the same as Pascal pointers except they appear more often.

C uses pointers in three main ways. First, they create *dynamic data structures*: data structures built up from blocks of memory allocated from the heap at runtime. Second, they handle *variable parameters* passed to functions. And third, they provide an alternative means of accessing information stored in arrays, which is especially valuable when you work with strings. There is an intimate link between arrays and pointers in C.

In many cases, programmers use pointers because they make the code slightly more efficient. Sometimes, they simply seem to make the code harder to understand. Once you have mastered the three uses of pointers in C, however, you "know" C for all practical purposes.

Pointer Basics

A normal variable is a location in memory that can hold a value. For example, when you declare a variable **i** as an integer, four bytes of memory are set aside for it. In your program, you refer to that location in memory by the name **i**. At the machine level, that location has a memory address, at which the four bytes can hold one integer value.

A pointer is a variable that points to another variable. This means that it holds the memory address of another variable. Put another way, the pointer does not hold a value in the traditional sense; instead, it holds the address of another variable. It points to that other variable by holding its address.

Because a pointer holds an address rather than a value, it has two parts. The pointer itself holds the address. That address points to a value. There is the pointer and the value pointed to. This fact can be a little confusing until you get used to it.

The following example code shows a typical pointer:

```
#include <stdio.h>

void main()
{
    int i,j;
    int *p;   /* a pointer to an integer */

    p = &i;
    *p=5;
    j=i;
    printf("%d %d %d\n",i,j,*p);
}
```

The line `int *p` declares a pointer. It asks the compiler to declare a variable **p** that is a pointer to an integer. The * indicates that a pointer is being declared rather than a normal variable. You can create a pointer to anything: a float, a structure, a char, and so on.

The line `p = &i;` will definitely be new to you. In C, & is called the *address operator*. The expression `&i` means "the memory address of the variable i." Thus, the expression `p = &i;` means "Assign to **p** the address of **i**." Once you execute this statement, **p** points to **i**. Before you do so, **p** contains a random, unknown address, and its use will likely cause a segmentation fault.

After the line `p = &i;`, the memory situation looks something like this:

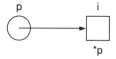

Note that **p** is represented by a circle to indicate that it is a pointer, while **i** is represented by a square to indicate that it is a normal variable.

Once **p** points to **i**, the memory location **i** has two names. It is still known as **i**, but now it is known as ***p** as well. This is how C talks about the two parts of a pointer variable: **p** is the location holding the address, while ***p** is the location pointed to by that address. Therefore `*p=5` means that the location pointed to by **p** should be set to 5. Because this location is also **i**, **i** also takes on the value 5. Consequently, `j=i;` sets **j** to 5, and the **printf** statement produces 5 5 5.

Try the following:

```
#include <stdio.h>

void main()
{
    int i,j;
    int *p;    /* a pointer to an integer */

    printf("%d %d\n",p,&i);
    p = &i;
    printf("%d %d\n",p,&i);
}
```

This code tells the compiler to print out the address held in **p**, along with the address of **i**. The variable **p** starts off with some crazy value or with 0. The address of **i** is generally a large value. For example, when I ran this code, I received the following output:

```
0    2147478276
2147478276    2147478276
```

which means that the address of **i** is 2147478276. Once the statement **p = &i;** has been executed, **p** contains the address of **i**. Try this as well:

```c
#include <stdio.h>

void main()
{
    int *p;    /* a pointer to an integer */

    printf("%d\n",*p);
}
```

This code tells the compiler to print the value **p** points to. However, **p** has not been initialized yet; it contains the address 0. A segmentation fault results, which means that you have used a pointer that points to an invalid area of memory. Almost always, an uninitialized pointer or a bad pointer address is the cause of segmentation faults.

Also note that if you type in the statement p=&i; without any spaces, you will probably get a warning like:

```
Warning: c.c, line 9: ambiguous assignment: simple assign,
         unary op assumed
```

When you see this warning, place blanks around the equal sign.

E.10   USING POINTERS FOR VARIABLE PARAMETERS

Most C programmers first need to use pointers for variable parameters. Suppose you have a simple procedure in Pascal that swaps two integer values:

```pascal
program samp;
var
    a,b:integer;

procedure swap(var i,j:integer);
var t:integer;
begin
    t:=i;
    i:=j;
    j:=t;
end;
```

```
begin
    a:=5;
    b:=10;
    writeln(a,b);
    swap(a,b);
    writeln(a,b);
end.
```

Because this code uses variable parameters, it swaps the values **a** and **b** correctly.

C has no formal mechanism for passing variable parameters: It passes everything by value. Enter and execute the following code and see what happens:

```
#include <stdio.h>

void swap(int i, int j)
{
    int t;

    t=i;
    i=j;
    j=t;
}

void main()
{
    int a,b;

    a=5;
    b=10;
    printf("%d %d\n",a,b);
    swap(a,b);
    printf("%d %d\n",a,b);
}
```

No swapping takes place. The values of **a** and **b** are passed to **swap**, but no values are returned.

To make this function work correctly, you must use pointers, as shown below:

```
#include <stdio.h>

void swap(int *i, int *j)
```

```
{
    int t;

    t = *i;
    *i = *j;
    *j = t;
}

void main()
{
    int a,b;

    a=5;
    b=10;
    printf("%d %d\n",a,b);
    swap(&a,&b);
    printf("%d %d\n",a,b);
}
```

To get an idea of what this code does, print it out, draw the two integers **a** and **b**, and enter 5 and 10 in them. Now draw the two pointers **i** and **j**, along with the integer **t**. When **swap** is called, it is passed the addresses of **a** and **b**. Thus, **i** points to **a** (draw an arrow from **i** to **a**) and **j** points to **b** (draw another arrow). Because the pointers have been established, ***i** is another name for **a**, and ***j** is another name for **b**. Now run the code in **swap**. When the code uses ***i** and ***j**, it really means **a** and **b**. When the function completes, **a** and **b** have been swapped.

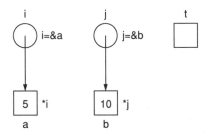

Suppose you accidentally forget the **&** when the **swap** function is called, and that the **swap** line accidentally reads swap(a,b);. This causes a segmentation fault. When you leave out the **&**, the value of **a** is passed instead of its address. Therefore, **i** points to an invalid location in memory and the system crashes when ***i** is used.

This is also why **scanf** crashes if you forget **&**—**scanf** is using pointers to put the value it reads back into the variable you have passed. Without **&**, **scanf** is passed a bad address and crashes.

E.11   USING POINTERS FOR DYNAMIC DATA STRUCTURES

Dynamic data structures—those that grow and shrink as you need them to by allocating and deallocating memory from the heap—are extremely important in C. If you have never seen them before, pick up a book on data structures so that you can learn about them in depth.

Dynamic data structures allocate blocks of memory from the heap as required and link those blocks together into some kind of structure that uses pointers. When a structure no longer needs a block, it will return it to the heap for reuse.

The following two examples show the correspondence between Pascal code and C code using the heap. The first example allocates an integer block, fills it, writes it, and disposes of it. In Pascal, it looks like this:

```
program samp;
var
    p:^integer;

begin
    new(p);
    p^:=10;
    writeln(p^);
    dispose(p);
end.
```

The same code in C looks like this:

```
#include <stdio.h>

void main()
{
    int *p;

    p=(int *) malloc (sizeof(int));
    *p=10;
    printf("%d\n",*p);
    free(p);
}
```

This code is really useful only for demonstrating the process of allocating, deallocating, and using a block in C. The `malloc` line does the same thing as the **new** statement does in Pascal. It allocates a block of memory of the size specified—in this case, `sizeof(int)` bytes. The **sizeof** command in C returns the size, in bytes, of any type. The code could just as easily have said `malloc(4)`, since `sizeof(int)` equals four bytes on most UNIX machines. Using **sizeof**, however, makes the code much more portable and readable.

The **malloc** function returns a pointer to the allocated block. This pointer is generic. Using the pointer without typecasting generally produces a type warning from the compiler. The (`int *`) typecast converts the generic pointer returned by **malloc** into a pointer to an integer, which is what **p** expects. The **dispose** statement in Pascal is replaced by **free** in C. It returns the specified block to the heap for reuse.

The second example illustrates the same functions as the previous example, but it uses a record instead of an integer. In Pascal, the code looks like this:

```
program samp;
type
    rec=record
        i:integer;
        f:real;
        c:char;
    end;
var
    p:^rec;
begin
    new(p);
    p^.i:=10;
    p^.f:=3.14;
    p^.c='a';
    writeln(p^.i,p^.f,p^.c);
    dispose(p);
end.
```

In C, the code looks like this:

```
#include <stdio.h>

struct rec
{
    int i;
    float f;
    char c;
};
```

```
void main()
{
    struct rec *p;

    p=(struct rec *) malloc (sizeof(struct rec));
    (*p).i=10;
    (*p).f=3.14;
    (*p).c='a';
    printf("%d %f %c\n",(*p).i,(*p).f,(*p).c);
    free(p);
}
```

Note the following line:

```
(*p).i=10;
```

Many wonder why the following doesn't work:

```
*p.i=10;
```

The answer has to do with the precedence of operators in C. The result of the calculation 5+3*4 is 17, not 32, because the * operator has higher precedence than + in most computer languages. In C, the . operator has higher precedence than *, so parentheses force the proper precedence. See E.14 for more information on precedence.

Most people tire of typing (*p).i all the time, so C provides a shorthand notation. The following two statements are exactly equivalent, but the second is easier to type:

```
(*p).i=10;
p->i=10;
```

You will see the second more often than the first when referencing records pointed to by a pointer.

A more complex example of dynamic data structures is a simple stack library, one that uses a dynamic list and includes functions to **init**, **clear**, **push**, and **pop**. The library's header file looks like this:

```
/* Stack Library -
   This library offers the minimal stack operations for a
   stack of integers (easily changeable) */

typedef int stack_data;
```

```
extern void stack_init();
/* Initializes this library. Call first before calling anything. */

extern void stack_clear();
/* Clears the stack of all entries. */

extern int stack_empty();
/* Returns 1 if the stack is empty, 0 otherwise. */

extern void stack_push(stack_data d);
/* Pushes the value d onto the stack. */

extern stack_data stack_pop();
/* Returns the top element of the stack, and removes that element.
   Returns garbage if the stack is empty. */
```

The library's code file follows:

```
#include "stack.h"
#include <stdio.h>

/* Stack Library - This library offers the minimal stack operations
   for a stack of integers */

struct stack_rec
{
    stack_data data;
    struct stack_rec *next;
};

struct stack_rec *top=NULL;

void stack_init()
/* Initializes this library. Call before calling anything else. */
{
    top=NULL;
}

void stack_clear()
/* Clears the stack of all entries. */
{
    stack_data x;
```

```
    while (!stack_empty())
        x=stack_pop();
}


int stack_empty()
/* Returns 1 if the stack is empty, 0 otherwise. */
{
    if (top==NULL)
        return(1);
    else
        return(0);
}


void stack_push(stack_data d)
/* Pushes the value d onto the stack. */
{
    struct stack_rec *temp;

    temp=(struct stack_rec *)malloc(sizeof(struct stack_rec));
    temp->data=d;
    temp->next=top;
    top=temp;
}


stack_data stack_pop()
/* Returns the top element of the stack, and removes that element.
   Returns garbage if the stack is empty. */
{
    struct stack_rec *temp;
    stack_data d=0;

    if (top!=NULL)
    {
        d=top->data;
        temp=top;
        top=top->next;
        free(temp);
    }
    return(d);
}
```

Note how this library practices information hiding: Someone who can see only the header file cannot tell if the stack is implemented with arrays, pointers, files, or in some other way. Note also that C uses NULL in place of the

Pascal nil. NULL is defined in `stdio.h`, so you will almost always have to include `stdio.h` when you use pointers.

C Errors to Avoid

1. Forgetting to include parentheses when you reference a record, as in `(*p).i` above.
2. Failing to dispose of any block you allocate. For example, you should not say `top=NULL` in the **stack_clear** function, because that orphans blocks that need to be disposed.
3. Forgetting to include `stdio.h` with any pointer operations.

Exercises

1. Add a **dup**, a **count**, and an **add** function to the stack library.
2. Build a driver program and a makefile, and compile the stack library with the driver to make sure it works.

E.12   USING POINTERS WITH ARRAYS

Arrays and pointers are intimately linked in C. To use arrays effectively, you have to know how to use pointers with them. Fully understanding the relationship between the two requires several weeks or even months of study, so do not get discouraged if you do not understand it right away. Kernighan and Ritchie have a good chapter on these topics.

Let's start with the treatment of arrays in Pascal and other languages. C is nothing like Pascal in this regard, so it will provide a good contrast. Following is an example of arrays in Pascal:

```
program samp;
const
    max=9;
var
    a,b:array[0..max] of integer;
    i:integer;
begin
    for i:=0 to max do
        a[i]:=i;
    b:=a;
end.
```

The elements of the array a are initialized, and then all elements in a are copied into b, so that a and b are identical.

Compare the C version:

```
#define MAX 10

void main()
{
    int a[MAX];
    int b[MAX];
    int i;

    for(i=0; i<MAX; i++)
        a[i]=i;
    b=a;
}
```

Enter this code and try to compile it. You will find that C will not compile it. If you want to copy a into b, you have to enter something like the following:

```
for (i=0; i<MAX; i++)
    a[i]=b[i];
```

Or, to put it more succinctly:

```
for (i=0; i<MAX; a[i]=b[i], i++);
```

Better yet, use the memcpy utility in string.h.

Arrays in C are unusual in that variables **a** and **b** are not technically arrays themselves but permanent pointers to arrays. Thus, they point to blocks of memory that hold the arrays. They hold the addresses of the actual arrays, but since they are *permanent* pointers, you cannot change their addresses. The statement a=b; therefore does not work.

Because **a** and **b** are pointers, you can do several interesting things with pointers and arrays. For example, the following code works:

```
#define MAX 10

void main()
{
    int a[MAX];
    int b[MAX];
    int i;
    int *p,*q;

    for(i=0; i<MAX; i++);
```

```
        a[i]=i;
    p=a;
    printf("%d\n",*p);
}
```

The statement p=a; works because **a** is a pointer. Technically, **a** points to the address of the 0th element of the actual array. This element is an integer, so **a** is a pointer to a single integer. Therefore, declaring **p** as a pointer to an integer and setting it equal to **a** works. Another way to say exactly the same thing would be to replace p=a; with p=&a[0];. Since **a** contains the address of a[0], **a** and &a[0] mean the same thing.

Now that **p** is pointing at the 0th element of **a**, you can do some rather strange things with it. The **a** variable is a permanent pointer and can not be changed, but **p** is not subject to such restrictions. C actually encourages you to move it around using *pointer arithmetic*. For example, if you say p++;, the compiler knows that **p** points to an integer, so this statement increments **p** the appropriate number of bytes to move it to the next element of the array. If **p** were pointing to an array of 100-byte-long records, p++; would move **p** over by 100 bytes. C takes care of the details of element size.

You can copy the array **a** into **b** using pointers as well. The following code can replace (for i=0; i<MAX; a[i]=b[i], i++);:

```
p=a;
q=b;
for (i=0; i<MAX; i++)
{
    *q = *p;
    q++;
    p++;
}
```

You can abbreviate this code as follows:

```
p=a;
q=b;
for (i=0; i<MAX; i++)
    *q++ = *p++;
```

and you can further abbreviate it to:

```
for (p=a,q=b,i=0; i<MAX; *q++ = *p++, i++);
```

What if you go beyond the end of the array **a** or **b** with the pointers **p** or **q**? C does not care—it blithely goes along incrementing **p** and **q**, copying away over other variables with abandon. You need to be careful when indexing into arrays in C, because C assumes that you know what you are doing.

You can pass an array such as **a** or **b** to a function in two different ways. Imagine a function **dump** that accepts an array of integers as a parameter and prints the contents of the array to stdout. There are two ways to code **dump**:

```
void dump(int a[],int nia)
{
    int i;

    for (i=0; i<nia; i++)
        printf("%d\n",a[i]);
}
```

or

```
void dump(int *p,int nia)
{
    int i;

    for (i=0; i<nia; i++)
        printf("%d\n",*p++);
}
```

The **nia** (**number_in_array**) variable is required so that the size of the array is known. Note that only a pointer to the array, rather than the contents of the array, is passed to the function. Also note that C functions can accept variable-size arrays as parameters, which is not possible in Pascal.

E.13   STRINGS IN C

E.13.1   USING STRINGS

Strings in C are intertwined with pointers to a large extent. You must become familiar with the pointer concepts covered in E.9 through E.12 to use C strings effectively. Once you get used to them, however, you can often perform string manipulations more efficiently than you can in Pascal.

A string in C is simply an array of characters (a string of characters held in an array). The following declares a string that can hold up to 99 characters:

```
char str[100];
```

It holds characters as you would expect: str[0] is the first character of the string, str[1] is the second character, and so on. But why is a 100-element array unable to hold up to 100 characters? Because C uses *null-terminated strings*, which means that the end of any string is marked by the ASCII value 0 (the null character), which is also represented in C as \0.

Null termination is very different from the way Pascal compilers such as Turbo Pascal handle strings. In Turbo, each string consists of an array of characters, with a length byte that keeps count of the number of characters stored in the array. The differences are shown below. In these diagrams, ˜ represents garbage.

Pascal String

```
 1  2  3  4  5  6  7  8  9
| H| e| l| l| o| ~| ~| ~| ~| etc.

| 5|  Length byte
```

C String

```
 0  1  2  3  4  5  6  7  8
| H| e| l| l| o|\0| ~| ~| ~| etc.
```

The structure above gives Pascal a definite advantage when you ask for the length of a string. Pascal can simply return the length byte, whereas C has to count the characters until it finds \0. This fact makes C much slower than Pascal in certain cases, but in others it makes it somewhat faster, as we will see in the examples below.

Because C provides no explicit support for strings in the language itself, all of the string-handling functions are implemented in libraries. The string I/0 operations (**gets**, **puts**, and so on) are implemented in <stdio.h>, and a set of fairly simple string manipulation functions are implemented in <string.h> (on some systems, <strings.h>).

The fact that strings are not native to C forces you to create some fairly roundabout code. For example, suppose you want to assign one string to another string; that is, you want to copy the contents of one string to another. In Pascal, this task is easy:

```
program samp;
var
    s1,s2:string;
begin
    s1:='hello';
    s2:=s1;
end.
```

In C, as we saw in E.12, you cannot simply assign one array to another. You have to copy it element by element. The string library (<string.h> or

<strings.h>) contains a function called **strcpy** for this task. The following code shows how to use **strcpy** to achieve the same results in C as in the Pascal code above:

```
#include <string.h>

void main()
{
    char s1[100],s2[100];

    strcpy(s1,"hello"); /* copy "hello" into s1 */
    strcpy(s2,s1);      /* copy s1 into s2 */
}
```

strcpy is used whenever a string is initialized in C. Another major difference between Pascal and C is the way they handle string comparisons. In Pascal, unlike in C, string compares are built into the language. In C, you use the **strcmp** function in the string library, which compares two strings and returns an integer that indicates the result of the comparison. Zero means the two strings are equal, a negative value means that s1 < s2, and a positive value means s1 > s2. In Pascal, the code looks like this:

```
program samp;
var
     s1,s2:string;
begin
     readln(s1);
     readln(s2);
     if s1=s2 then
         writeln('equal')
     else if (s1<s2) then
         writeln('s1 less than s2')
     else
         writeln('s1 greater than s2');
end.
```

Here is the same code in C:

```
#include <stdio.h>
#include <string.h>

void main()
{
    char s1[100],s2[100];
```

```
    gets(s1);
    gets(s2);
    if (strcmp(s1,s2)==0)
        printf("equal\n");
    else if (strcmp(s1,s2)<0)
        printf("s1 less than s2\n");
    else
        printf("s1 greater than s2\n");
}
```

Other common functions in the string library include **strlen**, which returns the length of a string, and **strcat** which concatenates two strings. The string library contains a number of other functions, which you can peruse by reading the man page. Note that many of the standard Pascal capabilities, such as copy, delete, pos, and so on, are missing.

To get you started building string functions, and to help you understand other programmers' codes—everyone seems to have his or her own set of string functions for special purposes in a program—we will look at two examples, **strlen** and **strcpy**. Following is a strictly Pascal-like version of **strlen**:

```
int strlen(char s[])
{
    int x;

    x=0;
    while (s[x] != '\0')
        x=x+1;
    return(x);
}
```

Most C programmers shun this approach because it seems inefficient. Instead, they often use a pointer-based approach:

```
int strlen(char *s)
{
    int x=0;

    while (*s != '\0')
    {
        x++;
        s++;
    }
    return(x);
}
```

You can abbreviate this code to the following:

```
int strlen(char *s)
{
    int x=0;

    while (*s++)
        x++;
    return(x);
}
```

I imagine a true C expert could make this code even shorter.

When I compile these three pieces of code on a MicroVAX with gcc, using no optimization, and run each 20,000 times on a 120-character string, the first piece of code yields a time of 12.3 seconds, the second 12.3 seconds, and the third 12.9 seconds! What does this mean? To me, it means that you should write the code in whatever way is easiest for you to understand. Pointers generally yield faster code, but the **strlen** code above shows that that is not always the case.

We can go through the same evolution with **strcpy**:

```
strcpy(char s1[],char s2[])
{
    int x;

    for (x=0; x<=strlen(s2); x++)
        s1[x]=s2[x];
}
```

Note here that <= is important in the for loop. Be sure to copy \0. Major bugs occur later on if you leave it out, because the string has no end and therefore an unknown length. Note also that this code is very inefficient, because **strlen** gets called every time through the for loop. To solve this problem, you could use the following code:

```
strcpy(char s1[],char s2[])
{
    int x,len;

    len=strlen(s2);
    for (x=0; x<=len; x++)
        s1[x]=s2[x];
}
```

The pointer version is similar.

```
strcpy(char *s1,char *s2)
{
    while (*s2 != '\0')
    {
        *s1 = *s2;
        s1++;
        s2++;
    }
}
```

You can compress this code further:

```
strcpy(char *s1,char *s2)
{
    while (*s2)
        *s1++ = *s2++;
}
```

If you wish, you can even say while(*s1++ = *s2++);. The first version of
strcpy takes 415 seconds to copy a 120-character string 10,000 times, the second version takes 14.5 seconds, the third version 9.8 seconds, and the fourth
10.3 seconds. As you can see, pointers provide a significant performance boost
here.

The prototype for the **strcpy** function in the string library indicates that it
is designed to return a pointer to a string:

```
char *strcpy(char *s1,char *s2)
```

Most of the string functions return a string pointer as a result, and **strcpy**
passes the value of s1 as its result.

Using pointers with strings can sometimes result in definite improvements
in speed and you can take advantage of these if you think about them a little.
For example, suppose you want to remove the leading blanks from a string. To
do this in Pascal, you might use the **delete** function in one of two ways, the
most obvious way being the following:

```
program samp;
var
    s:string;
begin
    readln(s);
    while (s[1] <> ' ') and (length(s)>0) do
        delete(s,1,1);
    writeln(s);
end;
```

This is inefficient because it moves the whole array of characters in the string over one position for each blank found at the beginning of the string. A better way follows:

```
program samp;
var
    s:string;
    x:integer;
begin
    readln(s);
    x:=0;
    while (s[x+1] <> ' ') and (x<length(s)) do
        x:=x+1;
    delete(s,1,x);
    writeln(s);
end;
```

With this technique, each of the letters moves only once. In C, you can avoid the movement altogether:

```
#include <stdio.h>
#include <string.h>

void main()
{
    char s[100],*p;

    gets(s);
    p=s;
    while (*p==' ')
        p++;
    printf("%s\n",p);
}
```

This is much faster than the Pascal technique, especially for long strings.

You will pick up many other tricks with strings as you go along and read other code. Practice is the key.

E.13.2   A SPECIAL NOTE ON STRING CONSTANTS

Suppose you create the following two code fragments and run them:

Fragment 1

```
{
    char *s;
```

```
    s="hello";
    printf("%s\n",s);
}
```

Fragment 2

```
{
    char s[100];

    strcpy(s,"hello");
    printf("%s\n",s);
}
```

These two fragments produce the same output, but their internal behavior is quite different. In fragment 2, you cannot say s="hello";. To understand the differences, you have to understand how the *string constant table* works in C.

When your program is compiled, the compiler forms the object code file, which contains your machine code and a table of all the string constants declared in the program. In fragment 1, the statement s="hello"; causes s to point to the address of the string hello in the string constant table. Since this string is in the string constant table, and therefore technically a part of the executable code, you cannot modify it. You can only point to it and use it in a read-only manner.

In fragment 2, the string hello also exists in the constant table, so you can copy it into the array of characters named s. Since s is not a pointer, the statement s="hello"; will not work in fragment 2. It will not even compile.

E.13.3   A SPECIAL NOTE ON USING STRINGS WITH MALLOC

Suppose you write the following program:

```
void main()
{
    char *s;

    s=(char *) malloc (100);
    s="hello";
    free(s);
}
```

It compiles properly, but gives a segmentation fault at the free line when you run it. The malloc line allocates a block 100 bytes long and points s at it, but now the s="hello"; line is a problem. It is syntactically correct because s is a pointer; however, when s="hello"; is executed, s points to the string in the string constant table and the allocated block is orphaned. Since **s** is pointing into the string constant table, the string cannot be changed; **free** fails because it cannot deallocate a block in an executable region.

The correct code follows:

```
void main()
{
    char *s;

    s=(char *) malloc (100);
    strcpy(s,"hello");
    free(s);
}
```

C Errors to Avoid

1. Losing the \0 character, which is easy if you aren't careful, and can lead to some very subtle bugs. Make sure you copy \0 when you copy strings. If you create a new string, make sure you put \0 in it. And if you copy one string to another, make sure the receiving string is big enough to hold the source string, including \0. Finally, if you point a character pointer to some characters, make sure they end with \0.

Exercises

1. Create a program that reads in a string containing a first name followed by a blank followed by a last name. Write functions to remove any leading or trailing blanks. Write another function that returns the last name.
2. Write a function that converts a string to uppercase.
3. Write a function that gets the first word from a string and returns the remainder of the string.

E.14   OPERATOR PRECEDENCE IN C

C contains many operators, and because of the way in which operator precedence works, the interactions between multiple operators can become confusing.

Most programmers learn about operator precedence from writing equations. For example, say the following statement exists in a C program:

```
x=5+3*6;
```

X receives the value 23, not 48, because in C multiplication and division have higher precedence than addition and subtraction.

Since C has so many operators, it is important to know how operator precedence works. For example, examine the following C declaration:

```
char *a[10];
```

Is a a single pointer to an array of 10 characters, or is it an array of 10 pointers to character? Unless you know the precedence conventions in C, there is no way to find out. Similarly, in E.11 we saw that because of precedence statements such as *p.i = 10; do not work. Instead, the form (*p).i = 10; must be used to force correct precedence.

The following table from Kernighan and Ritchie shows the precedence hierarchy in C. The top line has the highest precedence, the bottom line the lowest.

Operators	Associativity
() [] -> .	Left to right
! - ++ -- + * & (type-cast) sizeof	Right to left
(in the above line, +, - and * are the unary forms)	
* / %	Left to right
+ -	Left to right
<< >>	Left to right
< <= > >=	Left to right
== !=	Left to right
&	Left to right
^	Left to right
|	Left to right
&&	Left to right
||	Left to right
?:	Right to left
= += -= *= /= %= &= ^= |= <<= >>=	Right to left
,	Left to right

Using this table, you can see that char *a[10]; is an array of 10 pointers to character. You can also see why the parentheses are required if (*p).i is to be handled correctly. After some practice, you will memorize most of this table, but every now and again something will not work because you have been caught by a subtle precedence problem.

E.15   COMMAND LINE PARAMETERS USING ARGC AND ARGV

C on UNIX provides a fairly simple mechanism for retrieving command line parameters entered by the user. It passes an **argv** parameter to the main function in the program. **argv** structures appear in a fair number of the more advanced library calls, so you should understand them.

Enter the following code and compile it to a.out:

```
#include <stdio.h>

void main(int argc, char *argv[])
{
    int x;

    printf("%d\n",argc);
    for (x=0; x<argc; x++)
        printf("%s\n",argv[x]);
}
```

In this code, the main program accepts two parameters, **argv** and **argc**. The **argv** parameter is an array of pointers to string that contains the parameters entered when the program was invoked at the UNIX command line. The **argc** integer contains a count of the number of parameters. This particular piece of code types out the command line parameters. To try this, compile the code to a.out and type a.out **xxx yyy zzz**. The code will print the parameters, one per line.

The char *argv[] line is an array of pointers to string. In other words, each element of the array is a pointer, and each pointer points to a string (technically, to the first character of the string). Thus, argv[0] points to a string that contains the first parameter on the command line (the program's name), argv[1] points to the next parameter, and so on. The **argc** variable tells you how many of the pointers in the array are valid. You will find that the preceding code does nothing more than print each of the valid strings pointed to by **argv**.

Because **argv** exists, you can let your program react to command line parameters entered by the user fairly easily. For example, you might have your program detect the word help as the first parameter following the program name, and dump a help file to stdout. File names can also be passed in and used in your **fopen** statements.

E.16   RECORD-BASED (BINARY) FILES IN C

Record-based files are very similar to arrays of records, except the records are in a disk file rather than in an array in memory. Because the records in a record-based file are on disk, you can create very large collections of them (limited only by your available disk space). They are also permanent and always available. The only disadvantage is the slowness that comes from disk access time.

Record-based files have two features that distinguish them from text files: You can jump instantly to any record in the file, which provides random access as in an array; and you can change the contents of a record anywhere in the file at any time. Record-based files also usually have faster read and write times than text files, because a binary image of the record is stored directly from memory to disk (or vice versa). In a text file, everything has to be converted back and forth to text, and this takes time.

Pascal supports the file-of-records concept very cleanly. You declare a variable such as `var f:file of rec;` and then open the file. At that point, you can read a record, write a record, or seek to any record in the file. This file structure supports the concept of a *file pointer*. When the file is opened, the pointer points to record 0 (the first record in the file). Any read operation reads the currently pointed-to record and moves the pointer down one record. Any write operation writes to the currently pointed-to record and moves the pointer down one record. Seek moves the pointer to the requested record.

In C, the concepts are exactly the same but less concise. Keep in mind that C thinks of everything in the disk file as blocks of bytes read from disk into memory or read from memory onto disk. C uses a file pointer, but it can point to any byte location in the file.

The following program illustrates these concepts:

```c
#include <stdio.h>

/* random record description - could be anything */
struct rec
{
    int x,y,z;
};

/* writes and then reads 10 arbitrary records from the file "junk". */
void main()
{
    int i,j;
    FILE *f;
```

```
struct rec r;

/* create the file of 10 records */
f=fopen("junk","w");
for (i=1;i<=10; i++)
{
    r.x=i;
    fwrite(&r,sizeof(struct rec),1,f);
}
fclose(f);

/* read the 10 records */
f=fopen("junk","r");
for (i=1;i<=10; i++)
{
    fread(&r,sizeof(struct rec),1,f);
    printf("%d\n",r.x);
}
fclose(f);
printf("\n");

/* use fseek to read the 10 records in reverse order */
  f=fopen("junk","r");
for (i=9; i>=0; i--)
{
    fseek(f,sizeof(struct rec)*i,SEEK_SET);
    fread(&r,sizeof(struct rec),1,f);
    printf("%d\n",r.x);
}
fclose(f);
printf("\n");

/* use fseek to read every other record */
f=fopen("junk","r");
fseek(f,0,SEEK_SET);
for (i=0;i<5; i++)
{
    fread(&r,sizeof(struct rec),1,f);
    printf("%d\n",r.x);
    fseek(f,sizeof(struct rec),SEEK_CUR);
}
```

```
    fclose(f);
    printf("\n");

    /* use fseek to read 4th record, change it, and write it back */
    f=fopen("junk","r+");
    fseek(f,sizeof(struct rec)*3,SEEK_SET);
    fread(&r,sizeof(struct rec),1,f);
    r.x=100;
    fseek(f,sizeof(struct rec)*3,SEEK_SET);
    fwrite(&r,sizeof(struct rec),1,f);
    fclose(f);
    printf("\n");

    /* read the 10 records to insure 4th record was changed */
    f=fopen("junk","r");
    for (i=1;i<=10; i++)
    {
        fread(&r,sizeof(struct rec),1,f);
        printf("%d\n",r.x);
    }
    fclose(f);
}
```

In this program, a random record description **rec** has been used, but you can use any record description you want. You can see that **fopen** and **fclose** work exactly as they did for text files.

The new functions here are **fread**, **fwrite** and **fseek**. The **fread** function takes four parameters: a memory address, the number of bytes to read per block, the number of blocks to read, and the file variable. Thus, the line `fread(&r,sizeof(struct rec),1,f);` says to read 12 bytes (the size of **rec**) from the file **f** (from the current location of the file pointer) into memory address **&r**. One block of 12 bytes is requested. It would be just as easy to read 100 blocks from disk into an array in memory by changing 1 to 100.

The **fwrite** function works the same way, but moves the block of bytes from memory to the file. The **fseek** function moves the file pointer to a byte in the file. Generally, you move the pointer in `sizeof(struct rec)` increments to keep the pointer at record boundaries. You can use three options when seeking: SEEK_SET, SEEK_CUR, and SEEK_END. SEEK_SET moves the pointer *x* bytes down from the beginning of the file (from byte 0 in the file). SEEK_CUR moves the pointer *x* bytes down from the current pointer position. SEEK_END moves the pointer from the end of the file (so you must use negative offsets with this option).

Several different options appear in the code above. In particular, note the section where the file is opened with r+ mode. This opens the file for reading and writing, which allows records to be changed. The code seeks to a record, reads it, and changes a field; it then seeks back because the read displaced the pointer, and writes the change back.

F AN EDITOR EXAMPLE

To test some of the code and ideas in this book, I created an editor called NMG
Editor as the first release of the NCSU Motif Group (NMG). NMG is a group
of students who get together once a week to discuss Motif programming. The
group's goal is to learn about Motif. To that end I encourage students to work
on projects of a high enough quality to be released onto the network. This
editor code acts as a code formatting, documentation, and style baseline for
the group.

NMG Editor is a good example of a fairly large Motif program that works
well. It uses a number of widgets and combines material from Chapters 3
through 7, 10, 13, 14, and 15. Enjoy using it and customizing it for your own
needs.

```
/*------------------------------------------------------------------
    00    0   00000   0000   0    0      The North Carolina State
    0 0   0   0         0    0    0      University Motif Group
    0 0 0 0            0000   0    0      NCSU Box 8206
    0   00 0              0  0    0      Raleigh, NC 2695-8206
    0    00   00000   0000   0000

    0     0  0000  0000000 0  00000    0000  0000   000  0    0 0000
    00   00 0    0    0     0 0        0      0 0   0 0   0 0   0 0   0
    0 0 0 0 0    0    0     0 0  00000  0      0000 0   0 0   0 0000
    0 0 0 0 0    0    0     0 0        0 000 0 0   0   0 0    0 0
    0   0 0    0      0     0 0        0     0 0 0   0 0    0 0
    0     0  0000    0     0 0        0000  0   0  000   0000 0
------------------------------------------------------------------
```

        Title: NMG Editor demo

        File name: nmg_editor1.c

        File Type: Code

Lead Programmer: Marshall Brain, brain@eos.ncsu.edu

Testing by: Errol Casey, Dave Patterson, Rob Ward, Kelly Campbell
            Brian Casper, Lance Lovette, Aaron Nauman, Steve Loyer,
            Jerry Cox.

Version: 1.03
Date   : 11/5/91

Description: This program implements a Motif text editor. It
    includes File open, new, save, save as, close and quit;
    Clipboard cut, copy, paste and clear; and Navigate top,
    bottom, jump to cursor and jump to line. It also includes
    a utility menu containing a find dialog. Use it to learn
    about the text widget or to create a personalized editor.

Author's notes:
    I have written a book on Motif programming (due from Digital
    Press in early 1992). This program was written to prove some
    of the code in the book correct. For detailed descriptions
    of the code, please see the book (all chapter references in
    the comments refer to chapters in the book).

    The Find dialog used in this program will be more useful if
    it has a title bar that allows it to be moved. If dialog boxes
    on your system do not have title bars and other decorations,
    then add the following line to your ".Xdefaults" file:
        mwm*transientDecoration: all

    Occasionally the scroll bar in the text widget will not allow
    you to scroll all the way to the bottom of the text. I believe
    this is a problem inside the text widget. To solve this, use
    the Navigate/Bottom menu option. It will go to the bottom of
    the text and reset the scroll bar.

System Information:
    This text and code is based on the OSF/Motif widget set version
    1.1 and the X Window System version 4.

About the NCSU Motif Group:
    The NCSU Motif Group is a group of students at North Carolina
    State University who meet once a week to discuss Motif
    programming. Individual projects are used to help students

learn Motif. These projects are then released onto the network
to help others. All released code is available at our anonymous
FTP site: osl.csc.ncsu.edu, in the directory pub/ncsu_motif.
Questions and comments should be directed to the lead
programmer for the project in question, or to the faculty
advisor, Marshall Brain, at brain@eos.ncsu.edu.

```
**********************************************************************/

#include <stdio.h>
#include <sys/types.h>
#include <sys/stat.h>

#include <X11/cursorfont.h>

#include <Xm/Xm.h>
#include <Xm/Text.h>
#include <Xm/Form.h>
#include <Xm/PushB.h>
#include <Xm/Label.h>
#include <Xm/RowColumn.h>
#include <Xm/CascadeB.h>
#include <Xm/FileSB.h>
#include <Xm/SelectioB.h>
```

```
#include <Xm/MessageB.h>
#include <Xm/BulletinB.h>
#include <Xm/ToggleB.h>

/* constants for menu options and find dialog buttons. */
#define OPEN        11
#define CLOSE       12
#define NEW         13
#define SAVE        14
#define SAVE_AS     16
#define QUIT        17

#define CUT         21
#define CLEAR       22
#define COPY        23
#define PASTE       24

#define TOP         35
#define BOTTOM      36
#define JUMP_CURS   37
#define JUMP_LINE   38

#define ABOUT       41
#define HELP        42

#define FIND        51

#define OK          1
#define CANCEL      2

#define FIND_FIND          1
#define FIND_FIND_CHANGE 2
#define FIND_CHANGE        3
#define FIND_CANCEL        4
#define FIND_CASE          5

/* bitmap for icon */
#define nmg_width 50
#define nmg_height 50
static char nmg_bits[] = {
0x00, 0x00, 0x00, 0x00, 0x00, 0x00, 0x00, 0x0e, 0x98, 0x03, 0x0e, 0x7e,
0x00, 0x00, 0x1e, 0x98, 0x07, 0x8f, 0xff, 0x00, 0x00, 0x1e, 0x98, 0x07,
0x8f, 0x81, 0x01, 0x00, 0x36, 0x98, 0x8d, 0xcd, 0x80, 0x01, 0x00, 0x36,
```

```
0x98, 0x8d, 0xcd, 0x00, 0x00, 0x00, 0x66, 0x98, 0xd9, 0xcc, 0x00, 0x00,
0x00, 0x66, 0x98, 0xd9, 0xcc, 0x00, 0x00, 0x00, 0xc6, 0x98, 0x71, 0xcc,
0x00, 0x00, 0x00, 0xc6, 0x98, 0x71, 0xcc, 0xf8, 0x01, 0x00, 0x86, 0x99,
0x01, 0xcc, 0xf8, 0x01, 0x00, 0x86, 0x99, 0x01, 0xcc, 0x80, 0x01, 0x00,
0x06, 0x9b, 0x01, 0xcc, 0x80, 0x01, 0x00, 0x06, 0x9b, 0x01, 0xcc, 0x80,
0x01, 0x00, 0x06, 0x9e, 0x01, 0x8c, 0x81, 0x01, 0x00, 0x06, 0x9c, 0x01,
0x8c, 0xff, 0x00, 0x00, 0x06, 0x9c, 0x01, 0x0c, 0x7e, 0x00, 0x00, 0x00,
0x00, 0x00, 0x00, 0x00, 0x00, 0x00, 0x00, 0x00, 0x00, 0x00, 0x00, 0x00,
0x00, 0xff, 0xff, 0xff, 0xff, 0xff, 0xff, 0x03, 0xff, 0xff, 0xff, 0xff,
0xff, 0xff, 0x03, 0x00, 0x00, 0x00, 0x00, 0x00, 0x00, 0x00, 0x00, 0x00,
0x00, 0x00, 0x00, 0x00, 0x00, 0x42, 0x8e, 0x13, 0x01, 0x00, 0x00, 0x00,
0x46, 0x51, 0x14, 0x01, 0x00, 0x00, 0x00, 0x4a, 0x41, 0x10, 0x01, 0x00,
0x00, 0x00, 0x4a, 0x81, 0x11, 0x01, 0x00, 0x00, 0x00, 0x52, 0x01, 0x12,
0x01, 0x00, 0x00, 0x00, 0x52, 0x01, 0x14, 0x01, 0x00, 0x00, 0x00, 0x62,
0x51, 0x14, 0x01, 0x00, 0x00, 0x00, 0x42, 0x8e, 0xe3, 0x00, 0x00, 0x00,
0x00, 0x00, 0x00, 0x00, 0x00, 0x00, 0x00, 0x00, 0x00, 0x00, 0x00, 0x00,
0x00, 0x00, 0x00, 0x22, 0xe7, 0xeb, 0x03, 0x00, 0x00, 0x00, 0xb6, 0x88,
0x28, 0x00, 0x00, 0x00, 0x00, 0xaa, 0x88, 0x28, 0x00, 0x00, 0x00, 0x00,
0xa2, 0x88, 0xe8, 0x00, 0x00, 0x00, 0x00, 0xa2, 0x88, 0x28, 0x00, 0x00,
0x00, 0x00, 0xa2, 0x88, 0x28, 0x00, 0x00, 0x00, 0x00, 0x22, 0x87, 0x28,
0x00, 0x00, 0x00, 0x00, 0x00, 0x00, 0x00, 0x00, 0x00, 0x00, 0x00, 0x00,
0x00, 0x00, 0x00, 0x00, 0x00, 0x00, 0x9c, 0xc7, 0x89, 0x1e, 0x00, 0x00,
0x00, 0xa2, 0x28, 0x8a, 0x22, 0x00, 0x00, 0x00, 0x82, 0x28, 0x8a, 0x22,
0x00, 0x00, 0x00, 0xba, 0x27, 0x8a, 0x1e, 0x00, 0x00, 0x00, 0xa2, 0x22,
0x8a, 0x02, 0x00, 0x00, 0x00, 0xa2, 0x24, 0x8a, 0x02, 0x00, 0x00, 0x00,
0x9c, 0xc8, 0x71, 0x02, 0x00, 0x00, 0x00, 0x00, 0x00, 0x00, 0x00, 0x00,
0x00, 0x00};

/* general widgets. */
Widget toplevel, text, form, menu_bar;

/* dialog box widgets */
Widget open_dialog, new_dialog, jump_dialog, quit_dialog,
        readonly_dialog, error_dialog, close_dialog, save_as_dialog,
        about_dialog, help_dialog, find_dialog, finderror_dialog,
        overwrite_dialog;

/* widgets having to do with find dialog */
Widget find_label1, find_label2;
Widget find_edit1, find_edit2;
Widget find_button, find_change_button, change_button, find_top_button,
    cancel_button;
Widget case_toggle;
```

```
/* menu item widgets. */
Widget open_option, new_option, save_option, save_as_option,
        close_option, quit_option;
Widget cut_option, clear_option, copy_option, paste_option;
Widget top_option,bottom_option, jump_curs_option, jump_line_option;
Widget help_option, about_option;
Widget find_option, find_rc;


XtAppContext context;
XmStringCharSet char_set=XmSTRING_DEFAULT_CHARSET;


char *filename=NULL;          /* holds the current filename */
char *new_filename=NULL;      /* holds new filename for save as
                                 option. */
Boolean text_changed=False; /* tells whether file has been modified. */
Boolean case_matters=False; /* remembers case sensitivity for find. */


void change_menu_sensitivity(open_state)
    Boolean open_state;
/* changes the menu sensitivities between open and close states. */
{
    XtSetSensitive(open_option,open_state);
    XtSetSensitive(new_option,open_state);
    XtSetSensitive(close_option,!open_state);
    / *will get set true if text is modified. */
    XtSetSensitive(save_option,False);
    XtSetSensitive(save_as_option,!open_state);

    XtSetSensitive(cut_option,!open_state);
    XtSetSensitive(copy_option,!open_state);
    XtSetSensitive(paste_option,!open_state);
    XtSetSensitive(clear_option,!open_state);

    XtSetSensitive(top_option,!open_state);
    XtSetSensitive(bottom_option,!open_state);
    XtSetSensitive(jump_curs_option,!open_state);
    XtSetSensitive(jump_line_option,!open_state);

    XtSetSensitive(find_option,!open_state);
    XtSetSensitive(find_change_button,!open_state);
    XtSetSensitive(change_button,!open_state);
}
```

```
void watch_cursor(w)
    Widget w;
/* change the cursor to a wrist watch shape. */
/* See Chapter 15. */
{
    Cursor c1;

    c1 = XCreateFontCursor(XtDisplay(w),XC_watch);
    XDefineCursor(XtDisplay(w),XtWindow(w),c1);
    XFlush(XtDisplay(w));
}

void normal_cursor(w)
    Widget w;
/* return the cursor to its normal shape. */
/* See Chapter 15. */
{
    XUndefineCursor(XtDisplay(w),XtWindow(w));
    XFlush(XtDisplay(w));
}

void change_title()
/* changes the title on the window to file name. */
/* See Chapter 14. */
{
    int ac;
    Arg al[10];
    char s[1000];

    if (filename!=NULL)
    {
        strcpy(s,"NMG Editor - ");
        strcat(s,filename);
        ac = 0;
        XtSetArg(al[ac], XmNtitle, s); ac++;
        XtSetValues(toplevel,al,ac);
    }
    else
    {
        strcpy(s,"NMG Editor");
        ac = 0;
        XtSetArg(al[ac], XmNtitle, s); ac++;
```

```
        XtSetValues(toplevel,al,ac);
    }
}


Boolean read_file()
/* reads the file in filename into the text widget. */
/* See Chapter 10. */
{
    FILE *f;
    char *file_contents;
    int file_length;
    struct stat stat_val;

    /* open and read the file. */
    if (stat(filename, &stat_val) == 0)
    {
        watch_cursor(toplevel);
        file_length = stat_val.st_size;
        /* try to open file in "r+" mode. if OK then read it. */
        if ((f=fopen(filename,"r+"))==NULL)
        {
            /* if can't open with "r+", try to open with "r". This
               means the file is read-only. If can't open that way,
               then file is unreadable. */
            if ((f=fopen(filename,"r"))==NULL)
                return(False);
            else
                XtManageChild(readonly_dialog);
        }
        /* malloc a place for the string to be read to. */
        file_contents = (char *) XtMalloc(file_length+1);
        *file_contents = '\0';
        /* read the file string */
        fread(file_contents, sizeof(char), file_length, f);
        fclose(f);
        file_contents[file_length]='\0';
        /* give the string to the text widget. */
        XmTextSetString(text, file_contents);
        XtFree(file_contents);
        text_changed=False;
        XtSetSensitive(save_option,False);
        normal_cursor(toplevel);
    }
```

```
        else
            return(False);
        return(True);
}


void openCB(w, client_data, call_data)
        Widget w;
        int client_data;
        XmFileSelectionBoxCallbackStruct *call_data;
/* handles the file selection box callback and the new dialog callback.
   if the file is new, then read_file will do nothing and a blank
   file will be created. */
/* See Chapter 10. */
{
        if (client_data==CANCEL) /* do nothing if cancel is selected. */
        {
            XtUnmanageChild(open_dialog);
            return;
        }

        if (filename != NULL) /* free up filename if it exists. */
        {
            XtFree(filename);
            filename = NULL;
        }

        /* get the filename from the file selection box */
        XmStringGetLtoR(call_data->value, char_set, &filename);
        change_title();

        if (read_file()||(w==new_dialog))
        {
            change_menu_sensitivity(False);
            XtSetSensitive(text,True);
            XmTextSetEditable(text,True);
            XmTextSetInsertionPosition(text,0);
            XtUnmanageChild(open_dialog);
        }
}


void handle_close()
/* closes the file and returns text widget to blank state. */
/* See Chapter 10. */
```

```
{
    int ac;
    Arg al[10];

    XtSetSensitive(text,False);
    XmTextSetEditable(text,False);
    XmTextSetString(text,"");
    change_menu_sensitivity(True);
    text_changed=False;

    /* change title back to default. */
    ac=0;
    XtSetArg(al[ac], XmNtitle, "NMG Editor"); ac++;
    XtSetValues(toplevel,al,ac);
}


Boolean handle_save(filename)
    char *filename;
/* saves the text widget's string to a file. */
/* See Chapter 10. */
{
    FILE *f;
    char *s=NULL;

    /* otherwise, prepare to write the file. If cannot write the file,
       display an error dialog. */
    if ((f=fopen(filename,"w"))!=NULL)
    {
        watch_cursor(toplevel);
        /* get the string from the text widget */
        s = (char *)XmTextGetString(text);
        if (s!=NULL)
        {
            /* write the file. */
            fwrite(s, sizeof(char), strlen(s), f);
            /* make sure the last line is terminated by '\n'
               so that vi, compilers, etc. like it. */
            if (s[strlen(s)-1]!='\n')
                fprintf(f,"\n");
            XtFree(s);
        }
        fflush(f);
        fclose(f);
```

```
                text_changed=False;
                normal_cursor(toplevel);
                return True;
        }
        else
        {
                XtManageChild(error_dialog);
                return False;
        }
}


void text_changedCB(w, client_data, call_data)
        Widget w;
        int client_data;
        XmAnyCallbackStruct *call_data;
/* Each time text widget value is changed, this CB is called.
   It allows the quit option to detect that the text
   has been changed.*/
/* See Chapter 10. */
{
        if (!text_changed)
        {
                XtSetSensitive(save_option,True);
                text_changed=True;
        }
}


void overwriteCB(w, client_data, call_data)
        Widget w;
        int client_data;
        XmAnyCallbackStruct *call_data;
/* handles the "ok to overwrite" dialog for save as. */
{
        if (client_data==CANCEL)
        {
                XtUnmanageChild (overwrite_dialog);
                return;
        }
        else if (handle_save(new_filename))
        {
                if (filename != NULL) /* free up filename if it exists. */
                {
                        XtFree(filename);
```

```
                filename = NULL;
            }
            filename=new_filename;
            change_title();
            XtSetSensitive(save_option,False); /* will get set true if  */
                                              /* changed again.         */
        }
    }


    void save_asCB(w, client_data, call_data)
        Widget w;
        int client_data;
        XmSelectionBoxCallbackStruct *call_data;
    /* handles retrieval of new file name dialog box. */
    {
        FILE *f;

        if (client_data==CANCEL)
        {
            XtUnmanageChild (save_as_dialog);
            return;
        }

        /* get the filename from the dialog box */
        XmStringGetLtoR(call_data->value, char_set,
            &new_filename);

        if ((f=fopen(new_filename,"r"))!=NULL)
        {
            fclose(f);
            XtManageChild(overwrite_dialog);
        }
        else if (handle_save(new_filename))
        {
            if (filename != NULL) /* free up filename if it exists. */
            {
                XtFree(filename);
                filename = NULL;
            }
            filename=new_filename;
            change_title();
            XtSetSensitive(save_option,False); /* will get set true if  */
                                              /* changed again. */
```

```
        }
}

void jump_to_line(line_num)
    int line_num;
/* Counts '\n's so that cursor can be placed at correct line. */
/* See Chapters 10 and 13. */
{
    int x,l,curr;
    char *temp;
    Arg al[10];
    int ac;

    /* get string from text widget */
    temp=XmTextGetString(text);
    x=0;
    curr=1;
    l=strlen(temp);
    /* scan the string for '\n's, counting them. */
    while ((x<l)&&(curr<line_num))
        if (temp[x++]=='\n') curr++;
    /* set cursor position to beginning of the correct line. */
    XmTextSetInsertionPosition(text,(XmTextPosition)x);
    /* prevent memory leaks. */
    if (temp != NULL)
        XtFree(temp);
}

void jumpCB(w, client_data, call_data)
    Widget w;
    int client_data;
    XmSelectionBoxCallbackStruct *call_data;
/* handles jump-to-line dialog box. */
/* See Chapter 10. */
{
    char *jumpstr;

    if (client_data==CANCEL)
    {
        XtUnmanageChild (jump_dialog);
        return;
    }
```

```
    /* get the number entered */
    XmStringGetLtoR(call_data->value, char_set, &jumpstr);

    /* use the jump string to jump to a line */
    jump_to_line(atoi(jumpstr));

    /* popdown the file selection box */
    XtUnmanageChild (jump_dialog);
    XtFree(jumpstr);
}

void closeCB(w, client_data, call_data)
    Widget w;
    int client_data;
    XmAnyCallbackStruct *call_data;
/* handles the "OK to close" question. */
{
    if (client_data==OK)
      handle_close();
}


char *string_search(cs,ct)
    char *cs;
    char *ct;
/* searches for ct in cs. Returns a pointer to the beginning of the
   first instance of ct. */
/* See Chapter 14. */
{
    int done;
    char *ct2,*cs2;

    /* check for "no work" situations */
    if (cs==NULL || ct==NULL)
        return NULL;
    if (*cs=='\0' || *ct=='\0')
        return NULL;

    /* loop through each character of cs. */
    done=False;
    while ((!done)&&(*cs!='\0'))
    {
        /* check to see if the first char of ct is in *cs.
           If it is, proceed to check the rest of the letters
```

```
                    in ct against cs. */
          if (*cs!=*ct)
              cs++;
          else
          {
              cs2=cs;
              ct2=ct;
              do
              {
                  ct2++;
                  cs2++;
              } while ((*cs2==*ct2) && (*ct2!='\0') && (*cs2!='\0'));
              if (*ct2=='\0')
              {
                  done=True;
                  return cs;
              }
              else
                  cs++;
          }
      }
      if (!done)
          return NULL;
  }


  void lowercase(s)
      char *s;
  /* converts s to lower case. */
  /* See Chapter 14. */
  {
      int x,y;

      y=strlen(s);
      for (x=0; x<y; x++)
      {
          if (s[x]>='A' && s[x]<='Z')
              s[x]=s[x]+32;
      }
  }


  void do_find()
  /* finds the string in find_edit1 in the text starting at the current
     cursor position. */
```

```
/* See Chapter 14. */
{
    Arg al[10];
    int ac;
    XmTextPosition cursor_pos;
    char *find_string,*start,*temp,*p;
    Boolean found=False;
    int i;

    /* get the strings from the dialog box and the main text widget. */
    find_string=XmTextGetString(find_edit1);
    cursor_pos=XmTextGetInsertionPosition(text);
    start=XmTextGetString(text);
    temp=start+cursor_pos+1;
    if (!case_matters)
    {
      lowercase(temp);
      lowercase(find_string);
    }
    p=string_search(temp,find_string);
    /* if not found, display an error. */
    if (p==NULL)
    {
        ac=0;
        XtSetArg(al[ac], XmNmessageString, XmStringCreateLtoR(
          "String not found between current\ncursor location and end.",
          char_set)); ac++;
        XtSetValues(finderror_dialog,al,ac);
        XtManageChild(finderror_dialog);
    }
    /* if found, select the found string and scroll it to the top of
       the window. */
    else if (p!=NULL)
    {
        i=p-start;
        XmTextSetSelection(text,(XmTextPosition)i,
            (XmTextPosition)(i+strlen(find_string)),
            CurrentTime);
        XmTextSetInsertionPosition(text,(XmTextPosition)i);
        XmTextSetTopCharacter(text,(XmTextPosition)i);
        found=True;
    }
    XtFree(start);
```

```
    XtFree(find_string);
}


void do_change()
/* changes the found string to the new value. */
/* See Chapter 14. */
{
    Arg al[10];
    int ac;
    XmTextPosition cursor_pos;
    char *start,*temp,*p,*find_string,*replace_string;

    find_string=XmTextGetString(find_edit1);
    replace_string=XmTextGetString(find_edit2);
    cursor_pos=XmTextGetInsertionPosition(text);
    start=XmTextGetString(text);
    temp=start+cursor_pos;
    if (!case_matters)
    {
        lowercase(temp);
        lowercase(find_string);
    }
    if ((find_string==NULL)||
        (strncmp(temp,find_string,strlen(find_string))!=0))
    {
        ac = 0;
        XtSetArg(al[ac], XmNmessageString, XmStringCreateLtoR(
            "Change must be preceeded by a find.",
            char_set));  ac++;
        XtSetValues(finderror_dialog, al, ac);
        XtManageChild(finderror_dialog);
    }
    else
    {
        XmTextReplace(text,cursor_pos,cursor_pos+
            (XmTextPosition)strlen(find_string),replace_string);
        XmTextSetSelection(text,cursor_pos,
            cursor_pos+(XmTextPosition)strlen(replace_string),
            CurrentTime);
        XmTextSetInsertionPosition(text,(XmTextPosition)(cursor_pos+
            strlen(replace_string)));
    }
    XtFree(find_string);
```

```
        XtFree(replace_string);
    }

    void do_find_change()
    {
        do_change();
        do_find();
    }

    void do_case_sensitivity()
    /* get the new value of the case toggle button. */
    /* See Chapter 14. */
    {
        Arg al[10];
        int ac;

        ac=0;
        XtSetArg(al[ac],XmNset,&case_matters); ac++;
        XtGetValues(case_toggle,al,ac);
    }

    void findCB(w,client_data,call_data)
        Widget w;
        int client_data;
        XmAnyCallbackStruct *call_data;
    /* callback for any button in the find dialog box. */
    /* See Chapter 14. */
    {
        switch (client_data)
        {
            case FIND_FIND:
                do_find();
                break;
            case FIND_FIND_CHANGE:
                do_find_change();
                break;
            case FIND_CHANGE:
                do_change();
                break;
            case FIND_CANCEL:
                XtUnmanageChild(find_dialog);
                break;
            case FIND_CASE:
```

```
            do_case_sensitivity();
            break;
    }
}


void quitCB(w, client_data, call_data)
    Widget w;
    int client_data;
    XmAnyCallbackStruct *call_data;
/* handles the "OK to quit" question. */
{
    if (client_data==OK)
      exit(0);
}


void unmanageCB(w, client_data, call_data)
    Widget w;
    int client_data;
    XmAnyCallbackStruct *call_data;
/* handles the unmanagement of any dialog needing to
   simply disappear. */
{
    XtUnmanageChild(w);
}


void readonlyCB(w, client_data, call_data)
    Widget w;
    int client_data;
    XmAnyCallbackStruct *call_data;
/* handles menu options. */
{
    XtSetSensitive(save_option,False);
    XtSetSensitive(cut_option,False);
    XtSetSensitive(clear_option,False);
    XtSetSensitive(paste_option,False);
    XtSetSensitive(find_change_button,False);
    XtSetSensitive(change_button,False);
    XmTextSetEditable(text,False);
    XtUnmanageChild(readonly_dialog);
}


void menuCB(w, client_data, call_data)
    Widget w;
```

```
        int client_data;
        XmAnyCallbackStruct *call_data;
/* handles menu options. */
/* See Chapter 6, 10. */
{
    Time time;
    Arg al[10];
    int ac;
    XmString directory,dir_mask,pattern;
    char *s;

    switch (client_data)
    {
        case OPEN:
            /* make the file selection box appear. The DoSearch
               function is called each time so that new files are
               incorporated into the list of available files.*/
            ac=0;
            XtSetArg(al[ac],XmNdirMask,&dir_mask); ac++;
            XtGetValues(open_dialog,al,ac);

            XmFileSelectionDoSearch(open_dialog,dir_mask);

            XtManageChild(open_dialog);
            break;
        case CLOSE:
            if (text_changed)
                XtManageChild(close_dialog);
            else
                handle_close();
            break;
        case SAVE:
            handle_save(filename);
            XtSetSensitive(save_option,False); /* will get set true  */
                                               /* if file is changed */
                                               /* again.             */
            break;
        case SAVE_AS:
            /* get the directory from the open dialog filter so the
               user knows where the filter path is pointing when
               using save_as. */
            ac=0;
            XtSetArg(al[ac],XmNdirectory,&directory); ac++;
```

```
        XtGetValues(open_dialog,al,ac);
        ac=0;
        XtSetArg(al[ac],XmNtextString,directory); ac++;
        XtSetValues(save_as_dialog,al,ac);
        XtFree(directory);
        XtManageChild(save_as_dialog);
        break;
    case NEW:
        /* get the directory from the open dialog filter so the
           user knows where the filter path is pointing when
           using new. */
        ac=0;
        XtSetArg(al[ac],XmNdirectory,&directory); ac++;
        XtGetValues(open_dialog,al,ac);
        ac=0;
        XtSetArg(al[ac],XmNtextString,directory); ac++;
        XtSetValues(new_dialog,al,ac);
        XtFree(directory);
        XtManageChild(new_dialog);
        break;
    case QUIT:
        if (text_changed)
            XtManageChild(quit_dialog);
        else
            exit(0);
        break;

    case CUT:
        time=call_data->event->xbutton.time;
        XmTextCut(text,time);
        break;
    case CLEAR:
        XmTextRemove(text);
        break;
    case PASTE:
        XmTextPaste(text);
        break;
    case COPY:
        time=call_data->event->xbutton.time;
        XmTextCopy(text,time);
        break;

    case TOP:
```

```
        /* if the cursor is already at 0 and you have scrolled
           elsewhere with the scroll bar and then select top, the
           fact that you move the cursor from 0 to 0 will not
           cause the screen to update to the top of the file.
           To solve this problem, move to position 1 and then
           back to 0. Same technique is used in other options.*/
        XmTextSetInsertionPosition(text,(XmTextPosition)1);
        XmTextSetInsertionPosition(text,(XmTextPosition)0);
        break;
case BOTTOM:
{
    XmTextPosition y,z;
    char *temp;

    temp=XmTextGetString(text);
    y=z=XmTextGetLastPosition(text);
    if (y!=0) z--;
    XmTextSetInsertionPosition(text,z);
    XmTextSetInsertionPosition(text,y);
    if (temp != NULL)
        XtFree(temp);
    break;
}
case JUMP_CURS:
{
    XmTextPosition x,cursorPos;

    cursorPos=XmTextGetInsertionPosition(text);
    if (cursorPos>0) x=cursorPos-1; else x=cursorPos+1;
    XmTextSetInsertionPosition(text,x);
    XmTextSetInsertionPosition(text,cursorPos);
    break;
}
case JUMP_LINE:
    XtManageChild (jump_dialog);
    break;

case ABOUT:
    XtManageChild (about_dialog);
    break;
case HELP:
    XtManageChild (help_dialog);
    break;
```

```
        case FIND:
            XtManageChild(find_dialog);
            break;
    }
}


Widget make_help_menu(menu_name, mnemonic, menu_bar)
    char *menu_name;
    KeySym mnemonic;
    Widget menu_bar;
/* Creates a new menu on the menu bar. */
/* See Chapter 6. */
{
    int ac;
    Arg al[10];
    Widget menu, cascade;

    ac = 0;
    menu = XmCreatePulldownMenu (menu_bar, menu_name, al, ac);

    ac = 0;
    XtSetArg (al[ac], XmNsubMenuId, menu); ac++;
    XtSetArg (al[ac], XmNmnemonic, mnemonic); ac++;
    XtSetArg(al[ac], XmNlabelString,
        XmStringCreateLtoR(menu_name, char_set)); ac++;
    cascade = XmCreateCascadeButton (menu_bar, menu_name, al, ac);
    XtManageChild (cascade);

    ac=0;
    XtSetArg(al[ac],XmNmenuHelpWidget,cascade); ac++;
    XtSetValues(menu_bar,al,ac);

    return(menu);
}


void add_accelerator(w, acc_text, key)
    Widget w;
    char *acc_text;
    char *key;
/* adds an accelerator to a menu option. */
/* See Chapter 6. */
{
    int ac;
```

```
        Arg al[10];

        ac=0;
        XtSetArg(al[ac],XmNacceleratorText,
            XmStringCreate(acc_text,char_set)); ac++;
        XtSetArg(al[ac],XmNaccelerator,key); ac++;
        XtSetValues(w,al,ac);
}


Widget make_menu_option(option_name, mnemonic, client_data, menu)
        char *option_name;
        KeySym mnemonic;
        int client_data;
        Widget menu;
/* Adds an option to an existing menu. */
/* See Chapter 6. */
{
        int ac;
        Arg al[10];
        Widget b;

        ac = 0;
        XtSetArg(al[ac], XmNlabelString,
            XmStringCreateLtoR(option_name,
            char_set)); ac++;
        XtSetArg (al[ac], XmNmnemonic, mnemonic); ac++;
        b=XtCreateManagedWidget(option_name,xmPushButtonWidgetClass,
            menu,al,ac);
        XtAddCallback (b, XmNactivateCallback, menuCB, client_data);
        return(b);
}


Widget make_menu(menu_name, mnemonic, menu_bar)
        char *menu_name;
        KeySym mnemonic;
        Widget menu_bar;
/* Creates a new menu on the menu bar. */
/* See Chapter 6. */
{
        int ac;
        Arg al[10];
        Widget menu, cascade;
```

```
    ac = 0;
    menu = XmCreatePulldownMenu (menu_bar, menu_name, al, ac);

    ac = 0;
    XtSetArg (al[ac], XmNsubMenuId, menu); ac++;
    XtSetArg (al[ac], XmNmnemonic, mnemonic); ac++;
    XtSetArg(al[ac], XmNlabelString,
        XmStringCreateLtoR(menu_name, char_set)); ac++;
    cascade = XmCreateCascadeButton (menu_bar, menu_name, al, ac);
    XtManageChild (cascade);

    return(menu);
}

void create_menus(menu_bar)
    Widget menu_bar;
/* See Chapter 6. */
{
    int ac;
    Arg al[10];
    Widget menu;

    menu=make_menu("File",'F',menu_bar);
    open_option = make_menu_option("Open",'O',OPEN,menu);
    add_accelerator(open_option,"meta+o","Meta<Key>o:");
    new_option = make_menu_option("New",'N',NEW,menu);
    add_accelerator(new_option,"meta+w","Meta<Key>w:");
    save_option = make_menu_option("Save",'S',SAVE,menu);
    add_accelerator(save_option,"meta+s","Meta<Key>s:");
    save_as_option = make_menu_option("Save As",'A',SAVE_AS,menu);
    close_option = make_menu_option("Close",'C',CLOSE,menu);
    add_accelerator(close_option,"meta+l","Meta<Key>l:");
    quit_option = make_menu_option("Exit",'E',QUIT,menu);
    add_accelerator(quit_option,"meta+q","Meta<Key>q:");

    menu=make_menu("Edit",'E',menu_bar);
    cut_option = make_menu_option("Cut",'C',CUT,menu);
    /* my Mac heritage is showing through on these accelerators.
       Change them to something else if you want. */
    add_accelerator(cut_option,"meta+x","Meta<Key>x:");
    copy_option = make_menu_option("Copy",'o',COPY,menu);
    add_accelerator(copy_option,"meta+c","Meta<Key>c:");
    paste_option = make_menu_option("Paste",'P',PASTE,menu);
```

```
        add_accelerator(paste_option,"meta+v","Meta<Key>v:");
        clear_option = make_menu_option("Clear",'r',CLEAR,menu);

        menu=make_menu("Navigate",'N',menu_bar);
        top_option = make_menu_option("Top",'T',TOP,menu);
        add_accelerator(top_option,"meta+t","Meta<Key>t:");
        bottom_option = make_menu_option("Bottom",'B',BOTTOM,menu);
        add_accelerator(bottom_option,"meta+b","Meta<Key>b:");
        jump_curs_option = make_menu_option("Jump to Cursor",'C',
            JUMP_CURS,menu);
        jump_line_option = make_menu_option("Jump to Line",'L',
            JUMP_LINE,menu);
        add_accelerator(jump_line_option,"meta+j","Meta<Key>j:");

        menu=make_help_menu("Help",'H',menu_bar);
        about_option=make_menu_option("About",'A',ABOUT,menu);
        help_option=make_menu_option("Help",'H',HELP,menu);

        menu=make_menu("Utilities",'U',menu_bar);
        find_option = make_menu_option("Find/Change",'F',FIND,menu);

        change_menu_sensitivity(True);
}


void create_find_dialog()
/* creates all of the widgets in the find dialog box. */
/* See Chapter 13. */
{
    Arg al[10];
    int ac;

    /* create but do NOT manage the container dialog. */
    ac=0;
    XtSetArg(al[ac],XmNheight,200); ac++;
    XtSetArg(al[ac],XmNwidth,400); ac++;
    XtSetArg(al[ac],XmNautoUnmanage,False); ac++;
    XtSetArg(al[ac],XmNnoResize,True); ac++;
    XtSetArg(al[ac],XmNdialogStyle,XmDIALOG_MODELESS); ac++;
    XtSetArg(al[ac],XmNdialogTitle,XmStringCreateLtoR(
        "NMG Editor: Find",char_set)); ac++;
    find_dialog=XmCreateBulletinBoardDialog(toplevel,
        "find_dialog",al,ac);
```

```
/* create and manage the two labels. */
ac=0;
XtSetArg(al[ac],XmNx,10); ac++;
XtSetArg(al[ac],XmNy,10); ac++;
XtSetArg(al[ac], XmNlabelString,
    XmStringCreateLtoR("Find:", char_set));    ac++;
find_label1=XmCreateLabel(find_dialog,"find_label1",al,ac);
XtManageChild(find_label1);

ac=0;
XtSetArg(al[ac],XmNx,10); ac++;
XtSetArg(al[ac],XmNy,50); ac++;
XtSetArg(al[ac], XmNlabelString,
    XmStringCreateLtoR("Change to:", char_set));    ac++;
find_label2=XmCreateLabel(find_dialog,"find_label2",al,ac);
XtManageChild(find_label2);

/* Create and manage the two text widgets. */
ac=0;
XtSetArg(al[ac],XmNx,100); ac++;
XtSetArg(al[ac],XmNy,10); ac++;
find_edit1=XmCreateText(find_dialog,"find_edit1",al,ac);
XtManageChild(find_edit1);

ac=0;
XtSetArg(al[ac],XmNx,100); ac++;
XtSetArg(al[ac],XmNy,50); ac++;
find_edit2=XmCreateText(find_dialog,"find_edit2",al,ac);
XtManageChild(find_edit2);

/* create and manage the four pushbuttons in a rowcolumn widget. */
ac=0;
XtSetArg(al[ac],XmNx,0); ac++;
XtSetArg(al[ac],XmNy,90); ac++;
XtSetArg(al[ac],XmNorientation,XmHORIZONTAL); ac++;
XtSetArg(al[ac],XmNpacking,XmPACK_TIGHT); ac++;
XtSetArg(al[ac],XmNadjustLast,False); ac++;
find_rc=XmCreateRowColumn(find_dialog,"find_rc",al,ac);
XtManageChild(find_rc);

ac=0;
XtSetArg(al[ac], XmNlabelString,
    XmStringCreateLtoR("Find", char_set));    ac++;
```

```
find_button=XmCreatePushButton(find_rc,"find_button",al,ac);
XtManageChild(find_button);
XtAddCallback (find_button, XmNactivateCallback,
    findCB, FIND_FIND);

ac=0;
XtSetArg(al[ac], XmNlabelString,
    XmStringCreateLtoR("Change, then Find", char_set));    ac++;
find_change_button=XmCreatePushButton(find_rc,"find_change_button",
    al,ac);
XtManageChild(find_change_button);
XtAddCallback (find_change_button, XmNactivateCallback, findCB,
    FIND_FIND_CHANGE);

ac=0;
XtSetArg(al[ac], XmNlabelString,
    XmStringCreateLtoR("Change", char_set));    ac++;
change_button=XmCreatePushButton(find_rc,"change_button",al,ac);
XtManageChild(change_button);
XtAddCallback (change_button, XmNactivateCallback, findCB,
    FIND_CHANGE);

ac=0;
XtSetArg(al[ac], XmNlabelString,
    XmStringCreateLtoR("Top", char_set));    ac++;
find_top_button=XmCreatePushButton(find_rc,
    "find_top_button",al,ac);
XtManageChild(find_top_button);
XtAddCallback (find_top_button, XmNactivateCallback, menuCB,
    TOP);

ac=0;
XtSetArg(al[ac], XmNlabelString,
    XmStringCreateLtoR("Cancel", char_set));    ac++;
cancel_button=XmCreatePushButton(find_rc,"cancel_button",al,ac);
XtManageChild(cancel_button);
XtAddCallback (cancel_button, XmNactivateCallback, findCB,
    FIND_CANCEL);

/* create and manage the toggle button. */
ac=0;
XtSetArg(al[ac],XmNx,10); ac++;
XtSetArg(al[ac],XmNy,130); ac++;
```

```
    XtSetArg(al[ac], XmNlabelString,
        XmStringCreateLtoR("Case Matters", char_set));    ac++;
    case_toggle=XmCreateToggleButton(find_dialog,"case_toggle",al,ac);
    XtManageChild(case_toggle);
    XtAddCallback (case_toggle, XmNvalueChangedCallback, findCB,
        FIND_CASE);

    /* set the default and cancel button for the find dialog. */
    ac=0;
    XtSetArg(al[ac],XmNdefaultButton,find_button); ac++;
    XtSetArg(al[ac],XmNcancelButton,cancel_button); ac++;
    XtSetValues(find_dialog,al,ac);
}

void create_dialog_boxes()
/* See Chapter 7. */
{
    Arg al[10];
    int ac;

    /* create the file selection box used by open option. */
    ac=0;
    XtSetArg(al[ac],XmNmustMatch,True); ac++;
    XtSetArg(al[ac],XmNautoUnmanage,False); ac++;
    XtSetArg(al[ac],XmNdialogTitle,XmStringCreateLtoR(
        "NMG Editor: Open",char_set)); ac++;
    open_dialog=XmCreateFileSelectionDialog(toplevel,
        "open_dialog",al,ac);
    XtAddCallback (open_dialog, XmNokCallback, openCB, OK);
    XtAddCallback (open_dialog, XmNcancelCallback, openCB, CANCEL);
    XtUnmanageChild(XmSelectionBoxGetChild(open_dialog,
        XmDIALOG_HELP_BUTTON));

    /* create the new file prompt dialog. */
    ac = 0;
    XtSetArg(al[ac], XmNselectionLabelString, XmStringCreateLtoR
        ("Enter the name of the new file.", char_set));  ac++;
    XtSetArg(al[ac],XmNdialogStyle,XmDIALOG_APPLICATION_MODAL); ac++;
    XtSetArg(al[ac],XmNdialogTitle,XmStringCreateLtoR(
        "NMG Editor: New",char_set)); ac++;
    new_dialog = XmCreatePromptDialog(toplevel,
        "new_dialog", al, ac);
    XtAddCallback (new_dialog, XmNokCallback, openCB, OK);
```

```
XtAddCallback (new_dialog, XmNcancelCallback, openCB, CANCEL);
XtUnmanageChild(XmSelectionBoxGetChild(new_dialog,
    XmDIALOG_HELP_BUTTON));


/* create the overwrite error dialog. */
ac = 0;
XtSetArg(al[ac], XmNmessageString, XmStringCreateLtoR
    ("The file exists.\nOK to overwrite?",
    char_set)); ac++;
XtSetArg(al[ac],XmNdialogTitle,XmStringCreateLtoR(
    "NMG Editor: Overwrite",char_set)); ac++;
overwrite_dialog = XmCreateQuestionDialog(toplevel,
    "overwrite_dialog", al, ac);
XtAddCallback (overwrite_dialog, XmNokCallback, overwriteCB, OK);
XtAddCallback (overwrite_dialog, XmNcancelCallback,
    overwriteCB, CANCEL);
XtUnmanageChild(XmMessageBoxGetChild(overwrite_dialog,
    XmDIALOG_HELP_BUTTON));


/* create the jump prompt dialog. */
ac = 0;
XtSetArg(al[ac], XmNselectionLabelString, XmStringCreateLtoR
    ("Enter line number to jump to.", char_set)); ac++;
XtSetArg(al[ac],XmNdialogTitle,XmStringCreateLtoR(
    "NMG Editor: Jump to Line",char_set)); ac++;
jump_dialog = XmCreatePromptDialog(toplevel, "jump_dialog",
    al, ac);
XtUnmanageChild(XmSelectionBoxGetChild(jump_dialog,
    XmDIALOG_HELP_BUTTON));
XtAddCallback (jump_dialog, XmNokCallback, jumpCB, OK);
XtAddCallback (jump_dialog, XmNcancelCallback, jumpCB, CANCEL);


/* create the save_as prompt dialog. */
ac = 0;
XtSetArg(al[ac], XmNselectionLabelString, XmStringCreateLtoR
    ("Enter the new file name to save the file as.",
    char_set)); ac++;
XtSetArg(al[ac],XmNdialogTitle,XmStringCreateLtoR(
    "NMG Editor: Save As",char_set)); ac++;
save_as_dialog = XmCreatePromptDialog(toplevel, "save_as_dialog",
    al, ac);
XtUnmanageChild(XmSelectionBoxGetChild(save_as_dialog,
    XmDIALOG_HELP_BUTTON));
```

```
XtAddCallback (save_as_dialog, XmNokCallback, save_asCB, OK);
XtAddCallback (save_as_dialog, XmNcancelCallback,
    save_asCB, CANCEL);

/* create the quit question dialog. */
ac = 0;
XtSetArg(al[ac], XmNmessageString, XmStringCreateLtoR
    ("The file has been changed.\nOK to quit?", char_set));  ac++;
XtSetArg(al[ac],XmNdialogTitle,XmStringCreateLtoR(
    "NMG Editor: Quit Check",char_set)); ac++;
quit_dialog = XmCreateQuestionDialog(toplevel, "quit_dialog",
    al, ac);
XtUnmanageChild(XmMessageBoxGetChild(quit_dialog,
    XmDIALOG_HELP_BUTTON));
XtAddCallback (quit_dialog, XmNokCallback, quitCB, OK);
XtAddCallback (quit_dialog, XmNcancelCallback, quitCB, CANCEL);

/* create the close question dialog. */
ac = 0;
XtSetArg(al[ac], XmNmessageString, XmStringCreateLtoR
    ("The file has been changed.\nOK to close without saving?",
    char_set));  ac++;
XtSetArg(al[ac],XmNdialogTitle,XmStringCreateLtoR(
    "NMG Editor: Close Check",char_set)); ac++;
close_dialog = XmCreateQuestionDialog(toplevel, "close_dialog",
    al, ac);
XtUnmanageChild(XmMessageBoxGetChild(close_dialog,
    XmDIALOG_HELP_BUTTON));
XtAddCallback (close_dialog, XmNokCallback, closeCB, OK);
XtAddCallback (close_dialog, XmNcancelCallback, closeCB, CANCEL);

/* create the read only dialog. */
ac = 0;
XtSetArg(al[ac], XmNmessageString, XmStringCreateLtoR
    ("This file is read-only.", char_set));  ac++;
XtSetArg(al[ac],XmNdialogTitle,XmStringCreateLtoR(
    "NMG Editor: Read Only",char_set)); ac++;
readonly_dialog = XmCreateInformationDialog(toplevel,
    "readonly_dialog", al, ac);
XtUnmanageChild(XmMessageBoxGetChild(readonly_dialog,
    XmDIALOG_HELP_BUTTON));
XtUnmanageChild(XmMessageBoxGetChild(readonly_dialog,
    XmDIALOG_CANCEL_BUTTON));
```

```
XtAddCallback (readonly_dialog, XmNokCallback, readonlyCB, OK);

/* create the write error dialog. */
ac = 0;
XtSetArg(al[ac], XmNmessageString, XmStringCreateLtoR
    ("The file could not be written.", char_set));  ac++;
XtSetArg(al[ac],XmNdialogTitle,XmStringCreateLtoR(
    "NMG Editor: Write Error",char_set)); ac++;
error_dialog = XmCreateErrorDialog(toplevel, "error_dialog",
    al, ac);
XtUnmanageChild(XmMessageBoxGetChild(error_dialog,
    XmDIALOG_HELP_BUTTON));
XtUnmanageChild(XmMessageBoxGetChild(error_dialog,
    XmDIALOG_CANCEL_BUTTON));
XtAddCallback (error_dialog, XmNokCallback, unmanageCB, OK);

/* create the help dialog. */
ac = 0;
XtSetArg(al[ac], XmNmessageString, XmStringCreateLtoR
    ("This is a fairly simple program, and should be self-
explanatory.\nThe only question I've had is, 'What does Jump to
Cursor do?'\nIf you have used the scroll bar to move around in
the document,\nthen Jump to Cursor will take you back to the
current cursor\nposition and display it.\n   Occasionally the
scroll bar in the text widget will not allow\nyou to scroll all
the way to the bottom of the text. I believe\nthis is a problem
inside the text widget. To solve this, use\nthe Navigate/Bottom
menu option. It will go to the bottom of\nthe text and reset
the scroll bar.",
    char_set));  ac++;
XtSetArg(al[ac],XmNdialogTitle,XmStringCreateLtoR(
    "NMG Editor: Help",char_set)); ac++;
help_dialog = XmCreateInformationDialog(toplevel, "help_dialog",
    al, ac);
XtUnmanageChild(XmMessageBoxGetChild(help_dialog,
    XmDIALOG_HELP_BUTTON));
XtUnmanageChild(XmMessageBoxGetChild(help_dialog,
    XmDIALOG_CANCEL_BUTTON));
XtAddCallback (help_dialog, XmNokCallback, unmanageCB, OK);

/* create the find error dialog. */
ac=0;
```

```
    XtSetArg(al[ac],XmNdialogTitle,XmStringCreateLtoR(
        "NMG Editor: Find error",char_set)); ac++;
    finderror_dialog = XmCreateMessageDialog(find_dialog,
        "fr_error", al, ac);
    XtAddCallback (finderror_dialog, XmNokCallback,
        unmanageCB, OK);
    XtUnmanageChild(XmMessageBoxGetChild(finderror_dialog,
        XmDIALOG_CANCEL_BUTTON));
    XtUnmanageChild(XmMessageBoxGetChild(finderror_dialog,
        XmDIALOG_HELP_BUTTON));

    /* create the about box dialog. */
    ac = 0;
    XtSetArg(al[ac], XmNmessageAlignment, XmALIGNMENT_CENTER); ac++;
    XtSetArg(al[ac],XmNdialogTitle,XmStringCreateLtoR(
        "NMG Editor: About",char_set)); ac++;
    XtSetArg(al[ac], XmNmessageString, XmStringCreateLtoR
        ("NMG Editor\n\nPresented by the NCSU Motif Group\n\nVersion
1.03, released 11/5/91\nby Marshall Brain.\nemail: brain@eos.ncsu.edu",
        char_set));  ac++;
    about_dialog = XmCreateMessageDialog(toplevel, "about_dialog",
        al, ac);
    XtUnmanageChild(XmMessageBoxGetChild(about_dialog,
        XmDIALOG_HELP_BUTTON));
    XtUnmanageChild(XmMessageBoxGetChild(about_dialog,
        XmDIALOG_CANCEL_BUTTON));
    XtAddCallback (about_dialog, XmNokCallback, unmanageCB, OK);
}


void create_icon()
/* creates the icon pixmap and title. */
/* See Chapter 14. */
{
    Pixmap p;
    Arg al[10];
    int ac;

    p=XCreateBitmapFromData(XtDisplay(toplevel),
        RootWindowOfScreen(XtScreen(toplevel)),
        nmg_bits, nmg_width, nmg_height);
    ac=0;
    XtSetArg(al[ac], XmNiconPixmap, p); ac++;
```

```
        XtSetArg(al[ac], XmNiconName, "Editor"); ac++;
        XtSetValues(toplevel,al,ac);
}

void main(argc, argv)
    int argc;
    char *argv[];
/* See Chapter 2, 5, 10. */
{
    Arg al[10];
    int ac;
    XFontStruct *font=NULL;
    XmFontList fontlist=NULL;

    toplevel = XtAppInitialize(&context,"",NULL,0,&argc,argv,
        NULL,NULL,0);

    /* default window size and title. */
    ac=0;
    XtSetArg(al[ac], XmNtitle, "NMG Editor"); ac++;
    XtSetArg(al[ac],XmNheight,400); ac++;
    XtSetArg(al[ac],XmNwidth,600); ac++;
    XtSetValues(toplevel,al,ac);

    /* create a form widget. */
    ac=0;
    form=XtCreateManagedWidget("form",xmFormWidgetClass,
        toplevel,al,ac);

    /* create a menu bar and attach it to the form. */
    ac=0;
    XtSetArg(al[ac], XmNtopAttachment,   XmATTACH_FORM); ac++;
    XtSetArg(al[ac], XmNrightAttachment, XmATTACH_FORM); ac++;
    XtSetArg(al[ac], XmNleftAttachment,  XmATTACH_FORM); ac++;
    menu_bar=XmCreateMenuBar(form,"menu_bar",al,ac);
    XtManageChild(menu_bar);

    /* create a text widget and attach it to the form. */
    ac=0;
    XtSetArg(al[ac], XmNtopAttachment,   XmATTACH_WIDGET); ac++;
    XtSetArg(al[ac], XmNtopWidget, menu_bar); ac++;
    XtSetArg(al[ac], XmNrightAttachment, XmATTACH_FORM); ac++;
    XtSetArg(al[ac], XmNleftAttachment,  XmATTACH_FORM); ac++;
```

```
        XtSetArg(al[ac], XmNbottomAttachment,XmATTACH_FORM); ac++;
        XtSetArg(al[ac],XmNeditMode,XmMULTI_LINE_EDIT); ac++;
        text=XmCreateScrolledText(form, "text", al, ac);
        XtManageChild(text);
        XtSetSensitive(text,False);
        XmTextSetEditable(text,False);
        XtAddCallback(text, XmNvalueChangedCallback, text_changedCB, NULL);

        /* change the font used */
        ac=0;
        font=XLoadQueryFont(XtDisplay(text),"fixed");
        fontlist=XmFontListCreate(font,char_set);
        XtSetArg(al[ac],XmNfontList,fontlist); ac++;
        XtSetValues(text,al,ac);

        create_find_dialog();
        create_dialog_boxes();
        create_menus(menu_bar);
        create_icon();

        XtRealizeWidget(toplevel);
        XtAppMainLoop(context);
}
```

G X REFERENCE

This appendix contains a summary of all of the X function calls used in this book, along with several others. Most of this material is discussed in Chapter 17. Section G.1 contains the basic functions, while G.2 contains the drawing functions.

G.1   BASIC FUNCTIONS

XBlackPixel   *Returns the black pixel value for the specified screen. Use it to set foreground and background colors in a GC.*

```
unsigned long XBlackPixel(
    Display *display,
    int screen);
```

display   The display (use **XtDisplay**).
screen   The screen (use **XtScreen**).

XClearArea   *Clears an area in the given window.*

```
XClearArea(
    Display *display,
    Window window,
    int x,
    int y,
    unsigned int width,
    unsigned int height,
    Boolean exposures);
```

display   The display (use **XtDisplay**).
window   The window (use **XtWindow**).

x, y	The upper left corner of the rectangle to clear.
width, height	The width and height of the rectangle to clear.
exposures	If true, generates an exposure event on the cleared rectangle.

XClearWindow   *Clears the given window.*

```
XClearWindow(
    Display *display,
    Window window);
```

| display | The display (use **XtDisplay**). |
| window | The window (use **XtWindow**). |

XCopyArea   *Copies pixels from one drawable to another. The drawables must be the same depth and have the same root window.*

```
XCopyArea(
    Display *display,
    Drawable src,
    Drawable dst,
    GC gc,
    int src_x,
    int src_y,
    unsigned int width,
    unsigned int height,
    int dst_x,
    int dst_y);
```

display	The display (use **XtDisplay**).
src	The source drawable.
dst	The destination drawable.
src_x,src_y	The upper left corner of the rectangle from which to copy.
width, height	The width and height of the rectangle from which to copy.
dst_x,dst_y	The upper left corner of the destination rectangle.

XCreateBitmapFromData   *Copies a pixmap of depth 1 from the bitmap data specified.*

```
Pixmap XCreateBitmapFromData(
    Display *display,
    Drawable drawable,
    char *data,
    unsigned int width,
    unsigned int height);
```

display	The display (use **XtDisplay**).
drawable	A drawable (used to indicate the screen that will own the pixmap).
data	Bitmap data.
width, height	Width and height of the bitmap.

XCreateFontCursor   *Creates a cursor from the list in* /usr/X11/cursorfont.h.

```
Cursor XCreateFontCursor(
    Display *display,
    unsigned int shape);
```

display	The display (use **XtDisplay**).
shape	The shape of the cursor. See cursorfont.h for the available shapes.

XCreateGC   *Creates a modifiable GC.*

```
GC XCreateGC(
    Display *display,
    Drawable drawable,
    unsigned long value_mask,
    XGCValues *values);
```

display	The display (use **XtDisplay**).
drawable	The drawable (use **XtWindow**).
value_mask	Bit mask indicating which fields in **values** contain valid information.
values	GC values structure (pass an address).

XCreatePixmap   *Creates a pixmap.*

```
Pixmap XCreatePixmap(
    Display *display,
    Drawable drawable,
    unsigned int width,
    unsigned int height,
    unsigned int depth);
```

display	The display (use **XtDisplay**).
drawable	The drawable (use **XtWindow**).
width, height	The width and height of the pixmap.
depth	The depth of the pixmap.

XCreatePixmapFromBitmapData   *Creates a pixmap of the depth specified from the bitmap data specified.*

```
Pixmap XCreatePixmapFromBitmapData(
    Display *display,
    Drawable drawable,
    char *data,
    unsigned int width,
    unsigned int height,
    unsigned long fg,
    unsigned long bg,
    unsigned int depth);
```

display	The display (use **XtDisplay**).
drawable	A drawable (used to indicate the screen that will own the pixmap).
data	Bitmap data.
width, height	Width and height of the bitmap.
fg,bg	Foreground and background colors for pixmap.
depth	Depth of the pixmap.

XDefineCursor   *Defines which cursor to use in the specified window. See also **XUndefineCursor** and **XCreateFontCursor**.*

```
Cursor XDefineCursor(
    Display *display,
```

```
Window window,
Cursor cursor);
```

display   The display (use **XtDisplay**).
window   The window (use **XtWindow**).
cursor   The cursor to use.

XFlush   *Flushes the output buffer to the X server.*

```
XFlush(Display *display);
```

display   The display (use **XtDisplay**).

XFreeCursor   *Frees the specified cursor.*

```
XFreeCursor(
    Display *display,
    Cursor cursor);
```

display   The display (use **XtDisplay**).
cursor   The cursor to free.

XFreeFont   *Frees the specified font.*

```
XFreeFont(
    Display *display,
    XFontStruct *font);
```

display   The display (use **XtDisplay**).
font   The font to free.

XFreeGC   *Frees a previously created GC.*

```
XFreeGC(
    Display *display,
    GC gc);
```

display   The display (use **XtDisplay**).
gc   The GC to free.

XFreePixmap *Frees a previously created pixmap.*

```
XFreePixmap(
    Display *display,
    Pixmap pixmap);
```

display   The display (use **XtDisplay**).
pixmap   The pixmap to free.

XGetGeometry *Returns information about the given drawable.*

```
Status XGetGeometry(
    Display *display,
    Drawable drawable,
    Window *root,
    int *x,
    int *y,
    unsigned int *width,
    unsigned int *height,
    unsigned int *border_width,
    unsigned int *depth);
```

display	The display (use **XtDisplay**).
drawable	The drawable (use **XtWindow**).
root	Returns the root window for that display.
x,y	Returns the upper left corner of the drawable relative to the parent's origin.
width, height	Returns the width and height of the drawable.
border_width	Returns the border width of the drawable.
depth	Returns the depth of the drawable.

XLoadQueryFont *Gets and loads the specified font.*

```
XFontStruct *XLoadQueryFont(
    Display *display,
    char *font_name);
```

display	The display (use **XtDisplay**).
font_name	The font name (see Chapter 3).

XSetBackground   *Sets the background color in a GC.*

```
XSetBackground(
    Display *display,
    GC gc,
    unsigned long background);
```

display	The display (use **XtDisplay**).
gc	The GC to set.
background	The new background color.

XSetClipOrigin   *Sets the clip origin in a GC.*

```
XSetClipOrigin(
    Display *display,
    GC gc,
    int clip_x_origin,
    clip_y_origin);
```

display	The display (use **XtDisplay**).
gc	The GC to set.
clip_x_origin, clip_y_origin	The clip origin.

XSetForeground   *Sets the foreground color in a GC.*

```
XSetForeground(
    Display *display,
    GC gc,
    unsigned long foreground);
```

display	The display (use **XtDisplay**).
gc	The GC to set.
foreground	The new foreground color.

XUndefineCursor   *Replaces the cursor with its shape prior to the call to **XDefineCursor**.*

```
Cursor XUndefineCursor(
    Display *display,
    Window window);
```

display   The display (use **XtDisplay**).
window   The window (use **XtWindow**).

XWhitePixel   *Returns the white pixel value for the specified screen. Use it to set foreground and background colors in a GC.*

```
unsigned long XWhitePixel(
    Display *display,
    int screen);
```

display   The display (use **XtDisplay**).
screen   The screen (use **XtScreen**).

G.2   DRAWING FUNCTIONS

The following structures are useful:

```
typedef struct
{
  short x, y;
  unsigned short width, height;
  short angle1, angle2;
} XArc;

typedef struct
{
  short x, y;
} XPoint;

typedef struct
{
  short x, y;
```

```
      unsigned short width, height;
} XRectangle;

typedef struct
{
   short x1, y1, x2, y2;
} XSegment;
```

XDrawArc   *Draws the specified arc.*

```
XDrawArc(
   Display *display,
   Drawable drawable,
   GC gc,
   int x,
   int y,
   unsigned int width,
   unsigned int height
   int angle1,
   int angle2);
```

display	The display (use **XtDisplay**).
drawable	The drawable (use **XtWindow** or a pixmap).
gc	The GC.
x,y	The upper left corner of the arc's rectangle.
width, height	The width and height of the arc's rectangle.
angle1	Starting at three o'clock, the starting angle in the unit degree*64.
angle2	Starting at three o'clock, the ending angle in the unit degree*64.

XDrawArcs   *Draws the specified set of arcs.*

```
XDrawArcs(
   Display *display,
   Drawable drawable,
   GC gc,
   XArc *arcs,
   int num_arcs);
```

display	The display (use **XtDisplay**).
drawable	The drawable (use **XtWindow** or a pixmap).
gc	The GC.
arcs	An array of **XArc**.
num_arcs	The number of arcs in the array.

XDrawImageString *Draws the specified string. Draws pixels of characters as well as the surrounding box; see XDrawString).*

```
XDrawPoint(
   Display *display,
   Drawable drawable,
   GC gc,
   int x,
   int y,
   char *string,
   int length);
```

display	The display (use **XtDisplay**).
drawable	The drawable (use **XtWindow** or a pixmap).
gc	The GC.
x	The x coordinate of the left baseline of the text.
y	The y coordinate of the left baseline of the text.
string	The string to draw.
length	Number of characters in the string.

XDrawLine *Draws a line between specified points.*

```
XDrawLine(
   Display *display,
   Drawable drawable,
   GC gc,
   int x1,
   int y1,
   int x2,
   int y2);
```

display	The display (use **XtDisplay**).
drawable	The drawable (use **XtWindow** or a pixmap).
gc	The GC.

x1, y1   First end point of the line.
x2, y2   Second end point of the line.

XDrawLines *Draws a set of lines between points in a point array. See also **XDrawSegments**.*

```
XDrawLines(
    Display *display,
    Drawable drawable,
    GC gc,
    XPoint *points,
    int num_points,
    int mode);
```

display   The display (use **XtDisplay**).
drawable   The drawable (use **XtWindow** or a pixmap).
gc   The GC.
points   An array of **XPoints**.
num_points   The number of points in the array.
mode   Valid values: **CoordModeOrigin** (absolute) and **CoordModePrevious** (relative).

XDrawPoint *Draws the specified point.*

```
XDrawPoint(
    Display *display,
    Drawable drawable,
    GC gc,
    int x,
    int y);
```

display   The display (use **XtDisplay**).
drawable   The drawable (use **XtWindow** or a pixmap).
gc   The GC.
x   The x coordinate of the point.
y   The y coordinate of the point.

XDrawPoints *Draws the specified set of points.*

```
XDrawPoints(
    Display *display,
    Drawable drawable,
    GC gc,
    XPoint *points,
    int num_points,
    int mode);
```

display	The display (use **XtDisplay**).
drawable	The drawable (use **XtWindow** or a pixmap).
gc	The GC.
points	An array of **XPoint**.
num_points	The number of points in the array.
mode	Valid values: **CoordModeOrigin** (absolute) and **CoordModePrevious** (relative).

XDrawRectangle *Draws the specified rectangle.*

```
XDrawRectangle(
    Display *display,
    Drawable drawable,
    GC gc,
    int x,
    int y,
    unsigned int width,
    unsigned int height);
```

display	The display (use **XtDisplay**).
drawable	The drawable (use **XtWindow** or a pixmap).
gc	The GC.
x,y	The upper-left corner of the rectangle.
width, height	The width and height of the rectangle.

XDrawRectangles *Draws the specified set of rectangles.*

```
XDrawRectangles(
    Display *display,
```

```
    Drawable drawable,
    GC gc,
    XRectangle *rectangles,
    int num_rectangles);
```

display	The display (use **XtDisplay**).
drawable	The drawable (use **XtWindow** or a pixmap).
gc	The GC.
rectangles	An array of **XRectangle**.
num_rectangles	The number of rectangles in the array.

XDrawSegments   *Draws a set of line segments.*

```
XDrawSegments(
    Display *display,
    Drawable drawable,
    GC gc,
    XSegment *segments,
    int num_segments);
```

display	The display (use **XtDisplay**).
drawable	The drawable (use **XtWindow** or a pixmap).
gc	The GC.
segments	An array of **XSegments**.
num_segments	The number of segments in the array.

XDrawString   *Draws the specified string. Draws pixels of characters only; see **XDrawImage-String**.*

```
XDrawPoint(
    Display *display,
    Drawable drawable,
    GC gc,
    int x,
    int y,
    char *string,
    int length);
```

display	The display (use **XtDisplay**).

drawable	The drawable (use **XtWindow** or a pixmap).
gc	The GC.
x	The x coordinate of the left baseline of the text.
y	The y coordinate of the left baseline of the text.
string	The string to draw.
length	Number of characters in the string.

XFillArc *Draws the specified filled arc.*

```
XFillArc(
    Display *display,
    Drawable drawable,
    GC gc,
    int x,
    int y,
    unsigned int width,
    unsigned int height
    int angle1,
    int angle2);
```

display	The display (use **XtDisplay**).
drawable	The drawable (use **XtWindow** or a pixmap).
gc	The GC.
x,y	The upper-left corner of the arc's rectangle.
width, height	The width and height of the arc's rectangle.
angle1	Starting at three o'clock, the starting angle in the unit degree*64.
angle2	Starting at three o'clock, the ending angle in the unit degree*64.

XFillArcs *Draws the specified set of filled arcs.*

```
XFillArcs(
    Display *display,
    Drawable drawable,
    GC gc,
    XArc *arcs,
    int num_arcs);
```

display	The display (use **XtDisplay**).
drawable	The drawable (use **XtWindow** or a pixmap).
gc	The GC.
arcs	An array of **XArc**.
num_arcs	The number of arcs in the array.

XFillPolygon   *Draws the specified filled polygon.*

```
XFillPolygon(
    Display *display,
    Drawable drawable,
    GC gc,
    XPoint *points,
    int num_points,
    int shape,
    int mode);
```

display	The display (use **XtDisplay**).
drawable	The drawable (use **XtWindow** or a pixmap).
gc	The GC.
points	An array of **XPoint**.
num_points	The number of points in the array.
shape	Valid values: **Complex**, **Convex**, and **Nonconvex**.
mode	Valid values: **CoordModeOrigin** (absolute) and **CoordModePrevious** (relative).

XFillRectangle   *Draws the specified filled rectangle.*

```
XFillRectangle(
    Display *display,
    Drawable drawable,
    GC gc,
    int x,
    int y,
    unsigned int width,
    unsigned int height);
```

| display | The display (use **XtDisplay**). |
| drawable | The drawable (use **XtWindow** or a pixmap). |

gc	The GC.
x,y	The upper-left corner of the rectangle.
width, height	The width and height of the rectangle.

XFillRectangles *Draws the specified set of filled rectangles.*

```
XFillRectangles(
    Display *display,
    Drawable drawable,
    GC gc,
    XRectangle *rectangles,
    int num_rectangles);
```

display	The display (use **XtDisplay**).
drawable	The drawable (use **XtWindow** or a pixmap).
gc	The GC.
rectangles	An array of **XRectangle**.
num_rectangles	The number of rectangles in the array.

H   XT REFERENCE

XtAddCallback   *Adds a callback function to a widget.*

```
void XtAddCallback(
    Widget widget,
    String callback_name,
    XtCallbackProc callback,
    XtPointer client_data);
```

widget	The widget.
callback_name	The name of the callback.
callback	The function to call when the callback is triggered.
client_data	Programmer-specified data sent to the function.

XtAddEventHandler   *Adds an event handler to a widget.*

```
void XtAddEventHandler(
    Widget widget,
    EventMask mask,
    Boolean nonmaskable,
    XtEventHandler proc,
    XtPointer client_data);
```

widget	The widget to which to apply the event handler.
mask	An X event mask.
nonmaskable	If true, calls the handler if it receives a nonmaskable event.

proc   The function to be called.

client_data   A four-byte piece of data passed to the event-handling
                        function.

XtAppAddInput   *Specifies a callback function to be called when data becomes available.*

```
XtInputId XtAppAddInput(
    XtAppContext context,
    int source,
    XtPointer condition,
    XtInputCallbackProc proc,
    XtPointer client_data);
```

context   The application context.

source   The input stream.

condition   The condition for which to wait. Valid values
                        are **XtInputReadMask**, **XtInputWriteMask**, and
                        XtInputExceptMask.

proc   The callback function to call.

client_data   User-defined data.

XtAppAddTimeOut   *Adds a timeout to the application.*

```
XtIntervalId XtAppAddTimeOut(
    XtAppContext context,
    unsigned long interval,
    XtTimerCallbackProc proc,
    XtPointer client_data);
```

context   The context value for the application.

interval   The time interval of the delay, in milliseconds.

proc   The callback function to be called when the interval
                        expires.

client_data   A four-byte piece of data passed to the function.

XtAppAddWorkProc   *Adds a work proc to the application.*

```
XtWorkProcId XtAppAddWorkProc(
    XtAppContext context,
    XtWorkProc proc,
    XtPointer client_data);
```

context   The context value for the application.
proc   The function to be called.
client_data   A four-byte piece of data passed to the function.

XtAppErrorMsg   *Generates an error message and exits the program.*

```
void XtAppErrorMsg(
    XtAppContext context,
    String name,
    String type,
    String class,
    String default,
    String *params,
    Cardinal *num_params);
```

context   The application's context.
name   The name of the error.
type   The type of the error.
class   The class of the error (for example, the application's name).
default   The error message, possibly containing %s identifiers.
params   Substitution strings for %s identifiers.
num_params   The number of parameters in **params**.

XtAppInitialize   *Creates the application's toplevel shell.*

```
Widget XtAppInitialize(
    XtAppContext *context,
    String application_class,
    XrmOptionDescRec options[],
    Cardinal num_options,
    Cardinal *argc,
```

```
   String *argv,
   String *fallback_resources,
   ArgList args,
   Cardinal num_args);
```

context	Returns the context value; needed for calls to other **XtApp** functions.
application_class	The class name for loading resources.
options	Passed directly to the **XrmParseCommand** function.
num_options	Number of options.
argc	A pointer to the number of command line options (pass an address).
argv	The standard command line options array.
fallback_resources	A set of predefined resource strings.
args	An argument list for the toplevel shell.
num_args	Number of arguments in the argument list.

XtAppMainLoop   *Manages the Motif event loop.*

```
   void XtMainLoop(XtAppContext context)
```

context	The context variable for the application received from **XtAppInitialize.**

XtAppWarningMsg   *Generates a warning message.*

```
   void XtAppWarningMsg(
      XtAppContext context,
      String name,
      String type,
      String class,
      String default,
      String *params,
      Cardinal *num_params);
```

context	The application's context.
name	The name of the warning.
type	The type of the warning.
class	The class of the warning (for example, the application's name).

default	The warning message, possibly containing **%s** identifiers.
params	Substitution strings for **%s** identifiers.
num_params	The number of parameters in **params**.

XtCalloc   *Allocates memory for an array.*

```
char *XtCalloc(
    Cardinal num,
    Cardinal size);
```

| num | Number of elements to allocate. |
| size | Size of each element. |

XtCreateManagedWidget   *Creates and manages a widget. Use instead of **XmCreate** functions.*

```
Widget XtCreateWidget(
    String name,
    WidgetClass class,
    Widget parent,
    ArgList args,
    Cardinal num_args);
```

name	The name of the widget .
class	The class name of the widget from Appendix J.
parent	The parent of this widget.
args	A normal **al** argument list.
num_args	**ac.**

XtCreateWidget   *Creates a widget. Use instead of **XmCreate** functions.*

```
Widget XtCreateWidget(
    String name,
    WidgetClass class,
    Widget parent,
    ArgList args,
    Cardinal num_args);
```

name	The name of the widget.
class	The class name of the widget from Appendix J.
parent	The parent of this widget.
args	A normal **al** argument list.
num_args	**ac.**

XtDestroyWidget   *Destroys the specified widget.*

```
void XtDestroyChild(Widget widget);
```

widget   The widget to destroy.

XtDisplay   *Returns the X display for a widget.*

```
Display *XtDisplay(Widget widget);
```

widget   The widget.

XtFree   *Frees memory.*

```
void XtFree(char *ptr);
```

ptr   Pointer to block previously allocated.

XtGetGC   *Obtains a read-only graphics context.*

```
GC XtGetGC(
    Widget widget,
    XtGCMask value_mask,
    XGCValues *values)
```

widget	The widget used to find the screen for the GC.
value_mask	Specifies fields in the GC the default values of which will be modified.
values	Specifies the values to use during modification.

XtGetValues   *Retrieves resource values for a widget.*

```
void XtGetValues(
    Widget widget,
    ArgList arg,
    Cardinal num_args)
```

widget   The widget.

arg   The argument array of resources and values.

num_args   The number of arguments in the array.

XtIsManaged   *Indicates if the widget is managed.*

```
Boolean XtIsManaged(Widget widget);
```

widget   The widget.

XtIsRealized   *Indicates if the widget is realized.*

```
Boolean XtIsRealized(Widget widget);
```

widget   The widget.

XtIsSensitive   *Indicates if the widget is sensitive.*

```
Boolean XtIsSensitive(Widget widget);
```

widget   The widget.

XtLastTimestampProcessed   *Obtains a copy of the last time stamp displayed.*

```
Time XtLastTimestampProcessed(Display *display)
```

display   The display.

XtMalloc   *Allocates memory.*

```
char *XtMalloc(Cardinal size);
```

size   Number of bytes to allocate.

XtManageChild   *Manages the specified widget.*

```
void XtManageChild(Widget widget);
```

widget   The widget to manage.

XtManageChildren   *Manages the specified widgets.*

```
void XtManageChildren(
    WidgetList children,
    Cardinal num_children);
```

children   A list of widgets to manage, in an array.
num_children   The number of widgets in the list.

XtNew   *Allocates memory for the specified type.*

```
type *XtNew(type);
```

type   Type of block required.

XtNewString   *Allocates memory for the specified string and copies the string.*

```
String XtNewString(String s);
```

s   The string to be allocated.

XtNumber   *Returns the number of elements in an array.*

```
Cardinal XtNumber(ArrayVariable array);
```

array   The array.

XtParent   *Returns the parent of the widget.*

```
Widget XtParent(Widget widget);
```

widget   The widget.

XtRealizeWidget   *Realizes a widget. Creates a window for the widget and realizes all of its managed children.*

```
void XtRealizeWidget(Widget widget);
```

widget   The widget to be realized.

XtRealloc   *Allocates memory, copying old block to new.*

```
char *XtRealloc(
    char *ptr,
    Cardinal size);
```

ptr   Pointer to a block previously allocated.
size   New number of bytes to allocate.

XtReleaseGC   *Releases a read-only graphics context created by **XtGetGC**.*

```
GC XtReleaseGC(
    Widget widget,
    GC gc);
```

widget   A widget with the same display as the **gc**.
gc   Graphics context to free.

XtRemoveTimeOut *Removes a time out.*

```
void XtRemoveTimeOut(XtIntervalId id);
```

id   Identifier of time out from **XtAppAddTimeOut**.

XtRemoveWorkProc *Removes a work proc.*

```
void XtRemoveWorkProc(XtWorkProcId id);
```

id   Identifier of work proc from **XtAppAddWorkProc**.

XtScreen *Returns the screen of the widget.*

```
Screen *XtScreen(Widget widget);
```

widget   The widget.

XtSetArg *Sets a resource argument in the argument array.*

```
void XtSetArg(
    Arg arg,
    String resource_name,
    XtArgVal value);
```

arg   An argument variable. By convention, a location in an array.

resource_name   The name of the resource to set.

value   The value to which to set the resource.

XtSetSensitive *Sets a widget's sensitive resource.*

```
Boolean XtSetSensitive(
    Widget widget,
    Boolean value);
```

widget   The widget.

value   The Boolean value to which to set the sensitivity.

XtSetValues   *Passes an argument list to a widget.*

```
void XtSetValues(
    Widget widget,
    ArgList arg,
    Cardinal num_args)
```

widget   The widget to be set.
arg   The argument array of resources and values.
num_args   The number of arguments in the array.

XtUnmanageChild   *Unmanages the specified widget.*

```
void XtUnmanageChild(Widget widget);
```

widget   The widget to unmanage.

XtUnmanageChildren   *Unmanages the specified widgets.*

```
void XtUnmanageChildren(
    WidgetList children,
    Cardinal num_children);
```

children   A list of widgets to unmanage, in an array.
num_children   The number in the list.

XtWindow   *Returns the window for a widget.*

```
Window XtWindow(Widget widget);
```

widget   The widget.

I CONVENIENCE FUNCTIONS

This appendix summarizes five categories of special Motif convenience functions: **XmText**, **XmList**, **XmString**, **XmFontList**, and **XmClipboard**. These summaries are made from the *OSF/Motif Programmer's Reference*. For more information, please refer to the *OSF/Motif Programmer's Reference*.

I.1 THE XMTEXT CONVENIENCE FUNCTIONS

The *XmText* convenience functions provide easy ways to manipulate the text widget. Several also provide capabilities beyond the scope of the text widget itself. For example, **XmTextCut** manipulates the text widget as well as the Clipboard.

Several of the following functions request a parameter of type **Time**. In all of the functions that require **Time**, you can extract a valid time value from the event record associated with the callback function. The following code fragment demonstrates how to extract the `time` field from the event record contained in the **call_data** parameter of a menu callback function named **menuCB**.

```
void menuCB(Widget w, int client_data,
    XmAnyCallbackStruct *call_data);
{
  Time time;
    .
    .
  time = call_data->event->xbutton.time;
    .
    .
}
```

X also defines a special constant named **CurrentTime** that you can use as a **Time** parameter if no event record value is handy. Xt defines a function, **XtLastTimestampProcessed**, that is also useful.

Several of the functions deal with selected text, which is created when the user drags over a region of text in the text widget. It is normally displayed in reverse video.

All of the following functions accept a widget as a parameter. This widget must be a text widget.

XmCreateScrolledText

Creates a text widget with scroll bars. Several of the resources in the text widget control the position of the scroll bars.

```
Widget XmCreateScrolledText(
    Widget parent,
    char *name,
    ArgList arglist,
    Cardinal argcount);
```

XmCreateText

Creates a text widget.

```
Widget XmCreateText(
    Widget parent,
    char *name,
    ArgList arglist,
    Cardinal argcount);
```

XmTextClearSelection

Clears the selected region; that is, it unselects all text in the selected region so that no part of it remains highlighted.

```
void XmTextClearSelection(
    Widget widget,
    Time clear_time);
```

You can extract the **Time** parameter from the event record as explained at the beginning of this section.

XmTextCopy

Copies the currently selected region onto the Clipboard. The region remains selected and remains in the widget. Returns false if something goes wrong (for example, nothing is selected at the time of the call).

```
Boolean XmTextCopy(
   Widget widget,
   Time copy_time);
```

You can extract the **Time** parameter from the event record as explained at the beginning of this section.

XmTextCut

Deletes the selected text from the widget and places it on the Clipboard.

```
Boolean XmTextCut(
   Widget widget,
   Time cut_time);
```

You can extract the **Time** parameter from the event record as explained at the beginning of this section.

XmTextGetBaseline

Returns the y coordinate of the baseline of the first line of characters displayed in the text widget, in pixels.

```
int XmTextGetBaseline(Widget widget);
```

XmTextGetEditable

Returns the value of the **editable** resource.

```
Boolean XmTextGetEditable(Widget widget);
```

XmTextGetInsertionPosition

Returns the value of the current insertion position.

```
XmTextPosition XmTextGetInsertionPosition(Widget widget);
```

XmTextGetLastPosition

Returns the position of the last character in the text widget's **value** resource.

```
XmTextPosition XmTextGetLastPosition(Widget widget);
```

XmTextGetMaxLength

Returns the value of the **maxLength** resource.

```
int XmTextGetMaxLength(Widget widget);
```

XmTextGetSelection

Returns a pointer to a string that contains a copy of the currently selected region. The string is a standard null-terminated C string. You should eventually free the string with **XtFree**.

```
char *XmTextGetSelection(Widget widget);
```

XmTextGetSelectionPosition

Returns the left and right position values of the selected string within the full string held by the text widget. Returns false if something is wrong (for example, nothing is selected). Note that you must pass the *address* of the left and right parameters so that the function can return values.

```
Boolean XmTextGetSelectionPosition(
    Widget widget,
    XmTextPosition *left,
    XmTextPosition *right);
```

XmTextGetSource

In Motif, multiple text widgets can share the same source of text. This function gets the **source** resource from one text widget so you can pass it to another using the **XmTextSetSource** function.

```
XmTextSource XmTextGetSource(Widget widget);
```

XmTextGetString

Returns a pointer to a string that contains a copy of the current **value** resource. The string is a standard null-terminated C string. You should eventually free the string with **XtFree**.

```
char *XmTextGetString(Widget widget);
```

XmTextGetTopCharacter

Returns the position of the character currently appearing in the top left of the text widget's window.

```
XmTextPosition XmTextGetTopCharacter(Widget widget);
```

XmTextInsert

Inserts the string into **value** at the specified position.

```
void XmTextInsert(
   Widget widget,
   XmTextPosition position,
   char *value);
```

XmTextPaste

Pastes the contents of the Clipboard into the widget at the current insertion position. The function returns false if something is wrong (for example, the Clipboard is empty).

```
Boolean XmTextPaste(Widget widget);
```

XmTextPosToXY

Translates a position value in the string into x and y coordinate values on the current screen. If the position is not on the screen or is beyond **maxLength**, the function returns false. Note that you must pass the address of x and y so that the values can be returned.

```
Boolean XmTextPosToXY(
   Widget widget,
   XmTextPosition position,
   Position *x,
   Position *y);
```

XmTextRemove

Deletes the selected text from the text widget. Returns false if something is wrong (for example, nothing is selected).

```
Boolean XmTextRemove(Widget widget);
```

XmTextReplace

Replaces the text between **pos1** and **pos2** with the text to which **value** points.

```
void XmTextReplace(
   Widget widget,
   XmTextPosition pos1,
   XmTextPosition pos2,
   char *value);
```

XmTextScroll

Scrolls the text in the text window the number of lines specified in **n**. Positive values scroll upward; negative values scroll downward.

```
void XmTextScroll(
   Widget widget,
   int n);
```

XmTextSetAddMode

Sets **Add Mode** to true or false. When true, the insertion point can be moved without affecting selected text.

```
void XmTextSetAddMode(
   Widget widget,
   Boolean mode);
```

XmTextSetEditable

Sets the value of the **editable** resource.

```
void XmTextSetEditable(
   Widget widget,
   Boolean editable);
```

XmTextSetHighlight

Highlights regions of text. The **pos1** and **pos2** parameters specify the starting and ending positions of the region. You can set the mode parameter to XmHIGHLIGHT_NORMAL (turn off highlighting), XmHIGHLIGHT_SELECTED (highlight with reverse video), or XmHIGHLIGHT_SECONDARY_SELECTED (highlight with underlining).

```
void XmTextSetHighlight(
   Widget w,
   XmTextPosition pos1,
   XmTextPosition pos2,
   XmHighlightMode mode);
```

XmTextSetInsertionPosition

Sets the current insertion position.

```
void XmTextSetInsertionPosition(
   Widget widget,
   XmTextPosition position);
```

XmTextSetMaxLength

Sets the maximum size allowed for the text widget.

```
void XmTextSetMaxLength(
   Widget widget,
   int max_length);
```

XmTextSetSelection

Sets the selected region. It is equivalent to the user selecting an area of text with the mouse. The **pos1** and **pos2** parameters indicate the starting and ending point of the selected region.

```
void XmTextSetSelection(
   Widget widget,
   XmTextPosition pos1,
   XmTextPosition pos2,
   Time set_time);
```

You can extract the **Time** value from an event structure as shown at the beginning of the section.

XmTextSetSource

See **XmTextGetSource**. The **top** parameter indicates which character should appear in the top left postiion of the widget. The **cursor_position** parameter sets the initial cursor position.

```
void XmTextSetSource(
   Widget widget,
   XmTextSource source,
   XmTextPosition top,
   XmTextPosition cursor_position);
```

XmTextSetString

Sets the value of the text widget's **value** resource.

```
void XmTextSetString(
   Widget widget,
   char *value);
```

XmTextSetTopCharacter

Sets the position of the character displayed in the top left corner of the text widget's window.

```
void XmTextSetTopCharacter(
   Widget widget,
   XmTextPosition top);
```

XmTextShowPosition

Ensures that the position specified appears within the text widget's window. Scrolls the text if necessary.

```
void XmTextShowPosition(
    Widget widget,
    XmTextPosition position);
```

XmTextXYToPos

Translates a pair of x and y coordinates on the screen into a position in the **value** resource. This function is the converse of **XmTextPosToXY**.

```
XmTextPosition XmTextXYToPos(
    Widget widget,
    Position x,
    Position y);
```

I.2   THE XMLIST CONVENIENCE FUNCTIONS

Like the text widget, the list widget is fairly complicated and provides 25 convenience functions. All of these functions accept a widget, which must be a list widget.

XmListAddItem

Adds one item to the list at the position specified. If position 0 is specified, adds the item to the end of the list.

```
void XmListAddItem(
    Widget w,
    XmString item,
    int position);
```

XmListAddItems

Adds a set of items at the position specified. The **items** parameter is an array of **XmStrings**, with **item_count** indicating the number in the array. If position 0 is specified, adds the items to the end of the list.

```
void XmListAddItems(
    Widget w,
    XmString *items,
    int item_count,
    int position);
```

XmListAddItemUnselected

Same as **XmListAddItem**, but the added item does not appear selected even if it belongs to the set held in the **selectedItems** resource.

```
void XmListAddItemUnselected(
   Widget w,
   XmString item,
   int position);
```

XmListDeleteAllItems

Clears all items from the list widget.

```
void XmListDeleteAllItems(Widget w);
```

XmListDeleteItem

Removes the indicated item from the list.

```
void XmListDeleteItem(
   Widget w,
   XmString item);
```

XmListDeleteItems

Deletes a set of items. The **items** parameter is an array of **XmStrings**, with **item_count** indicating the number in the array.

```
void XmListDeleteItems(
   Widget w,
   XmString *items,
   int item_count);
```

XmListDeleteItemsPos

Deletes **item_count** items starting at the position indicated.

```
void XmListDeleteItemsPos(
   Widget w,
   int item_count,
   int position);
```

XmListDeletePos

Deletes one item at the position indicated.

```
void XmListDeletePos(
    Widget w,
    int position);
```

XmListDeselectAllItems

Undoes all item highlighting and clears the **selectedItems** resource.

```
void XmListDeselectAllItems(Widget w);
```

XmListDeselectItem

Undoes the highlighting of the item specified and removes that item from the **selectedItems** resource.

```
void XmListDeselectItem(
    Widget w,
    XmString item);
```

XmListDeselectPos

Undoes the highlighting of the item at the specified position and removes that item from the **selectedItems** resource.

```
void XmListDeselectPos(
    Widget w,
    int position);
```

XmListGetMatchPos

Finds the specified item in the list and returns an array of positions at which the item exists. The **pos_count** parameter indicates the number of items in the array. The return value is true if memory was allocated to create the array. If so, you should free the **pos_list** pointer with **XtFree**.

```
Boolean XmListGetMatchPos(
    Widget w,
    XmString item,
    int **pos_list,
    int *pos_count);
```

XmListGetSelectedPos

Returns an array containing the positions of all selected items in the list (the contents of the **selectedItems** resource). The **pos_count** parameter indicates the number of items in the array. The return value is true if memory was allocated to create the array. If so, you should free the **pos_list** pointer using **XtFree**.

```
Boolean XmListGetSelectedPos(
   Widget w,
   int **pos_list,
   int *pos_count);
```

XmListItemExists

Returns true if **item** exists in the list.

```
Boolean XmListItemExists(
   Widget w,
   XmString item);
```

XmListItemPos

Returns the position of the first occurrence of the item in the list.

```
int XmListItemPos(
   Widget w,
   XmString item);
```

XmListReplaceItems

Receives two arrays of items in **old_items** and **new_items**. These arrays must both contain **item_count** items. All occurrences of the first item of **old_item** are replaced by the first item of **new_item**, the second item by the second, and so on.

```
void XmListReplaceItems(
   Widget w,
   XmString *old_items,
   int item_count,
   XmString *new_items);
```

XmListReplaceItemsPos

Replaces **item_count** items, starting at the specified position, with the items in the **new_items** array.

```
void XmListReplaceItemsPos(
   Widget w,
```

```
XmString *new_items,
int item_count,
int position);
```

XmListSelectItem

Highlights the specified item and adds it to the **selectedItems** resource. If the **notify** parameter is true when the function is called, the appropriate selection callback is triggered.

```
void XmListSelectItem(
    Widget w,
    XmString item,
    Boolean notify);
```

XmListSelectPos

Highlights the specified position and adds it to the **selectedItems** resource. If the **notify** parameter is true when the function is called, the appropriate selection callback is triggered.

```
void XmListSelectPos(
    Widget w,
    int position,
    Boolean notify);
```

XmListSetAddMode

Sets the add mode on or off. This mode controls keyboard and mouse functionality in extended selection mode.

```
void XmListSetAddMode(
    Widget w,
    Boolean mode);
```

XmListSetBottomItem

Makes the specified item the last item visible in the list.

```
void XmListSetBottomItem(
    Widget w,
    XmString item);
```

XmListSetBottomPos

Makes the item at the specified position the last item visible in the list.

```
void XmListSetBottomPos(Widget w, int position);
```

XmListSetHorizPos

Moves the scroll bar to the indicated position.

```
void XmListSetHorizPos(
   Widget w,
   int position);
```

XmListSetItem

Makes the specified item the first item visible in the list.

```
void XmListSetItem(
   Widget w,
   XmString item);
```

XmListSetPos

Makes the item at the specified position the first item visible in the list.

```
void XmListSetPos(Widget w, int position);
```

I.3   THE XMSTRING CONVENIENCE FUNCTIONS

This section lists and describes the Motif functions you can use to manipulate compound strings. The prototypes come from the `Xm.h` file. The list is alphabetical, but you might want to start with the creation functions and fan out from there.

XmStringBaseline

Accepts a font list and a compound string. This function determines the height of the first segment of text in the string in pixels, measuring from the top of the character box to the baseline of the text.

```
Dimension XmStringBaseline(
   XmFontList fontlist,
   XmString string);
```

XmStringByteCompare

Compares two compound strings byte by byte and returns true if they are identical.

```
Boolean XmStringByteCompare(
   XmString a1,
   XmString b1);
```

XmStringCompare

Compares two strings semantically to see if they contain the same components, directions, and separators. Returns true if they are the same.

```
Boolean XmStringCompare(
    XmString a,
    XmString b);
```

XmStringConcat

Concatenates **b** to **a** and returns the result. Does not change the original strings.

```
XmString XmStringConcat(
    XmString a,
    XmString b);
```

XmStringCopy

Copies the string passed and returns the result.

```
XmString XmStringCopy(XmString string);
```

XmStringCreate

Creates a new compound string from the null-terminated C string passed in. The new string has one segment containing the text.

```
XmString XmStringCreate(
    char *text,
    XmStringCharSet charset);
```

XmStringCreateLtoR

Creates a new compound string from the null-terminated C string passed in. The function recognizes \n characters, places a separator in the string, and starts a new segment for each \n character it finds. All segments have the same **charset**.

```
XmString XmStringCreateLtoR(
    char *text,
    XmStringCharSet charset);
```

XmStringCreateSimple

Same as **XmStringCreate**, but derives its character set from the current language environment.

```
XmString XmStringCreateSimple(char *text);
```

XmStringDirectionCreate

Creates a compound string that contains only a direction component (no text). The **direction** parameter can have the value XmSTRING_DIRECTION_ L_TO_R or XmSTRING_DIRECTION_R_TO_L.

```
XmString XmStringDirectionCreate(XmStringDirection direction);
```

XmStringDraw

Draws the specified string in a drawing area widget. See Chapter 17 for information on drawing areas, graphics contexts, and so on. See Chapter 14 for information on this function. The parameters **XmStringDraw** uses are defined as follows:

d	The X display.
w	The drawable in which to draw.
fontlist	The font list for drawing.
string	The compound string to draw.
gc	A graphics context.
x, y	The coordinates at which to start drawing.
width	The width of a rectangle that determines the right margin for the text.
align	Valid values: XmALIGNMENT_BEGINNING, XmALIGNMENT_ CENTER, and XmALIGNMENT_END.
lay_dir	Direction in which segments are laid out. Use XmSTRING_DI- RECTION_L_TO_R or XmSTRING_DIRECTION_R_TO_L.
clip	A clipping rectangle. Pass NULL for no clipping.

This function draws only the characters' pixels. See **XmStringDrawImage** to draw the background pixels as well.

```
void XmStringDraw(
    Display *d,
    Window w,
    XmFontList fontlist,
    XmString string,
    GC gc,
    Position x,
    Position y,
    Dimension width,
```

```
    unsigned char align,
    unsigned char lay_dir,
    XRectangle *clip);
```

XmStringDrawImage

Same as **XmStringDraw**, except that it draws the background pixels surrounding each character as well as the foreground pixels. The parameters are the same as for **XmStringDraw**.

```
void XmStringDrawImage(
    Display *d,
    Window w,
    XmFontList fontlist,
    XmString string,
    GC gc,
    Position x,
    Position y,
    Dimension width,
    unsigned char align,
    unsigned char lay_dir,
    XRectangle *clip);
```

XmStringDrawUnderline

Searches for the string in **under** in the string **str**, draws **str**, and underlines the characters in **under** if they are found. Underlines only the first instance of **under** in **str**.

```
void XmStringDrawUnderline(
    Display *d,
    Window w,
    XmFontList fntlst,
    XmString str,
    GC gc,
    Position x,
    Position y,
    Dimension width,
    unsigned char align,
    unsigned char lay_dir,
    XRectangle *clip,
    XmString under);
```

XmStringEmpty

Returns true if all text segments in the compound string have a length of 0.

```
Boolean XmStringEmpty(XmString string);
```

XmStringExtent

Returns the width and height of the smallest rectangle that can contain the string when drawn with the given font list.

```
void XmStringExtent(
   XmFontList fontlist,
   XmString string,
   Dimension *width,
   Dimension *height);
```

XmStringFree

Deallocates the memory associated with a compound string.

```
void XmStringFree(XmString string);
```

XmStringFreeContext

Frees a string context. See **XmStringInitContext**.

```
void XmStringFreeContext(XmStringContext context);
```

XmStringGetLtoR

Returns a null-terminated C string containing the contents of all of the segments in the compound string that have the matching character set.

```
Boolean XmStringGetLtoR(
   XmString string,
   XmStringCharSet charset,
   char **text));
```

XmStringGetNextComponent

Returns the characters and type of the next component in a compound string, using the context parameter to identify the string (see **XmStringInitContext**). Returns one of five values: XmSTRING_COMPONENT_UNKNOWN, XmSTRING_COMPONENT_CHARSET,   XmSTRING_COMPONENT_SEPARATOR, XmSTRING_COMPONENT_DIRECTION, or XmSTRING_COMPONENT_

TEXT. If the return type indicates that the component is a character set, text, or direction component, the function sets the appropriate field. Deallocate the space with **XtFree** when finished. If the component is of an unknown type, the unknown fields will be filled.

```
XmStringComponentType XmStringGetNextComponent(
    XmStringContext context,
    char **text,
    XmStringCharSet *charset,
    XmStringDirection *direction,
    XmStringComponentType *unknown_tag,
    unsigned short *unknown_length,
    unsigned char **unknown_value);
```

XmStringGetNextSegment

Returns characters and type of the next segment in a compound string, using the context parameter to identify the string (see **XmStringInitContext**). Returns all information about each segment, including a null-terminated C string, its character set, and direction. The function returns false when no segments remain.

```
Boolean XmStringGetNextSegment(
    XmStringContext context,
    char **text,
    XmStringCharSet *charset,
    XmStringDirection *direction,
    Boolean *separator);
```

XmStringHasSubstring

Tries to find **substring** in any one segment of **string**. If found, returns true.

```
Boolean XmStringHasSubstring(
    XmString string,
    XmString substring);
```

XmStringHeight

Returns the height, in pixels, of the block consisting of all lines in string for the specified font list.

```
Dimension XmStringHeight(
    XmFontList fontlist,
    XmString string);
```

XmStringInitContext

Returns a string context for the given string. Functions that pull separate segments from the string use the context so that the library can remember its current position in the string from call to call. The return value false indicates that something went wrong (for example, the string is invalid).

```
Boolean XmStringInitContext(
   XmStringContext *context,
   XmString string);
```

XmStringLength

Returns the number of bytes in the string.

```
int XmStringLength(XmString string);
```

XmStringLineCount

Returns the number of separators plus one in the string.

```
int XmStringLineCount(XmString string);
```

XmStringNConcat

Concatenates **n** bytes from **second** onto the end of **first** and returns the result.

```
XmString XmStringNConcat(
   XmString first,
   XmString second,
   int n);
```

XmStringNCopy

Returns a string containing the first **n** bytes of **str**.

```
XmString XmStringNCopy(
   XmString str,
   int n);
```

XmStringPeekNextComponent

Returns the type of the next component that **XmStringGetNextComponent** gets. See **XmStringGetNextComponent**.

```
XmStringComponentType XmStringPeekNextComponent(
   XmStringContext context);
```

XmStringSegmentCreate

Creates a compound string. The string has the text, character set, and direction specified. If **separator** is true, the segment is followed by a separator.

```
XmString XmStringSegmentCreate(
    char *text,
    XmStringCharSet charset,
    XmStringDirection direction,
    Boolean separator);
```

XmStringSeparatorCreate

Creates a compound string that contains only a separator.

```
XmString XmStringSeparatorCreate (void);
```

XmStringWidth

Returns the width of the widest segment in the string, given the specified font list.

```
Dimension XmStringWidth(
    XmFontList fontlist,
    XmString string);
```

I.4   THE XMFONT CONVENIENCE FUNCTIONS

The convenience functions in this section can be used to create and manipulate Motif font lists.

XmFontListAdd

Adds the specified font and character set to **old** and returns the augmented font list. Deallocates the **old** parameter.

```
XmFontList XmFontListAdd(
    XmFontList old,
    XFontStruct *font,
    XmStringCharSet charset);
```

XmFontListCopy

Returns a copy of the specified font list.

```
XmFontList XmFontListCopy(XmFontList fontlist);
```

XmFontListCreate

Returns a new font list containing the specified font and character set.

```
XmFontList XmFontListCreate(
   XFontStruct *font,
   XmStringCharSet charset);
```

XmFontListFree

Deallocates the memory associated with a font list.

```
void XmFontListFree(XmFontList fontlist);
```

XmFontListFreeFontContext

Deallocates the memory allocated to a context. See **XmFontListInitFont-Context**.

```
void XmFontListFreeFontContext(XmFontContext context);
```

XmFontListGetNextFont

Retrieves the next font from the font list, returning its font and character set. See **XmFontListInitFontContext**. You should eventually free the **charset** string with **XtFree**. The function returns false if something goes wrong (for example, no fonts remain).

```
Boolean XmFontListGetNextFont(
   XmFontContext context,
   XmStringCharSet *charset,
   XFontStruct **font);
```

XmFontListInitFontContext

Returns a font context variable. **XmFontListGetNextFont** uses the context so that the library can keep track of where it is in the font list as each font is extracted. You should eventually free the context with **XmFontListFreeFont-Context**. The function returns false if something goes wrong (for example, the font list is invalid).

```
Boolean XmFontListInitFontContext(
   XmFontContext *context,
   XmFontList fontlist);
```

I.5   THE XM CLIPBOARD CONVENIENCE FUNCTIONS

This section lists and describes the functions available for manipulating the Clipboard, which you can access by including the file <Xm/CutPaste.h>. All of these functions require a display and a window parameter. The easiest way to obtain these parameters is to use **XtDisplay** and **XtWindow**: When you pass these functions a widget, they return the display and window of that widget. For example, for the widget w, you can call the function **XmClipboardStart-Copy** with the line:

```
XmClipboardStartCopy(XtDisplay(w), XtWindow(w), ...
```

All of these functions also return an integer result. You can compare the result with the constants **ClipboardSuccess, ClipboardLocked,**and **Clipboard-Fail** (along with several others, as described below). The **Success** and **Fail** constants have obvious meanings. You should use the **Locked** constant as a spin lock. Since multiple applications that run simultaneously often access the Clipboard in competition with one another, this constant provides a locking mechanism for the Clipboard. If a Clipboard function is called and returns the value **ClipboardLocked**, that function should be called repeatedly until **ClipboardSuccess** is returned.

The application gives an item a name when it copies the item to the Clipboard—generally the name of the application itself. The application also gives the item a format name. A single item can exist on the Clipboard in multiple formats: For example, an advanced word processor might store an item on the Clipboard in its own native format, in some standard format for transfer to other word processor programs, and in raw text format for copying to simple editors. The format name can be an arbitrary string, but should comply with ICCCM standards if you want the item to interact appropriately with other applications. (See Scheifler and Gettys for ICCCM standards.)

The following functions manipulate the Clipboard. They appear in logical rather than alphabetical order.

XmClipboardStartCopy

Begins transferring data to the Clipboard during a cut or copy operation. You can copy data either *directly* or *by callback function*. The latter is used so that large pieces of data are not actually copied to the Clipboard unless and until they are pasted somewhere else. This process is also called *copying by name*. To copy directly, a **NULL** parameter is passed to **callback**. To copy by name, a callback function name is passed.

The **label** parameter contains the name of the data item. In general, the name is the originating application's name. The **timestamp** parameter must be derived from the event record that generated the cut or copy request or from **XtLastTimestampProcessed** (see Section 10.3); you cannot use the **CurrentTime** constant. The **widget** parameter should contain the widget from which the data item will be copied.

You should use the **itemid** value in subsequent calls to other functions involved in the copy operation, such as **XmClipboardCopy**.

```
int XmClipboardStartCopy(
    Display *display,
    Window window,
    XmString label,
    Time timestamp,
    Widget widget,
    VoidProc callback,
    long *itemid);
```

XmClipboardCopy

You must precede the **XmClipboardCopy** function with a call to **XmClipboardStartCopy**. The **XmClipboardCopy** function puts the data into temporary space so that **XmClipboardEndCopy** can copy it onto the Clipboard.

```
int XmClipboardCopy(
    Display *display,
    Window window,
    long itemid,
    char *format,
    char *buffer,
    unsigned long length,
    int private_id,
    int *dataid);
```

The **itemid** parameter should be the value returned by the **XmClipboardStartCopy** function. The **format** parameter is a string identifying the format of the data; for raw text, the standard name is STRING (see the ICCCM for other formats). The **buffer** parameter points to the memory location containing the data, and **length** indicates the number of bytes there. The **private_data** parameter is a piece of application-specific data that you can use in any way you choose.

The **dataid** parameter returns an identifier that Motif uses when passing data by name (with the callback function described in the **XmClipboardStart-Copy** function). To pass data by name, set the **buffer** parameter to NULL. When an application pastes the data item from the Clipboard, the callback function specified in the **XmClipboardStartCopy** function is called. It should have the following format :

```
void clipboard_callback_function(
    Widget w;
    int *dataid;
    int *private;
    int *reason);
```

When the callback function is called, it receives the widget that contains the data, the **dataid** value (which you can match against the **dataid** value returned by the **XmClipboardCopy** function), the private data specified in the call to the **XmClipboardCopy** function, and a reason value with either the value XmCR_CLIPBOARD_DATA_DELETE or the value XmCR_CLIPBOARD_DATA_REQUEST. The DELETE value says that the data item has been removed from the Clipboard and will no longer be referenced. The REQUEST value says that the item is needed on the Clipboard and should be put there by a call to the **XmClipboardCopyByName** function.

If you copy the same data to the Clipboard in multiple formats, you should make multiple calls to **XmClipboardCopy** within the same **StartCopy** and **EndCopy** pair, using a different format string for each format.

XmClipboardEndCopy

Moves the Clipboard data from temporary storage to the Clipboard itself. The **itemid** parameter comes from the original call to the **XmClipboardStartCopy** function that started this copy operation.

```
int XmClipboardEndCopy(
    Display *display,
    Window window,
    long itemid);
```

XmClipboardCancelCopy

When copying, you can call this function any time prior to a call to **XmClip-boardEndCopy** to halt the copy operation and free up temporary space. The **itemid** parameter comes from the original call to the **XmClipboardStartCopy** function that started this copy operation.

```
int XmClipboardCancelCopy(
   Display *display,
   Window window,
   long itemid);
```

XmClipboardCopyByName

This function resembles the **XmClipboardCopy** function. It should be called from within the callback function triggered by a call by name to actually put the desired data onto the Clipboard. See **XmClipboardCopy** for a description of the parameters.

```
int XmClipboardCopyByName(
   Display *display,
   Window window,
   int data,
   char *buffer,
   unsigned long length,
   int private_id);
```

XmClipboardUndoCopy

Removes the last item placed onto the Clipboard if it has the same display and window as those passed to this function.

```
int XmClipboardUndoCopy(
   Display *display,
   Window window);
```

XmClipboardLock

Locks the Clipboard to prevent other applications from changing it. You do *not* need to use this function between calls to **StartCopy** and **EndCopy** or **StartRetrieve** and **EndRetrieve** because these functions handle locking themselves.

The lock is a counter rather than a Boolean value. Multiple calls to a lock must be followed by an equal number of unlock calls.

```
int XmClipboardLock(
   Display *display,
   Window window);
```

XmClipboardUnlock

Unlocks the Clipboard. See **XmClipboardLock**. If **all_levels** is true, all prior locks are removed.

```
int XmClipboardUnlock(
    Display *display,
    Window window,
    Boolean all_levels);
```

XmClipboardStartRetrieve

You must call this function at the start of a retrieve (paste) operation. The **timestamp** parameter comes from the event record generating the retrieve request (see **XmClipboardStartCopy**).

```
int XmClipboardStartRetrieve(
    Display *display,
    Window window,
    Time timestamp);
```

XmClipboardRetrieve

Incrementally retrieves all data with the matching format name from the Clipboard. The **format** parameter specifies the format of the data the application wants to retrieve. The **buffer** parameter points to a preallocated memory area that will hold the returned data. The **length** parameter is the size of the preallocated buffer. The **outlength** parameter returns the length of the data copied to the buffer. The **private_id** parameter returns the private data passed during the copy operation. Call this function multiple times to get all data of the specified format.

Besides returning the normal **ClipboardLocked** and **ClipboardSuccess** values, this function can also return **ClipboardTruncate** (the buffer was not big enough) and **ClipboardNoData** (nothing of that format is in the Clipboard, or a value copied by name is no longer available).

```
int XmClipboardRetrieve(
    Display *display,
    Window window,
    char *format,
    char *buffer,
    unsigned long length,
    unsigned long *outlength,
    int *private_id);
```

XmClipboardEndRetrieve

You should call this function at the end of a retrieve operation started by **XmClipboardStartRetrieve** to unlock the Clipboard.

```
int XmClipboardEndRetrieve(
   Display *display,
   Window window);
```

XmClipboardInquireCount

Returns a count of the number of different formats in which the current clipboard item is stored. The **count** parameter returns the count, and the **maxlength** parameter returns the length of the longest format name.

```
int XmClipboardInquireCount(
   Display *display,
   Window window,
   int *count,
   int *maxlength);
```

XmClipboardInquireFormat

Gets the name of the format for the specified item. The **n** parameter is an index specifying which format's name to retrieve. The **buffer** parameter is a pointer to a preallocated buffer that will contain the name once this function returns. The **bufferlength** parameter is the length of the supplied buffer. The **outlength** parameter is the length of the string placed into the buffer. Call **XmClipboardInquireCount** first to get the number of formats and the size of the buffer.

```
int XmClipboardInquireFormat(
   Display *display,
   Window window,
   int n,
   char *buffer,
   unsigned long bufferlength,
   unsigned long *outlength);
```

XmClipboardInquireLength

When you pass this function a format name, it returns the length of the data item with that name.

```
int XmClipboardInquireLength(
   Display *display,
   Window window,
   char *format,
   unsigned long *length);
```

XmClipboardInquirePendingItems

Finds out if any items passed by name still need to be copied to the Clipboard before the application terminates. The **format** parameter specifies the format of interest. The function returns a structure containing a list of the **privateid** and **dataid** values passed by the **XmClipboardCopy** function for data of the specified format. The count parameter returns the number of items in the list. Free the list itself with **XtFree** when you no longer need it.

```
int XmClipboardInquirePendingItems(
    Display *display,
    Window window,
    char *format,
    XmClipboardPendingList *list,
    unsigned long *count);
```

XmClipboardRegisterFormat

Registers a new format (that is, formats not specified in the ICCCM) and makes the format known to other applications.

```
int XmClipboardRegisterFormat(
    Display *display,
    String format_name,
    unsigned long format_length);
```

XmClipboardWithdrawFormat

Tells the Clipboard that the application can no longer supply data previously passed by name by a call to **XmClipboardCopy**. The **dataid** parameter specifies the id of that item.

```
int XmClipboardWithdrawFormat(
    Display *display,
    Window window,
    int dataid);
```

J   MOTIF WIDGET REFERENCE

This appendix represents a summary of the *Motif Programmer's Reference* manual (*PRM*). It contains enough information to allow you to program and use the widgets if you do not have the *PRM*. The *PRM* contains more information.

This appendix is divided into two parts. Section J.1 lists Motif widgets, while J.2 lists Xt widgets (which are common to all widget sets). Figure J.1 shows the relationships among all the widgets.

This will probably be the appendix that you use most often. I had wanted it to be printed on colored paper to make it easier to find, but this was not possible. You may want to pinch the pages together and color their edges with a magic marker to make them stand out.

J.1   MOTIF WIDGETS

XmArrowButton Widget

See Chapter 11. Also available as a gadget.

Description	A push button that displays an arrow rather than a label.
Class Pointer	xmArrowButtonWidgetClass
Class Name	XmArrowButton
Include File	<Xm/ArrowB.h>
Superclass	XmPrimitive

RESOURCES

Name	Type	Default
XmNarrowDirection	unsigned char	XmARROW_UP
XmNmultiClick	unsigned char	dynamic

523

Figure J.1   The Inheritance Hierarchy of the Motif and Xt Widgets

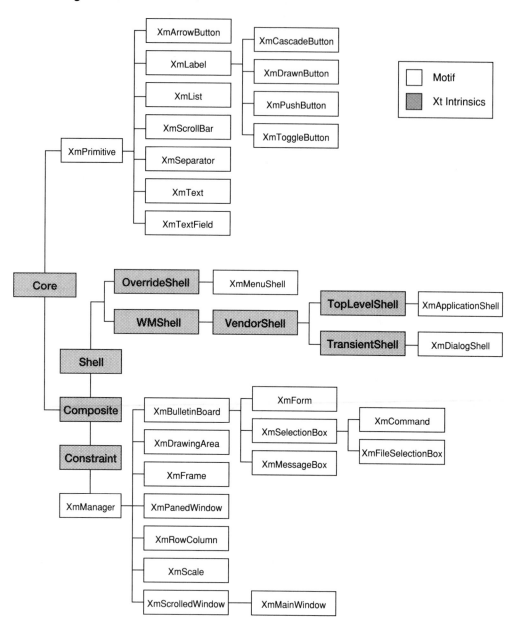

RESOURCE DESCRIPTIONS

XmNarrowDirection	Valid values: XmARROW_UP, XmARROW_DOWN, XmARROW_LEFT, XmARROW_RIGHT.
XmNmultiClick	See multiClick resource for push button.

CALLBACKS

Callback List	Call Data Type	Reason
XmNactivateCallback	XmArrowButtonCallbackStruct	XmCR_ACTIVATE
XmNarmCallback	XmArrowButtonCallbackStruct	XmCR_ARM
XmNdisarmCallback	XmArrowButtonCallbackStruct	XmCR_DISARM

CALLBACK DESCRIPTIONS

XmNactivateCallback, XmNarmCallback, XmNdisarmCallback	See push-button widget.

CALLBACK STRUCTURE

```
typedef struct
{
    int reason;
    XEvent *event;
    int click_count;
} XmArrowButtonCallbackStruct;
```

CONVENIENCE FUNCTIONS

```
Widget XmCreateArrowButton(Widget parent,String name,
    ArgList arglist,Cardinal argcount);
Widget XmCreateArrowButtonGadget(Widget parent,String name,
    ArgList arglist,Cardinal argcount);
```

XmBulletinBoard Widget

See Chapter 5, Chapter 13.

Description	A basic manager widget that lets you "tack on" other widgets at any position.
Class Pointer	xmBulletinBoardWidgetClass
Class Name	XmBulletinBoard
Include File	<Xm/BulletinB.h>
Superclass	XmManager

RESOURCES

Name	Type	Default
XmNallowOverlap	Boolean	True
XmNautoUnmanage	Boolean	True
XmNbuttonFontList	XmFontList	dynamic
XmNcancelButton	Window	NULL
XmNdefaultButton	Window	NULL
XmNdefaultPosition	Boolean	True
XmNdialogStyle	unsigned char	dynamic
XmNdialogTitle	XmString	NULL
XmNlabelFontList	XmFontList	dynamic
XmNmarginHeight	Dimension	10
XmNmarginWidth	Dimension	10
XmNnoResize	Boolean	False
XmNresizePolicy	unsigned char	XmRESIZE_ANY
XmNshadowType	unsigned char	XmSHADOW_OUT
XmNtextFontList	XmFontList	dynamic
XmNtextTranslations	XtTranslations	NULL

RESOURCE DESCRIPTIONS

XmNallowOverlap	Determines whether children are allowed to overlap.
XmNautoUnmanage	If the bulletin board is in a dialog shell, then if a button within the bulletin board is activated, the shell is unmanaged automatically if this resource is true. Must be set at widget creation.
XmNbuttonFontList	Determines the font for any buttons in the bulletin board.
XmNcancelButton	Holds the widget value for the Cancel button.
XmNdefaultButton	Determines which button is the Default button.
XmNdefaultPosition	If true, automatically positions the bulletin board if it is within a dialog shell.
XmNdialogStyle	Possible values: XmDIALOG_SYSTEM_MODAL (system waits for user to answer dialog); XmDIALOG_PRIMARY_APPLICATION_MODAL and XmDIALOG_APPLICATION_MODAL (user must answer dialog before anything can happen in ancestors); XmDIALOG_FULL_APPLICATION_MODAL

	(application waits for user to answer dialog); XmDIALOG_MODELESS (for dialogs that coexist with application); XmDIALOG_WORK_AREA (for bulletin boards not in a dialog shell).
XmNdialogTitle	Title in title bar of dialog shell.
XmNlabelFontList	Font list for labels in the bulletin board.
XmNmarginHeight	Margin used at top and bottom of dialog.
XmNmarginWidth	Margin used at left and right of dialog.
XmNnoResize	Determines if dialog shell around bulletin board can be resized.
XmNresizePolicy	Possible values: XmRESIZE_NONE; XmRESIZE_ANY (grow or shrink); XmRESIZE_GROW (grow only)
XmNshadowType	Possible values: XmSHADOW_IN (shadow appears inset); XmSHADOW_OUT (shadow appears outset); XmSHADOW_ETCHED_IN (double-line shadow inset); XmSHADOW_ETCHED_OUT (double-line shadow outset).
XmNtextFontList	Font for child text widgets.
XmNtextTranslations	Translations added to text children.

CALLBACKS

Callback List	Call Data Type	Reason
XmNfocusCallback	XmAnyCallbackStruct	XmCR_FOCUS
XmNmapCallback	XmAnyCallbackStruct	XmCR_MAP
XmNunmapCallback	XmAnyCallbackStruct	XmCR_UNMAP

CALLBACK DESCRIPTIONS

XmNfocusCallback	Triggered when bulletin board accepts focus.
XmNmapCallback	If in a dialog shell, triggered when bulletin board is mapped.
XmNunmapCallback	If in a dialog shell, triggered when bulletin board is unmapped.

CALLBACK STRUCTURE

```
typedef struct
{
    int reason;
    XEvent *event;
} XmAnyCallbackStruct;
```

CONVENIENCE FUNCTIONS

```
XmCreateBulletinBoard(Widget parent,String name,
    ArgList arglist,Cardinal argcount);
XmCreateBulletinBoardDialog(Widget parent,String name,
    ArgList arglist,Cardinal argcount);
```

XmCascadeButton Widget

See Chapter 6. Also available as a gadget.

Description	A button that can call up a menu pane. Must have a rowColumn parent as part of a menu.
Class Pointer	xmCascadeButtonWidgetClass
Class Name	XmCascadeButton
Include File	<Xm/CascadeB.h>
Superclass	XmLabel

RESOURCES

Name	Type	Default
XmNcascadePixmap	Pixmap	dynamic
XmNmappingDelay	int	180
XmNsubMenuId	Widget	NULL

RESOURCE DESCRIPTIONS

XmNcascadePixmap	Determines the pixmap displayed when the cascade button appears in a hierarchical menu. Default is a right arrow.
XmNmappingDelay	Time in milliseconds before submenu appears. Applies only if widget is in a pop-up or pull-down menu.
XmNsubMenuId	Widget that appears when this button is armed.

CALLBACKS

Callback List	Call Data Type	Reason
XmNactivateCallback	XmAnyCallbackStruct	XmCR_ACTIVATE
XmNcascadingCallback	XmAnyCallbackStruct	XmCR_CASCADING

CALLBACK DESCRIPTIONS

XmNactivateCallback	Triggered when button is activated.
XmNcascadingCallback	Called immediately before submenu is mapped.

CALLBACK STRUCTURE

```
typedef struct
{
   int reason;
   XEvent *event;
} XmAnyCallbackStruct;
```

CONVENIENCE FUNCTIONS

```
Widget XmCreateCascadeButton(Widget parent,String name,
    ArgList arglist,Cardinal argcount);
Widget XmCreateCascadeButtonGadget(Widget parent,String name,
    ArgList arglist,Cardinal argcount);
void XmCascadeButtonHighlight(Widget cascadeButton,
    Boolean highlight);
void XmCascadeButtonGadgetHighlight(Widget cascadeButton,
    Boolean highlight);
```

XmCommand Widget

See Chapter 11.

Description	A widget that accepts commands from the user.
Class Pointer	xmCommandWidgetClass
Class Name	XmCommand
Include File	<Xm/Command.h>
Superclass	XmSelectionBox

RESOURCES

Name	Type	Default
XmNcommand	XmString	""
XmNhistoryItems	XmStringTable	NULL
XmNhistoryItemCount	int	0
XmNhistoryMaxItems	int	100
XmNhistoryVisibleItemCount	int	8
XmNpromptString	XmString	dynamic

RESOURCE DESCRIPTIONS

XmNcommand	Current command's text.
XmNhistoryItems	Values in the history list.
XmNhistoryItemCount	Numbers of values in historyItems.

XmNhistoryMaxItems	Maximum items in history list.
XmNhistoryVisible-ItemCount	Number of visible lines in history list.
XmNpromptString	Prompt displayed in the widget.

CALLBACKS

Callback List	Call Data Type	Reason
XmNcommandChangedCallback	XmCommand CallbackStruct	XmCR_COMMAND_ CHANGED
XmNcommandEnteredCallback	XmCommand CallbackStruct	XmCR_COMMAND_ ENTERED

CALLBACK DESCRIPTIONS

| XmNcommandChanged-Callback | Triggered each time user changes current command. |
| XmNcommandEntered-Callback | Triggered when user enters command. |

CALLBACK STRUCTURE

```
typedef struct
{
    int reason;
    XEvent *event;
    XmString value;
    int length;
} XmCommandCallbackStruct;
```

CONVENIENCE FUNCTIONS

```
Widget XmCreateCommand(Widget parent,String name,
    ArgList arglist,Cardinal argcount);
void XmCommandAppendValue(Widget widget,XmString command);
void XmCommandError(Widget widget,XmString error);
Widget XmCommandGetChild(Widget widget,unsigned char child);
    Valid values for child:
        XmDIALOG_COMMAND_TEXT
        XmDIALOG_PROMPT_LABEL
        XmDIALOG_HISTORY_LIST
void XmCommandSetValue(Widget widget, XmString command);
```

XmDrawingArea Widget

See Chapter 17.

Description	An area in which an application can draw using X drawing commands. Also acts like a bulletin board manager.
Class Pointer	xmDrawingAreaWidgetClass
Class Name	XmDrawingArea
Include File	<Xm/DrawingA.h>
Superclass	XmManager

RESOURCES

Name	Type	Default
XmNmarginHeight	Dimension	10
XmNmarginWidth	Dimension	10
XmNresizePolicy	unsigned char	XmRESIZE_ANY

RESOURCE DESCRIPTIONS

XmNmarginHeight	Spacing between edge of drawing area and any child widget on top and bottom. Does not include drawn elements, such as lines and arcs, which do not require margins.
XmNmarginWidth	Spacing between edge of drawing area and any child widget on left and right. Does not include drawn elements such as lines and arcs, which do not require margins.
XmNresizePolicy	Possible values: XmRESIZE_NONE; XmRESIZE_ANY (grow or shrink); XmRESIZE_GROW (grow only).

CALLBACKS

Callback List	Call Data Type	Reason
XmNexposeCallback	XmDrawingAreaCallbackStruct	XmCR_EXPOSE
XmNinputCallback	XmDrawingAreaCallbackStruct	XmCR_INPUT
XmNresizeCallback	XmDrawingAreaCallbackStruct	XmCR_RESIZE

CALLBACK DESCRIPTIONS

XmNexposeCallback	Triggered when part of the widget is exposed.
XmNinputCallback	Triggered when the widget receives a keyboard or mouse event.
XmNresizeCallback	Triggered when the widget is resized.

CALLBACK STRUCTURE

```
typedef struct
{
    int reason;
    XEvent *event;
    Window w;
} XmDrawingAreaCallbackStruct;
```

CONVENIENCE FUNCTIONS

```
Widget XmCreateDrawingArea(Widget parent,String name,
    ArgList arglist,Cardinal argcount);
```

XmDrawnButton Widget

See Chapter 11.

Description	A push button with a drawing area on its face.
Class Pointer	xmDrawnButtonWidgetClass
Class Name	XmDrawnButton
Include File	<Xm/DrawnB.h>
Superclass	XmLabel

RESOURCES

Name	Type	Default
XmNmultiClick	unsigned char	dynamic
XmNpushButtonEnabled	Boolean	False
XmNshadowType	unsigned char	XmSHADOW_ETCHED_IN

RESOURCE DESCRIPTIONS

XmNmultiClick	See push-button widget.
XmNpushButtonEnabled	Enables and disables shadow drawing (the appearance of a button going in and out) when button is clicked.
XmNshadowType	See XmBulletinBoard.

CALLBACKS

Callback List	Call Data Type	Reason
XmNactivateCallback	XmDrawnButtonCallbackStruct	XmCR_ACTIVATE
XmNarmCallback	XmDrawnButtonCallbackStruct	XmCR_ARM

XmNdisarmCallback	XmDrawnButtonCallbackStruct	XmCR_DISARM
XmNexposeCallback	XmDrawnButtonCallbackStruct	XmCR_EXPOSE
XmNresizeCallback	XmDrawnButtonCallbackStruct	XmCR_RESIZE

CALLBACK DESCRIPTIONS

XmNactivateCallback,	
XmNarmCallback,	
XmNdisarmCallback	See push-button widget.
XmNexposeCallback	Triggered whenever part of the button is exposed.
XmNresizeCallback	Triggered whenever button is resized.

CALLBACK STRUCTURE

```
typedef struct
{
    int reason;
    XEvent *event;
    Window w;
    int click_count;
} XmDrawnButtonCallbackStruct;
```

CONVENIENCE FUNCTIONS

```
Widget XmCreateDrawnButton(Widget parent,String name,
    ArgList arglist,Cardinal argcount);
```

XmFileSelectionBox Widget

See Chapter 7.

Description	A selection box for file and directory handling.
Class Pointer	xmFileSelectionBoxWidgetClass
Class Name	XmFileSelectionBox
Include File	<Xm/FileSB.h>
Superclass	XmSelectionBox

RESOURCES

Name	Type	Default
XmNdirectory	XmString	dynamic
XmNdirectoryValid	Boolean	dynamic
XmNdirListItems	XmStringTable	dynamic
XmNdirListItemCount	int	dynamic

XmNdirListLabelString	XmString	"Directories"
XmNdirMask	XmString	dynamic
XmNdirSearchProc	(*)()	default proc
XmNdirSpec	XmString	dynamic
XmNfileListItems	XmStringTable	dynamic
XmNfileListItemCount	int	dynamic
XmNfileListLabelString	XmString	"Files"
XmNfileSearchProc	(*)()	default proc
XmNfileTypeMask	unsigned char	XmFILE_REGULAR
XmNfilterLabelString	XmString	"Filter"
XmNlistUpdated	Boolean	dynamic
XmNnoMatchString	XmString	"[ ]"
XmNpattern	XmString	dynamic
XmNqualifySearchDataProc	(*)()	default proc

RESOURCE DESCRIPTIONS

XmNdirectory	Current directory being used. If NULL, then current working directory.
XmNdirectoryValid	Used by dirSearchProc. If true, dirSearchProc can search the directory.
XmNdirListItems	List of items in directory list.
XmNdirListItemCount	Number of items in directory list.
XmNdirListLabelString	String displayed above directory list.
XmNdirMask	Mask that determines which files and directories are displayed.
XmNdirSearchProc	Custom directory search procedure that user specifies.
XmNdirSpec	Full file path name, which replaces the **textString** resource in the selection box ancestor.
XmNfileListItems	List of names in the file list.
XmNfileListItemCount	Number of items in the file list.
XmNfileListLabelString	The label displayed over the file names.
XmNfileSearchProc	Custom file search procedure that the user specifies.
XmNfileTypeMask	Valid values: XmFILE_REGULAR (file list contains only files); XmFILE_DIRECTORY (file list contains only directories); XmFILE_ANY_TYPE (file list contains both files and directories).
XmNfilterLabelString	Label displayed over filter string.
XmNlistUpdated	Set to true when search procedures update file lists.

XmNnoMatchString	Label displayed in file list when file list is empty.
XmNpattern	Filter pattern used to select files.
XmNqualifySearchDataProc	Custom search procedure that the user specifies.

CALLBACK STRUCTURE

```
typedef struct
{
    int reason;
    XEvent *event;
    XmString value;
    int length;
    XmString mask;
    int mask_length;
    XmString dir;
    int dir_length;
    XmString pattern;
    int pattern_length;
} XmFileSelectionBoxCallbackStruct;
```

CONVENIENCE FUNCTIONS

```
Widget XmCreateFileSelectionBox(Widget parent,String name,
     ArgList arglist,Cardinal argcount);
Widget XmCreateFileSelectionDialog(Widget parent,String name,
     ArgList arglist,Cardinal argcount);
void XmFileSelectionDoSearch(Widget w, XmString dirmask);
Widget XmFileSelectionBoxGetChild(Widget w, unsigned char child);
     Valid values for child:
          XmDIALOG_APPLY_BUTTON
          XmDIALOG_CANCEL_BUTTON
          XmDIALOG_DEFAULT_BUTTON
          XmDIALOG_DIR_LIST
          XmDIALOG_DIR_LIST_LABEL
          XmDIALOG_FILTER_LABEL
          XmDIALOG_FILTER_TEXT
          XmDIALOG_HELP_BUTTON
          XmDIALOG_LIST
          XmDIALOG_LIST_LABEL
          XmDIALOG_OK_BUTTON
          XmDIALOG_SELECTION_LABEL
          XmDIALOG_SEPARATOR
          XmDIALOG_TEXT
          XmDIALOG_WORK_AREA
```

XmForm Widget

See Chapter 5.

Description	A manager widget that lets children attach themselves in various ways.
Class Pointer	xmFormWidgetClass
Class Name	XmForm
Include File	<Xm/Form.h>
Superclass	XmBulletinBoard

RESOURCES

Name	Type	Default
XmNfractionBase	int	100
XmNhorizontalSpacing	Dimension	0
XmNrubberPositioning	Boolean	False
XmNverticalSpacing	Dimension	0

RESOURCE DESCRIPTIONS

XmNfractionBase	The divisor used when attaching to a position. The default value of 100 makes attach positions behave like percentages.
XmNhorizontalSpacing	Offset for right and left attachments.
XmNrubberPositioning	If false, top and left attachments default to XmATTACH_FORM. If true, attachments default to XmATTACH_POSITION.
XmNverticalSpacing	Offset for top and bottom attachments.

CONSTRAINT RESOURCES

Name	Type	Default
XmNbottomAttachment	unsigned char	XmATTACH_NONE
XmNleftAttachment	unsigned char	XmATTACH_NONE
XmNrightAttachment	unsigned char	XmATTACH_NONE
XmNtopAttachment	unsigned char	XmATTACH_NONE
XmNbottomWidget	Window	NULL
XmNleftWidget	Window	NULL
XmNrightWidget	Window	NULL

XmNtopWidget	Window	NULL
XmNbottomPosition	int	0
XmNleftPosition	int	0
XmNrightPosition	int	0
XmNtopPosition	int	0
XmNbottomOffset	int	0
XmNleftOffset	int	0
XmNrightOffset	int	0
XmNtopOffset	int	0
XmNresizable	Boolean	True

CONSTRAINT RESOURCE DESCRIPTIONS

XmNbottomAttachment, XmNleftAttachment, XmNrightAttachment, XmNtopAttachment

Valid values: XmATTACH_NONE (don't attach); XmATTACH_FORM (attach to same side of form); XmATTACH_OPPOSITE_FORM (attach to opposite side of form); XmATTACH_WIDGET (attach specified side of this widget to opposite side of specified widget); XmATTACH_OPPOSITE_WIDGET (attach specified side of this widget to same side of specified widget); XmATTACH_POSITION (attach to specified position); and XmATTACH_SELF (attach specified side of widget to position proportional to size of widget divided by form size).

XmNbottomOffset, XmNleftOffset, XmNrightOffset, XmNtopOffset

Determines the offset between the side of the widget and its attachment point.

XmNbottomPosition, XmNleftPosition, XmNrightPosition, XmNtopPosition

Position used when attachment resource is set to XmATTACH_POSITION.

XmNbottomWidget, XmNleftWidget, XmNrightWidget, XmNtopWidget

Widget used when attachment resource is set to XmATTACH_WIDGET or XmATTACH_OPPOSITE_WIDGET.

XmNresizable

If set true, the child's resizing requests are granted when possible.

CONVENIENCE FUNCTIONS

```
XmCreateForm(Widget parent,String name,
    ArgList arglist,Cardinal argcount);
XmCreateFormDialog(Widget parent,String name,
    ArgList arglist,Cardinal argcount);
```

XmFrame Widget

See Chapter 11.

Description	Frames the child widget.
Class Pointer	xmFrameWidgetClass
Class Name	XmFrame
Include File	<Xm/Frame.h>
Superclass	XmManager

RESOURCES

Name	Type	Default
XmNmarginWidth	Dimension	0
XmNmarginHeight	Dimension	0
XmNshadowType	unsigned char	dynamic

RESOURCE DESCRIPTIONS

XmNmarginWidth	Margin to left and right of the frame.
XmNmarginHeight	Margin to top and bottom of frame.
XmNshadowType	See XmBulletinBoard.

CONVENIENCE FUNCTIONS

```
Widget XmCreateFrame(Widget parent,String name,
    ArgList arglist,Cardinal argcount);
```

XmGadget Widget

See Chapter 14.

Description	Basic object from which all gadgets are built.
Class Pointer	xmGadgetClass
Class Name	XmGadget
Include File	<Xm/Xm.h>
Superclass	RectObj

RESOURCES

Name	Type	Default
XmNHighlightOnEnter	Boolean	False
XmNhighlightThickness	Dimension	2
XmNnavigationType	XmNavigationType	XmNONE
XmNshadowThickness	Dimension	2
XmNtraversalOn	Boolean	True
XmNunitType	unsigned char	dynamic
XmNuserData	Pointer	NULL

RESOURCE DESCRIPTIONS

XmNhighlightOnEnter	When true, gadget highlights when cursor enters it.
XmNhighlightThickness	Thickness of highlighting rectangle.
XmNnavigationType	Valid values: XmNONE, XmTAB_GROUP, Xm-STICKY_TAB_GROUP, XmEXCLUSIVE_TAB_GROUP.
XmNshadowThickness	Size of border shadow.
XmNtraversalOn	When true, gadget can be traversed.
XmNunitType	Valid values: XmPIXELS, Xm100TH_MILLIMETERS, Xm1000TH_INCHES, XM100TH_POINTS, Xm-100TH_FONT_UNITS. Specifies how to interpret sizing requests.
XmNuserData	Pointer to user data.

XmLabel Widget

See Chapter 3. Also available as a gadget.

Description	Displays a compound string or pixmap.
Class Pointer	xmLabelWidgetClass
Class Name	XmLabel
Include File	<Xm/Label.h>
Superclass	XmPrimitive

RESOURCES

Name	Type	Default
XmNaccelerator	String	NULL
XmNacceleratorText	XmString	NULL

XmNalignment	unsigned char	XmALIGNMENT_CENTER
XmNfontList	XmFontList	dynamic
XmNlabelInsensitive-Pixmap	Pixmap	XmUNSPECIFIED_PIXMAP
XmNlabelPixmap	Pixmap	XmUNSPECIFIED_PIXMAP
XmNlabelString	XmString	dynamic
XmNlabelType	unsigned char	XmSTRING
XmNmarginBottom	Dimension	0
XmNmarginHeight	Dimension	2
XmNmarginLeft	Dimension	0
XmNmarginRight	Dimension	0
XmNmarginTop	Dimension	0
XmNmarginWidth	Dimension	2
XmNmnemonic	KeySym	NULL
XmNmnemonicCharSet	String	dynamic
XmNrecomputeSize	Boolean	True
XmNstringDirection	XmStringDirection	dynamic

RESOURCE DESCRIPTIONS

XmNaccelerator	The accelerator character to use when the label is part of a push button or a toggle button in a menu.
XmNacceleratorText	Text that tells the user what the accelerator is.
XmNalignment	Alignment of string in the label. Valid values: XmALIGNMENT_BEGINNING, XmALIGNMENT_CENTER, and XmALIGNMENT_END.
XmNfontList	Font of labelString.
XmNlabelInsensitivePixmap	Pixmap used if label is insensitive and contains a pixmap (labelType=XmPIXMAP).
XmNlabelPixmap	Pixmap used if label is sensitive and contains a pixmap (labelType=XmPIXMAP).
XmNlabelString	String displayed in the label if labelType=XmSTRING.
XmNlabelType	Specifies whether label displays a string (XmSTRING) or a pixmap (XmPIXMAP).
XmNmarginBottom	Space below labelString.
XmNmarginHeight	Height of margin above and below labelstring.
XmNmarginLeft	Space to the left of labelString.
XmNmarginRight	Space to the right of labelString.

XmNmarginTop	Space above labelString.
XmNmarginWidth	Width of margin to left and right of labelString.
XmNmnemonic	Specifies the mnemonic character that activates the button when the label is part of a push button or toggle button in a menu.
XmNmnemonicCharSet	Mnemonic's charset.
XmNrecomputeSize	When true, any change to the label automatically readjusts its size. When false, no readjustment occurs.
XmNstringDirection	Determines direction in which string is drawn. Valid values: XmSTRING_DIRECTION_L_TO_R and XmSTRING_DIRECTION_R_TO_L.

CONVENIENCE FUNCTIONS

```
Widget XmCreateLabel(Widget parent,String name,
    ArgList arglist,Cardinal argcount);
Widget XmCreateLabelGadget(Widget parent,String name,
    ArgList arglist,Cardinal argcount);
```

XmList Widget

See Chapter 11.

Description	Lets the user choose single or multiple items from a list.
Class Pointer	xmListWidgetClass
Class Name	XmList
Include File	<Xm/List.h>
Superclass	XmPrimitive

RESOURCES

Name	Type	Default
XmNautomaticSelection	Boolean	False
XmNdoubleClickInterval	int	dynamic
XmNfontList	XmFontList	dynamic
XmNitemCount	int	0
XmNitems	XmStringTable	NULL
XmNlistMarginHeight	Dimension	0
XmNlistMarginWidth	Dimension	0
XmNlistSizePolicy	unsigned char	XmVARIABLE

XmNlistSpacing	Dimension	0
XmNscrollBarDisplayPolicy	unsigned char	XmAS_NEEDED
XmNselectedItemCount	int	0
XmNselectedItems	XmStringTable	NULL
XmNselectionPolicy	unsigned char SELECT	XmBROWSE_
XmNstringDirection	XmStringDirection	dynamic
XmNtopItemPosition	int	1
XmNvisibleItemCount	int	1

RESOURCE DESCRIPTIONS

XmNautomaticSelection	If true, then a selection callback is triggered when an item is armed (in browse and extended modes). When false, item must be activated to get callback.
XmNdoubleClickInterval	Time (in milliseconds) within which second click must occur to be interpreted as a double-click.
XmNfontList	Font for items in list.
XmNitemCount	Number of items currently in list.
XmNitems	XmString items held in the list.
XmNlistMarginHeight, XmNlistMarginWidth	Margins around list.
XmNlistSizePolicy	Possible values: XmCONSTANT, XmVARIABLE, and XmRESIZE_IF_POSSIBLE. Determines what happens when a new item in the list forces the list widget to resize horizontally. Must be set at creation.
XmNlistSpacing	Space between items.
XmNscrollBarDisplayPolicy	Possible values: XmAS_NEEDED and XmSTATIC.
XmNselectedItemCount	Number of selected items.
XmNselectedItems	XmString array holding selected items.
XmNselectionPolicy	Possible values: XmSINGLE_SELECT, XmMULTI-PLE_SELECT, XmEXTENDED_SELECT, and Xm-BROWSE_SELECT.
XmNstringDirection	Possible values: XmSTRING_DIRECTION_L_TO_R and XmSTRING_DIRECTION_R_TO_L.
XmNtopItemPosition	Holds the number of the item at the top of the list displayed by the widget.
XmNvisibleItemCount	Maximum number of items visible at once.

CALLBACKS

Callback List	Call Data Type	Reason
XmNbrowseSelectionCallback	XmListCallbackStruct	XmCR_BROWSE_SELECT
XmNdefaultActionCallback	XmListCallbackStruct	XmCR_DEFAULT_ACTION
XmNextendedSelectionCallback	XmListCallbackStruct	XmCR_EXTENDED_SELECT
XmNmultipleSelectionCallback	XmListCallbackStruct	XmCR_MULTIPLE_SELECT
XmNsingleSelectionCallback	XmListCallbackStruct	XmCR_SINGLE_SELECT

CALLBACK DESCRIPTIONS

XmNbrowseSelection-Callback	Triggered in browse mode when a user selects an item.
XmNdefaultActionCallback	Triggered when user double-clicks an item.
XmNextendedSelection-Callback	Triggered when user selects an item in extended selection mode.
XmNmultipleSelection-Callback	Triggered when user selects an item in multiple selection mode.
XmNsingleSelectionCallback	Triggered when user selects an item in single selection mode.

CALLBACK STRUCTURE

```
typedef struct
{
    int reason;
    XEvent *event;
    XmString item;
    int item_length;
    int item_position;
    XmString *selected_items;
    int selected_item_count;
    int *selected_item_positions;
    int selection_type;
} XmListCallbackStruct;
```

CONVENIENCE FUNCTIONS

```
Widget XmCreateList(Widget parent,String name,
    ArgList arglist,Cardinal argcount);
Widget XmCreateScrolledList(Widget parent,String name,
    ArgList arglist,Cardinal argcount);
void XmListAddItem(Widget w, XmString item, int position);
void XmListAddItems(Widget w, XmString *items, int item_count,
    int position);
void XmListAddItemUnselected(Widget w, XmString item, int position);
void XmListDeleteAllItems(Widget w);
void XmListDeleteItem(Widget w,XmString item);
void XmListDeleteItems(Widget w, XmString *items, int item_count);
void XmListDeleteItemsPos(Widget w, int item_count, int position);
void XmListDeletePos(Widget w, int position);
void XmListDeselectAllItems(Widget w);
void XmListDeselectItem(Widget w, XmString item);
void XmListDeselectPos(Widget w, int position);
Boolean XmListGetMatchPos(Widget w, XmString item, int **pos_list,
    int *pos_count);
Boolean XmListGetSelectedPos(Widget w, int **pos_list, int *pos_count);
Boolean XmListItemExists(Widget w, XmString item);
int XmListItemPos(Widget w, XmString item);
void XmListReplaceItems(Widget w, XmString *old_items, int item_count,
    XmString *new_items);
void XmListReplaceItemsPos(Widget w, XmString *new_items, int item_count,
    int position);
void XmListSelectItem(Widget w, XmString item, Boolean notify);
void XmListSelectPos(Widget w, int position, Boolean notify);
void XmListSetAddMode(Widget w, Boolean mode);
void XmListSetBottomItem(Widget w, XmString item);
void XmListSetBottomPos(Widget w, int position);
void XmListSetHorizPos(Widget w, int position);
void XmListSetItem(Widget w, XmString item);
void XmListSetPos(Widget w, int position);
```

XmMainWindow Widget

See Chapter 11.

Description   A widget that builds a main application window.

Class Pointer   xmMainWindowWidgetClass

Class Name	XmMainWindow
Include File	<Xm/MainW.h>
Superclass	XmScrolledWindow

RESOURCES

Name	Type	Default
XmNcommandWindow	Window	NULL
XmNcommandWindowLocation	unsigned char	XmCOMMAND_ABOVE_ WORKSPACE
XmNmainWindowMarginHeight	Dimension	0
XmNmainWindowMarginWidth	Dimension	0
XmNmenuBar	Window	NULL
XmNmessageWindow	Window	NULL
XmNshowSeparator	Boolean	False

RESOURCE DESCRIPTIONS

XmNcommandWindow	The widget child that is the command window.
XmNcommandWindow- Location	Possible values: XmCOMMAND_ABOVE_ WORKSPACE and XmCOMMAND_BELOW_ WORKSPACE.
XmNmainWindowMargin- Height, XmNmainWindow- MarginWidth	Margins around main window.
XmNmenuBar	The widget child that is the menu bar.
XmNmessageWindow	The widget child that is the message area.
XmNshowSeparator	If true, displays separators between the parts.

CONVENIENCE FUNCTIONS

```
Widget XmCreateMainWindow(Widget parent,String name,
    ArgList arglist,Cardinal argcount);
Widget XmMainWindowSep1(Widget w);
Widget XmMainWindowSep2(Widget w);
Widget XmMainWindowSep3(Widget w);
void XmMainWindowSetAreas(Widget w, Widget menu_bar,
    Widget command_window, Widget horizontal_scrollbar,
    Widget vertical_scrollbar, Widget work_area);
```

XmManager Widget

Description	A widget type that builds managers of other widgets (for example, rowColumn, form, and so on).
Class Pointer	xmManagerWidgetClass
Class Name	XmManager
Include File	<Xm/Xm.h>
Superclass	Constraint

RESOURCES

Name	Type	Default
XmNbottomShadowColor	Pixel	dynamic
XmNbottomShadowPixmap	Pixmap	XmUNSPECIFIED_PIXMAP
XmNforeground	Pixel	dynamic
XmNhighlightColor	Pixel	dynamic
XmNhighlightPixmap	Pixmap	dynamic
XmNnavigationType	XmNavigationType	XmTAB_GROUP
XmNshadowThickness	Dimension	0
XmNstringDirection	XmStringDirection	dynamic
XmNtopShadowColor	Pixel	dynamic
XmNtopShadowPixmap	Pixmap	dynamic
XmNtraversalOn	Boolean	True
XmNunitType	unsigned char	dynamic
XmNuserData	Pointer	NULL

RESOURCE DESCRIPTIONS

XmNbottomShadowColor	Color of border shadow.
XmNbottomShadowPixmap	Pixmap for border shadow.
XmNforeground	Foreground color.
XmNhighlightColor	Highlight rectangle color.
XmNhighlightPixmap	Highlight rectangle pixmap.
XmNnavigationType	Valid values: XmNONE, XmTAB_GROUP, XmSTICKY_TAB_GROUP, and XmEXCLUSIVE_TAB_GROUP.
XmNshadowThickness	Border shadow thickness.
XmNstringDirection	Possible values: XmSTRING_DIRECTION_L_TO_R and XmSTRING_DIRECTION_R_TO_L.
XmNtopShadowColor	Color of border shadow.

XmNtopShadowPixmap	Pixmap for border shadow.
XmNtraversalOn	Transversal activation.
XmNunitType	Valid values: XmPIXELS, Xm100TH_MILLIMETERS, Xm1000TH_INCHES, XM100TH_POINTS, and Xm100TH_FONT_UNITS. Specifies how to interpret sizing requests.
XmNuserData	A pointer to anything.

CALLBACKS

Callback List	Call Data Type	Reason
XmNhelpCallback	XmAnyCallbackStruct	XmCR_HELP

CALLBACK DESCRIPTIONS

| XmNhelpCallback | Activated when user presses Help key. |

CALLBACK STRUCTURE

```
typedef struct
{
    int reason;
    XEvent *event;
} XmAnyCallbackStruct;
```

XmMenuShell Widget

Description	A widget designed to handle menus.
Class Pointer	xmMenuShellWidgetClass
Class Name	XmMenuShell
Include File	<Xm/XmMenuShell.h>
Superclass	OverrideShell

RESOURCES

Name	Type	Default
XmNdefaultFontList	XmFontList	dynamic

RESOURCE DESCRIPTIONS

| XmNdefaultFontList | Font for any text, label, or button widget held in the menu, unless the child widget specifies a font. |

XmMessageBox Widget

See Chapter 7.

Description	A widget that displays messages, yes/no questions, and so on to the user.
Class Pointer	xmMessageBoxWidgetClass
Class Name	XmMessageBox
Include File	<Xm/MessageB.h>
Superclass	XmBulletinBoard

RESOURCES

Name	Type	Default
XmNcancelLabelString	XmString	"Cancel"
XmNdefaultButtonType	unsigned char	XmDIALOG_OK_BUTTON
XmNdialogType	unsigned char	XmDIALOG_MESSAGE
XmNhelpLabelString	XmString	"Help"
XmNmessageAlignment	unsigned char	XmALIGNMENT_BEGINNING
XmNmessageString	XmString	""
XmNminimizeButton	Boolean	False
XmNokLabelString	XmString	"OK"
XmNsymbolPixmap	Pixmap	dynamic

RESOURCE DESCRIPTIONS

XmNcancelLabelString	String on cancel button.
XmNdefaultButtonType	Possible values: XmDIALOG_CANCEL_BUTTON, XmDIALOG_OK_BUTTON, and XmDIALOG_HELP_BUTTON. Determines which button is the default.
XmNdialogType	Possible values: XmDIALOG_ERROR, XmDIALOG_INFORMATION, XmDIALOG_MESSAGE, XmDIALOG_QUESTION, XmDIALOG_WARNING, and XmDIALOG_WORKING.
XmNhelpLabelString	String on Help button.
XmNmessageAlignment	Possible values: XmALIGNMENT_BEGINNING, XmALIGNMENT_CENTER, and XmALIGNMENT_END. Alignment of message.
XmNmessageString	String displayed by the message box.

XmNminimizeButtons	If false, buttons are all the same size as the largest button displayed. If true, they take on their minimum sizes.
XmNokLabelString	String on OK button.
XmNsymbolPixmap	Pixmap used for icon in message box.

CALLBACKS

Callback List	Call Data Type	Reason
XmNcancelCallback	XmAnyCallbackStruct	XmCR_CANCEL
XmNokCallback	XmAnyCallbackStruct	XmCR_OK

CALLBACK DESCRIPTIONS

| XmNcancelCallback | Triggered when user clicks Cancel button. |
| XmNokCallback | Triggered when user clicks OK button. |

CALLBACK STRUCTURE

```
typedef struct
{
   int reason;
   XEvent *event;
} XmAnyCallbackStruct;
```

CONVENIENCE FUNCTIONS

```
Widget XmCreateMessageBox(Widget parent,String name,
    ArgList arglist,Cardinal argcount);
Widget XmMessageBoxGetChild(Widget w,
    unsigned char child);
    Valid values for child:
        XmDIALOG_CANCEL_BUTTON
        XmDIALOG_DEFAULT_BUTTON
        XmDIALOG_HELP_BUTTON
        XmDIALOG_MESSAGE_LABEL
        XmDIALOG_OK_BUTTON
        XmDIALOG_SEPARATOR
        XmDIALOG_SYMBOL_LABEL
Widget XmCreateMessageDialog(Widget parent,String name,
    ArgList arglist,Cardinal argcount);
Widget XmCreateErrorDialog(Widget parent,String name,
    ArgList arglist,Cardinal argcount);
```

```
Widget XmCreateInformationDialog(Widget parent,String name,
    ArgList arglist,Cardinal argcount);
Widget XmCreateQuestionDialog(Widget parent,String name,
    ArgList arglist,Cardinal argcount);
Widget XmCreateWarningDialog(Widget parent,String name,
    ArgList arglist,Cardinal argcount);
Widget XmCreateWorkingDialog(Widget parent,String name,
    ArgList arglist,Cardinal argcount);
```

XmPanedWindow Widget

See Chapter 11

Description	A manager widget that places multiple widgets, separated by draggable sashes, in a single window.
Class Pointer	xmPanedWindowWidgetClass
Class Name	XmPanedWindow
Include File	<Xm/PanedW.h>
Superclass	XmManager

RESOURCES

Name	Type	Default
XmNmarginHeight	Dimension	3
XmNmarginWidth	Dimension	3
XmNrefigureMode	Boolean	True
XmNsashHeight	Dimension	10
XmNsashIndent	Position	-10
XmNsashShadowThickness	Dimension	dynamic
XmNsashWidth	Dimension	10
XmNseparatorOn	Boolean	True
XmNspacing	Dimension	8

RESOURCE DESCRIPTIONS

XmNmarginHeight, XmNmarginWidth	Margin between widget and its children.
XmNrefigureMode	When true, changes to panes affect the children immediately.
XmNsashHeight	Height of sash.
XmNsashIndent	Spacing between sash and window.

XmNsashShadowThickness   Thickness of shadow on sash.
XmNsashWidth   Width of sash.
XmNseparatorOn   When true, separators appear between panes.
XmNspacing   Spacing between panes.

CONSTRAINT RESOURCES

Name	Type	Default
XmNallowResize	Boolean	False
XmNpaneMaximum	Dimension	1000
XmNpaneMinimum	Dimension	1
XmNskipAdjust	Boolean	False

CONSTRAINT RESOURCE DESCRIPTIONS

XmNallowResize   When true, pane tries to follow size of child. When
                              false, children cannot resize themselves.
XmNpaneMaximum   Maximum size of pane.
XmNpaneMinimum   Minimum size of pane.
XmNskipAdjust   When true, pane will not be adjusted.

CONVENIENCE FUNCTIONS

```
Widget XmCreatePanedWindow(Widget parent,String name,
    ArgList arglist,Cardinal argcount);
```

XmPrimitive Widget

See Chapter 3.

Description   The widget from which all simple Motif widgets are built. All
                   simple Motif widgets inherit these resources.
Class Pointer   xmPrimitiveWidgetClass
Class Name   XmPrimitive
Include File   <Xm/Xm.h>
Superclass   Core

RESOURCES

Name	Type	Default
XmNbottomShadowColor	Pixel	dynamic
XmNbottomShadowPixmap	Pixmap	XmUNSPECIFIED_PIXMAP

XmNforeground	Pixel	dynamic
XmNhighlightColor	Pixel	dynamic
XmNhighlightOnEnter	Boolean	False
XmNhighlightPixmap	Pixmap	dynamic
XmNhighlightThickness	Dimension	2
XmNnavigationType	unsigned char	XmNONE
XmNshadowThickness	Dimension	2
XmNtopShadowColor	Pixel	dynamic
XmNtopShadowPixmap	Pixmap	dynamic
XmNtraversalOn	Boolean	True
XmNunitType	unsigned char	dynamic
XmNuserData	Pointer	NULL

RESOURCE DESCRIPTIONS

XmNbottomShadowColor	Color of border shadow.
XmNbottomShadowPixmap	Pixmap for border shadow.
XmNforeground	Foreground color.
XmNhighlightColor	Highlight color.
XmNhighlightOnEnter	If true, highlight appears when cursor enters widget.
XmNhighlightPixmap	Highlight pixmap.
XmNhighlightThickness	Highlight thickness.
XmNnavigationType	See XmManager widget.
XmNshadowThickness	Border shadow thickness.
XmNtopShadowColor	Color of border shadow.
XmNtopShadowPixmap	Pixmap for border shadow.
XmNtraversalOn	See XmManager widget.
XmNunitType	See XmManager widget.
XmNuserData	A pointer to anything.

CALLBACKS

Callback List	Call Data Type	Reason
XmNhelpCallback	XmAnyCallbackStruct	XmCR_HELP

CALLBACK DESCRIPTIONS

| XmNhelpCallback | Activated when user presses Help button. |

CALLBACK STRUCTURE

```
typedef struct
{
   int reason;
   XEvent *event;
} XmAnyCallbackStruct;
```

XmPushButton Widget

See Chapter 4. Also available as a gadget.

Description	Lets user issue a command by clicking a push button.
Class Pointer	xmPushButtonWidgetClass
Class Name	XmPushButton
Include File	<Xm/PushB.h>
Superclass	XmLabel

RESOURCES

Name	Type	Default
XmNarmColor	Pixel	dynamic
XmNarmPixmap	Pixmap	XmUNSPECIFIED_PIXMAP
XmNdefaultButton-ShadowThickness	Dimension	0
XmNfillOnArm	Boolean	True
XmNmultiClick	unsigned char	dynamic
XmNshowAsDefault	Dimension	0

RESOURCE DESCRIPTIONS

XmNarmColor	Color of button when armed.
XmNarmPixmap	If labelType inherited from label widget is XmPIXMAP, this pixmap appears on the button when armed.
XmNdefaultButton-ShadowThickness	The thickness of the border around the default button.
XmNfillOnArm	When true, the button fills when armed. When false, only shadow borders change appearance when armed.

XmNmultiClick

Possible values: XmMULTICLICK_DISCARD and XmMULTICLICK_KEEP. If you use DISCARD and the program receives a second click within the multiclick time, the second click is ignored.

XmNshowAsDefault

Any value greater than 0 marks the button as the default button.

CALLBACKS

Callback List	Call Data Type	Reason
XmNactivateCallback	XmPushButtonCallbackStruct	XmCR_ACTIVATE
XmNarmCallback	XmPushButtonCallbackStruct	XmCR_ARM
XmNdisarmCallback	XmPushButtonCallbackStruct	XmCR_DISARM

CALLBACK DESCRIPTIONS

XmNactivateCallback   Called when button is successfully activated.

XmNarmCallback   Called when button is armed.

XmNdisarmCallback   Called when button is disarmed.

CALLBACK STRUCTURE

```
typedef struct
{
    int reason;
    XEvent *event;
    int click_count;
} XmPushButtonCallbackStruct;
```

CONVENIENCE FUNCTIONS

```
Widget XmCreatePushButton(Widget parent,String name,
    ArgList arglist,Cardinal argcount);
Widget XmCreatePushButtonGadget(Widget parent,String name,
    ArgList arglist,Cardinal argcount);
```

XmRowColumn Widget

See Chapter 5.

Description   A manager widget that automatically arranges its children in rows and columns.

Class Pointer   xmRowColumnWidgetClass

Class Name   XmRowColumn

Include File   <Xm/RowColumn.h>
Superclass   XmManager

RESOURCES

Name	Type	Default
XmNadjustLast	Boolean	True
XmNadjustMargin	Boolean	True
XmNentryAlignment	unsigned char	XmALIGNMENT_BEGINNING
XmNentryBorder	Dimension	0
XmNentryClass	WidgetClass	dynamic
XmNisAligned	Boolean	True
XmNisHomogeneous	Boolean	dynamic
XmNlabelString	XmString	NULL
XmNmarginHeight	Dimension	dynamic
XmNmarginWidth	Dimension	dynamic
XmNmenuAccelerator	String	dynamic
XmNmenuHelpWidget	Widget	NULL
XmNmenuHistory	Widget	NULL
XmNmenuPost	String	NULL
XmNmnemonic	KeySym	NULL
XmNmnemonicCharSet	String	dynamic
XmNnumColumns	short	1
XmNorientation	unsigned char	dynamic
XmNpacking	unsigned char	dynamic
XmNpopupEnabled	Boolean	True
XmNradioAlwaysOne	Boolean	True
XmNradioBehavior	Boolean	False
XmNresizeHeight	Boolean	True
XmNresizeWidth	Boolean	True
XmNrowColumnType	unsigned char	XmWORK_AREA
XmNspacing	Dimension	dynamic
XmNsubMenuId	Widget	NULL
XmNwhichButton	unsigned int	dynamic

RESOURCE DESCRIPTIONS

XmNadjustLast   When true, adjusts last widget in row or column to
                                 end of RowColumn widget. When false, does not
                                 adjust last widget.

XmNadjustMargin	When true, inner margins for all children of the RowColumn have the same value.
XmNentryAlignment	Possible values: XmALIGNMENT_BEGINNING, XmALIGNMENT_CENTER, and XmALIGNMENT_END. If XmNisAligned is true, all label widgets use this value for their alignment resource.
XmNentryBorder	Gives all children the same border. Disabled if set to 0.
XmNentryClass	If XmNisHomogeneous is true, this resource specifies the allowed class.
XmNisAligned	If true, any child widget that is a label uses the alignment specified in XmNentryAlignment.
XmNisHomogeneous	If true, RowColumn forces all children to be of the type specified in XmNentryClass.
XmNlabelString	If XmNrowColumnType is set to XmMENU_OPTION, this string is displayed to the side of the selection area.
XmNmarginHeight	Determines margin between RowColumn and its children at the top and bottom of each column.
XmNmarginWidth	Determines margin between RowColumn and its children to the left and right of each row.
XmNmenuAccelerator	If RowColumn is a pop-up menu or a menu bar, this key activates the menu.
XmNmenuHelpWidget	If RowColumn is a menu bar and this resource is set to a cascade button widget, the cascade button specified appears at the far right of the menu bar.
XmNmenuHistory	Holds the widget ID of the last child activated.
XmNmenuPost	Determines which type of event activates the menu (that is, which button on the mouse activates a pop-up).
XmNmnemonic	If type is XmMENU_OPTION, holds the menu's mnemonic character.
XmNmnemonicCharSet	Character set for XmNmnemonic.
XmNnumColumns	Indicates the preferred number of columns or rows, depending on the orientation, used to arrange the children. XmNpacking must be XmPACK_COLUMN.
XmNorientation	Possible values: XmVERTICAL and XmHORIZONTAL.

XmNpacking	Possible values: XmPACK_TIGHT (packs as tight as possible, using minimum sizes); XmPACK_COLUMN (places all children in boxes of the same size); or XmPACK_NONE (reverts to bulletin board behavior, with x and y resources controlling placement).
XmNpopupEnabled	Allows pop-up behavior.
XmNradioAlwaysOne	Forces one toggle in a radio box always to be on.
XmNradioBehavior	Makes all of the toggle children have radio box behavior.
XmNresizeHeight, XmNresizeWidth	When true, changes to widget or children cause the widget to resize.
XmNrowColumnType	Valid values: XmMENU_BAR, XmMENU_PULLDOWN, XmMENU_POPUP, XmMENU_OPTION, and XmWORK_AREA (the default).
XmNspacing	Spacing between children.
XmNsubMenuId	The rowColumnType resource must be set to XmMENU_OPTION. Determines which menu is activated.
XmNwhichButton	Determines which mouse button activates a pop-up. This resource is obsolete; use XmNmenuPost instead.

CALLBACKS

Callback List	Call Data Type	Reason
XmNentryCallback	XmRowColumnCallbackStruct	XmCR_ACTIVATE
XmNmapCallback	XmRowColumnCallbackStruct	XmCR_MAP
XmNunmapCallback	XmRowColumnCallbackStruct	XmCR_UNMAP

CALLBACK DESCRIPTIONS

XmNentryCallback	Remaps a widget's XmNactivateCallback or XmNvalueChangedCallback to the RowColumn's entry callback. Must be set before creating children.
XmNmapCallback	Activated when RowColumn is mapped.
XmNUnmapCallback	Activated when RowColumn is unmapped.

CALLBACK STRUCTURE

```
typedef struct
{
    int reason;
    XEvent *event;
    Widget widget;
    char *data;
    char *callbackstruct;
} XmRowColumnCallbackStruct;
```

CONVENIENCE FUNCTIONS

```
Widget XmCreateRowColumn(Widget parent,String name,
    ArgList arglist,Cardinal argcount);
```
Related convenience functions:
```
Widget XmCreateMenuBar(Widget parent,String name,
    ArgList arglist,Cardinal argcount);
Widget XmCreateOptionMenu(Widget parent,String name,
    ArgList arglist,Cardinal argcount);
Widget XmCreatePopupMenu(Widget parent,String name,
    ArgList arglist,Cardinal argcount);
Widget XmCreatePulldownMenu(Widget parent,String name,
    ArgList arglist,Cardinal argcount);
Widget XmCreateRadioBox(Widget parent,String name,
    ArgList arglist,Cardinal argcount);
Widget XmCreateSimpleCheckBox(Widget parent,String name,
    ArgList arglist,Cardinal argcount);
Widget XmCreateSimpleMenuBar(Widget parent,String name,
    ArgList arglist,Cardinal argcount);
Widget XmCreateSimpleOptionMenu(Widget parent,String name,
    ArgList arglist,Cardinal argcount);
Widget XmCreateSimplePopupMenu(Widget parent,String name,
    ArgList arglist,Cardinal argcount);
Widget XmCreateSimplePulldownMenu(Widget parent,String name,
    ArgList arglist,Cardinal argcount);
Widget XmCreateSimpleRadioBox(Widget parent,String name,
    ArgList arglist,Cardinal argcount);
Widget XmCreateWorkArea(Widget parent,String name,
    ArgList arglist,Cardinal argcount);
Cursor XmGetMenuCursor(Display *display);
Widget XmGetPostedFromWidget(widget menu);
void XmMenuPosition(Widget menu,XmButtonPressedEvent *event);
```

```
Widget XmOptionButtonGadget(Widget option_menu);
Widget XmOptionLabelGadget(Widget option_menu);
void XmSetMenuCursor(Display *display, Cursor cursor);
```

XmScale Widget

See Chapter 4.

Description	Creates a slider that lets users change a value.
Class Pointer	xmScaleWidgetClass
Class Name	XmScale
Include File	<Xm/Scale.h>
Superclass	XmManager

RESOURCES

Name	Type	Default
XmNdecimalPoints	short	0
XmNfontList	XmFontList	dynamic
XmNhighlightOnEnter	Boolean	False
XmNhighlightThickness	Dimension	2
XmNmaximum	int	100
XmNminimum	int	0
XmNorientation	unsigned char	XmVERTICAL
XmNprocessingDirection	unsigned char	dynamic
XmNscaleHeight	Dimension	0
XmNscaleMultiple	int	dynamic
XmNscaleWidth	Dimension	0
XmNshowValue	Boolean	False
XmNtitleString	XmString	NULL
XmNvalue	int	0

RESOURCE DESCRIPTIONS

XmNdecimalPoints	Location of decimal point from the right.
XmNfontList	Font of title.
XmNhighlightOnEnter	When true, widget highlights when cursor enters it.
XmNhighlightThickness	Thickness of highlight.
XmNmaximum	Maximum value of slider.

XmNminimum	Minimum value of slider.
XmNorientation	Valid values: XmVERTICAL and XmHORIZONTAL.
XmNprocessingDirection	Valid values: XmMAX_ON_TOP, XmMAX_ON_BOTTOM, XmMAX_ON_LEFT, and XmMAX_ON_RIGHT.
XmNscaleHeight	Height of slider.
XmNscaleMultiple	Amount slider moves when clicking in trough. (XmNmaximum-XmNminimum)/10 is the default.
XmNscaleWidth	Width of slider.
XmNshowValue	When true, creates a label that displays the current value.
XmNtitleString	Message displayed above slider.
XmNvalue	Holds current value of slider.

CALLBACKS

Callback List	Call Data Type	Reason
XmNdragCallback	XmScaleCallbackStruct	XmCR_DRAG
XmNvalueChangedCallback	XmScaleCallbackStruct	XmCR_VALUE_CHANGED

CALLBACK DESCRIPTIONS

XmNdragCallback	Triggered each time a change occurs as slider is dragged.
XmNvalueChangedCallback	Triggered when value changes.

CALLBACK STRUCTURE

```
typedef struct
{
    int reason;
    XEvent *event;
    int value;
} XmScaleCallbackStruct;
```

CONVENIENCE FUNCTIONS

```
Widget XmCreateScale(Widget parent,String name,
    ArgList arglist,Cardinal argcount);
void XmScaleGetValue(Widget w, int *value);
void XmScaleSetValue(Widget w, int value);
```

XmScrollBar Widget

See Chapter 11.

Description	Implements a Motif-style scroll bar.
Class Pointer	xmScrollBarWidgetClass
Class Name	XmScrollBar
Include File	<Xm/ScrollBar.h>
Superclass	XmPrimitive

RESOURCES

Name	Type	Default
XmNincrement	int	1
XmNinitialDelay	int	250
XmNmaximum	int	100
XmNminimum	int	0
XmNorientation	unsigned char	XmVERTICAL
XmNpageIncrement	int	10
XmNprocessingDirection	unsigned char	dynamic
XmNrepeatDelay	int	50
XmNshowArrows	Boolean	True
XmNsliderSize	int	dynamic
XmNtroughColor	Pixel	dynamic
XmNvalue	int	0

RESOURCE DESCRIPTIONS

XmNincrement	Amount value changes when user clicks arrow of the scroll bar.
XmNinitialDelay	Milliseconds of delay before repetition starts when user clicks arrow or shaft.
XmNmaximum	Maximum value of scroll bar.
XmNminimum	Minimum value of scroll bar.
XmNorientation	Valid values: XmVERTICAL and XmHORIZONTAL.
XmNpageIncrement	Amount value changes when user clicks shaft of the scroll bar.
XmNprocessingDirection	See scale widget.
XmNrepeatDelay	Milliseconds between repetitions.
XmNshowArrows	Determines if scroll bar's arrows are visible.
XmNsliderSize	Size of the slider.

| XmNtroughColor | Color of shaft. |
| XmNvalue | Current value of the scroll bar. |

CALLBACKS

Callback List	Call Data Type	Reason
XmNdecrementCallback	XmScrollBar-CallbackStruct	XmCR_DECREMENT
XmNdragCallback	XmScrollBar-CallbackStruct	XmCR_DRAG
XmNincrementCallback	XmScrollBar-CallbackStruct	XmCR_INCREMENT
XmNpageDecrementCallback	XmScrollBar-CallbackStruct	XmCR_PAGE_DECREMENT
XmNpageIncrementCallback	XmScrollBar-CallbackStruct	XmCR_PAGE_INCREMENT
XmNtoBottomCallback	XmScrollBar-CallbackStruct	XmCR_TO_BOTTOM
XmNtoTopCallback	XmScrollBar-CallbackStruct	XmCR_TO_TOP
XmNvalueChangedCallback	XmScrollBar-CallbackStruct	XmCR_VALUE_CHANGED

CALLBACK DESCRIPTIONS

XmNdecrementCallback	Triggered when scroll bar value decreases by one increment.
XmNdragCallback	Triggered each time value changes when user drags scroll bar.
XmNincrementCallback	Triggered when scroll bar value increases by one increment.
XmNpageDecrement-Callback	Triggered when user clicks to move scroll bar back by one page.
XmNpageIncrement-Callback	Triggered when user clicks to advance scroll bar by a page.
XmNtoTopCallback, XmNtoBottomCallback	Triggered when the slider reaches the top or the bottom.
XmNvalueChangedCallback	Triggered each time XmNvalue changes.

CALLBACK STRUCTURE

```
typedef struct
{
    int reason;
    XEvent *event;
    int value;
    int pixel;
} XmScrollBarCallbackStruct;
```

CONVENIENCE FUNCTIONS

```
Widget XmCreateScrollBar(Widget parent,String name,
    ArgList arglist,Cardinal argcount);
void XmScrollBarGetValues(Widget w, int *value, int *slider_size,
    int *increment, int *page_increment);
void XmScrollBarSetValues(Widget w, int value, int slider_size,
    int increment, int page_increment, Boolean notify);
```

XmScrolledWindow Widget

See Chapter 11.

Description	A work area combined with two scroll bars.
Class Pointer	xmScrolledWindowWidgetClass
Class Name	XmScrolledWindow
Include File	<Xm/ScrolledW.h>
Superclass	XmManager

RESOURCES

Name	Type	Default
XmNclipWindow	Window	NULL
XmNhorizontalScrollBar	Window	NULL
XmNscrollBarDisplayPolicy	unsigned char	dynamic
XmNscrollBarPlacement	unsigned char	XmBOTTOM_RIGHT
XmNscrolledWindowMarginHeight	Dimension	0
XmNscrolledWindowMarginWidth	Dimension	0
XmNscrollingPolicy	unsigned char	XmAPPLICATION_ DEFINED
XmNspacing	Dimension	4
XmNverticalScrollBar	Window	NULL

| XmNvisualPolicy | unsigned char | dynamic |
| XmNworkWindow | Window | NULL |

RESOURCE DESCRIPTIONS

XmNclipWindow	Set automatically if XmNvisualPolicy is Xm-CONSTANT.
XmNhorizontalScrollBar	Identifier of horizontal scroll bar.
XmNscrollBarDisplayPolicy	Valid values: XmAS_NEEDED (removes scroll bars from view if window is large enough to display entire pixmap); XmSTATIC (always displays scroll bars).
XmNscrollBarPlacement	Valid values: XmTOP_LEFT, XmBOTTOM_LEFT, XmTOP_RIGHT, XmBOTTOM_RIGHT.
XmNscrolledWindow-MarginHeight, XmN-scrolledWindow-MarginWidth	Margins in window.
XmNscrollingPolicy	Causes widget to handle all scrolling itself using an oversized pixmap. Also handles normal scroll callbacks to the application. Valid values: XmAUTOMATIC and XmAPPLICATION_DEFINED.
XmNspacing	Space between scroll bars and window.
XmNverticalScrollBar	Identifier of vertical scroll bar.
XmNvisualPolicy	Valid values: XmVARIABLE and XmCONSTANT.
XmNworkWindow	Identifier of work area.

CONVENIENCE FUNCTIONS

```
Widget XmCreateScrolledWindow(Widget parent,String name,
    ArgList arglist,Cardinal argcount);
void XmScrolledWindowSetAreas(Widget w, Widget horiz_scrollbar,
    Widget vert_scrollbar,Widget work_area);
```

XmSelectionBox Widget

See Chapter 7.

Description	Creates a list of options from which the user can make selections.
Class Pointer	xmSelectionBoxWidgetClass
Class Name	XmSelectionBox

Include File	<Xm/SelectioB.h>
Superclass	XmBulletinBoard

RESOURCES

Name	Type	Default
XmNapplyLabelString	XmString	"Apply"
XmNcancelLabelString	XmString	"Cancel"
XmNdialogType	unsigned char	dynamic
XmNhelpLabelString	XmString	"Help"
XmNlistItemCount	int	0
XmNlistItems	XmStringTable	NULL
XmNlistLabelString	XmString	NULL
XmNlistVisibleItemCount	int	8
XmNminimizeButtons	Boolean	False
XmNmustMatch	Boolean	False
XmNokLabelString	XmString	"OK"
XmNselectionLabelString	XmString	"Selection"
XmNtextAccelerators	XtAccelerators	default
XmNtextColumns	short	20
XmNtextString	XmString	""

RESOURCE DESCRIPTIONS

XmNapplyLabelString	String for Apply button.
XmNcancelLabelString	String for Cancel button.
XmNdialogType	Possible values: XmDIALOG_PROMPT, Xm-DIALOG_COMMAND, XmDIALOG_SELECTION, XmDIALOG_FILE_SELECTION, and XmDIALOG_WORK_AREA.
XmNhelpLabelString	String for Help button.
XmNlistItems	Items in the list.
XmNlistItemCount	Number of items in list.
XmNlistLabelString	String displayed above list.
XmNlistVisibleItemCount	Number of items visible in list.
XmNminimizeButtons	If false, buttons are all the size of the largest. If true, buttons take on minimum sizes.
XmNmustMatch	When true, value entered in text area must match one of the items in the list.

XmNokLabelString	String for OK button.
XmNselectionLabelString	Label displayed above text field.
XmNtextAccelerators	Normal accelerators for text widget.
XmNtextColumns	Width of list.
XmNtextString	Value held in text widget.

CALLBACKS

Callback List	Call Data Type	Reason
XmNapplyCallback	XmSelectionBoxCallbackStruct	XmCR_APPLY
XmNcancelCallback	XmSelectionBoxCallbackStruct	XmCR_CANCEL
XmNnoMatchCallback	XmSelectionBoxCallbackStruct	XmCR_NO_MATCH
XmNokCallback	XmSelectionBoxCallbackStruct	XmCR_OK

CALLBACK DESCRIPTIONS

XmNapplyCallback	Triggered when user clicks Apply button.
XmNcancelCallback	Triggered when user clicks Cancel button.
XmNnoMatchCallback	Triggered when value in text area does not match a value in the list.
XmNokCallback	Triggered when user clicks OK button.

CALLBACK STRUCTURE

```
typedef struct
{
    int reason;
    XEvent *event;
    XmString value;
    int length;
} XmSelectionBoxCallbackStruct;
```

CONVENIENCE FUNCTIONS

```
Widget XmCreateSelectionBox(Widget parent,String name,
    ArgList arglist,Cardinal argcount);
Widget XmCreateSelectionDialog(Widget parent,String name,
    ArgList arglist,Cardinal argcount);
Widget XmCreatePromptDialog(Widget parent,String name,
    ArgList arglist,Cardinal argcount);
Widget XmSelectionBoxGetChild(Widget w, unsigned char child);
```

Valid values for child:
```
XmDIALOG_APPLY_BUTTON
XmDIALOG_CANCEL_BUTTON
XmDIALOG_DEFAULT_BUTTON
XmDIALOG_HELP_BUTTON
XmDIALOG_LIST
XmDIALOG_LIST_LABEL
XmDIALOG_OK_BUTTON
XmDIALOG_SELECTION_LABEL
XmDIALOG_SEPARATOR
XmDIALOG_TEXT
XmDIALOG_WORK_AREA
```

XmSeparator Widget

See Chapter 5. Also available as a gadget.

Description	Creates a separation line on the screen. Be sure to attach this widget to a form, or assign it a width, or it will appear as a dot and not a line.
Class Pointer	xmSeparatorWidgetClass
Class Name	XmSeparator
Include File	<Xm/Separator.h>
Superclass	XmPrimitive

RESOURCES

Name	Type	Default
XmNmargin	Dimension	0
XmNorientation	unsigned char	XmHORIZONTAL
XmNseparatorType	unsigned char	XmSHADOW_ETCHED_IN

RESOURCE DESCRIPTIONS

XmNmargin	Margin at end of separator.
XmNorientation	Valid values: XmVERTICAL and XmHORIZONTAL.
XmNseparatorType	Valid values: XmSINGLE_LINE, XmDOUBLE_LINE, XmSINGLE_DASHED_LINE, XmDOUBLE_DASHED_LINE, XmNO_LINE, XmSHADOW_ETCHED_IN, and XmSHADOW_ETCHED_OUT.

CONVENIENCE FUNCTIONS

```
Widget XmCreateSeparator(Widget parent,String name,
    ArgList arglist,Cardinal argcount);
Widget XmCreateSeparatorGadget(Widget parent,String name,
    ArgList arglist,Cardinal argcount);
```

XmText Widget

See Chapter 10.

Description	Provides text editing capabilities.
Class Pointer	xmTextWidgetClass
Class Name	XmText
Include File	<Xm/Text.h>
Superclass	XmPrimitive

RESOURCES

Name	Type	Default
XmNautoShowCursorPosition	Boolean	True
XmNblinkRate	int	500 (milliseconds)
XmNcolumns	Short	dynamic
XmNcursorPosition	XmTextPosition	0
XmNcursorPositionVisible	Boolean	True
XmNeditable	Boolean	True
XmNeditMode	int	XmSINGLE_LINE_EDIT
XmNfontList	XmFontList	dynamic
XmNmarginHeight	Dimension	5
XmNmarginWidth	Dimension	5
XmNmaxLength	int	largest int
XmNpendingDelete	Boolean	True
XmNresizeHeight	Boolean	False
XmNresizeWidth	Boolean	False
XmNrows	short	dynamic
XmNscrollHorizontal	Boolean	True
XmNscrollLeftSide	Boolean	dynamic
XmNscrollTopSide	Boolean	False
XmNscrollVerticle	Boolean	True
XmNselectThreshold	int	5
XmNselectionArray	Pointer	default array

XmNselectionArrayCount	int	4
XmNsource	XmTextSource	Default source
XmNtopCharacter	XmTextPosition	0
XmNvalue	String	" "
XmNverifyBell	Boolean	True
XmNwordWrap	Boolean	False

RESOURCE DESCRIPTIONS

XmNautoShowCursor-Position	When true, text scrolls to make cursor visible if cursorPosition resource changes.
XmNblinkRate	Rate of cursor blinking (in milliseconds).
XmNcolumns	Width of text widget in columns of characters.
XmNcursorPosition	Position of the cursor in the text string.
XmNcursorPositionVisible	When true, blinking cursor marks insert point.
XmNeditable	When true, text can be modified. When false, text is read-only.
XmNeditMode	Possible values: XmSINGLE_LINE_EDIT and XmMULTI_LINE_EDIT.
XmNfontList	Font for widget.
XmNmarginHeight, XmNmarginWidth	Size of margin around text.
XmNmaxLength	Maximum length of the text.
XmNpendingDelete	When true, selected area is deleted at next insert.
XmNresizeHeight	When true, widget tries to display all text it owns in one window by readjusting its height.
XmNresizeWidth	When true, widget tries to display all text it owns in one window by readjusting its width.
XmNrows	Height of widget in rows of characters.
XmNscrollHorizontal	When true, creates horizontal scroll bar.
XmNscrollLeftSide	When true, positions horizontal scroll bar on the left side.
XmNscrollTopSide	When true, positions horizontal scroll bar on top.
XmNscrollVertical	When true, uses vertical scroll bar.
XmNselectThreshold	Number of pixels that user must move mouse to select a character.
XmNselectionArray	Holds an array containing the actions that occur on multiple mouse clicks. The default array contains the values XmSELECT_POSITION, XmSELECT_WORD, XmSELECT_LINE, and XmSELECT_ALL.

XmNselectionArrayCount	Number of elements in selection array.
XmNsource	Allows sharing of text sources.
XmNtopCharacter	Holds the location of the first visible character in the text string.
XmNvalue	Holds the text string.
XmNverifyBell	When true, sounds bell.
XmNwordWrap	When true, turns on automatic word wrapping.

CALLBACKS

Callback List	Call Data Type	Reason
XmNactivateCallback	XmAny-CallbackStruct	XmCR_ACTIVATE
XmNfocusCallback	XmAny-CallbackStruct	XmCR_FOCUS
XmNgainPrimaryCallback	XmAny-CallbackStruct	XmCR_GAIN_PRIMARY
XmNlosePrimaryCallback	XmAny-CallbackStruct	XmCR_LOSE_PRIMARY
XmNlosingFocusCallback	XmTextVerify-CallbackStruct	XmCR_LOSING_FOCUS
XmNmodifyVerifyCallback	XmTextVerify-CallbackStruct	XmCR_MODIFYING_TEXT_VALUE
XmNmotionVerifyCallback	XmTextVerify-CallbackStruct	XmCR_MOVING_INSERT_CURSOR
XmNvalueChangedCallback	XmAny-CallbackStruct	XmCR_VALUE_CHANGED

CALLBACK DESCRIPTIONS

XmNactivateCallback	Triggered when widget is activated.
XmNfocusCallback	Triggered when widget receives focus.
XmNgainPrimaryCallback	Triggered when widget gains primary selection.
XmNlosePrimaryCallback	Triggered when widget loses primary selection.
XmNlosingFocusCallback	Triggered when widget loses focus.
XmNmodifyVerifyCallback	Called prior to changes in text due to insertion or deletion.
XmNmotionVerifyCallback	Triggered each time cursor moves.
XmNvalueChangedCallback	Called following text changes due to insertion or deletion.

CALLBACK STRUCTURE

```
typedef struct
{
    int reason;
    XEvent *event;
} XmAnyCallbackStruct;

typedef struct
{
    int reason;
    XEvent *event;
    Boolean doit;
    XmTextPosition currInsert, newInsert;
    XmTextPosition startPos, endPos;
    XmTextBlock text;
} XmTextVerifyCallbackStruct;
```

CONVENIENCE FUNCTIONS

```
Widget XmCreateText(Widget parent,String name,
    ArgList arglist,Cardinal argcount);
Widget XmCreateScrolledText(Widget parent,String name,
    ArgList arglist,Cardinal argcount);
void XmTextClearSelection (Widget widget, Time clear_time);
Boolean XmTextCopy (Widget widget, Time copy_time);
Boolean XmTextCut (Widget widget, Time cut_time);
int XmTextGetBaseline (Widget widget);
Boolean XmTextGetEditable (Widget widget);
XmTextPosition XmTextGetInsertionPosition (Widget widget);
XmTextPosition XmTextGetLastPosition (Widget widget);
int XmTextGetMaxLength (Widget widget);
char *XmTextGetSelection (Widget widget);
Boolean XmTextGetSelectionPosition (Widget widget,
    XmTextPosition *left, XmTextPosition *right);
XmTextSource XmTextGetSource (Widget widget);
char *XmTextGetString(Widget widget);
XmTextPosition XmTextGetTopCharacter (Widget widget);
void XmTextInsert (Widget widget, XmTextPosition position,
    char *value);
Boolean XmTextPaste (Widget widget);
Boolean XmTextPosToXY (Widget widget, XmTextPosition position,
    Position *x, Position *y);
Boolean XmTextRemove (Widget widget);
```

```
void XmTextReplace (Widget widget, XmTextPosition frompos,
    XmTextPosition topos, char *value);
void XmTextScroll (Widget widget, int n);
void XmTextSetAddMode (Widget widget, Boolean state);
void XmTextSetEditable (Widget widget, Boolean editable);
void XmTextSetHighlight (Widget w, XmTextPosition left,
    XmTextPosition right, XmHighlightMode mode);
void XmTextSetInsertionPosition (Widget widget, XmTextPosition position);
void XmTextSetMaxLength (Widget widget, int max_length);
void XmTextSetSelection (Widget widget, XmTextPosition first,
    XmTextPosition last, Time set_time);
void XmTextSetSource (Widget widget, XmTextSource source,
    XmTextPosition top_character, XmTextPosition cursor_position);
void XmTextSetString (Widget widget, char *value);
void XmTextSetTopCharacter (Widget widget, XmTextPosition top_character);
void XmTextShowPosition (Widget widget, XmTextPosition position);
XmTextPosition XmTextXYToPos (Widget widget, Position x, Position y);
```

XmToggleButton Widget

See Chapter 11. Also available as a gadget.

Description	Lets user flip a two-state variable. Provides a visual indicator.
Class Pointer	xmToggleButtonWidgetClass
Class Name	XmToggleButton
Include File	<Xm/ToggleB.h>
Superclass	Xmlabel

RESOURCES

Name	Type	Default
XmNfillOnSelect	Boolean	True
XmNindicatorOn	Boolean	True
XmNindicatorSize	Dimension	XmINVALID_DIMENSION
XmNindicatorType	unsigned char	dynamic
XmNselectColor	Pixel	dynamic
XmNselectInsensitivePixmap	Pixmap	XmUNSPECIFIED_PIXMAP
XmNselectPixmap	Pixmap	XmUNSPECIFIED_PIXMAP
XmNset	Boolean	False
XmNspacing	Dimension	4
XmNvisibleWhenOff	Boolean	dynamic

RESOURCE DESCRIPTIONS

XmNfillOnSelect	When true, fills indicator with selectColor.
XmNindicatorOn	When true, makes indicator visible.
XmNindicatorSize	Sets indicator's size. Special value XmINVALID_DIMENSION scales indicator to label's font size.
XmNindicatorType	Valid values: XmONE_OF_MANY (diamond shape) and XmN_OF_MANY (square shape).
XmNselectColor	Fill color for indicator.
XmNselectInsensitive-Pixmap	Pixmap for selected and insensitive button.
XmNselectPixmap	Pixmap for selected and sensitive button.
XmNset	Current value of the toggle.
XmNspacing	Space between toggle indicator and button.
XmNvisibleWhenOff	When false, makes indicator invisible if not selected.

CALLBACKS

Callback List	Call Data Type	Reason
XmNarmCallback	XmToggleButtonCallbackStruct	XmCR_ARM
XmNdisarmCallback	XmToggleButtonCallbackStruct	XmCR_DISARM
XmNvalueChangedCallback	XmToggleButtonCallbackStruct	XmCR_VALUE_CHANGED

CALLBACK DESCRIPTIONS

armCallback	Called when button is armed.
disarmCallback	Called when button is disarmed.
valueChangedCallback	Called when value of set resource flips.

CALLBACK STRUCTURE

```
typedef struct
{
    int reason;
    XEvent *event;
    int set;
} XmToggleButtonCallbackStruct;
```

CONVENIENCE FUNCTIONS

```
Widget XmCreateToggleButton(Widget parent,String name,
    ArgList arglist,Cardinal argcount);
Widget XmCreateToggleButtonGadget(Widget parent,String name,
    ArgList arglist,Cardinal argcount);
```

J.2   X TOOLKIT WIDGETS

The following widgets come from the X Toolkit. They are included because you will need to use them often, and because they make up the hierarchy to an application shell widget. See Section 14.5 for more information.

ApplicationShell Widget

Description	The toplevel shell for any application.
Class Pointer	applicationShellWidgetClass
Class Name	ApplicationShell
Include File	<Xm/Xm.h>, <X11/Shell.h>
Superclass	TopLevelShell

RESOURCES

Name	Type	Default
XmNargc	int	0
XmNargv	String *	NULL

RESOURCE DESCRIPTIONS

XmNargc	Number of strings held in argv.
XmNargv	Applications argument list. Contains a copy of the command line arguments used to invoke the application.

Composite Widget

Description	The basis of all container widgets.
Class Pointer	compositeWidgetClass
Class Name	Composite
Include File	<Xm/Xm.h>
Superclass	Core

RESOURCES

Name	Type	Default
XmNchildren	WidgetList	NULL
XmNinsertPosition	(*)()	NULL
XmNnumChildren	Cardinal	0

RESOURCE DESCRIPTIONS

XmNchildren	List of child widgets.
XmNinsertPosition	Pointer to a function determining insert position of children.
XmNnumChildren	Number of children.

Constraint Widget

Description	The basis of all constraint widgets.
Class Pointer	constraintWidgetClass
Class Name	Constraint
Include File	<Xm/Xm.h>
Superclass	Composite

This widget defines no resources of its own.

Core Widget

See Chapter 3.

Description	The superclass of all widgets. All widgets have the core widget's resources and callbacks.
Class Pointer	widgetClass
Class Name	Core
Include File	<Xm/Xm.h>
Superclass	None

RESOURCES

Name	Type	Default
XmNaccelerators	XtAccelerators	NULL
XmNancestorSensitive	Boolean	dynamic
XmNbackground	Pixel	dynamic

XmNbackgroundPixmap	Pixmap	XmUNSPECIFIED_PIXMAP
XmNborderColor	Pixel	XtDefaultForeground
XmNborderPixmap	Pixmap	XmUNSPECIFIED_PIXMAP
XmNborderWidth	Dimension	1
XmNcolormap	Colormap	copy from parent
XmNdepth	int	dynamic
XmNheight	Dimension	dynamic
XmNinitialResourcesPersistent	Boolean	True
XmNmappedWhenManaged	Boolean	True
XmNscreen	Screen*	dynamic
XmNsensitive	Boolean	True
XmNtranslations	XtTranslations	NULL
XmNwidth	Dimension	dynamic
XmNx	Position	0
XmNy	Position	0

RESOURCE DESCRIPTIONS

XmNaccelerators	Translation table for accelerators.
XmNancestorSensitive	If true, the parent of this widget can receive input events.
XmNbackground	Background color.
XmNbackgroundPixmap	Pixmap for tiling background of widget.
XmNborderColor	Color of widget's border.
XmNborderPixmap	Pixmap for the border.
XmNborderWidth	Width of border in pixels.
XmNcolormap	Colormap table for widget.
XmNdepth	Depth of pixels in widget.
XmNheight	Height of widget.
XmNinitialResources-Persistent	Set to true if widget will not be destroyed during the life of the application. Set to false if it will.
XmNmappedWhenManaged	When true, widget is mapped as soon as it is managed. When false, widget must be mapped explicitly.
XmNscreen	Screen that displays widget.
XmNsensitive	When true, widget receives input events.
XmNtranslations	Pointer to translation list.
XmNwidth	Width of the widget.
XmNx	X coordinate of the widget.
XmNy	Y coordinate of the widget.

CALLBACK DESCRIPTIONS

XmNdestroyCallback   Triggered when widget is destroyed.

Shell Widget

Description	Toplevel widget that works with the window manager.
Class Pointer	shellWidgetClass
Class Name	Shell
Include File	<Xm/Xm.h>, <X11/Shell.h>
Superclass	Composite

RESOURCES

Name	Type	Default
XmNallowShellResize	Boolean	False
XmNcreatePopupChildProc	(*)()	NULL
XmNgeometry	String	NULL
XmNoverrideRedirect	Boolean	False
XmNsaveUnder	Boolean	False
XmNvisual	Visual*	CopyFromParent

RESOURCE DESCRIPTIONS

XmNallowShellResize	When false, shell size cannot be changed.
XmNcreatePopupChildProc	Function called when shell is popped up.
XmNgeometry	Geometry for the shell.
XmNoverrideRedirect	Do not change.
XmNsaveUnder	Hint to window manager if it has a backing store that determines if the screen under this widget should be saved or not.
XmNvisual	Visual used when widget is created.

CALLBACKS

Callback List

XmNpopdownCallback
XmNpopupCallback

CALLBACK DESCRIPTIONS

XmNpopupCallback	Triggered when widget is popped up.
XmNpopdownCallback	Triggered when widget is popped down.

TopLevelShell Widget

Description	Creates additional decorated shells on the screen.
Class Pointer	topLevelShellWidgetClass
Class Name	TopLevelShell
Include File	<Xm/Xm.h>, <X11/Shell.h>
Superclass	VendorShell

RESOURCES

Name	Type	Default
XmNiconic	Boolean	False
XmNiconName	String	NULL
XmNiconNameEncoding	Atom	XA_STRING

RESOURCE DESCRIPTIONS

XmNiconic	When true, widget appears as icon at startup.
XmNiconName	Title of widget's icon.
XmNiconNameEncoding	Encoding of icon name string.

VendorShell Widget

Description	Shell widget superclass for all shells visible to window manager.
Class Pointer	vendorShellWidgetClass
Class Name	VendorShell
Include File	<Xm/Xm.h>, <X11/Shell.h>
Superclass	WMShell

RESOURCES

Name	Type	Default
XmNdefaultFontList	XmFontList	dynamic
XmNdeleteResponse	unsigned char	XmDESTROY
XmNkeyboardFocusPolicy	unsigned char	XmEXPLICIT
XmNmwmDecorations	int	-1

XmNmwmFunctions	int	-1
XmNmwmInputMode	int	-1
XmNmwmMenu	String	NULL
XmNshellUnitType	unsigned char	XmPIXELS
XmNuseAsyncGeometry	Boolean	False

RESOURCE DESCRIPTIONS

XmNdefaultFontList	Font for any text, label, or button child unless some other font is specified for the widget.
XmNdeleteResponse	Valid values: XmDESTROY, XmUNMAP, and XmDO_NOTHING. Specifies what happens when the shell receives a destroy message from the window manager.
XmNkeyboarFocusPolicy	Valid values: XmEXPLICIT (click-to-type) and XmPOINTER (pointer-driven).
XmNmwmDecorations	Specifies which window decorations are in effect.
XmNmwmFunctions	Specifies functions in the system menu.
XmNmwmInputMode	Specifies the input mode flag.
XmNmwmMenu	Items to be added to the end of the system menu.
XmNshellUnitType	Valid values: XmPIXELS, Xm100TH_MILLIMETERS, Xm1000TH_INCHES, XM100TH_POINTS, and Xm100TH_FONT_UNITS.
XmNuseAsyncGeometry	When set to true, XmNwaitForWm is set to false and XmNwmTimeout is set to 0. When false, nothing happens.

WMShell Widget

Description	Shell widget providing interface to window manager.
Class Pointer	wmShellWidgetClass
Class Name	WMShell
Include File	<Xm/Xm.h>, <X11/Shell.h>
Superclass	Shell

RESOURCES

Name	Type	Default
XmNbaseHeight	int	XtUnspecifiedShellInt
XmNbaseWidth	int	XtUnspecifiedShellInt
XmNheightInc	int	XtUnspecifiedShellInt

XmNiconMask	Pixmap	NULL
XmNiconPixmap	Pixmap	NULL
XmNiconWindow	Window	NULL
XmNiconX	int	-1
XmNiconY	int	-1
XmNinitialState	int	NormalState
XmNinput	Boolean	False
XmNmaxAspectX	int	XtUnspecifiedShellInt
XmNmaxAspectY	int	XtUnspecifiedShellInt
XmNmaxHeight	int	XtUnspecifiedShellInt
XmNmaxWidth	int	XtUnspecifiedShellInt
XmNminAspectX	int	XtUnspecifiedShellInt
XmNminAspectY	int	XtUnspecifiedShellInt
XmNminHeight	int	XtUnspecifiedShellInt
XmNminWidth	int	XtUnspecifiedShellInt
XmNtitle	String	dynamic
XmNtitleEncoding	Atom	XA_STRING
XmNtransient	Boolean	False
XmNwaitForWm	Boolean	True
XmNwidthInc	int	XtUnspecifiedShellInt
XmNwindowGroup	Window	dynamic
XmNwinGravity	int	dynamic
XmNwmTimeout	int	5000 ms.

RESOURCE DESCRIPTIONS

XmNbaseHeight	Starting point for height progression. Widget height starts here and goes up by XmNheightInc.
XmNbaseWidth	Starting point for width progression. Widget width starts here and goes up by XmNwidthInc.
XmNheightInc	Increments in which height increases and decreases.
XmNiconMask	Bitmap for clipping face of icon.
XmNiconPixmap	Pixmap on face of icon.
XmNiconWindow	Window holding icon.
XmNiconX	Preferred X location of icon.
XmNiconY	Preferred Y location of icon.
XmNinitialState	Valid values: NormalState and IconicState.

XmNinput	Helps determine input model for widget.
XmNmaxAspectX, XmNmaxAspectY	Maximum aspect ratio (X/Y) of widget.
XmNmaxHeight, XmNmaxWidth	Maximum height and width of widget.
XmNminAspectX, XmNminAspectY	Minimum aspect ratio (X/Y) of widget.
XmNminHeight, XmNminWidth	Minimum height and width of widget.
XmNtitle	Title displayed in window border.
XmNtitleEncoding	Encoding for XmNtitle.
XmNtransient	If widget is a pop-up, this is true.
XmNwaitForWm	Determines whether widget waits for window manager to respond to actions.
XmNwidthInc	Increments in which width increases and decreases.
XmNwindowGroup	Window to which this widget belongs.
XmNwinGravity	Valid values: NorthGravity, NorthEastGravity, EastGravity, and so on. Determines which way window manager places widget.
XmNwmTimeout	Time in milliseconds to wait for window manager.

INDEX